4/93

To Rabbi Goldman,
With best wishes,
& hopes for a more
"enlightened" world

Richard Shen

*Church and University
in the Scottish Enlightenment*

William Robertson by Sir Joshua Reynolds

Church and University in the Scottish Enlightenment

THE MODERATE LITERATI
OF EDINBURGH

❁

Richard B. Sher

PRINCETON UNIVERSITY PRESS

PRINCETON, NEW JERSEY

Copyright © 1985 by Princeton University Press
Published by Princeton University Press, 41 William Street,
Princeton, New Jersey 08540

All Rights Reserved
Library of Congress Cataloging in Publication Data will be
found on the last printed page of this book

ISBN 0-691-05445-2

Publication of this book has been aided by
the Whitney Darrow Fund of Princeton University Press

This book has been composed in Linotron Baskerville

Clothbound editions of Princeton University Press books
are printed on acid-free paper, and binding materials are
chosen for strength and durability. Paperbacks, although satisfactory
for personal collections, are not usually suitable for library rebinding

Printed in the United States of America
by Princeton University Press
Princeton, New Jersey

FOR
Doris and Jeremy

CONTENTS

Contents

LIST OF ILLUSTRATIONS

NOTE ON THE ILLUSTRATIONS

The frontispiece by Sir Joshua Reynolds (courtesy of the Scottish National Portrait Gallery, Edinburgh) portrays William Robertson with clerical gown, writing materials, and powdered wig symbolic of the Moderates' commitment to religion, learning, and politeness, respectively. First exhibited at the Royal Academy in 1772, it depicts the university principal at the height of his power and influence and admirably captures both his intelligence and craftiness.

Besides Reynolds (who also painted a portrait of Adam Ferguson that may now be lost), artists such as David Martin, William Millar, Sir Henry Raeburn, and Archibald Skirving painted the subjects of this book at various times in their lives. Several of their works—including Millar's pleasant portrait of John Home at the age of forty, Martin's two splendid portraits of Alexander Carlyle in his prime, Skirving's striking portrait of Carlyle near the end of his life, and Raeburn's full-length portrait of a heavy-set, baggy-eyed Hugh Blair—are reproduced in James Kinsley's edition of Carlyle's *Anecdotes and Characters of the Times* (London, 1973); others, such as Raeburn's fine portraits of Ferguson and Robertson from the early 1790s (both on display at the University of Edinburgh, as is Martin's mid-1770s portrait of Blair with hand on heart), may be found in various other publications.

The illustrations on pages 142–46 in this book reveal different aspects of the personalities and appearances of the Moderate literati of Edinburgh. The portrait of Adam Ferguson by William Millar (1763; courtesy of a private Scottish collection) shows the professor at the age of forty, the year before his switch from the natural philosophy to the moral philosophy chair at the University of Edinburgh. Millar's portrait of William Robertson on the next page (courtesy of a private Scottish collection) probably dates from the same period, when its subject was just beginning his illustrious academic career. John Home is perhaps sixty years old in the Raeburn portrait that follows (courtesy of Mr. Guy Ross-Lowe of Malpas, Cheshire). This is neither the sprightly young playwright whose entrance into company Alexander Carlyle once compared to "opening a window and letting the sun into a dull room," nor the sad, worn-out old man pictured in a Raeburn painting of Home in the National Portrait Gallery, London. Raeburn painted two excellent, yet very different,

xi

late eighteenth-century portraits of Hugh Blair in the identical pose (seated with hands clasped, looking to the right): in one of them (current whereabouts unknown) Blair dons a powdered wig and clerical gown; in the other (reproduced below from a private collection) he wears an ordinary suit and an elegant velvet nightcap. The portrait that Raeburn painted of Alexander Carlyle at a stately seventy-four years of age (1796; courtesy of the present earl of Haddington, whose ancestor of that title commissioned it) demonstrates why Carlyle's appearance as an older man was sometimes likened to that of the Roman god Jupiter ("the grandest demigod I ever saw," Sir Walter Scott said of him in this context). But good looks were no defense against the witty caricaturist John Kay, whose satirical etching "Faithful Service Rewarded" (1793; reproduced from Kay's *Series of Original Portraits and Caricature Etchings*, 2 vols. [Edinburgh, 1837–1842], 2:118) renders Carlyle and fellow Moderate Henry Grieve not as gods or demigods but as asses ridden by Scotland's political boss, Henry Dundas.

Other likenesses of the Moderate literati of Edinburgh, including pencil and chalk drawings, medallions, engravings, and additional caricature etchings by John Kay, are listed by Elaine Kilmurray in volume 2 of the *Dictionary of British Portraiture*, ed. Richard Ormond and Malcolm Rogers, 4 vols. (London, 1979).

TABLES

ABBREVIATIONS

AC	Alexander Carlyle, *Anecdotes and Characters of the Times*, ed. James Kinsley (London, 1973).
Annals	*Annals of the General Assembly of the Church of Scotland, 1739–1766*, ed. Nathaniel Morren, 2 vols. (Edinburgh, 1838–1840).
Auto.	*The Autobiography of Dr. Alexander Carlyle of Inveresk, 1722–1805*, new ed., ed. John Hill Burton (London and Edinburgh, 1910).
BL	British Library
Brougham	Henry, Lord Brougham, "William Robertson," in *Lives of Men of Letters and Science Who Flourished in the Time of George III*, 2 vols. (London, 1845), 1:256–323.
Bute	Bute Papers, Mount Stuart, Isle of Bute
Clark diss.	Ian D. L. Clark, "Moderatism and the Moderate Party in the Church of Scotland, 1752–1805" (Ph.D. diss., Cambridge University, 1963).
EBS	*Supplement to the Fourth, Fifth, and Sixth Editions of the Encyclopedia Britannica* (London, 1824).
EC	*The Eighteenth Century: Theory and Interpretation* (formerly *Studies in Burke and His Time*).
Erskine	John Erskine, "The Agency of God in Human Greatness," in *Discourses Preached on Several Occasions*, 2d ed., 2 vols. (Edinburgh, 1801–1804), 1:240–77.
Essay	Adam Ferguson, *An Essay on the History of Civil Society*, ed. Duncan Forbes (Edinburgh, 1966).
EUL	Edinburgh University Library
Fagg	Jane Bush Fagg, "Adam Ferguson: Scottish Cato" (Ph.D. diss., University of North Carolina, 1968).
HL	*The Letters of David Hume*, ed. J.Y.T. Greig, 2 vols. (Oxford, 1932).
Insts.	Adam Ferguson, *Institutes of Moral Philosophy*, 3d ed. (Edinburgh, 1785).
JHI	*Journal of the History of Ideas*
Lects.	Hugh Blair, *Lectures on Rhetoric and Belles Lettres*, ed. Harold F. Harding, 2 vols. (Carbondale and Edwardsville, Ill., 1965).
Mackenzie	Henry Mackenzie, "Account of the Life of Mr. John Home" (1822), in *WJH*, 1:1–184.

Mossner   Ernest Campbell Mossner, *The Life of David Hume*, 2d ed. (Oxford, 1980).

NLS   National Library of Scotland

NP   *New Perspectives on the Politics and Culture of Early Modern Scotland*, ed. John Dwyer, Roger Mason, and Alexander Murdoch (Edinburgh, 1982).

ONSE   *The Origins and Nature of the Scottish Enlightenment*, ed. R. H. Campbell and Andrew S. Skinner (Edinburgh, 1982).

Parl. Hist.   *The Parliamentary History of England . . . to the Year 1803*, 36 vols. (London, 1806–1820).

Princs.   Adam Ferguson, *Principles of Moral and Political Science*, 2 vols. (London, 1792).

RSCHS   *Records of the Scottish Church History Society*

RSE   Royal Society of Edinburgh

SAI   *Scotland in the Age of Improvement: Essays in Scottish History in the Eighteenth Century*, ed. N. T. Phillipson and Rosalind Mitchison (Edinburgh, 1970).

Sers.   Hugh Blair, *Sermons*, 5 vols. (London, 1818).

SHR   *Scottish Historical Review*

SM   *Scots Magazine*

Somerville   Thomas Somerville, *My Own Life and Times, 1741–1814* (Edinburgh, 1861).

SRO   Scottish Record Office

Stewart   Dugald Stewart, "Account of the Life and Writings of William Robertson" (1801), in *The Works of William Robertson*, 2 vols. (Edinburgh, 1829), 1:v–lxxvi.

SVEC   *Studies on Voltaire and the Eighteenth Century*

Tour   James Boswell, *Journal of a Tour to the North of Scotland with Samuel Johnson*, ed. Frederick A. Pottle and Charles H. Bennett (New York, 1961).

TRSE   *Transactions of the Royal Society of Edinburgh*

WJH   *The Works of John Home*, ed. Henry Mackenzie, 3 vols. (Edinburgh, 1822).

WLCL   William L. Clements Library, University of Michigan

WV   *Wealth and Virtue: The Shaping of Political Economy in the Scottish Enlightenment*, ed. Istvan Hont and Michael Ignatieff (Cambridge, 1983).

WWR   *The Works of William Robertson*, 8 vols. (Oxford, 1825).

YUL   Yale University Library

PREFACE

My initial encounter with the Scottish Enlightenment occurred at the University of Chicago in 1970. I was then pursuing a master's degree in the history and philosophy of social science, and my interest in the Scottish literati was limited to topics of concern to the historian of social theory. Further course work and research on the social and intellectual history of eighteenth-century France, however, transformed my thinking about the Scottish Enlightenment. Impressed by the manner in which historians of the French Enlightenment were bringing together materials relating to ideas, institutions, and ideologies in order to create a comprehensive picture of French cultural life, I began to ponder the very different treatment accorded to the Enlightenment in Scotland. If the ideological battles of the Encyclopedists, the controversies over the claims of the king and *parlements*, and the struggles against religious intolerance and injustice in cases like the Calas affair were considered central to the French Enlightenment, why were comparable instances of involvement with contemporary issues by the literati in Scotland so often regarded as mere appendages to the Enlightenment there? Why was the French Enlightenment defined chiefly in terms of *philosophes* fighting for "enlightened" principles, whereas the Scottish Enlightenment was usually confined to an intellectual "awakening" in social theory, political economy, and related fields? Why were the French *philosophes* studied in a multiplicity of social and cultural contexts—with due attention to their affiliations and coteries, their aspirations and enterprises, their attempts to redefine words and influence the society in which they lived—whereas the Scottish literati generally were not? After reflecting on such questions, I set out to apply some of the conceptual and methodological perspectives of French social and intellectual history to eighteenth-century Scotland. Out of that endeavor came the rudiments of the cultural interpretation of the Scottish Enlightenment sketched in the Introduction and the origins of my special interest in a group of literary men who appeared to me to be at the center of the Scottish Enlightenment when so defined— the "Moderate literati of Edinburgh."

These remarks do not begin to convey the full extent of my indebtedness to postgraduate professors at the University of Chicago, only a few of whom can be thanked here. George Stocking first introduced me to the Scottish Enlightenment and remained a helpful critic and friend throughout my dissertation years. Bill Sewell opened my eyes to social and cultural history of the *Annales* variety. William McNeill was a great source of encouragement in the final stages of my dissertation preparation. Above all, my principal mentor Keith Baker guided my research with a rare mixture of rigor and warmth and provided an inspirational model for practicing the social history of ideas and ideologies. I was also extremely fortunate to have had the chance to spend the 1973–1974 academic year at the University of Edinburgh. There I attended Nicholas Phillipson's stimulating seminar on eighteenth-century Scottish thought and culture, which usually had a way of spilling over into an Edinburgh pub for many additional hours of instructive and convivial conversation—in the best tradition of the Scottish literati. Many others, including David Kettler, Steven Shapin, and Norah Smith, aided my early investigations in various ways, but special thanks must go to Ian D. L. Clark for his hospitality and willingness to share the fruits of his extensive research on the Moderates. Then, as well as later, my parents were tremendously supportive; I only wish my father could have lived to see the final product, which would have meant so much to him.

The fact that this book differs substantially from the doctoral dissertation on which it is based has much to do with the constant stream of information, criticism, and moral support offered by numerous friends and scholars during the past five years. I am particularly grateful to Roger Emerson for his trenchant criticisms of the entire manuscript, but especially of chapter 3, and to John Robertson for valuable guidance and debate on the militia issue and other matters. John Dwyer, Roger Mason, Nick Phillipson, David Raynor, Sandy Stewart, Rick Teichgraeber, and Paul Wood are among those who helped by revealing unsuspected sources, checking references in inaccessible places, and exchanging ideas about various topics. Istvan Hont kindly provided prepublication copies of several papers originally presented at a colloquium and seminars held at King's College, Cambridge, in 1979 and 1980. For the illustrations I owe a double debt: to the owners of the pictures reproduced below and to the person most responsible for advising me about them and in some cases making them available to me, Rosalind Marshall of the Scottish National Portrait Gallery. From Becky Daniels I received assistance with typing, partly with funds granted for that purpose by the New Jersey Institute of Technology. I also wish to thank David Norton and John Pocock for steering me to Princeton University Press, where I was lucky enough to work with several helpful and very patient editors: Joanna Hitchcock, Gretchen Oberfranc, and Cathie Brettschneider.

Any book making as much use as this one does of manuscripts and rare publications owes its very existence to the repositories of such materials and the people who own and manage them. I am grateful to them all, but particularly to T. I. Rae of the manuscript department at the National Library of Scotland; to the marquess of Bute and his charming archivist, Miss Catherine Armet, who permitted me to examine and cite the Bute Papers at Mount Stuart on the Isle of Bute; to Yale University and McGraw-Hill Book Company (William Heinemann, Ltd.) for permission to cite unpublished letters in the Boswell Papers (including one by Hugh Blair quoted in epigraphs at the beginning of chapters 5 and 8) that were brought to my attention by Nicholas Phillipson; to Mrs. Donald F. Hyde for permission to use materials in the Hyde Collection in Somerville, New Jersey; to the Huntington Library, San Marino, California, and the William L. Clements Library, University of Michigan, for permission to cite manuscripts housed in special collections there; and to the interlibrary loan librarians at the New Jersey Institute of Technology, without whose efficiency the bibliographical essay at the conclusion of this book would have suffered.

There are, finally, two people who have done more for this book than words can express. The contributions of my dear friend Alex Murdoch have been indispensable for more than a decade. I can never adequately thank him for sending me countless sources, guiding me through the maze of eighteenth-century British politics, accompanying me on memorable research jaunts to London and Mount Stuart, and sharing with me his abounding love for things Scottish. Closer to home, my wife Doris has supported me in every conceivable way while this study was taking shape. Without her constructive criticism, constant encouragement, and loving care, I would have given it all up many drafts ago.

Church and University
in the Scottish Enlightenment

The Problem of
the Scottish Enlightenment

"Je regarde Edinbourg comme la grande école de la philosophie." So wrote the French *philosophe* J.-B.-A. Suard in 1772,[1] when names like Hume, Smith, Kames, Blair, and Robertson had catapulted the literati of Scotland generally, and Edinburgh in particular, to international prominence. In the previous decade Carlo Denina of the Royal School of Turin had bestowed glowing acclaim on Scottish men of letters, and the Irish elocutionist Thomas Sheridan had christened Edinburgh "the Athens of Great Britain."[2] Even Voltaire, whose earlier account of British culture in the *Philosophical Letters* had ignored Scotland except for a snipe or two at Presbyterian fanaticism, now acknowledged, albeit with a touch of irony, that "today it is from Scotland that we get rules of taste in all the arts, from epic poetry to gardening."[3] In Voltaire's view the sudden ascendancy of Scottish polite literature and taste was a consequence of the progress of "l'esprit humain," which seemed to be extending itself to the very fringes of civilization. Scotland could no longer be dismissed by disparaging foreigners as a semicivilized center of Presbyterian enthusiasm, Highland barbarism, and incessant Jacobite intrigue. The old stereotypes were breaking down under the impetus of a profound cultural transformation that has come to be known as the Scottish Enlightenment.

[1] Suard to William Robertson, 6 April 1772, NLS, 3942:106–107.

[2] Carlo Denina, *An Essay on the Revolutions of Literature* (1763), trans. John Murdoch (London, 1771), chap. 11. "Sheridan has told us that Edinburgh is the Athens of Great Brittain," wrote Alexander Carlyle to Gilbert Elliot in London on 29 July 1761 (NLS, 11015:106), to which he added, "& we believe him." By the early nineteenth century the phrase had been broadened to "Athens of the North."

[3] *Philosophical Letters* (1732), trans. Ernest Dilworth (Indianapolis, 1961), 25, and Voltaire's review of Kames's *Elements of Criticism* (1762), quoted in Alexander Fraser Tytler, Lord Woodhouselee, *Memoirs of the Life and Writings of the Honourable Henry Home of Kames*, 2 vols. (Edinburgh, 1807), 2:84. Although Voltaire's words were tinged with sarcasm—for Kames had presumed to criticize his *Henriade*—other references to the Scottish literati leave no doubt that Voltaire was genuinely impressed by their achievements.

It is something of a paradox that for all the attention that has recently been showered on eighteenth-century Scottish men of letters for their achievements in philosophy, science, political economy, law, literary criticism, history, and sociology, the Scottish Enlightenment as such remains an enigma. Ever since that term was introduced by William Robert Scott in 1900 there has been no consensus about its meaning. Scott himself defined it rather vaguely as "the diffusion of philosophic ideas in Scotland and the encouragement of speculative tastes" among the generation of Scottish men of letters that reached maturity around the middle of the eighteenth century.[4] For the next fifty years the term was rarely used, but during the third quarter of this century it made a dramatic reappearance, bested its unfortunate rival "Scottish Renaissance,"[5] and won a place for itself in scholarly vocabularies. Yet widespread acceptance of the term has not cleared up the ambiguity associated with it. For this reason it is necessary to begin with the most basic of questions: just what was the Scottish Enlightenment?

In an influential paper presented at the Second International Congress on the Enlightenment in 1967, Hugh Trevor-Roper (now Lord Dacre) stated what is probably the most widely accepted general definition of the Scottish Enlightenment today: "that efflorescence of intellectual vitality that became obvious after the defeat of the last Jacobite rebellion in 1745" and continued for four or five succeeding decades.[6] A criterion such as "intellectual vitality," however, is bound to breed confusion, not only about *what* the Scottish Enlightenment was but also about *when* it occurred and *whom* it included. Although everyone agrees that the second half of the eighteenth century was a period of great intellectual achievement in Scotland, there is disagreement about just when that period of achievement began and ended. On one side of the historical divide, Scottish scholars offended by Trevor-Roper's allusions to Scotland's "dark age in the seventeenth century" have been at pains to demonstrate the unappreciated richness and continuity of early modern Scottish culture, as shown by the accomplishments of late seventeenth- and early eighteenth-century Scots such as Sir Robert Sibbald and Andrew Fletcher, as well as by progressive developments in

[4] *Francis Hutcheson: His Life, Teaching and Position in the History of Philosophy* (Cambridge, 1900), 265.

[5] Although some historians of literature have continued to apply "Scottish Renaissance" to the eighteenth century, as well as to the twentieth-century revival of Scottish literature discussed in Maurice Lindsay, *The Scottish Renaissance* (Edinburgh, 1948), the most appropriate usage of this term refers to the historical age of the Renaissance in the sixteenth century, as in Arthur H. Williamson, *Scottish National Consciousness in the Age of James VI* (Edinburgh, 1979), 86.

[6] "The Scottish Enlightenment," *SVEC* 58 (1967): 1635–58, esp. 1637.

the universities of that era.[7] A stronger case for a pre-'45 intellectual "awakening" can be made for the second quarter of the eighteenth century—the years of David Hume's *Treatise of Human Nature*, Francis Hutcheson's entire career as a moral philosopher, and much else besides. On the other side of the divide, the era of Francis Jeffrey, Henry Cockburn, Sir Walter Scott, Sir William Hamilton, and Sir David Brewster in the early nineteenth century can hardly be called one of intellectual decline. Considerations like these may be chiefly responsible for the current vogue of extending the dates of the Scottish Enlightenment all the way back to the Union of 1707, if not earlier, and as far forward as the 1830s, if not later,[8] even though this expanded chronology seems to spread the term too thin and to sever its chronological ties with the Enlightenment in France and elsewhere. So long as one's sole criterion is a concept like "intellectual vitality," one is obliged to begin the Scottish Enlightenment at the end of one "dark age" and to extend it all the way to the start of the next "dark age," regardless of the length of time covered or the changing nature of intellectual activity during the period in question. And chronology is only part of the problem. Even during the mid- and late eighteenth century there were some Scottish figures of undisputed "intellectual vitality," such as the Jacobite classicist Thomas Ruddiman and the Scots poets Robert Fergusson and Robert Burns, whose relationship to the Scottish Enlightenment was at best ambiguous and at worst antagonistic.

For Trevor-Roper and many others, including most social scientists who have treated the subject, the solution to the problem of how to use "intellectual vitality" as the basis for a viable definition of the Scottish Englightenment lies in restricting the conceptual field to a particular type of intellectual inquiry and to the relatively few authors deemed responsible for it. Searching for "the peculiar character of the Scottish Enlightenment," Trevor-Roper purports to find it by separating the "camp-followers" from the "real intellectual pioneers," whom he identifies as Francis Hutcheson, David Hume, Adam Ferguson, William Robertson, Adam Smith, and John Millar. "For together," he writes, "these are the Scottish Enlightenment."[9] The

---

[7] See the introduction to *ONSE* by Andrew Skinner and William Ferguson's remarks in *Scotland's Relations with England: A Survey to 1707* (Edinburgh, 1977), 242–43.

[8] See N. T. Phillipson, "The Scottish Enlightenment," in *A Companion to Scottish Culture*, ed. David Daiches (London, 1981), 340. But Phillipson is on firmer ground when he locates the "high period" of the Scottish Enlightenment between the 1750s and the 1780s.

[9] "Scottish Enlightenment," 1639–40. The same thesis was reformulated by Trevor-Roper a decade later in another article titled "The Scottish Enlightenment," in *Blackwood's Magazine* 322 (1977): 371–88, and it is endorsed in chapter 1 of *The Scottish*

"peculiar character of the Scottish Enlightenment" turns out to be the inquiry into "the social behaviour of mankind" that was the ruling passion and unifying interest of these pioneering Scottish thinkers. Beginning with Hutchesonian psychology and ethics, it spread to sociology and political economy, often approached in historical terms as a concern with progress. In this way, Trevor-Roper arrives at a definition that is compatible with Gladys Bryson's classic interpretation of the Scottish "school" of moralists and with J. G. A. Pocock's recent characterization of the Scottish Enlightenment as "a marvelous explosion of ideas in moral philosophy and historical sociology."[10]

Definitions like these quite properly draw attention to the remarkable range and primacy of place of moral philosophy in eighteenth-century Scottish intellectual life and the widespread concern of the Scottish literati with problems of "man and society." They may easily degenerate, however, into narrowly social scientific conceptions that distort the thought of some thinkers, and even at their best they exclude from the Scottish Enlightenment the many instances of intellectual vitality in other fields of polite literature and learning, such as literary criticism, natural science, medicine, drama, religion, and poetry. They therefore cannot accommodate Hugh Blair, John Home, Alexander Gerard, George Campbell, Joseph Black, William Cullen, and numerous other "enlightened" men of intellectual achievement whose contributions lay outside moral philosophy and social science. Nor can they accommodate enlightened musicians, artists, and architects, such as Robert Adam and Allan Ramsay. If they help to provide a somewhat clearer idea of the chronology and composition of the Scottish Enlightenment, they do so only at the expense of much that was undeniably vital in the culture of the eighteenth-century literati.

Moreover, whether it is used broadly, to include all varieties of "formal" thought, or narrowly, to include only moral philosophy and social science, the concept of "intellectual vitality" is inadequate as the sole criterion of the Scottish Enlightenment for other reasons. First, Trevor-Roper's distinction between the "real intellectual pioneers" who are worthy of further study and the "camp-followers" who are not shows the danger of this definition encouraging a simplistic equation

---

Enlightenment and the Militia Issue (Edinburgh, 1985) by John Robertson, who kindly allowed me to read portions of his manuscript.

[10] Gladys Bryson, *Man and Society: The Scottish Inquiry of the Eighteenth Century* (1945; reprint, New York, 1968); J. G. A. Pocock, "Post-Puritan England and the Problem of the Enlightenment," in *Culture and Politics: From Puritanism to the Enlightenment*, ed. Perez Zagorin (Berkeley, 1980), 92.

of "intellectual vitality" with genius. So does his claim that most of the Scottish men of letters who attracted attention during the eighteenth century were in fact "thoroughly second-rate" and are now "very properly forgotten."[11] One problem with such an approach is the difficulty of sorting out the innovating geniuses from the rest. That Trevor-Roper could exclude Thomas Reid, the high priest of common sense philosophy, from the ranks of the notable intellectuals proves that one scholar's intellectual pioneer may be another's camp-follower. Even if it were somehow possible to identify the intellectual pioneers or men of genius with reasonable accuracy, restricting investigations of the Scottish Enlightenment to their books and treatises would invariably produce a distorted impression of the nature of eighteenth-century Scottish intellectual life. Treating the brilliant but often idiosyncratic thought of David Hume as if it were the epitome of the age is probably the most common example of the sort of problem that is likely to arise when genius becomes the standard for defining the Scottish Enlightenment.[12]

Another difficulty with a definition based solely on "intellectual vitality" is its tendency to yield a Scottish Enlightenment that is confined to the realm of formal thought and discernible only through the study of formal texts—a Scottish Enlightenment that is narrowly intellectual rather than broadly cultural and narrowly textual rather than broadly contextual. Such an approach is apt to discourage careful consideration of the full range of values, ideologies, ulterior motives, linguistic nuances, and *mentalités* that constitute the essence of what Quentin Skinner has called the "ultimate framework" within which a text must be read in order to discover the author's meaning or meanings.[13] It also tends to discourage serious interest in archival research, pamphlet literature, and "low" intellectual history generally. It is especially likely to cut off the Scottish Enlightenment from its own national roots, since "high" or "pure" intellectual history is frequently written with little concern for local institutions and traditions. And it serves to isolate the Scottish Enlightenment from the Enlightenment as a whole, which is rarely defined now in terms of intellect alone.

---

[11] "Scottish Enlightenment" (1967): 1638, and (1977): 372–73.

[12] Duncan Forbes has issued repeated warnings against regarding Hume's thought as typical of the Scottish Enlightenment, but there are as yet few signs that his words have made much impression. On the other hand, J. David Hoeveler, Jr., goes too far by effectively banishing Hume from the Scottish Enlightenment in *James McCosh and the Scottish Intellectual Tradition* (Princeton, 1981), 20–21.

[13] "Meaning and Understanding in the History of Ideas," *History and Theory* 8 (1969): 3–53.

A satisfactory definition of the Scottish Enlightenment must avoid the pitfalls of previous definitions like Trevor-Roper's by including, yet transcending, the intellectual achievements of great Scottish thinkers. It must be capable of integrating those intellectual achievements with other relevant aspects of Scottish culture as well as with the general values and beliefs of the international Enlightenment. With these points in mind, I shall define the Scottish Enlightenment quite simply as *the culture of the literati of eighteenth-century Scotland.* Each term in this definition requires amplification. "Literati" signifies men of arts and letters who adhered to a broad body of "enlightened" values and principles held in common by European and American *philosophes.* These included a love of learning and virtue; a faith in reason and science; a dedication to humanism and humanitarianism; a style of civilized urbanity and polite cosmopolitanism; a preference for social order and stability; a respect for hard work and material improvement; an attraction to certain types of worldly pleasures and amusements; a taste for classical serenity tempered by sentimentalism; a distrust of religious enthusiasm and superstition; an aversion to slavery, torture, and other forms of inhumanity; a commitment to religious tolerance and freedom of expression; and at least a modicum of optimism about the human prospect if people would take the trouble to abide by these principles and cultivate their gardens as best they can. By the term "literati," then, I mean not merely men of letters but men of the Enlightenment.

"Eighteenth century" refers in this definition primarily to the second half of the eighteenth century, when the culture of the Scottish literati was at its height in almost every respect, and secondarily to the formative phase in the preceding two or three decades. This chronological schema meshes nicely with Peter Gay's contention that the Enlightenment spanned the careers of "three overlapping, closely associated generations" of *philosophes.*[14] In Scotland it began with the coming of age of Francis Hutcheson's pioneering generation of literati—Lord Kames, Colin Maclaurin, Alexander Monro *primus*, George Turnbull, and Robert Wallace, among others—who were born, like Voltaire, in the 1690s. It reached its peak under the leadership of the impressive array of literati born between 1710 and the mid- or late 1720s, including (in order of age) Thomas Reid, William Cullen, David Hume, Lord Monboddo, Hugh Blair, George Campbell, William Robertson, Adam Smith, Alexander Carlyle, John Home, Adam Ferguson, John Gregory, Sir John and Sir David Dalrymple (Lord Hailes), James Hutton, Joseph Black, Alexander Gerard, and Robert

---

[14] Peter Gay, *The Enlightenment: An Interpretation*, 2 vols. (New York, 1966–1969), 1:17.

Adam—who were the contemporaries of Diderot, d'Alembert, d'Holbach, and Kant. And it received a final thrust from a number of literati born after 1735, such as the controversial James Beattie, Henry Mackenzie, John Millar, John Playfair and, at the chronological limits of the Enlightenment, Dugald Stewart (born 1753)—who were roughly the same ages as Gibbon, Beccaria, Condorcet, Jefferson, and Goethe.

"Culture" is used here to encompass every aspect of life and thought. A cultural definition of the Scottish Enlightenment is therefore a multidimensional one in which the celebrated "efflorescence" of eighteenth-century "intellectual vitality" appears to be just one of several interrelated components or dimensions. It was unquestionably the most spectacular dimension, and I do not wish to minimize its significance or imply that it should be reduced to a mere reflection of the social context from which it sprang. Yet neither would I wish to mistake a part for the whole or treat one in isolation from the other. Besides the intellectual dimension of the Scottish Enlightenment (broadly defined to include literary criticism and rhetoric, natural science and jurisprudence, and other branches of polite literature and learning that students of social thought sometimes neglect), it is possible to identify a social and institutional dimension, embracing everything from the literati's clubs and colleges to their clothing and claret. There was also an economic and technological dimension, including the practical application of rational or scientific principles of medicine, industry, farming, estate management, landscape gardening, and many other improving endeavors. There was a dimension of the fine, applied, and performing arts, consisting of the different varieties of drama, music, painting, and architecture that flourished among Scottish men of arts and letters during the eighteenth century. And there was what may loosely be called an ideological dimension: for the Scottish Enlightenment was as much a revolution in values and ideals as it was a philosophical, literary, scientific, artistic, economic, technological, or social and institutional phenomenon.

Lastly, "Scotland" in the sense of this definition denotes a particular geographical context in which the Enlightenment flourished in a unique manner. Although the underlying values of the Enlightenment were roughly the same everywhere, and although the men of letters who professed them may justly be considered members of the same international "family,"[15] local circumstances altered the balance. The performance of the Scottish literati can be likened to a

---

[15] Ibid., 3–4.

variation on a common theme played by *philosophes* throughout Europe and America.

To understand the distinctive character of the Scottish Enlightenment, it is necessary to consider the special nature of eighteenth-century Scottish institutions and the special status of eighteenth-century Scottish men of arts and letters. Although Scotland ceased to exist as a sovereign state after 1707, it retained a number of institutions and traditions that distinguished the country from England and gave its inhabitants a sense of Scottish national identity. Scotland had its own cultural traditions, including distinctive foods, games, and manners, and its own spoken languages—Gaelic in the Highlands and Scots, or some combination of Scots and English, in Lowland regions. It had its own legal system, which owed more to the civilian law of the Continent than to the common law of England; its own schools and universities—Edinburgh, Glasgow, St. Andrews, and King's and Marischal Colleges in Aberdeen—with their own pedagogical policies; and its own national church, which had reverted to Presbyterianism soon after the Revolution of 1688–1689. It even had a surprising amount of political and administrative autonomy—or "semi-independence"—for most of the eighteenth century.[16] In short, Scotland was in many ways still a nation though not a nation-state.

With a few exceptions such as David Hume (who was himself bred for the bar until that prospect made him "nauseous" and who twice tried unsuccessfully to secure an academic chair), the Scottish literati earned their livelihoods in one or more of several professions affiliated with distinctively Scottish institutions, notably law, medicine, the universities, and the established church. This fact helps to explain the Weltanschauung of the Scottish Enlightenment. The literati of eighteenth-century Scotland were not angry or alienated intellectuals, eking out a living as hack writers or translators, satirizing the elite of their society, or dodging the censors and authorities. They were not bureaucratic state officials struggling to institute legal, political, and economic reforms. They were not Freemasons, pantheists, or republicans dreaming of a new order. They were not highborn dilettantes who could afford and perhaps relish the notoriety associated with daringly progressive ideas. Rather, the literati of the Scottish Enlightenment were nearly all what one would now call

---

[16] See N. T. Phillipson, "Nationalism and Ideology," in *Government and Nationalism in Scotland*, ed. J. N. Wolfe (Edinburgh, 1969), 167–88, and the detailed substantiation of Phillipson's argument in Alexander Murdoch, *"The People Above": Politics and Administration in Mid-Eighteenth-Century Scotland* (Edinburgh, 1980), chap. 1.

middle- and upper middle-class professional men. Their outlook was, if not a function of, certainly appropriate to their place as leading members of the liberal professions in a "provincial" society. Compared with most of their better-known counterparts in Paris, they appear less witty, less urbane, and often less critical of their country's religious, political, social, and educational establishments. Yet so long as one does not follow Peter Gay in mistaking the skeptical, anticlerical, reformist Enlightenment of certain French *philosophes* and a few men of letters elsewhere for the Enlightenment as a whole, there will be no difficulty accommodating regional variations of this kind.[17] In fact, further research on the Enlightenment in Germany, America, the French provinces, and other places may well reveal that the particular version of the Enlightenment that Gay has made a universal paradigm was the exception rather than the rule.[18]

The multidimensional or cultural definition of the Scottish Enlightenment that I am recommending has the capacity to situate that phenomenon within an international framework of values and beliefs while still allowing for the uniqueness of the Scottish experience. It can encompass the many "schools" of thought (e.g. Bryson's school of Scottish moralists, the "common sense" school of Scottish philosophy, the "Scottish historical school" of social evolutionary thought, the Scottish school of political economy) and modes of discourse and paradigmatic concepts (e.g., civic humanism, natural jurisprudence, "improvement," and "independence and universalism") that have been emphasized by various commentators over the years, but it does not pretend to reduce the entire movement to any one or

---

[17] Gay, *Enlightenment*, passim. Cf. Gay's remarks in *The Party of Humanity: Essays in the French Enlightenment* (New York, 1971), 112–13, where, in an essay deemed applicable to the Enlightenment everywhere, it is asserted that the *philosophes'* two primary enemies were "the institutions of Christianity and the idea of hierarchy"—both of which were actually vital features of the Enlightenment in Scotland, among other places.

[18] I owe this insight to Keith Baker, but similar points have been made elsewhere, most recently in the preface to Roy Porter and Mikuláš Teich, eds., *The Enlightenment in National Context* (Cambridge, 1981). That Gay's paradigm is too radical even for the Enlightenment in France—indeed, even for the Enlightenment in Paris—is suggested by recent studies such as Daniel Roche, *Le Siècle des lumières en province: Académies et académiciens provinciaux, 1680–1789*, 2 vols. (Paris, 1978) and Alan Charles Kors, *D'Holbach's Coterie: An Enlightenment in Paris* (Princeton, 1976). Of course, even Gay's *philosophes* appear tame next to some of the radicals discussed by Margaret C. Jacob in *The Radical Enlightenment: Pantheists, Freemasons, and Republicans* (London, 1981); but there are as yet only vague hints of possible links between this radical fringe and the so-called "High Enlightenment" with which I, like Gay, am chiefly concerned.

two of them.[19] It can also encompass the individual achievements of Scottish literati in a wide variety of fields—"from epic poetry to gardening," in Voltaire's memorable phrase. It helps to solve the problems of chronology and composition by justifying the exclusion from the Scottish Enlightenment of a Sibbald or a Fletcher, a Scott or a Jeffrey, a Ruddiman or a Burns, not because these men lacked "intellectual vitality" but because they stood for different values, spoke different intellectual and ideological languages, and inhabited different social and cultural worlds from the literati of the Enlightenment. Finally, this approach encourages an interdisciplinary yet truly historical method that meets the Scottish literati on their own ground, treats their formal thought as but one of several interesting aspects of their lives, and makes use of the manuscripts, pamphlets, institutional records, newspaper and magazine articles, and similar sources that often enable a researcher to penetrate the surface of things.

In this way, the history of ideas can be transformed into the social history of ideas, which is the avowed methodology of this study. Here, however, that term means something quite different from what Anand Chitnis has in mind when he claims to have written the first book-length account of "the social history of the Enlightenment in Scotland."[20] Since Chitnis defines the Scottish Enlightenment as an exclusively intellectual, and essentially philosophical and scientific, phenomenon,[21] he is forced to exclude from it not only the arts, rhetoric, and belles lettres but also the values and ideologies, personal relationships and interests, that give social and cultural meaning to the intellectual and institutional developments with which he is concerned. Recapturing that meaning—rather than merely describing, as Chitnis attempts to do, the institutional background against which the play of philosophical and scientific inquiry was set—is in my view the primary objective of the social history of ideas. In this sense, the social history of ideas is really another name for the history of cultural meaning:[22] it investigates the different ways in which individuals and groups from past societies employed various forms of expression—chiefly the written and spoken word, but perhaps also

[19] See Richard B. Sher, "A Northern Republic of Letters: Scotland and Her Literati," forthcoming in *American Historical Association Proceedings*, no. 10485.

[20] Anand Chitnis, *The Scottish Enlightenment: A Social History* (London, 1976), 246.

[21] Ibid., 6.

[22] William J. Bouwsma, "From History of Ideas to History of Meaning," *Journal of Interdisciplinary History* 12 (1980): 279–92.

pictorial representations, musical compositions, and the like—to clarify, interpret, explain, and influence their culture and their world, as well as the different ways in which contemporary audiences responded to their efforts.

Unlike Chitnis's book, this work does not claim to be a comprehensive social history of the entire Scottish Enlightenment. It does, however, seek to make a significant contribution to our understanding of that subject by depicting, in accordance with the general principles of definition and methodology just discussed, the culture of one important segment of the literati of eighteenth-century Scotland—the "Moderate literati of Edinburgh." It should be made clear that this label was not in use during the eighteenth century, though it is likely that the individuals to whom it now refers would have understood and perhaps appreciated it. In any event it is intended not as an inflexible category but as a handy device for drawing attention to significant social, ideological, and intellectual configurations among the Scottish literati. In a society as small, inbred, and sociable as mid-eighteenth-century Scotland—with perhaps a million and a quarter people nationwide and no town more populous than Edinburgh with its fifty or sixty thousand residents—there is a sense in which nearly all men of arts and letters were part of the same social milieu. Yet important distinctions arise when the Scottish literati are considered in terms of such factors as age, social background, education, occupation, geographical residence, personal relations, and ideology, as well as formal thought. The principal assumption of this book is that it makes sense, on the basis of such factors, to view the Moderate literati of Edinburgh as a distinctive group whose interests and activities require careful consideration if the nature of the Scottish Enlightenment is to be understood.

As defined here, the Moderate literati of Edinburgh consisted of Hugh Blair (1718–1800), professor of rhetoric and belles lettres and internationally known preacher at St. Giles Church in Edinburgh; Alexander Carlyle (1722–1805), minister at Inveresk near Edinburgh and author of numerous pamphlets and occasional sermons, as well as a remarkable set of memoirs; Adam Ferguson (1723–1816), military chaplain, professor of natural and later moral philosophy, and author of several books on moral philosophy and Roman history; John Home (1722–1808), minister at Athelstaneford, playwright and poet, secretary to the third earl of Bute, and historian of the Jacobite rebellion of 1745; and William Robertson (1721–1793), Edinburgh minister, university principal, ecclesiastical leader, and author of four celebrated works of history. A sixth candidate, Rev.

John Jardine of Edinburgh (1716–1766), has been excluded chiefly because of his premature death and a paucity of information about his activities and beliefs.

If these five men have not previously been recognized as a cohesive group, the reason may be that they have usually been studied either as individuals or as representatives of particular academic disciplines, institutions, schools of thought, or paradigms. They have not been studied from the standpoint of the totality of their values, interests, and relationships, and for this reason the deeper and more significant connections among them have not been fully appreciated or thoroughly investigated. All of them were born around the year 1720, which William Law Mathieson identified long ago as the time when the most important generation of Scottish literary men entered the world.[23] They were educated for careers in the ministry of the established church. They were intimate friends who settled in the Edinburgh vicinity during the 1740s and 1750s. They were affiliated with the Moderate party in ecclesiastical affairs. They secured positions of prestige and authority in the Church of Scotland and the University of Edinburgh. They played decisive roles in the intellectual and cultural life of Scotland during the second half of the eighteenth century, both as ecclesiastical politicians and academic administrators and as men of letters in their own right. And they contributed to the propagation of an identifiable, if not always rigorously systematic, set of moral, religious, philosophical, and ideological principles that would later be termed "Moderatism."

Within the matrix of professional men who gave the Scottish Enlightenment its distinctive character, the Moderate literati of Edinburgh occupied a central position. Their centrality was at once geographical, in that they lived in or near the cultural capital of Scotland; social and institutional, in that they came to dominate the two most important Scottish institutions for the dissemination of knowledge and beliefs—the Church of Scotland and the University of Edinburgh—as well as important clubs such as the Poker; intellectual, in that they published works in history, moral philosophy, rhetoric and belles lettres, drama, and religion that were among the most highly acclaimed, influential, and characteristic productions of eighteenth-century Scottish polite literature; and ideological, in that they successfully employed their institutional authority and intellectual talents to make the ideals and values of Moderatism preeminent in the Scotland of their day. This is not to say, of course, that the Mod-

[23] William Law Mathieson, *The Awakening of Scotland: A History from 1747 to 1797* (Glasgow, 1910), 200.

erate literati *were* the Scottish Enlightenment. By now it should be clear that the definition of the Scottish Enlightenment being espoused here is not reducible to *any* particular group, discipline, paradigm, school, ideology, or activity. It is to suggest, however, that Enlightenments, like societies, have what Edward Shils has called "centers and peripheries,"[24] and that the task of differentiating them is both legitimate and worthwhile. Examining the collective thought and practice of the Moderate literati of Edinburgh, then, serves not only to elucidate a particular intellectual and ideological program but also to substantiate Ernest Mossner's observation that "the philosophy of Moderatism . . . was part-and-parcel of the philosophy of the Scottish Enlightenment."[25]

In order to prevent misunderstanding, several points of qualification and clarification should be made. First, collective biography of this kind is no substitute for individual biography, for it must be selective in its treatment of biographical data and cannot possibly capture all the subtle nuances of each member of the group. Although the emphasis here is on uniformity and collaboration, the Moderate literati of Edinburgh obviously had their differences. There were contrasts in personality and temperament, style and appearance. And there were occasional disagreements about the best choices for particular academic or ecclesiastical offices, as was probably inevitable given the scarcity of such positions in eighteenth-century Scotland. Since competition for these positions was usually fierce, it is remarkable that disagreements of this type were so infrequent and amicable. Even when members of the group were in direct competition with each other, they maintained their friendly relations. Moreover, their differences almost never involved important intellectual or ideological issues, on which they nearly always agreed.

Besides the danger of minimizing individual differences within the group, a study of this type runs the risk of exaggerating its subjects' uniqueness and separateness from others. It is therefore worth reiterating that the Moderate literati of Edinburgh were not a closed or isolated group. There were scores of other clergymen, professors, lawyers, landowners, politicians, merchants, physicians, civil servants, and men of letters with whom they regularly associated, often on terms of great intimacy. Some of these individuals, such as David Hume, Adam Smith, Gilbert Elliot, Lord Kames, and Joseph Black, may be considered members of a larger social and literary circle to

[24] Edward Shils, "Center and Periphery," in *Center and Periphery: Essays in Macrosociology* (Chicago, 1975), 3–16.
[25] Ernest Campbell Mossner, *The Life of David Hume*, 2d ed. (Oxford, 1980), 284.

which the Moderate literati belonged. My contention is not that these wider relationships were insignificant but that, in spite of them, the five subjects of this book shared among themselves an extensive network of experiences, beliefs, values, and sentiments that defined their collective identity as a distinctive coterie.

Third, no claims are being made to elevate the Moderate literati of Edinburgh to the level of some of their more famous countrymen, such as David Hume, Adam Smith, or Robert Burns, as creative intellects or men of "genius." One might say that the methodology and objectives of this study render the concept of genius irrelevant. Whereas the "pure" history of ideas tends to concentrate on those few individuals from the past who appear in retrospect to have possessed the most penetrating or inventive minds or to have made the most important contributions in their chosen fields, the "social" history of ideas must throw its net wider. It must seek to uncover and analyze, to the extent that this is possible, the underlying patterns of ideas and values that actually existed in the society and period under investigation. Gone are the days when authors of studies of "second-rate" thinkers felt compelled to demonstrate the previously unappreciated philosophical, literary, or scientific brilliance of their subjects. From the point of view of the social history of ideas, a more useful task is to explain how rarely read, nearly forgotten works such as Home's *Douglas*, Robertson's *History of Scotland*, Ferguson's *Institutes*, Macpherson's *Fingal*, and Blair's *Sermons* could have been among the most popular and influential writings in Great Britain and abroad two hundred years ago.[26]

Finally, it will be useful to clarify the definitions of several potentially misleading terms that figure prominently in this study. The term "Moderate" is employed in the contemporary, partisan sense on which Ian D. L. Clark has rightly insisted. It applies to the party of Scottish Presbyterian churchmen that emerged shortly after 1750 under the leadership of William Robertson and his friends,[27] and it excludes a number of older ministers distinguished for their learning and moderation (i.e. Robert Wallace, William Wishart *secundus*, and even the Moderates' philosophical mentor Francis Hutcheson and early ally

---

[26] Cf. Dominick LaCapra, *Rethinking Intellectual History: Texts, Contexts, Language* (Ithaca, N.Y., 1983), esp. chap. 1. Though I disagree with LaCapra's critique of the social history of ideas, I have found it a stimulating and useful challenge, particularly in its insistence that every text is open to more than one sort of interpretation and that reading a text in historical "context" is a more complicated undertaking than some intellectual historians have been accustomed to think. In my view, however, such insights represent means of refining and improving—rather than grounds for abandoning—the social history of ideas.

[27] Clark diss., i–viii, 49–54.

Patrick Cuming)—who have frequently been designated "Moderates," "Old Moderates," or "Early Moderates" despite the fact that they so rarely supported the specific policies and programs of what came to be called the Moderate party. "Moderatism," a term that did not appear until the nineteenth century, is used in a somewhat narrower sense than that suggested by Clark. Here it denotes not a general mood of moderation in the kirk but the particular beliefs and ideological principles of the Robertson Moderates. Since there is no satisfactory term for an individual member of the anti-Moderate or "Popular" party in the Church of Scotland during the second half of the eighteenth century, wordy phrases such as "member of the Popular party" have deliberately been used instead of misleading labels like the pejorative "Highflyer" and the anachronistic "Evangelical." I have occasionally employed John Witherspoon's word "orthodox" to refer loosely to the Moderates' opponents in the kirk, but this usage is not meant to suggest that the Moderates themselves were necessarily *un*orthodox in their doctrine.

Like "Moderatism," "conservatism" and "nationalism" are nineteenth-century terms that I have applied to a somewhat earlier period for want of satisfactory alternatives. "Conservatism," or more precisely "Whig conservatism," is used both formally, in the sense of support for the status quo as such, and substantively, in the special eighteenth-century British sense of veneration for order and orders grounded in the constitution that was thought to have been secured and perfected following the "Glorious" Revolution of 1688–1689. "Conservative," "constitutional," or "establishment" Whigs of this sort must be distinguished from Jacobite reactionaries, who were the only true Tories in the Scottish context, as well as from various other types of eighteenth-century Whigs—ranging from "skeptical" Whigs like David Hume at one extreme to "radical" Whigs at the other. The addition of the word "Presbyterian" to this terminological complex is meant to suggest an ecclesiastical component—once again both formal (i.e. support for the established church as such) and substantive (i.e. support for the Presbyterian system of worship, doctrine, and above all church polity)—that narrows the focus to eighteenth-century Scotland.

Insofar as they approved of the Revolution Settlement of 1688–1690, the Union of 1707, the Hanoverian Succession of 1714, and the eighteenth-century constitution generally, all Whig-Presbyterian conservatives in Scotland were British patriots, eager to defend established institutions against perceived threats from Jacobites, radical Whigs, and foreign foes. Yet those same British patriots could sometimes be driven to espouse a very different set of values that

17

may—with caution—be called "Scottish nationalism." As used here, this term is stripped of the "romantic" and politically separatist connotations that it would later have. It refers chiefly to the passionate attachment and deep pride that many eighteenth-century Scots felt for their native land, particularly when they believed it was being unjustly maligned by "John Bull." In their efforts to resolve, or at least ease, this tension between British patriotism and Scottish nationalism, the Moderate literati of Edinburgh struggled with a dilemma that has remained troublesome for many Scots from the time of the Enlightenment to the present day.

In an effort to effect a balance between historical and topical analysis, this book has been divided into two parts, one of which is structured chronologically, the other thematically. Part I traces the development of the Moderate literati of Edinburgh from birth around 1720 to the establishment of Moderate hegemony in the Church of Scotland and the University of Edinburgh about forty years later. The opening chapter surveys the first thirty years of their lives, with emphasis on the similarity of their backgrounds and the emergence of their common identity as militant, conservative Whig-Presbyterians during the era of the '45. Chapter 2 concentrates on their coming of age as ecclesiastical politicians and defenders of enlightened principles in the period from 1751 to 1757. It was during those critical years that the Moderate party came into existence and attained prominence, originally as a rallying point for Presbyterian ministers and lay elders striving to bring order and regularity to the Church of Scotland, and later as a means of reconciling Presbyterianism with politeness and enlightenment. Part I culminates in chapter 3 with an examination of the manner in which the Moderate literati of Edinburgh secured prestigious and relatively lucrative academic and ecclesiastical offices and then used those offices to establish what has sometimes been called the "Moderate Regime" in the Church of Scotland and the University of Edinburgh.

The second part of the book considers the role of the Moderate literati of Edinburgh as propagators of a distinctive ideology during their years as an academic and ecclesiastical elite. Chapter 4 deals first with their role as leaders of the remarkable "awakening" of polite literature and enlightened values that occurred among the clergy in the Church of Scotland during the age of the Scottish Enlightenment. It then suggests similarities in the spirit and style of Moderate moral teaching and preaching, particularly as practiced by Adam Ferguson and Hugh Blair, respectively. Chapter 5 explores the message of Moderate moral teaching and preaching in greater depth, with attention focused on the cardinal doctrines of Christian-Stoicism and Whig-Presbyterian conservatism. Chapters 6 and 7 treat the involvement of the Moderate literati of Edinburgh with four issues of great contemporary concern: the Scots militia, Ossian, the American Revolution, and the "No Popery" affair of 1778–1779. In addition to demonstrating the unity and cohesiveness of the Moderate literati of Edinburgh, these contemporary controversies provide an opportunity for examining the practical applications of specific elements of Moderate ideology, such as Scottish nationalism, political conservatism, civic humanism, and religious tolerance. The final chapter sketches the gradual decline of the Moderate literati of Edinburgh and the Scottish Enlightenment in the closing years of the eighteenth century and concludes with a brief summary of the fundamental features of Moderatism.

PART I

THE MAKING OF
THE MODERATE REGIME

Students, Ministers, Volunteers

———— ❁ ————

POINTS OF
BIOGRAPHICAL CONVERGENCE

At the Revolution [of 1688–1689] the churches had been most filled with vulgar and illiterate men, Presbytery having been depressed and sometimes persecuted for twenty-eight years. . . . But after the secession [of the 1730s] the fear of the people gradually abated, and a set of young men entered into orders who had no need to put on the mask of hypocrisy. They added some degree of politeness and knowledge of the world to their superior learning.

Alexander Carlyle,
Memorial on the Church of Scotland, 1784

Scotland in 1720 stood at the threshold of a new age. In the past lay the upheavals and insecurity of the sixteenth and seventeenth centuries, when political instability, economic impoverishment, religious animosity, and an ambiguous, frustrating relationship with England had fostered a reputation for strife, confusion, and backwardness. The Revolution Settlement of 1688–1690, the Union of the Scottish and English Parliaments in 1707, and the Hanoverian Succession in 1714 had paved the way for a new era of stability and progress. There was the promise of economic prosperity and political participation as partners with England in a free and stable "united" kingdom. There was the guarantee of religious and legal autonomy that was built into the terms of the Union. There was the hope that Presbyterianism, restored as the national religion of Scotland in the aftermath of the Revolution, would put an end to the bitter religious struggles that had been such a critical factor in Scottish life since the days of John Knox. There was the prospect of significant educational reform, as demonstrated already by the major academic reorganization that Principal William Carstares had engineered at the University of

Edinburgh in 1708. And there was the trend toward a revolution in manners as the *Spectator*'s ideals of refinement and politeness steadily took hold.[1]

This, at least, is how an enlightened Presbyterian Whig might have assessed Scotland's condition in 1720. Others might have seen the matter in a different light. They might have argued that the Union had neither worked the economic miracles that some had predicted nor solved the problem of Anglo-Scottish relations, which had deteriorated rather than improved in the decade after 1707. They might have asserted that Scotland had become a virtual province of her larger, wealthier, and more powerful southern neighbor. They might have pointed out that English guarantees of religious autonomy had already been proved false by the patronage act of 1712, which had transferred the right of selecting ministers for most vacant Scottish churches from the local Protestant heritors (landowners) and Presbyterian elders who had been granted that right in 1690 to the traditional lay patrons who had exercised it in Roman Catholic and Episcopalian times. They might have observed that the fanaticism of many Presbyterians and the Episcopalian purges that followed the Revolution did not suggest the advent of a new age of moderation in religious affairs. They might have contended that Presbyterian enthusiasm and rigidity had retarded the development of Scottish education while the celebrated reforms of Principal Carstares had brought little real improvement to the University of Edinburgh. Above all, they might have noted that opposition in Scotland to the Hanoverian and Presbyterian establishments and the Union had remained strong among disaffected Roman Catholics, Episcopalians, and Highlanders, who had threatened rebellion under the banner of Jacobitism in 1708 and had carried out their threat in the Jacobite uprising of 1715.

It was into this world of hope and promise, but also of lingering discontent, tension, and uncertainty, that the five subjects of this study—the "Moderate literati of Edinburgh"—were born between 1718 and 1723. William Robertson, Hugh Blair, Adam Ferguson, John Home, and Alexander Carlyle all came from respectable Whig-Presbyterian families of moderate means that could claim distant kinship ties to one or another of the ancient clans or great families of Scotland. A good deal of clerical blood ran in their veins: three of them were sons of Presbyterian ministers, and a fourth was descended from

---

[1] On the impact of the *Spectator*, see Nicholas Phillipson, "The Scottish Enlightenment," in *The Enlightenment in National Context*, ed. Roy Porter and Mikuláš Teich (Cambridge, 1981), 26–27.

an illustrious line of Presbyterian divines. Most of them followed family tradition in deciding to enter the ministry, just as later in life they tended to marry ministers' daughters who frequently were also their cousins or distant relations. Four of them grew up in the vicinity of Edinburgh and took the arts course at Edinburgh University during the 1730s. All five were enrolled in the divinity course at the same university and were ordained ministers in the Church of Scotland during the 1740s. By the middle of the century they were practicing clergymen and close personal friends of about thirty years of age, gradually beginning to distinguish themselves as preachers and men of letters.

The eldest of the five was Hugh Blair. Born in Edinburgh in 1718, he was the only child of a once-prominent merchant who had lost his money in financial speculation and subsequently been reduced to a minor position in the excise. His family, which was descended from the Blairs of Blair, had produced numerous Presbyterian ministers of note, including the poet Robert Blair and Hugh's uncle James Bannatine of Trinity Church, Edinburgh. Bannatine's sons George and Hugh were to become Moderate ministers themselves, and their sister Katherine would later become Hugh Blair's wife. Another Moderate clergyman among Blair's relations was the historian Robert Watson, a professor, and later principal, at St. Andrews University. Still another relation, John Blair, was an early member of the Moderate circle who took orders in the Church of England and eventually became prebendary of Westminster.

Like Blair, to whom he seems to have been distantly related,[2] William Robertson was descended on his father's side from a distinguished Scottish family, the Robertsons of Gladney. He was born near Edinburgh in 1721 in the parish of Borthwick, where his father was then minister. Though a strict Calvinist, the senior William Robertson was liberal enough to keep a library well stocked with the works of continental Arminian divines, and his historical research on Mary Queen of Scots may have stimulated his son's interest in the history of Scotland.[3] Robertson's mother had an equally strong influence on young William.[4] The union of his mother's sister Mary Pitcairn with Rev. James Nisbet of Edinburgh produced a daughter who would one day become Robertson's wife and a son who, as a member of the Edinburgh town council, would wield political influence on Robertson's behalf. His father's sister, meanwhile, married into the Adam

[2] Hew Scott, ed., *Fasti Ecclesiæ Scoticanæ: The Succession of Ministers in the Church of Scotland*, new ed., 7 vols. (Edinburgh, 1915–28), 1:71.

[3] Ibid., 40; Erskine, 264.

[4] *The Life and Times of Henry, Lord Brougham*, 2d ed., 3 vols. (Edinburgh, 1871), 1:32.

family of architects, with whom Robertson was very close.[5] It was through the Adam family that Robertson came to be connected by ties of marriage to his future assistant in the administration of ecclesiastical affairs, Rev. John Drysdale, and to Drysdale's protégé and son-in-law Andrew Dalzel.

Alexander Carlyle was also the son of the minister of a parish in the Edinburgh vicinity, in this case Prestonpans in East Lothian. Although Carlyle described his father as "orthodox and popular," the strictness of his upbringing was mitigated somewhat by the influence of his mother and his mother's father, Rev. Alexander Robison, a Dumfriesshire clergyman of relatively liberal sentiments.[6] Carlyle's kinship ties on his mother's side included his cousin and close friend Rev. William Wight, later professor of ecclesiastical history at Glasgow University, and Provost George Bell of Dumfries, who had political links with the duke of Queensberry. Carlyle's grandmothers were connected with prominent Border families, such as Queensberry, Douglas, and Jardine, and through the last of these connections Alexander may have been related to a clergyman who would become a member of the Moderate literati's inner circle until his premature death in 1766—John Jardine.[7] Carlyle's patrilineal ancestry could be traced to the Carlyles of Brydekirk, a branch of the Carlyle (or Carlisle) family of northern English origin. One of his father's sisters had married into the English gentry, and another who resided in London taught him "to read English, with just pronunciation and a very tolerable accent—an accomplishment which in those days was very rare."[8] Finally, the Carlyle family was connected through marriage to the Johnstones of Westerhall,[9] giving rise to distant kinship ties with several of the Moderates' good friends of wealth and influence, including Sir William Johnstone Pulteney, his uncle Patrick Murray, Lord Elibank, and his younger brother George Johnstone.

John Home had fewer clerical ties than did the other members of the group. His father was town clerk of Leith, where John was born in 1722. Able to trace his ancestry directly back to Sir James Home of Cowdenknows and indirectly to the earls of Home, he could, with poetic license, boast of being "sprung from the ancient nobles of the land."[10] It has been said (though never demonstrated) that he was a

---

[5] John Fleming, *Robert Adam and His Circle* (Cambridge, Mass., 1962), 337–38.

[6] *Auto.*, 2, 14, 31–32.

[7] Ibid., Prefatory Note.

[8] Ibid., 4.

[9] Ibid., Prefatory Note.

[10] Quoted in Sir Walter Scott, "Life and Works of John Home" (1827), in *The Miscellaneous Prose Works of Sir Walter Scott*, 28 vols. (Edinburgh, 1834–1835), 19:286.

kinsman of the philosopher David Hume, with whom he bantered good-naturedly about the proper spelling of their common surname. The one Presbyterian clergyman among his close relations was his cousin Rev. William Home, whose niece would eventually marry Alexander Carlyle at the instigation of John Home. John himself married William Home's daughter Mary, the first cousin of Carlyle's wife. Another important marital bond was to the Moderate minister Henry Grieve, who married John Home's sister in 1762.

Adam Ferguson, born in 1723, was the youngest child of the minister of Logierait, a Gaelic-speaking parish in Perthshire at the foothills of the Highlands. His father, the son of an artisan, was a strict Calvinist and firm Whig who was linked by friendship and patronage to the duke of Atholl. His mother was a woman of genteel birth through whom Adam was distantly related to several noble families, including, perhaps, the dukes of Argyll.[11] She was also the aunt of two eminent Scottish scientists who were to number among Adam's closest friends: James Russel and Joseph Black. When Ferguson finally married at the age of forty-three, after being rebuffed by the sister of Carlyle's wife, his bride was a niece of Black from Aberdeen. On his father's side Ferguson may have been related to a Moderate minister and close family friend who shared his name, Rev. Adam Fergusson of Moulin, as well as to William Robertson.[12]

These brief biographical sketches suggest the importance of kinship in preparing these young men for successful careers as ministers and professors in the Whig-Presbyterian world of eighteenth-century Scotland. The Presbyterian clergy and Scottish professoriate of this era were marked by an extraordinarily high degree of inbreeding and clannishness. Among Church of Scotland clergymen active in Edinburgh between 1725 and 1775, for example, more than two-thirds of those for whom data are available were the sons of ministers,[13] and many owed their advancement within the church to family connections. Roger Emerson's research reveals a similar pattern among eighteenth-century Scottish professors, whose fathers were Presbyterian clergymen in more than a third of the cases for which data are available and whose kinship ties with other professors were remarkably extensive.[14] Examining the careers of the Moderate literati of Edinburgh provides, inter alia, a case study of the role of

---

[11] John Small, "Biographical Sketch of Adam Ferguson," *TRSE* 23 (1864): 599; Fagg, 7.

[12] "Adam Ferguson," *Edinburgh Review* 125 (1867): 50.

[13] These data have been compiled from Scott, *Fasti*, vol. 1.

[14] I am grateful to Professor Emerson for providing me with data from a projected study of Scottish professors.

kinship and connection in Scottish ecclesiastical and academic politics during the age of the Scottish Enlightenment.

In addition to suitable family backgrounds and connections, a second factor that helped to qualify these young men for distinction in the clerical and academic professions was education. Hugh Blair attended the large and prestigious High School of Edinburgh, John Home the nearby Leith Grammar School, and William Robertson the grammar school at Dalkeith, which was then considered the finest school in Scotland.[15] These grammar, high, or "burgh" schools offered a Latin-based, college-preparatory curriculum to young boys who might well find themselves in one of Scotland's five universities at fourteen, thirteen, or even twelve years of age. Although it was considerably more difficult for boys educated in country or "parish" schools to attain the same degree of scholarly preparation available in the grammar schools, Alexander Carlyle and Adam Ferguson both managed to overcome this obstacle. Carlyle studied at the parish school in Prestonpans, where an outstanding teacher whom his father had brought to the parish taught him Greek as well as Latin.[16] Ferguson began his education at the humble parish school in Logiarait but at age nine was sent to live with a relative in Perth in order to attend the grammar school there.[17]

When it came to selecting a college arts course, the choices followed patterns dictated by family tradition and geography. Like his father before him and most other college-bound Perthshire lads, Ferguson enrolled at St. Andrews University, where he studied Greek, mathematics, logic, metaphysics, and ethics and took an M.A. in 1742. The others attended their regional college, the University of Edinburgh.[18] By the time of their arrival there in the 1730s, the system of specialized professorships that Principal Carstares had introduced in 1708 was beginning to bear fruit.[19] The practice of taking formal degrees had virtually died out, but the arts curriculum remained a good deal more structured throughout the century than is some-

---

[15] Alexander Carlyle, "A Comparison of Two Eminent Characters Attempted after the Manner of Plutarch," in *AC*, 277.

[16] *Auto.*, 34n.

[17] Fagg, 10–11.

[18] Robert Noyes Smart, "Some Observations on the Provinces of the Scottish Universities, 1560–1850," in *The Scottish Tradition*, ed. G. W. S. Barrow (Edinburgh, 1974), 91–106.

[19] On the transition from the regenting system, in which each regent taught all subjects to a particular class of students over a four-year period, to the modern system of specialized chairs in various disciplines, see the accounts in Alexander Bower, *The History of the University of Edinburgh*, 3 vols. (Edinburgh, 1817), vol. 2, chap. 9, and Sir Alexander Grant, *The Story of the University of Edinburgh*, 2 vols. (London, 1884), vol. 1, chap. 5.

times thought. Though a certain amount of variation and specialization was possible, all Edinburgh arts students were expected to take a basic sequence of courses that remained unchanged throughout the century: humanity or Latin, Greek, mathematics, logic, natural philosophy, and moral philosophy. At this time the humanity course was taught by John Kerr, whom Carlyle considered "very much master of his business."[20] As the name implies, this was a comprehensive introduction to Latin grammar and literature, ranging from the usual assortment of classical Roman authors to later Christian works.[21] John Stevenson's logic class, which so impressed Robertson, John Erskine, and many of their contemporaries, was equally broad in scope, including as it did literary criticism, the history of philosophy, and much else in addition to logic proper.[22] The mathematics classes were taught by the renowned Colin Maclaurin, a brilliant teacher whose courses treated not only algebra, geometry, and calculus but also surveying, fortification, geography, optics, astronomy, and gunnery. John Pringle's moral philosophy class dealt mainly with the moral theory of Cicero, Marcus Aurelius, Pufendorf, and Bacon, but some attention was also paid to natural theology and politics. Two equally broad "electives" in history were offered by Charles Mackie: a survey of European political and intellectual history from the fall of Rome to the Reformation and a Roman antiquities class that covered all aspects of Roman culture.[23] Rounding out the curriculum were various supplementary classes in subjects like modern languages and dancing, taught by instructors to whom the town council allowed use of the college rooms but granted no salary.

Here was a comprehensive educational program designed to acquaint students with a wide range of academic disciplines. It was, as Samuel Johnson observed with characteristic condescension, not the sort of education that bred outstanding classical scholars of the Oxford variety.[24] But that was not its intent. Although Latin and Greek were by no means ignored, the core of the eighteenth-century arts

[20] *Auto.*, 35.

[21] The class descriptions presented here are drawn chiefly from Robert Henderson's account in *SM* 3 (August 1741): 371–74.

[22] Among Stevenson's collection of prize student essays is one by William Robertson, dated 30 April 1737, bearing the significant title "De probabilitate historica, sive evidentia morali" (EUL, Dc. 4.54; courtesy of Roger Emerson). For more on Stevenson and his student essays, as well as other topics concerning the Edinburgh arts faculty during this period, see Peter Jones, "The Scottish Professoriate and the Polite Academy, 1720–46," in *WV*, 89–117.

[23] On Mackie see L. W. Sharp, "Charles Mackie, the First Professor of History at Edinburgh University," *SHR* 41 (1961): 23–45.

[24] Samuel Johnson, *A Journey to the Western Islands of Scotland* (1773), ed. Mary Lascelles (New Haven, 1971), 160–61.

curriculum at Edinburgh and other Scottish universities was the philosophy sequence of logic, natural philosophy, and moral philosophy. Mathematics and the ancient languages were regarded less as ends in themselves than as the necessary foundation for philosophical attainments.[25] The chief objective was the production of well-rounded gentlemen, imbued with Christian humanist values and familiar with all branches of polite learning. Though only one of the Edinburgh arts professors of this era (Maclaurin) possessed a European reputation, good teaching was the rule, and the growth of the Scottish Enlightenment was in part the consequence of this fact.

During the late 1730s and early 1740s, these prospective clergymen matriculated at Divinity Hall in the University of Edinburgh. Since formal course work was limited to dull theological discourses on Pictet and Turrettini, read in Latin by Professors John Gowdie and Patrick Cuming, the Edinburgh divinity students of this period were inadvertently encouraged to provide their own stimulation and direction.[26] It was during these years that the ministers who would form the nucleus of the Moderate party became intimate with one another. A student society called the Hen (or Hens) Club was frequented, and enough independent literary projects were begun to justify applying the inscription on William Robertson's commonplace books from the late 1730s—*vita sine literis mors est*—to some of Robertson's classmates. Several of them, including Blair, Home, and Carlyle, were dedicated enough to earn M.A. degrees by writing substantial Latin theses.[27] Robertson attended Mackie's European history class (as did Home) and began a translation of the *Meditations* of Marcus Aurelius.[28] Blair wrote at least two long poems that were published but have not survived.[29] Home started working on a draft of his first tragedy, *Agis*, which he completed in 1747. Ferguson pursued a variety of intellectual activities and served as secretary to the influential Lord Milton.[30] Carlyle took leave to study for a year at

[25] John Veitch, "Philosophy in the Scottish Universities," *Mind* 2 (1877): 74–91, 207–34, esp. 74; George Elder Davie, *The Democratic Intellect: Scotland and Her Universities in the Nineteenth Century* (Edinburgh, 1961), 13.

[26] *Auto.*, 63; Somerville, 18–19.

[27] Printed copies of Blair's thesis, *De fundamentis & obligatione legis naturæ* (1739), and Home's thesis, *De republica vel imperio civili* (1742), are in the Edinburgh University Library. Carlyle's thesis of 1746 does not appear to have survived, but his degree is noted in *A Catalogue of the Graduates in the Faculties of Arts, Divinity, and Law of the University of Edinburgh*, ed. David Laing (Edinburgh, 1858), 208.

[28] EUL, Dc. 5.24:203. A brief excerpt from Robertson's translation of the *Meditations*, dated 21 January 1742, is printed in Brougham, 321–23. The complete manuscript is in the NLS, 3955.

[29] Robert Morrell Schmitz, *Hugh Blair* (New York, 1948), 139.

[30] John Lee, "Adam Ferguson," *EBS*, 4:240. Though the story of Ferguson serving as Milton's secretary at the age of nineteen has been doubted by some of his biogra-

Leyden and then for two years under William Leechman and Francis Hutcheson at Glasgow University, where he received a better education in divinity and moral philosophy than was available at Edinburgh but found that even the best students "had neither the strength nor the polish of the Blairs, and Robertsons, and Fergusons, and Homes."[31]

While these university students were developing their minds and personal relationships a powerful wave of evangelicalism was sweeping through parts of America and Great Britain. In Scotland the evangelical movement reached its peak in 1742, when tens of thousands were stirred by the preaching of William McCulloch and George Whitefield at Cambuslang, near Glasgow. With its open-air and itinerant preaching, its mass conversions, its emotionalism, and its occasional instances of mysticism, the "Cambus'lang Wark" was an unusual form of Scottish religious behavior.[32] For this reason it was subject to attack not only from theological liberals but also from some orthodox, scholastic Calvinists who were suspicious of enthusiasm and more concerned with election than with conversion.[33] When the controversy over Cambuslang was at its height, students at the University of Edinburgh took up the issue in their debating society. The anti-Cambuslang forces were led by William Robertson, and John Erskine headed the pro-Cambuslang cause. Although the precise content of the debate is not known, Erskine's position is indicated by the title of his pamphlet of 1742: *The Signs of the Times Considered; or the High Probability that the present appearances in New England and the West of Scotland are a prelude to the glorious things promised to the church in the latter ages.* Against this view, Robertson most likely argued that Whitefield's brand of evangelicalism violated the principles of enlightened Christianity and threatened to revive the fanaticism and

---

phers, I am inclined to believe it for several reasons. First, the story comes from Ferguson's own son, as reported in *Chambers's Journal* (24 February 1855):113. Second, it seems believable, considering Ferguson's intellectual precociousness and family ties with the earl of Ilay (Milton's patron) and duke of Atholl (Ilay's ally). Third, it helps explain why Ferguson suddenly transferred from St. Andrews to Edinburgh divinity school in 1742 and how he subsequently became so intimate with Milton and his family.

[31] *Auto.*, 95–96.

[32] Robert Sherman Rutter, "The New Birth: Evangelicalism in the Transatlantic Community during the Great Awakening, 1739–1745" (Ph.D. diss., Rutgers University, 1982), esp. 113–30, 337–407; Arthur Fawcett, *The Cambuslang Revival: The Scottish Evangelical Revival of the Eighteenth Century* (London, 1971), esp. chaps. 6 and 7. But see Ian A. Muirhead, "The Revival as a Dimension of Scottish Church History," *RSCHS* 20 (1978): 179–96, for instances of earlier revivals.

[33] See the remarkably popular *Letter from a Blacksmith to the Ministers and Elders of the Kirk of Scotland* (London, 1758), which attacks field preaching from an orthodox Calvinist perspective and recommends "solemn awe" instead of enthusiasm.

disorder of the seventeenth century. He may also have invoked orthodox Presbyterian arguments against field preaching and revival-
ism. It is said that the debate was sufficiently heated to bring about
the dissolution of this debating club as well as a temporary break in
personal relations between Robertson and Erskine, who would later
become leaders of the rival parties in the church.[34]

In the opinion of William Robertson and his closest friends, the
new evangelicalism that flourished at Cambuslang was but one of
several serious challenges to the Church of Scotland during the 1730s
and 1740s. Equally troublesome were the unresolved and potentially
explosive question of church patronage and the stubborn protest
against the policies and regulations of the highest church courts by
a group of devout dissidents led by Ebenezer Erskine. Just as the
evangelical movement threatened to dissolve the distinctive character of Scottish Presbyterianism in a flood of nondenominational, re-
vivalist enthusiasm, the secession that resulted from Erskine's protest
raised the specter of an endless series of small, rigid, Presbyterian
splinter groups, each claiming a monopooly over religious truth and
salvation. To Robertson's band of Edinburgh divinity students—young
men who would one day form the heart of the Moderate party in the
Church of Scotland—the enthusiasm of the evangelicals, the narrow
sectarianism of the seceders, and the widespread opposition to the
law of patronage were all manifestations of the disorderly and de-
structive tendencies latent in radical Presbyterianism. As we shall see
in the next chapter, their response to such tendencies was not to renounce Christianity or Presbyterianism but to direct their energies
toward building a strong, unified, orderly Scottish Presbyterian church
that would be capable of withstanding every variety of fanatical behavior and of providing a cure for the ecclesiastical instability of the
1730s and 1740s.

Upon completion of six years of divinity school, young men pursuing a career in the ministry were expected to take qualifying examinations or "trials," after which they would be licensed to preach
the gospel as "probationers." The trials, consisting mainly of a sermon and scriptural exegeses, do not appear to have constituted a serious obstacle in most cases. But a license to preach did not guarantee ordination and a church living, and many a probationer spent
several difficult and demeaning years as a private tutor, school-
teacher, or assistant minister before obtaining a parish of his own. If
the five probationers under discussion managed to secure respect-

---

[34] Sir Henry Moncreiff Wellwood, *Account of the Life and Writings of John Erskine*
(Edinburgh, 1818), 16, 100.

able ecclesiastical positions within a relatively short time, the reason has as much to do with their family backgrounds and connections as with their intellectual promise and preaching skills.

Ferguson's case was the most unusual. At the request of the duchess of Atholl, the general assembly of the Church of Scotland voted in 1745 to permit Ferguson to take his trials after just three years of divinity school so that he could qualify for a chaplaincy in her son's Highland regiment, the Black Watch. He was accordingly licensed and ordained by the Presbytery of Dunkeld and joined his regiment in Flanders to begin a decade of military life that would earn him the sobriquet "the Warlike Chaplain."[35] Blair, after briefly serving as a private tutor and as minister of the little parish of Collessie in Fife, was soon back in the Edinburgh vicinity as one of the ministers at the Canongate Church. Robertson and Home secured livings in rural East Lothian parishes situated in the Presbytery of Haddington: Home was presented in 1746 by Alexander Home of Eccles to replace Blair's cousin at Athelstaneford (ordained in 1747); Robertson was chosen in 1743 by the earl of Hopetoun to succeed his own uncle at Gladsmuir (ordained in 1744). Carlyle was ordained as the minister of Inveresk in the Presbytery of Dalkeith in 1748. While still in their mid twenties, then, all of them except Ferguson were settled at parishes within an hour or two's ride from Edinburgh, earning incomes that were quite respectable by the standards of their age and profession (see Table 1).

The case of Carlyle's contested settlement at Inveresk, a large, wealthy parish quite close to Edinburgh, throws light on the primary point of contention in the eighteenth-century kirk: church patronage. When Carlyle's father learned of an impending vacancy at Inveresk, he quickly got in touch with his friend Lord Drummore of the Court of Session, who recommended Alexander to the duke of Buccleuch (the patron) and his brother-in-law the duke of Queensbury. The people of the parish, however, objected that Carlyle was "too young, and too full of levity, and too much addicted to the company of [his] superiors." There were also complaints that he "danced frequently in a manner prohibited by the laws of the Church," wore his hat "agee," and "had been seen galloping through the Links one day between one and two o'clock," and there were doubts about whether he possessed the "grace of God."[36] Though Carlyle made light of these objections in his memoirs, it appears that only the fortuitous inter-

---

[35] Fagg, 17–18, 20–22. Fagg argues, however, that Ferguson was not at the Battle of Fontenoy despite the popular legend that he led the charge there.

[36] *Auto.*, 216–17.

TABLE 1

Annual Incomes (in pounds sterling) of Blair, Carlyle, and
Robertson, ca. 1750

Source of Income	Blair (Canongate pop. 3,600)	Carlyle (Inveresk pop. 4,400)	Robertson (Gladsmuir pop. 1,700)
Victual (wheat, barley, oats)	0	25	53
Cash stipend	103	61	16
Total	103	86	69
Value of glebe (farmland)	0	7	3
Value of grass (pasture)	0	1	3
Total (excluding value of manse and money for communion elements)	103	94	75

NOTE. The survey calculated the values of victual, glebe, and grass in pounds
sterling on the basis of current prices. Figures have been rounded off to the
nearest pound. John Home's parish, Athelstaneford, was not included in the
survey, but it can be assumed that the minister of that small rural parish
(population under 700) received a relatively low stipend that was mostly, if
not entirely, in the form of victual.

SOURCE: Church of Scotland Stipend Survey, 1750, SRO, CH 1/5/43.

vention of a devout seceder woman prevented a popular outcry that
might have cost him the parish. The whole incident illustrates both
the usefulness of family connections for obtaining church patronage
and the tension inherent in the struggles between pious parishioners
and landed patrons over the right to fill vacant churches.

Yet the fact that his settlement at Inveresk encountered widespread opposition should not be taken to mean that Carlyle neglected his pastoral duties. On the contrary, most of the available
evidence suggests that Carlyle, like the Reverend Balwhidder in John
Galt's novel *Annals of the Parish*, overcame the initial opposition to his
presentation by means of diligent pastoral service.[37] He excelled as a
preacher, helped to establish a Sunday school in his presbytery, used
his connections frequently on behalf of his parishioners, and was actively involved in the allocation of poor money and the administration of the poor house at Musselburgh. Other Moderate ministers of
Carlyle's generation shared these or similar pastoral concerns and were
usually popular with all but the most rigid or zealous of their parish-

[37] John Galt, *Annals of the Parish*, ed. James Kinsley (London, 1967).

ioners.[38] It is significant that when Carlyle and Home came under fire during the playhouse controversy of 1756–1757, their congregations stood fast behind them, prompting Home to remark that his one regret about resigning his charge stemmed from "leaving my poor Plebeians, whose attachment to me is as extraordinary as it is extreme."[39]

The extent of the group's piety is more difficult to assess. In the only thorough treatment of eighteenth-century Moderate theology, Ian D. L. Clark has shown that the Moderates' religious beliefs were not nearly so superficial or unorthodox as their opponents, along with all too many careless scholars, have claimed.[40] None of the Moderates in the William Robertson circle had any scruples about subscribing to the church's rigorously Calvinist creed, the Westminster Confession of Faith, and none of them ever overtly denied its fundamental tenets. On the other hand, insofar as they were quite willing to tolerate other churches and religious viewpoints, and insofar as the main thrust of their religion involved moral preaching and teaching rather than doctrine, they were frequently accused of impiety by the strictest and most zealous of their fellow churchmen. "No wonder that mankind are strangers to the power and knowledge of Religion," wrote one anonymous critic of Alexander Carlyle, "when the lean harangues of Moral Philosophy is all that is presented to them from day to day."[41] Although this charge was certainly exaggerated, as anyone who has perused the manuscripts of Carlyle's religious devotions can attest, it is undeniable that Carlyle and his friends lacked the religious fervor of many of their brethren. Without explicitly rejecting Calvinist doctrine, they sought to shift the emphasis of Scottish Presbyterianism from predestination and election to individual and social morality. And without surrendering the fundamental Christian ideal of salvation, they attempted to supplement this otherworldly goal with ethical and ideological objectives designed to increase virtue and happiness while strengthening the prevailing social, political, and ecclesiastical orders.

In pursuing their vision of an enlightened, tolerant Scottish kirk serving as a bulwark of virtue and stability, these young Presbyterian

---

[38] Clark diss., app. B; Andrew J. Campbell, *Two Centuries of the Church of Scotland, 1707–1929* (Paisley, 1930), 100–101; William Thomas Cairns, "Jupiter Carlyle and the Scottish Moderates," in *The Religion of Dr. Johnson and Other Essays* (1946; reprint, Freeport, N.Y., 1969), 81–110; John Kay, *A Series of Original Portraits and Caricature Etchings*, 2 vols. (Edinburgh, 1837–1842), 1:65.

[39] Home to Gilbert Elliot, 1 June [1757], NLS, 11009:141–42.

[40] Clark diss., esp. chaps. 7 and 8.

[41] Letter to Carlyle from "a very scurrilous anonymous," n.d., NLS, 3431:238.

divines had to prepare for war on two fronts. On one front stood rigid Calvinists, evangelicals of the Cambuslang variety, seceders such as Ebenezer Erskine, and other pious Presbyterians who tended, whatever the differences among them, to be more devout, more doctrinaire, more hostile to the law of patronage, less tolerant of religious and intellectual deviations, and less conservative in politics than the Moderates. It was on this front that the Moderate literati of Edinburgh would wage most of their ecclesiastical battles, particularly against the loose coalition of anti-Moderate forces within the established church that came to be called the Popular party. Yet bloody as these battles sometimes were, they were fought by men who assumed, as a point of common ground, a shared preference for Presbyterianism and the Hanoverian or Whig establishment. They were literally struggles among brethren. On the other front, however, the Moderate literati were pitted against men seeking to undermine the very foundations of the Whig-Presbyterian order. It was this Jacobite challenge to the political and religious status quo that provided the first major opportunity for the Moderate literati of Edinburgh to formulate in words and defend with deeds the principles of their emerging ideology.

CRISIS AND COMMITMENT:
THE '45

A band of fierce Barbarians, from the hills,
Rush'd like a torrent down upon the vale.

John Home, *Douglas*, 1757

Let every Scotchman recollect the terror and disgrace of the year
1745, and let him congratulate his country on the certain assur-
ance of never beholding such a scene any more.

Alexander Carlyle,
The Question Relating to a Scots Militia, 1760

Like the American War of Independence later in the century, the
Scottish Jacobite uprising of 1745 was essentially a struggle between
England and one of her rebellious provinces set in the international
context of continuous Anglo-French rivalry. The differences between these two rebellions reveal why one failed as completely as the
other succeeded. Whereas the American cause eventually received
concrete support from the French, the Scottish Jacobites of 1745 obtained little French aid other than the inadvertent diversions furnished by the War of Austrian Succession, which kept British troops
occupied on the Continent while Charles Edward Stuart was gathering his forces in the Highlands.[42] Ideologically, the American
revolutionaries were generally progressive, whereas the Jacobites were
thoroughly reactionary in seeking to restore the royal family that had
become synonymous with absolutism in politics and religion. Geo-
graphically, there was an enormous difference between a rebellion
occurring far across the sea and one happening just across the Tweed.
Finally, whereas the cause of American independence was popular
in the colonies, the Jacobite cause met with indifference or active opposition from most Scots, particularly in the Lowlands, where Presbyterian and Hanoverian sympathies had taken hold.

The ultimate futility of the rebellion, however, should not be allowed to mask its profound psychological impact at the time it occurred. As the Jacobite army approached Edinburgh in the late summer of 1745, the inhabitants were seized, in David Hume's words,

---

[42] The story of France's indecisiveness in this matter is told in F. J. McLynn, *France
and the Jacobite Rising of 1745* (Edinburgh, 1981).

with "an universal Panic, and that not groundless."[43] Some, like Provost Archibald Stewart, thought it best that the town fall to the Jacobites with as little bloodshed as possible. Others viewed Stewart himself as a secret Jacobite and opted for defending the capital at all costs. Despite the provost's lack of enthusiasm, a local regiment and several companies of volunteers were raised, including one company partially composed of older college students under the command of Stewart's political and personal rival, George Drummond. Zealous Whig-Presbyterians like Drummond and Professor Colin Maclaurin hoped that these raw recruits, together with improved fortifications, the town guard, an honorific organization of burgesses with the misleading name "trained bands," and two regiments of regular army dragoons posted outside the city, would be sufficient to deter the Jacobite forces until government troops commanded by General John Cope could intervene. In truth, the town was as good as defenseless, but it is easy to see how rational judgment and moderation could be suppressed or interpreted as treason under the pressure of such trying circumstances.

Among the members of the College Company of Edinburgh Volunteers were William Robertson, John Home, Alexander Carlyle, and several of their divinity school classmates such as William Cleghorn, Hugh Bannatine, William Wilkie, and George Logan. Like Bonnie Prince Charlie himself, these young men were approximately twenty-five years old and just beginning to assert themselves at their chosen life's work after many years of preparation. Wilkie and Home were probationers awaiting presentations to parish churches; Robertson was the minister at Gladsmuir; Cleghorn had recently bested David Hume for the moral philosophy chair at the University of Edinburgh; Carlyle, Bannatine, and Logan were still students of divinity. Their hostility to Jacobitism was the logical result of their family backgrounds and their identification with the avidly anti-Jacobite Presbyterian clergy. Even by Scottish Presbyterian standards, however, these young men demonstrated exceptional courage and zeal in their opposition to the rebellion.

On 15 September Drummond's company of volunteers prepared to join the dragoons and confront the Jacobite army outside the city limits. This foolhardy plan engendered an emotional appeal by a

---

[43] David Hume, *A True Account of the Behaviour and Conduct of Archibald Stewart* (1748), reprinted in John Valdimir Price, *The Ironic Hume* (Austin, Texas, 1965), app. A, esp. 164. Hume's assessment of the situation is corroborated in *AC*, 64, and John Home, *The History of the Rebellion in the Year 1745* (1802), in *WJH*, 3:50. See also W. A. Speck, *The Butcher: The Duke of Cumberland and the Suppression of the '45* (Oxford, 1981), 43–48.

delegation of the senior clergy under the leadership of Principal William Wishart of Edinburgh University. Realizing that a relatively small number of untried volunteers could scarcely be of much consequence against an army of warlike Highlanders, Wishart and his colleagues warned against the folly of exposing "the flower of the youth of Edinburgh" to so much danger in a hopeless cause.[44] This sound advice was heeded, and the volunteers remained in the town. But at least a dozen of them, including Home, Carlyle, Robertson, Cleghorn, and Bannatine, met at Turnbull's Tavern and resolved to fight elsewhere if the capital should surrender without a struggle.[45]

Their resolution was soon put to the test. On 16 September the dragoons posted outside Edinburgh moved to join Cope's army on the East Lothian coast, leaving the city to fend for itself. A town meeting was hastily convened, and amid general hysteria the defense of the capital was formally given up. The volunteers were then ordered to deliver their arms to Edinburgh Castle and disband. Early the next morning a band of Highlanders entered Edinburgh without opposition. Meanwhile, the group of volunteers that had met at Turnbull's the previous day hastened to join General Cope, who employed them as night watchmen while preparing for battle against the Jacobites. At dawn on the twenty-first the two armies engaged near the manse of Carlyle's father at Prestonpans, where Cope's forces were quickly routed by the ferocious Highland charge.[46] Despite their enthusiastic efforts on behalf of the Hanoverian cause, the young Presbyterian volunteers found that, for the time being at least, Charles Stuart was the sole sovereign of Scotland.

On the day following the Battle of Prestonpans, Alexander Carlyle had occasion to observe at close quarters the Highlanders who had put Cope's regulars to flight with such ease. "In general," he later wrote,

> they were of low stature and dirty, and of a contemptible appearance. . . . This view I had of the rebel army confirmed me in the prepossession that nothing but the weakest and most unaccountable bad conduct on our part could have possibly given them the victory. God forbid that Britain should ever again be in danger of being overrun by such a despicable enemy, for, at

[44] *Auto.*, 128.

[45] Carlyle put the number of volunteers present at Turnbull's at twelve or thirteen, whereas Home recalled a somewhat larger group of about twenty. Ibid., 130; *WJH*, 3:53–54.

[46] Katherine Tomasson and Francis Buist, *Battles of the '45*, 2d ed. (London, 1974), 39–80.

the best, the Highlanders were at that time but a raw militia, who were not cowards.[47]

John Home was equally disturbed by the lack of effective resistance offered by Lowland Scots in 1745. In the *History of the Rebellion in the Year 1745* that he published late in life, Home traced the root of the problem to the union of the Scottish and English crowns in 1603. Before that date, he argued, Lowlanders were as warlike as Highlanders because all male Lowlanders between the ages of sixteen and sixty were trained in the use of arms and expected to possess their own armor. Only after 1603, when the Lowland militia became "totally neglected" and arms "little regarded," did the Lowlanders become inferior to the Highlanders in fighting ability.[48]

Carlyle's and Home's remarks reflect the belief that a loyal and efficient militia could have prevented the easy Jacobite conquest of the Lowlands in 1745. As is suggested in chapter 6, the frustration and humiliation of that experience help explain the zeal later shown by the Moderate literati of Edinburgh for proposals to establish a national militia. Yet agitation for a militia and use of the civic humanist rhetoric that often accompanied it constituted only one aspect of the Moderates' response to the problems raised by this last and greatest Jacobite uprising. Another aspect of their response to the '45 drew on the rhetoric of religion rather than on that of the civic tradition. In both cases their goal was public virtue and social well-being, but whereas one approach sought to reach that goal by means of a secular, political ideology and its appropriate institutional embodiment, the other placed its faith in a religiously inspired commitment to morality that would follow from a proper understanding of the ways of Providence. At the time of the '45 it was this religious or spiritual approach to questions of moral and social responsibility that found expression among the Moderate literati, particularly in a pair of sermons preached and published by Adam Ferguson and Hugh Blair.

Ferguson preached in Gaelic or "Ersh" to his regiment of Highlanders on 18 December 1745—a day of public fasting and penance for the rebellion. He translated the sermon into English and had it published in London at the request of his patroness the duchess of Atholl.[49] The purpose of the sermon was to convince the troops of "the Duty of every Man to defend his Country when in Danger" and of the special relevance of this principle in "the present Circumstances of our Country." Before developing these points, Ferguson

---

[47] *Auto.*, 156–57.   [48] *WJH*, 3:396–98.

[49] Adam Ferguson, *A Sermon Preached in the Ersh Language to His Majesty's Highland Regiment of Foot . . . on the 18th Day of December, 1745* (London, 1746).

40

provided an explanation and justification of fast days squarely in the providential tradition of orthodox Presbyterianism. "Though we are not rashly to judge of Mens Merit by their Misfortunes in particular Instances," he stated, "yet Sacred History gives sufficient Authority to presume, that *publick Calamities are the Effect of publick Corruption,* and that there is no way of thoroughly averting the Punishment but by a general Reformation of Manners." Fast days are proclaimed in times of "general Distress" to encourage people "to humble themselves before God in a solemn and open manner, that he may avert his deserved Judgments from us, and bless our Resolutions towards a better Conduct for the future." In this sense the '45 constitutes divine retribution for the collective sins of the Scottish nation and Great Britain generally—sins that could be atoned for only by means of collective penance and moral regeneration.

Ferguson then set out to show that all people have a responsibility to defend the society to which they belong. His basic premise will be familiar to readers of Ferguson's later "sociological" writings: human beings are thoroughly social animals, or, in the language of Presbyterian moral preaching, "Society . . . is the State for which Providence has calculated our Natures."[50] Since people owe to society all the advantages they have come to enjoy, it follows that each member of society "is bound, both on account of his own and the publick Welfare, to maintain that League from which he derives so many Blessings." Turning next to the matter of "present Circumstances," Ferguson warned that "our present happy Establishment" is "in danger of being subverted unless we exert ourselves in its Support." The failure of some subjects to appreciate the excellence of the British constitution is due to their unfamiliarity with the evils of "Anarchy" and "Tyranny" that enslave other nations. Fortunately, Britain has laws, duly executed, that "secure our civil Liberties, and shelter us from Injury." "Nor are we less happy in our Religious Establishment," Ferguson added. Would not a "Popish King" bring about "the Subversion of our Liberty, and the entire Corruption of our Religion?" Would not "Ignorance and Superstition again resume their Tyranny in these lands"? In sum, Ferguson told his troops, "your Persons and Liberty is secured, your Religion is established pure and undefiled, according to the Word of God. What Change for the better this Rebellion would bring, is not easily conceived." Why, then, would anyone support a venture "which looks rather like the daring Attempt of desperate Men, to advance their own Fortunes at the Expense of their Country?" In the end the Jacobites and their French

---

[50] Cf. *Essay*, 1–16.

allies will discover "that they are only made Tools to serve Purposes very different from the Ends they propose to themselves."

Preached while the rebellion was still in progress, to Highland soldiers whose loyalties were suspect, Ferguson's sermon was fundamentally a piece of Hanoverian propaganda. Fragmentary evidence suggests that Ferguson's friends among the Presbyterian clergy in Scotland were also active in the service of the Hanoverian cause during the critical winter of 1745–1746. A letter from John Jardine dated Christmas day 1745 reports that Jardine and "Mr Blair" (presumably Hugh) were accompanying and aiding the duke of Cumberland's army, which recently had driven Charles Stuart's forces out of England and was now camped in southern Scotland.[51] When the Jacobites had their final moment of triumph at the Battle of Falkirk in mid-January, John Home fought as an officer in a regiment of volunteers and, after being captured and imprisoned in Doune Castle, led his men in a daring escape.[52]

After the Battle of Culloden put an end to hostilities in April 1746, there remained the task of explaining why God had allowed the rebellion to occur and permitted it so much initial success. The sermon that Hugh Blair preached before the general assembly of the Church of Scotland on 18 May 1746—scarcely one month after Cumberland's decisive victory at Culloden—offered a classical Presbyterian answer to these questions that centered on the theme of divine retribution for moral and religious transgressions.[53] Beholding a nation blessed with a "happy Constitution" and "pure Religion" sunk into "Luxury," "Corruption of Manners," and religious apathy, "God sent forth the *wrath of man*"—in the form of the Jacobites—"to work a Cure for all these Evils." By the "wrath of man" Blair means the passions of the wicked, in this case the Jacobites. Despite their evil intentions, the Jacobite rebels are actually part of the providential plan, for God "makes the unruly Passions of bad Men *work* in a secret Way, towards Ends, by them altogether unseen." We are not then to lose faith in divine justice because of any "seeming Disorders of the World." Like the ancient Hebrews, the people of Britain, and especially of Scotland, were dealt a divine blow so that they might acknowledge their sinfulness and reform their corrupt ways. This, for Blair, constitutes the true cosmic significance of the '45.

---

[51] Jardine to Milton, 25 December 1745, NLS, 16609:138. Jardine was apparently part of Milton's "intelligence network" of clerical spies noted in John Stuart Shaw, *The Management of Scottish Society, 1707–1764* (Edinburgh, 1983), 168.

[52] *WJH*, 3:169–70.

[53] Hugh Blair, *The Wrath of Man Praising God. A Sermon Preached in the High Church of Edinburgh, May 18, 1746* (Edinburgh, 1746).

By seeking to explain the rebellion in terms of a providential logic of history, Blair's and Ferguson's sermons employed a traditional Calvinist and Scottish Presbyterian mode of moral and political preaching: the jeremiad. Like Jeremiah himself, the preacher using this mode regards national misfortunes as punishments by God for "publick Corruption," in the sense of excessive selfishness, luxury, ir-religion, apathy, and general immorality. Underlying this view is the assumption that God has a special relationship or covenant with his people and that other nations are sometimes the unknowing agents or instruments of God's will. Only a widespread moral regeneration can restore the chosen people to their special place in the eyes of God and prevent similar instances of God's wrath in the future. In this way political events like the '45 are endowed with moral and re-ligious meaning, and seemingly profane occurrences become part of sacred history.

More will be said in chapter 5 about the role of the jeremiad in the moral and political thought of the Moderate literati of Edin-burgh, but three implications of this mode of preaching may be noted here. First, it seems clear from the preceding discussion that several of the concepts for which the Scottish Enlightenment generally and Adam Ferguson in particular are best known today among social sci-entists had Presbyterian or Calvinist foundations. Scottish Presbyter-ianism particularly emphasized the Calvinist concern with scrutiniz-ing a society's political and economic record for signs of God's judgments: correlations between worldly success, or the lack of it, and righteousness in the eyes of the Lord were considered much more meaningful on a social than on a personal level.[54] Such a view im-plied that human beings constitute integral parts of the particular societies in which they live and cannot be studied apart from them; that God frequently uses people (or peoples) for divine purposes that remain unknown to them, such as punishing the sinful and reward-ing the righteous (the famous concept of "unintended conse-quences"); and that the study of collectivities—nations, tribes, and the like—is rich with moral and religious significance. Although it is true that concepts like these may have derived in part from other sources and eventually came to be expressed in a somewhat more secular and "sociological" form by Ferguson and other Scottish philosophers, it is also true that Ferguson qua social scientist owed more to his Pres-byterian roots than has usually been thought.

[54] There is a clear statement of this view by an orthodox Calvinist in the introduc-tion to John Bonar's unpublished "History of Tyre" [1758], New College Library, X156, 1/5, box 27.

The second implication concerns the ethical dictates of the Calvinist theory of society and history that the Moderate literati endorsed. In this regard the critical challenge posed by crises like the '45 was how to raise the level of virtue in order to earn for Scotland God's blessing instead of his wrath. The Moderates' preoccupation with moral teaching and preaching is at least partially attributable to their steadfast belief that moral transgressions are to blame for national misfortunes and that moral regeneration is necessary for national well-being. The injunction to bring about a national regeneration of virtue was therefore implicit in the Presbyterian tradition of moral and social thought. Scottish moral philosophy, like Scottish "social science," had orthodox Presbyterian roots.

Finally, the jeremiad's dialectical pattern of national transgression/divine retribution/national atonement had broader ideological significance. For the Moderate literati of Edinburgh, moral regeneration was not simply a matter of raising the level of personal or private virtue. Equally vital was civic or public virtue, in the sense of patriotism and active support for the existing institutional order, including a willingness to fight for it in times of national emergency. The Moderate literati practiced what they preached on this topic by energetically serving as Hanoverian soldiers and propagandists during the '45. Much of what they wrote, taught, and preached in later years was intended to promote a similar spirit of militant, conservative, public virtue. The jeremiad was an excellent vehicle for spreading such an ideology. Moral urgency and commitment were built into it, as was association of the individual with the welfare of the entire nation. Since in this context the "nation" normally meant both Scotland and England, the Moderate jeremiad encouraged a sense of *British* national identity. Yet it was also a respectable Presbyterian mode of discourse that could, in the cases of particular events like the '45 and particular institutions like the Church of Scotland, deliver its patriotic message with a decidedly Scottish accent. Though God's punishments and rewards were usually bestowed on the whole island, Scotland had its own role to play in the regeneration process. The Moderate literati believed that the time had come for the Scottish people to end the dissension and disunity of the past by uniting behind the Whig-Presbyterian establishment. And if that establishment was itself racked by dissension and disunity, they were prepared to take matters into their own hands by assuming positions of national leadership. The Moderate revolution was about to begin.

CHAPTER TWO

The Moderate Revolution

❋

PATRONAGE AND POLITENESS

There can be no union, and by consequence there can be no society, where there is no subordination.

William Robertson et al.,
"Reasons of Dissent," 1752

A minister must endeavour to acquire as great a degree of politeness, in his carriage and behaviour, and to catch as much of
the air and manner of a fine gentleman, as possibly he can.

John Witherspoon,
Ecclesiastical Characteristics, 1753

The defeat of Charles Edward Stuart's Jacobite army in 1746 was a
mixed blessing for Scottish Presbyterians. On the one hand, it ended
once and for all the threat of a Roman Catholic or Episcopal restoration and ensured the Presbyterian character of the Church of
Scotland. On the other hand, making Presbyterianism secure brought
to light some serious problems and divisions within the kirk. The spirit
of Presbyterian unity that had flourished immediately after the Revolution of 1688–1689 had been steadily eroding for several decades,
and since the death of William Carstares in 1715 the church had
spawned no ecclesiastical leaders capable of reviving it. The problem
was not simply a crisis in leadership but also a lack of consensus about
the church's role in a society that had finally attained religious and
political stability and was slowly beginning to experience economic
and cultural development. Though old-school Calvinists like Robert
Wodrow tried their best to keep the kirk on the straight and narrow
path of their forefathers,[1] unanswered questions about the church's
relations with the modern, secular world made this a formidable task.
Should the church sanction theater in Edinburgh? Should it tolerate
an infidel philosopher? Should it allow its ministers to relax their strict

[1] Robert Wodrow, *Analecta*, 4 vols. (Edinburgh, 1842–1843).

code of behavior and mingle freely in polite society? As the Moderate literati of Edinburgh began their ecclesiastical careers toward the middle of the century, none of these issues had been clearly resolved, and the future of the Church of Scotland was very much in doubt.

The element of uncertainty in the kirk was compounded by the nature of Scottish Presbyterian church polity. The absence of episcopacy; the prominent role of lay elders; the "republican" organization of ecclesiastical authority, rising from local kirk sessions to regional presbyteries and synods and finally to the annual general assembly (and its commission, or standing committee, that met three times between assemblies); the mechanism for automatically adjusting general assembly representation in response to demographic changes; the strict rotations used by most presbyteries to ensure an equitable distribution of assembly seats among the ministers in their jurisdictions—all contributed to the open and democratic character of the kirk, in marked contrast to the authoritarian structure of episcopal churches and the corrupt state of British electoral politics during the eighteenth century. Yet these same features weakened the kirk's ability to remain unified and autonomous. For if the ultimate authority in the church was an annual assembly of several hundred parish ministers and lay elders from all parts of Scotland, most of whom had not attended the previous assembly and would not attend the next one, how could ecclesiastical order and continuity be maintained? Since indigenous, principled ecclesiastical parties were so difficult to organize, the advantage lay with small groups of ministers associated with the interests of "great men" outside the church.

By far the most powerful of these ecclesiastical interest groups during the second quarter of the eighteenth century represented Archibald Campbell, earl of Ilay and (after 1743) third duke of Argyll, who served as Sir Robert Walpole's Scottish manager. In his capacity as ecclesiastical agent for this "Argathelian" interest, Rev. Patrick Cuming was for many years responsible for implementing the policies of Argyll and his Edinburgh subminister Andrew Fletcher, Lord Milton.[2] His connection with Milton and Argyll, together with the Edinburgh church history chair that the latter procured for him in 1736, made Cuming a prominent figure in the general assembly of the church as long as his patron continued in favor at Westminster. Yet all important policy decisions seem to have been made by

---

[2] Henry R. Sefton, "Lord Ilay and Patrick Cuming: A Study in Eighteenth-Century Ecclesiastical Management," *RSCHS* 19 (1977): 203–16. On the rise of the Argathelian interest in the kirk, see John Stuart Shaw, *The Management of Scottish Society, 1707–1764* (Edinburgh, 1983), 99–100.

Argyll and Milton rather than by Cuming. As Ian D. L. Clark has argued, the Argathelian interest in the church should not be considered a true ecclesiastical party because "it was controlled from outside and had no consistent policy or common outlook on ecclesiastical affairs."[3] The same may be said of the "Squadrone," or anti-Argathelian, interest in the kirk. During the brief Squadrone administration of the fourth marquess of Tweeddale (1742–1746), Rev. Robert Wallace played a role analogous to Cuming's with the Argathelians. Like Cuming, Wallace was selected for reasons having little or nothing to do with ecclesiastical policy. What counted most were his political loyalties (in 1742 he had written a pamphlet against Walpole and dedicated it to Tweeddale) and his personal connections with the Dundases of Arniston, a prominent Squadrone family.[4]

During the 1730s and 1740s—the years in which Cuming and Wallace wielded power as ecclesiastical managers for rival political factions—the question of patronage began to emerge as the critical issue dividing the Church of Scotland.[5] The focus of the controversy was the notorious patronage law enacted by a Tory Parliament in 1712, despite assurances of Scottish ecclesiastical autonomy written into the Treaty of Union of 1707. The effect of this act was to restore the traditional procedure for filling vacant churches that had been practiced in Scotland before 1649. In the royal burghs this usually meant that the right of selecting or presenting a new minister reverted to the town council, in place of a broader base of burghers active in ecclesiastical affairs as elders and deacons. In "landward" or country parishes, which accounted for more than ninety percent of Scotland's churches, the power of presentation passed almost entirely to members of the nobility and gentry, who were sole or joint patrons of about two-thirds of Scotland's more than nine hundred churches and normally were de facto patrons of more than two-hundred fifty additional churches where the crown was the official patron. For at least a decade after 1712, and much longer in the case of many burghs, patrons were slow to exercise their right of presentation in the face of popular hostility. It was only when Ilay began systematically enforcing the law of patronage during the second quarter of the cen-

---

[3] Clark diss., 52.

[4] Norah Smith, "Clerical Corridors of Power: Extracts from Letters concerning Robert Wallace's Involvement in Ecclesiastical Politics, 1742–43," *Notes and Queries*, n.s., 20 (1973): 214–19.

[5] For a fuller discussion of the patronage issue see Richard Sher and Alexander Murdoch, "Patronage and Party in the Church of Scotland, 1750–1800," in *Church, Politics and Society: Scotland 1408–1929*, ed. Norman Macdougall (Edinburgh, 1983), 197–220.

tury that the full impact of the issue was felt. From then on government managers continued to regard patronage as a right worth fighting for, partly because it gave them leverage among the Scottish landed interest, and partly because it was thought to encourage social stability and religious moderation.

Matters were further complicated by the fact that opponents of the law of patronage were themselves divided as to the best alternative to it. The most radical position held that a new minister should be elected by "the people," as John Knox and his associates had proposed in the *First Book of Discipline* (1560–1561). A somewhat more conservative and theocratic version of this radically Calvinist position, with roots in Andrew Melville's *Second Book of Discipline* (1578) and the parliamentary act and general assembly directory of 1649, restricted the right of selection to the elders of the church (i.e. the kirk session), whose choice was to be guided by the local presbytery and ratified by male heads of households under the presbytery's supervision. Between these radical Calvinist alternatives and the law of patronage lay the view that local Protestant heritors should have an equal say with church elders in the nomination process, once again subject to the consent of male heads of households in the congregation. This was the procedure enacted by the Scots Parliament and reluctantly approved by William III in 1690 in an effort to achieve a workable compromise.[6] It was the logical position for Revolution Whig and "commonwealthman" Presbyterians who looked to local men of property for political and ecclesiastical leadership. Although favored by Wallace, Cuming, William Hamilton, Francis Hutcheson, and other liberal clergymen during the 1730s, as well as by the dominant faction in the popular party (its name notwithstanding) throughout the second half of the century, this alternative was doomed by the failure of small and middle-sized landowners to endorse it and by the resurgence of both radical Calvinist and propatronage forces. To Ebenezer Erskine, any concessions to the landed interest as such were unacceptable in a Presbyterian church. The controversy leading to the original secession began with Erskine's protest not against the law of patronage per se but against the general assembly's controversial act of 1732, which essentially reasserted the compromise of 1690 in the event a patron failed to present a minister within the six-month time limit. To Ilay, the government, and the great landowners, on the other hand, the concessions of 1690 did not go far enough toward restoring the traditional rights of the government and the landed elite.

[6]Thomas Maxwell, "William III and the Scots Presbyterians," *RSCHS* 15 (1966): 169–91.

Caught between two disagreeable extremes, churchmen who favored the compromise of 1690 could not maintain a strong center party. Many of them elected to side with Ilay and the government as the lesser of two evils. Thus, a spokesman for the Cuming circle later explained that he and his friends had come to see collaboration with the Argathelian interest as a temporary expedient for "repelling the usurpations of the people,"[7] meaning particularly Ebenezer Erskine and others who were then proclaiming vote by male heads of households to be the only legitimate method for filling vacant churches. They believed they could best serve the compromise ideal of 1690 and the cause of religious moderation by accepting positions of influence that would allow them to combat the new evangelical radicalism of the "Marrow Men"[8] and to adopt conciliatory measures designed to mitigate the worst effects of ecclesiastical patronage. The same explanation accounts for the defection to the Argathelian camp of prominent churchmen such as William Hamilton, James Smith, and John Gowdie—all of whom became principals of Edinburgh University through Ilay's influence—and for Robert Wallace's willingness to manage the Tweeddale interest in the church during the 1740s.[9] Cuming and Wallace both insisted that every "presentee" obtain a "call" or invitation from the heritors and elders of the parish before being inducted as minister. Similarly, in the event of local resistance to a patron's choice, Cuming was especially fond of appointing ministers from other presbyteries to "riding committees" that would induct or "settle" the presentee in place of the local clergy. The call, however, was at best not legally binding and at worst a sham,[10] and riding committees were in express violation of the laws of the church, which stipulated that the settlement of a minister was to be carried out by the local presbytery. By employing these expe-

---

[7] James Oswald, *Letters concerning the Present State of the Church of Scotland* (Edinburgh, 1767), esp. letters v, vi, and vii.

[8] Scottish republication in 1718 of *The Marrow of Modern Divinity*, a mid-seventeenth-century English tract with antinomian implications, touched off a long, fierce controversy that signaled the emergence of a new breed of religious extremists within the Church of Scotland. The "Marrow Men" were also among the leaders of the successful campaign to oust the theologically liberal Glasgow divinity professor John Simson on grounds of heresy during the 1720s, and they had close ties with the seceders of the 1730s.

[9] Henry R. Sefton, "Rev. Robert Wallace: An Early Moderate," *RSCHS* 16 (1969): 1–22; Shaw, *Management of Scottish Society*, 101–103. Shaw's account of how the Argathelian interest bought off Hamilton and other ministers with places may be accurate as far as politicians like Milton and Ilay are concerned, but there was more at issue for the clergymen themselves.

[10] Cuming's acceptance of calls signed by a few elders and nonresident heritors suggests that for him the call was little more than a face-saving device.

dients, Cuming and Wallace were doing their best to ease tensions in the church under extremely trying circumstances, but the actual result of their policies was increased ambiguity and confusion about the patronage question. The law of patronage was neither renounced nor enforced wholeheartedly by either Cuming or Wallace, and in the absence of any fixed procedure the number of parish settlement disputes proliferated in the church courts during the 1740s while the authority of the general assembly over its own presbyteries sank lower and lower.[11] In time even Wallace and Cuming seem to have wished for a way out of the situation they had helped to create.

That way out came when a small group of young clergymen and lay elders initiated a revolution in Scottish ecclesiastical politics in the early 1750s. This "little band of earnest men," as they were once called,[12] was troubled by the church's failure to enforce the law of patronage in a vigorous and consistent manner. They were particularly dismayed by the leniency shown toward presbyters who, on pretense of "conscience," boldly refused to obey the general assembly's instructions to induct unpopular presentees. That in such cases the assembly resorted to the expedient of riding committees was, in their view, a plain indication of the extent to which the Church of Scotland had deviated from the fundamental principles of Presbyterian church government, which they took to be the parity of ministers and the strict subordination of ecclesiastical bodies or courts, culminating in the general assembly. Meeting at an Edinburgh tavern in May 1751, they resolved, in Alexander Carlyle's words, "that it was necessary to use every means in our power to restore the authority of the Church, otherwise her government would be degraded, and everything depending on her authority would fall into confusion."[13] With this resolution, it is fair to say, the Moderate party was born. Years later Carlyle was able to recall the names of eleven members of the "select company of fifteen" that attended this seminal party gathering.[14] Seven were ministers—all approximately thirty years old and members of Carlyle's circle of friends educated at the University of Edinburgh. These included Carlyle himself, William Robertson, John Home, Hugh Blair, John Jardine, Adam Dickson,

[11] Details of thirty-eight disputed presentations that reached the general assembly during the 1740s are recorded in *Annals*, 1:345–67. See also John Cunningham, *The Church History of Scotland*, 2 vols. (Edinburgh, 1859), 2:484.

[12] George F. S. Elliot, *The Border Elliots and the Family of Minto* (Edinburgh, 1897), 333.

[13] *Auto.*, 258.

[14] Ibid., 257; Clark diss., 66–67.

and George Logan.[15] Among the lay elders present were Jardine's father-in-law George Drummond, William, Baron Ross, and two young advocates who would be of great service to the Moderates: Gilbert Elliot (later third baronet of Minto) and Andrew Pringle (later Lord Alemoor of the Court of Session).

The strategy of these men was to raise the issue of church discipline in reference to a specific settlement dispute due to come before the next general assembly. The case in question concerned the parish of Torphichen in the Presbytery of Linlithgow, which was dominated by ministers hostile to the law of patronage.[16] In 1748 Lord Torphichen had exercised his legal right as patron by presenting one James Watson, who was so unacceptable to the people of the parish that only five or six heads of households out of about one thousand would sign his call. The Presbytery of Linlithgow referred the case to the Synod of Lothian and Tweeddale, which ruled in favor of Watson. Yet the recalcitrant presbyters refused to proceed with Watson's induction, even after the general assemblies of 1749 and 1750 ordered them to do so. Their position, as articulated before the general assembly of 1751, was that the authority of church courts did not apply in matters involving "conscience, of which God alone is Lord," and that therefore a riding committee should be appointed by the assembly to induct Watson and spare their consciences.[17] The assembly did appoint a riding committee, with Robertson, Blair, and Home among its members, and Watson was inducted by it on 30 May 1751.[18] But intense debate ensued as to whether or not the Linlithgow presbyters deserved to be censured for their disobedience.

Three distinct points of view emerged during the course of this debate in the general assembly of 1751. The great majority of the delegates favored a mild rebuke of the presbytery for its insubordination. This measure was easily adopted by the assembly, perhaps because it represented an ambiguous middle ground between the two extremes. One extreme position contended that the Linlithgow presbyters should not have been censured at all since they had acted according to the will of Christ as they understood it. Under the leadership of Principal William Wishart of Edinburgh University, twenty-

---

[15] Adam Dickson (1721–1776) would eventually gain fame for his writings on agriculture. For the little that is known about George Logan (1723–1754) see *Auto.*, 244–48.

[16] For details of the Torphichen case, as well as the Inverkeithing case discussed below, see *Annals*, 1:198–291.

[17] Ibid., 199.

[18] Ibid., 211, 367.

three members of the assembly adhering to this view submitted a statement of dissent against the assembly's decision to administer even a mild rebuke. The other extreme position, the Moderate one, held that the assembly had not gone far enough in censuring presbyters who had deliberately and repeatedly disobeyed its instructions. Following a plan devised by proponents of this view at their secret tavern meeting, John Home moved that the general assembly suspend the rebellious Linlithgow presbyters for six months. William Robertson seconded the motion in a speech that brought him recognition as a first-rate orator.[19] Although Gilbert Elliot and Andrew Pringle also spoke well for the motion, in the final tally it was overwhelmingly defeated, 200 to 11 votes.[20]

The "little band" had apparently failed in its first attempt at managing ecclesiastical politics; but by clearly and persistently setting forth a consistent policy platform in 1751, it had laid the groundwork for a decisive assembly contest in the following year. That contest concerned the parish of Inverkeithing in the Presbytery of Dunfermline, Fife. The presbytery had repeatedly refused, on grounds of "conscience," to induct Rev. Andrew Richardson, who had been lawfully presented by the patron of the parish in 1749. At the meeting of the general assembly's commission in November 1751, a "very high censure" had been threatened if the presbytery did not induct Richardson by the time of the commission's next meeting in March. When March came, however, the commission relented and chose not to censure the disobedient presbyters. This act of leniency was another setback for the emerging Moderates, who responded with a major policy paper explaining the grounds for their dissent. Dubbed "the Manifesto of the Moderate Party" by a nineteenth-century ecclesiastical historian, this dissenting paper was said to be the work of William Robertson, assisted by Blair, Carlyle, Home, Jardine, Pringle, and a handful of other commission members.[21] Its publication in the early spring of 1752 took the debate on ecclesiastical order out of the church courts and into the public eye.

The first three arguments in Robertson's "Reasons of Dissent" are essential for understanding the Moderate position on the absolute necessity for strict discipline and subordination. In the first place, Robertson argued, the lenient sentence of the commission violated "the nature and first principles of society." With the establishment of society, unrestricted individual freedom must give way to regulated

---

[19] *Auto.*, 258–59.
[20] Ibid.; *Annals*, 1:211.
[21] *Annals*, 1:231; *Auto.*, 470.

authority for the sake of social order and public good. Every man is accorded the right to seek the abolition of a particular form of society under extreme circumstances; "but as long as he continues in it, professes regard for it, and reaps the emoluments of it, if he refuses to obey its laws, he manifestly acts both a disorderly and dishonest part" and should be censured accordingly. To allow disobedience to go unpunished is to reject "government and order" and to justify "licentiousness" in the church and "rebellion and disorder in civil government." Second, it was argued that discipline and subordination form the basis not only of society in general but of ecclesiastical society in particular. A church is a society unto itself and therefore "can only subsist by those fundamental maxims by which all society subsists," including above all "discipline and authority." A member of a church has the right to disagree with its policies but is not entitled to defy those policies in practice under the cloak of "liberty of conscience." Finally, Robertson argued that discipline and authority are particularly important in a *Presbyterian* church. It is because Presbyterian ministers are all equal in rank that Presbyterian church courts assume far greater importance than comparable ecclesiastical bodies in episcopal churches. Above all, the annual general assembly must function as the undisputed final authority in all ecclesiastical affairs in order to maintain a true Presbyterian system of church polity. As the interim representative of the general assembly, the commission has a responsibility to enforce the laws of the church, if necessary by means of the various forms of censure recorded in the Westminster Confession of Faith.[22]

Taken together, these three arguments reveal a fundamentally conservative view of civil and ecclesiastical organization from which the Moderate literati of Edinburgh never deviated. From the outset the Moderates were strongly supportive of law and order and eager to prevent a recurrence of the religious and political unrest of their early years. They believed, as Robertson put it, that "there can be no society"—either civil or ecclesiastical—"where there is no subordination."[23] As loyal Hanoverian subjects, they praised the British constitution as a nearly perfect blend of order and liberty and accepted without question the prevailing notion of the inequality of ranks. In ecclesiastical matters they retained a firm commitment both to the law of patronage and to the Presbyterian principle of the absolute

[22] William Robertson et al., "Reasons of Dissent from the Judgment and Resolution of the Commission, March 11, 1752," in *Annals*, 1:231–37.
[23] Ibid., 233.

authority of the general assembly.[24] They were, in short, Whig-Presbyterian conservatives. If their "Reasons of Dissent" of March 1752 is entitled to the designation "Manifesto of the Moderate Party," it is because it set forth with remarkable clarity and logic the ideology of Whig-Presbyterian conservatism that formed the cornerstone of Moderate thinking about church and society.

The "Reasons of Dissent" was also a masterly piece of party propaganda. Tactfully confining its arguments to the issue of order and discipline and avoiding any discussion of the relative merits of patronage as such, it helped to win widespread support for the Moderates' position. Nine days before the meeting of the general assembly in mid-May, Rev. Gilbert Hamilton, one of the sons of William Hamilton, warned the Synod of Lothian and Tweeddale of serious consequences if the authority of the church was not reestablished.[25] Robert Wallace and most other churchmen associated with the principles of 1690 and 1732 agreed.[26] Most important, the ruling Argathelian interest decided to throw its weight behind Robertson's policy. This decision brought into the fray both Patrick Cuming, who won election as moderator of the general assembly, and the government's official representative in the assembly, Lord Commissioner Leven, whose opening speech contained a strong plea for ecclesiastical law and order. Freely drawing on Robertson's "Reasons of Dissent," Leven warned against the danger of "anarchy and confusion" and asserted that "subordination is the link of society, without which there can be no order in government."[27] A day or two later Principal Wishart and his party retaliated by publishing "Answers to the Reasons of Dissent," a vigorous defense of the right of every man to follow the dictates of his conscience in religious matters that seems to have been composed primarily by John Witherspoon.[28] But the attempt to refute Robertson's logic did not succeed. In this assembly there would be no leniency shown toward ministers who continued to disobey the direct orders of the highest authority in the church. After six such ministers once again refused to settle Richardson, proudly defended their actions on the basis of conscience when called before the bar of the assembly, and steadfastly refused to modify or retract their views on the matter, it was decided to set an example by

[24] Ian D. L. Clark, "From Protest to Reaction: The Moderate Regime in the Church of Scotland, 1752–1805," in *SAI*, 200–24, and Clark diss., chap. 2; Sher and Murdoch, "Patronage and Party," 211–14.

[25] Gilbert Hamilton, *The Disorders of a Church* (Edinburgh, 1752), 31.

[26] Sefton, "Robert Wallace," 14–15.   [27] *SM* 14 (May 1752): 239.

[28] Reproduced in *Annals*, 1:243–60. On the question of authorship see Varnum Lansing Collins, *President Witherspoon*, 2 vols. (Princeton, 1925), 1:33.

deposing one of them, later identified as Thomas Gillespie of Carnock.[29] The subsequent settlement of Andrew Richardson at Inverkeithing by the remaining ministers in the Presbytery of Dunfermline appeared to seal the victory of the forces of "order" over the proponents of "conscience."

No sooner had the general assembly of 1752 come to a close, however, than Gillespie's supporters began working to have him reinstated or "reponed" at the next assembly. Several pamphlets appeared criticizing ecclesiastical patronage and emphasizing the fallibility of church courts and the primacy of conscience. Some cited precedents in Scottish ecclesiastical history to strengthen their case.[30] Others, noting that the party of order had triumphed in the Inverkeithing affair by means of superior management of the eldership, set guidelines for the "proper" selection and conduct of elders.[31] Supporters of the assembly's policy countered with three or four pamphlets of their own.[32] In addition to pointing out ambiguities in the alleged precedents cited by their adversaries and castigating the opposition for blatantly trying to inflame the eldership, these pamphlets followed the authoritarian line of argument laid down in Robertson's "Reasons of Dissent." "The Moment that Individuals are allowed to follow the Direction of their own Judgment in all cases, Society disbands, and Government is set aside," wrote the anonymous author of one such pamphlet.[33] In the end the overture to repone Gillespie was defeated in the assembly of 1753 by three votes, thanks largely to effective political management by Cuming and Leven.[34]

[29] *Annals*, 1:276. On the deposition of Gillespie, who would become one of the founders of the Relief Church in the next decade, see Hugh Watt, "Thomas Gillespie," *RSCHS* 15 (1966): 89–101, and Gavin Struthers, *The History of the Rise of the Relief Church* (Edinburgh, 1848), 219–23.

[30] *A Letter from a Gentleman in Town to His Friend in the Country* (Edinburgh, 1752), 8; *A Letter from Several Elders, Lovers of Peace and Moderation, to their Brethren of the Same Principles* (Edinburgh, 1752).

[31] John Maclaurin, *A Loud Cry for Help to the Struggling Church of Scotland* (Glasgow, 1753), 30–31; John Lawson, *The Discovery of a Most Enormous Evil* (Edinburgh, 1752).

[32] James Nasmyth, *The General Assembly of the Church of Scotland Vindicated* (Edinburgh, 1753); John Hyndman, *A Just View of the Constitution of the Church of Scotland* (Edinburgh, 1753), which provoked *A Juster View of the Constitution of the Church of Scotland* (Edinburgh, 1753) and the appendix to *The Terms of Ministerial and Christian Communion* (Glasgow, 1753), which is sometimes attributed to John Maclaurin.

[33] *Some Thoughts Relating to that Submission and Obedience Due to the Authority and Decisions of the Supreme Judicatories of the Church* (Edinburgh, 1753), 8.

[34] Lord Drummore to Lord Milton, 11 December 1753, NLS, 16682:151; Clark diss., 70; *Annals*, 2:20; Struthers, *Relief Church*, 244–48. Carlyle exaggerates the magnitude of the Moderates' victory and errs in claiming that the matter never came to a vote again in *Auto.*, 284–85.

Who were the real victors in the Inverkeithing case of 1752–1753? The Argathelian interest, led in the general assembly by Patrick Cuming, won only the appearance of victory. This was true, first of all, because Cuming and his faction were associated more closely with the harsh sentence meted out to Thomas Gillespie than with the Presbyterian principles that had inspired it. It was also true because the Inverkeithing affair was not a conflict between rival political interests in the pre-1750 sense. The decline of the Squadrone after 1746 had left the Argathelians without any strong competing political interest in Scotland, so they had come to be identified more closely with government in general than with any particular political faction.[35] In the Inverkeithing dispute the sides divided chiefly on the basis of principle, with the result that some Squadrone supporters found themselves allied with the Argathelians, and vice versa. And since the points at issue in 1752 reflected fundamental differences within the kirk, the new sides formed the rudiments of a bifurcated system of stable ecclesiastical parties characterized by permanence, reasonably consistent policies, and a lack of dependence on any particular political faction or interest outside the church.[36] It is therefore significant that the initiative for the challenge to the Dunfermline presbyters had come, not from the government or from Argathelian political managers or from older churchmen like Robert Wallace and Patrick Cuming, who never fit comfortably into the new ecclesiastical party structure, but from the little band of young ministers and elders who had forged the Moderate party. "I know it will be a prejudice against what the Assembly have done, that the argument was supported by several young members," Cuming stated in his closing address to the general assembly of 1752, "but it was by young members in defence of our old constitution."[37] It was these "young members," William Robertson and his friends, who emerged as the biggest victors in the Inverkeithing affair. They had instigated the campaign for patronage and church discipline at their secret tavern meeting of May 1751, and they had articulated the main arguments of that campaign in speeches before the general assembly and in their "Reasons of Dissent" of March 1752. If Cuming viewed them as welcome new recruits for his old-guard Argathelian army, he would soon discover that he had underestimated both their degree of independence and their capacity for leadership.

· · ·

---

[35] John Simpson, "Who Steered the Gravy Train, 1707–1766?" in *SAI*, 58.
[36] Clark diss., 46–47, and Clark, "From Protest to Reaction," 209–10.
[37] *Annals*, 1:290.

Besides church patronage and church polity, the emerging Moderate and Popular parties disagreed about numerous matters of piety, style, decorum, and attitude that may be considered parts of a wider controversy over the principle of "politeness." Formally defined by Adam Ferguson as "a behaviour intended to please, or to oblige,"[38] this elusive term actually had broader connotations. Polite society meant well-bred people of taste and refinement; polite literature and learning meant the rational, elegant, polished poetry and prose and empirical scientific investigations that appealed to polite society; polite preaching meant the sensible, restrained religious instruction that polite society appreciated. The Moderate literati of Edinburgh recognized that the cultivation of politeness was fraught with danger, since it could all too easily lapse into overrefinement or affectation.[39] Within proper bounds, however, and combined with enlightened principles, politeness was in their view the distinctive mark of a fully civilized individual and the happy medium between "effeminacy" and "enthusiasm."

William Robertson and the "little band of earnest men" who founded the Moderate party were conspicuous for their commitment to such polite, enlightened values as genteel manners, religious moderation and tolerance, and high esteem for scientific and literary accomplishments. They envisaged a polite Presbyterian clergy overturning the persistent stereotype of Scottish Presbyterian ministers as ignorant, bigoted, and narrow-minded fanatics while guiding Scotland toward virtue, order, and enlightenment. Their enemies accused them of sacrificing the essentials of Christian doctrine and pastoral service for the sake of moral preaching, profane learning, and the impious affectations and amusements of polite society. This conflict was implicit in the Inverkeithing affair,[40] but it was the publication in October 1753 of John Witherspoon's famous satire of the Moderates, *Ecclesiastical Characteristics*, that did the most to bring it into the open. "What first induced me to write [*Ecclesiastical Characteristics*]," Witherspoon later wrote, "was a deep concern for the declining interest of religion in the Church of Scotland, mixed with some indignation at what appeared to me a strange abuse of church-authority in the years 1751 and 1752."[41] He particularly resented the

---

[38] *Insts.*, 246.

[39] Ibid.; *Princs.*, 2:374; Alexander Carlyle, "Recollections," NLS, 3463:71–72; *Sers.*, 1:158, 301, 2:261–62, 3:34.

[40] See, for example, Maclaurin, *Loud Cry for Help*, 4, where some younger clergymen are ridiculed for using fine language in the general assembly debates of 1752.

[41] John Witherspoon, *A Serious Apology for the Ecclesiastical Characteristics* (1763), in *The Works of John Witherspoon*, 9 vols. (Edinburgh, 1804–1805), 6:232.

fact that several of his former Edinburgh University classmates who prided themselves on their sentiments of "moderation" had demonstrated such severity in their handling of Thomas Gillespie. *Ecclesiastical Characteristics* was designed to expose the hypocrisy of these so-called "Moderate Men" and to contrast them unfavorably with "orthodox" or "popular" ministers like Witherspoon himself. Passing through no fewer than eight editions during the 1750s and 1760s, Witherspoon's book was probably responsible for bringing the term "Moderate" into general use as a party label.[42]

The first edition of *Ecclesiastical Characteristics* lists twelve basic maxims attributed to Moderate churchmen.[43] Three of these maxims (nos. 8–10) concern ecclesiastical patronage and church discipline, with the Moderates accused of totally disregarding the "inclinations of the common people." The remaining nine maxims deal with the general theme of politeness in one form or another. In regard to religion, the Moderate man must sneer at the Westminster Confession of Faith (no. 3) and "put off all appearances of devotion, and avoid all unnecessary exercises of religious worship" (no. 7). He should honor and protect heretics (no. 1) and libertines (no. 2) and show contempt for all those who have "a high profession of religion, and a great pretence to strictness in their walk and conversation" (nos. 11 and 12). As a preacher, the Moderate minister must follow four fundamental rules (no. 4):

> 1. His subjects must be confined to social duties. 2. He must recommend them only from rational considerations, viz., the beauty and comely proportions of virtue, and its advantages in the present life, without any regard to a future state of more extended self-interest. 3. His authorities must be drawn from heathen writers, *none*, or as few as possible, from Scripture. 4. He must be very unacceptable to the common people.

In short, his sermons should be about "moral virtues" rather than "the graces of the spirit." His learning should be limited to Leibniz, Collins, Hutcheson, Hume's *Essays*, and of course Shaftesbury's *Characteristicks*, which accounts for the title of Witherspoon's book (no. 6). Finally, a Moderate minister must cultivate politeness and emulate "the air and manner of a fine gentleman" (no. 5). To this maxim Witherspoon adds sarcastically, "I believe I might have spared myself the trouble of inserting this maxim, the present rising generation being of themselves sufficiently disposed to observe it."

---

[42] Clark diss., 49; Collins, *President Witherspoon*, 1:39.

[43] Witherspoon, *Works*, 6:138–222.

Clearly, the phrase "present rising generation" was meant to refer to Robertson, Home, Carlyle, and their circle of friends. Witherspoon had been acquainted with most of them since childhood and had followed what would seem to have been a similar pattern of education and development. He had attended the prestigious grammar school at Haddington, boarded with Carlyle in his first years at Edinburgh University, excelled in his college studies, taken an M.A. along with Blair in 1739, and entered the Edinburgh University divinity course in the same year. But Witherspoon's stern manner and strict Calvinist principles had alienated him from this close-knit circle of Moderates.[44] Apparently resentful of a union that he could not or would not join, he lashed out at the clannishness of the Moderates in the introduction to *Ecclesiastical Characteristics*. "The moderates are remarkable for the most perfect union and harmony," he wrote, "and for a firm and stedfast adherence to each other, in the prosecution of their designs."[45] In the second edition that appeared a few months later Witherspoon elevated this principle into a thirteenth maxim of Moderate policy.[46] Even as he taunted the Moderates for their clannishness, however, Witherspoon realized that this very characteristic had given them a decisive advantage over their disorganized opponents in the Inverkeithing affair.

Like all satires, *Ecclesiastical Characteristics* is highly exaggerated, and one must therefore be wary of accepting Witherspoon's maxims at face value. There is no truth to the charge that Moderate preachers preferred "heathen writers" to scripture for their authorities; nor were the Moderates anywhere near as impious and irreligious as Witherspoon suggested. Yet beneath the exaggeration lay a considerable amount of truth about Moderatism. The Moderates did tend to be clannish; they did favor lay patronage as the best means of filling parish vacancies; they did emphasize morality over doctrine in their sermons; and they did believe that ministers in the Church of Scotland should mix freely in polite society and aspire to politeness in their learning, speech, taste, religious views, and deportment.

As Witherspoon implied, the association of the Moderate literati with polite society was already well under way when *Ecclesiastical Characteristics* appeared. The original Moderate planning session of

---

[44] William Oliver Brackett, "John Witherspoon: His Scottish Ministry" (Ph.D. diss., Edinburgh University, 1935), 36. Carlyle's unflattering assessment of Witherspoon (*Auto.*, 34–35, 72–73) was apparently one reason for his executors' decision not to publish his memoirs at the time of his death. John Lee to Carlyle Bell, 6 January 1806, NLS, 3464:5–9.

[45] Witherspoon, *Works*, 6:152.

[46] Ibid., 215.

May 1751 had begun a tradition of annual "Assembly parties" that brought together enlightened ministers and like-minded lay elders in convivial settings.[47] Other Edinburgh literati soon began to attend these assembly parties, as well as similar informal dinners held throughout the year. Half a century later Alexander Carlyle fondly recollected these meetings of the Moderate literati's circle:

> Robertson and John Home and [Hugh] Bannatine and I lived all in the country, and came only periodically to the town. Blair and Jardine both lived in it, and supper being the only fashionable meal at that time, we dined where we best could, and by cadies [messengers] assembled our friends to meet us in a tavern by nine o'clock; and a fine time it was when we could collect David Hume, Adam Smith, Adam Ferguson, Lord Elibank, and Drs. Blair and Jardine, on an hour's warning.[48]

The two most conspicuous figures at such gatherings were Lord Elibank and David Hume, neither of whom had previously been in the habit of associating very much with Presbyterian clergymen. Elibank, a man of enormous intellect and learning, was as much an Episcopalian and sentimental Jacobite as Hume was an anticlerical skeptic. Yet both men were soon won over by the Moderate literati. Elibank became an early patron of Home and Robertson, whose parishes lay next to his estate in East Lothian and whose companionship, according to Carlyle, "cured him of his contempt for the Presbyterian clergy."[49] Hume likewise

> took much to the company of the younger [Moderate] clergy, not from a wish to bring them over to his opinions, for he never attempted to overturn any man's principles, but they best understood his notions, and could furnish him with literary conversation. . . . This intimacy of the young clergy with David Hume enraged the zealots on the opposite side, who little knew how impossible it was for him, had he been willing, to shake their principles.[50]

---

[47] *Auto.*, 259–60, 323–24.

[48] Ibid., 288.

[49] Ibid., 280; *Tour*, 378.

[50] *Auto.*, 288–89. There is ample evidence to support Carlyle's contention that the Moderate literati never allowed their friendship with Hume and respect for his intellectual prowess to obscure their religious and metaphysical differences with him. See, for example, *Auto.*, 247–48; Hume to Blair, [1761], *HL*, 1:351; Ferguson to Adam Smith, 2 September 1773, in *The Correspondence of Adam Smith*, ed. Ernest Campbell Mossner and Ian Simpson Ross (Oxford, 1977), 169; Stewart, xix.

The "zealots" in the church were indeed "enraged" by this mingling of their brethen with the likes of Elibank and Hume. In 1753 a school chaplain named George Anderson published a lengthy attack on the writings of Hume and another well-known man of letters suspected of religious deviations, Henry Home, Lord Kames, in which it was declared the obligation of devout Christians to exclude such infidel authors "from their communion and fellowship, not only in sacred things, but likewise from all unnecessary conversation upon other subjects."[51] Ignoring Anderson's advice, the Moderates intensified their ties with the lay literati of Edinburgh in the following year by taking part in the celebrated Select Society. Robertson, Home, Blair, and Carlyle, along with Jardine, Hume, Adam Smith, James Burnett (later Lord Monboddo), Sir David Dalrymple (later Lord Hailes), Alexander Wedderburn (later Lord Loughborough and earl of Rosslyn), and James Russel were among the first thirty-two members.[52] By the time Adam Ferguson joined the club shortly after his return to Scotland in the spring of 1756,[53] the Select Society included Kames, Elibank, Robert Wallace, William Wilkie, and virtually every other prominent man of letters and taste in the Edinburgh vicinity, as well as a host of physicians, architects, military officers, merchants, magistrates, and above all lawyers. Although Presbyterian clergymen constituted less than ten percent of the total membership of the Select, they quickly distinguished themselves as able administrators and debaters. When a special committee on belles lettres and criticism was established in August 1755, for example, Blair, Wilkie, and George Wishart were appointed along with Hume and Smith.[54] Blair and Wilkie were joined by Robertson on another special committee of 1755 to formulate questions suitable for debate.[55] In the debates themselves, Wilkie and especially Robertson excelled, as a result of which, Carlyle believed, "a new lustre was thrown on their order."[56] Since nearly all the fourteen or fifteen clerical members of the Select Society were affiliated with the Moderates, the luster was thrown chiefly on them. Moreover, by distinguishing themselves in the Select Society, these Moderate ministers not only improved the image of the Presbyterian clergy

[51] George Anderson, *An Estimate of the Profit and Loss of Religion* (Edinburgh, 1753), 77–78, 391.

[52] On the membership and significance of the Select Society, see Roger L. Emerson, "The Social Composition of Enlightened Scotland: The Select Society of Edinburgh, 1754–1764," *SVEC* 114 (1973): 291–329.

[53] Ferguson applied for membership on 23 June 1756 and was unanimously elected six weeks later. Select Society Minutes, NLS, Adv. 23.1.1.

[54] Ibid., 6 August 1755.

[55] Ibid., 12 November 1755.

[56] Quoted in Stewart, 1:li.

in the eyes of many laymen but also established friendships and connections that would prove invaluable for their ecclesiastical policies and personal careers.

Meanwhile, the Moderate literati were continuing to display initiative in various types of literary endeavors. The publication in 1753 of the first complete Scottish edition of Shakespeare's works, anonymously edited by Hugh Blair, was indicative of their willingness to enter a field still considered by many to be improperly suited to the character of Presbyterian clergymen: drama. Several years earlier John Home had dared to compose a play of his own, *Agis*, which had been rejected for the stage in the winter of 1749 by the renowned David Garrick of London's Drury Lane Theatre. Through the patronage of Gilbert Elliot, the play had then been read and criticized by Lord Kames, James Oswald of Dunnikier, William Pitt, and other eminent men. By the summer of 1754 it had been entirely revised by the author, and there was talk of a stage production during the coming winter despite the likelihood of provoking strong opposition from the orthodox wing of the kirk.[57] This production never occurred, but the play was sufficiently well known by 1753 for Witherspoon to ridicule it in *Ecclesiastical Characteristics*. In the tragedy of *Agis*, he commented sarcastically, "dramatic poetry is carried to the summit of perfection: and it is believed, by the author's friends, that there never will be a tragedy published after it, unless by somebody that is delirious."[58]

Set in ancient Sparta, *Agis* was a call for the renewal of British public virtue and martial spirit. Home had begun writing the play in the aftermath of the '45, when the totally defenseless state of the Scottish Lowlands had made such a strong impression on the playwright and his friends. It is significant that all of Home's earliest literary patrons were zealous supporters of the militia ideal in one form or another. The Moderate literati shared this promilitia sentiment, not only out of considerations of national defense but also because they considered the militia a necessary corrective to the harmful effects of modernization. "We are in danger of becoming *populus mercatorum, sine armis et ingenio*," Home wrote to James Oswald in response to the latter's letter on *Agis* of June 1750.[59] Similarly, during the militia debates of 1756 Adam Ferguson published a pamphlet castigating the

---

[57] Elliot to Oswald, 18 August 1754, in *Memorials of the Public Life and Character of the Right Hon. James Oswald of Dunnikier* (Edinburgh, 1825), 94–96.

[58] Witherspoon, *Works*, 6:184. It would appear from Home's letter to Carlyle in Mackenzie, 136, that Witherspoon was thinking specifically of Hugh Blair, Alexander Carlyle, and George Logan.

[59] Home to Oswald, 1 August 1750; Oswald to Home, 15 June 1750; and Pitt to Home [May or June 1750]—all in *Oswald Memorials*, 97–106, 110–11, 112–14.

nobility of Great Britain for relinquishing its traditional martial spirit in exchange for "the views of profit and interest alone."[60] More is said about the militia controversy and civic humanist ideology in chapter 6, but it is important to note here that for all their attention to the advantages of politeness the Moderate literati were always on their guard against that species of overrefinement that contemporaries quaintly termed "effeminacy."

While Home and Ferguson were advocating Spartan virtue Blair and Robertson were developing the ideal of polite Presbyterianism in sermons preached before the Scottish branch of the Society for Propagating Christian Knowledge (S.P.C.K.). Blair's sermon, preached in 1750, emphasized the constructive function of religion as a socializing and humanizing force, tending "to improve the social Intercourse of Men, and to assist them in co-operating for common Good." According to Blair, religion, and especially Christianity, "forms [men] for Society. It civilizes Mankind. It tames the Fierceness of their Passions, and wears off the Barbarity of their Manners."[61] The point of Robertson's S.P.C.K. sermon of 1755 was that God gave Christianity to the world at the precise historical moment "when the world stood most in need of such a revelation, and was best prepared for receiving it." Despotism and slavery, superstition and ignorance, luxury and licentiousness, and polygamy and divorce had replaced the ancient virtues of "temperance, frugality, decency, public spirit, love to their fellow-citizens, magnanimity" that had flourished during the era of the Greek city-states. Appearing at a time of widespread degeneration and barbarity, Christianity could be appreciated for its civilizing effects. It checked the growth of despotism, discouraged slavery, softened the practice of war, tightened the bonds of marriage, revitalized morality, and transformed superstition and ignorance into reason and light. When Robertson pondered possible explanations for "the mildness and humanity of modern manners," he found that Christianity alone was responsible for this happy phenomenon: for "Christianity not only sanctifies our souls, but refines our manners; and while it gives the promise of the next life, it improves and adorns the present."[62]

By emphasizing the positive role of Christianity in the civilization

---

[60] Adam Ferguson, *Reflections Previous to the Establishment of a Militia* (Edinburgh, 1756), 13–14.

[61] Hugh Blair, *The Importance of Religious Knowledge to the Happiness of Mankind* (Edinburgh, 1750), 26. Cf. *Sers.*, 1:144, 2:136.

[62] William Robertson, *The Situation of the World at the Time of Christ's Appearance, and Its Connexions with the Success of His Religion Considered* (1755), in *The Works of William Robertson*, 2 vols. (Edinburgh, 1829), 1:lxxvii–lxxxvi.

process, the s.p.c.k. sermons of Blair and Robertson sought to reconcile Christian principles with those of the Enlightenment. The fact that these sermons and others like them were so frequently reprinted in subsequent decades indicates the extent to which this strain of thought reflected the dominant mood of Scotland in the second half of the eighteenth century. Of course, a similar spirit of reconciliation between Christianity and the Enlightenment flourished elsewhere at this time—for example, in the discourses that Turgot delivered at the Sorbonne in 1750.[63] But whereas in France the gap between the established church and the Enlightenment grew wider during the second half of the eighteenth century—culminating in the complete renunciation of organized religion by Turgot's foremost disciple, Condorcet—in Scotland the established church came to terms with the Enlightenment after a series of bitter conflicts in the mid-1750s over issues involving the proper relation of church and churchmen with polite society. As we shall see, the triumph of the Moderate literati of Edinburgh in these ecclesiastical controversies was also the triumph of their vision of enlightened Christianity, or polite Presbyterianism. Having begun in 1751 as a campaign for ecclesiastical law and order, the Moderate Revolution was becoming as well a crusade for politeness and enlightenment.

[63] Cf. Ann-Robert-Jacques Turgot, "Discours sur les avantages que l'établissement du Christianisme a procurés au genre humain," in *Oeuvres de Turgot et documents le concernant*, ed. Gustave Schelle, 5 vols. (Paris, 1913–1923), 1:194–214, and "A Philosophical Review of the Successive Advances of the Human Mind," in *Turgot: On Progress, Sociology, and Economics*, ed. and trans. Ronald L. Meek (Cambridge, 1973), 53.

FROM INFIDEL PHILOSOPHY
TO VIRTUOUS TRAGEDY

To affect zeal against heresy, and at the same time to disregard truth, must appear to every one highly culpable and very unchristian.

Hugh Blair, *Observations,* 1755

Is there aught better than the Stage,
To mend the Follies of the Age,
If manag'd as it ought to be,
Frae ilka Vice and Blaidry free?

Allan Ramsay,
"To the Honourable Duncan Forbes
of Culloden," 1737

The muse once cherish'd, happier Bards shall rise,
And future Shakespears light our northern skies!

Alexander Carlyle,
Prologue to *Herminus and Espansia,* 1754

The first major ecclesiastical challenge to the Scottish Enlightenment and the Moderate party was the campaign of 1755–1756 to censure the writings of David Hume and Lord Kames for their alleged infidelity.[64] The offensive began on the second day of the general assembly of 1755 with the publication in Edinburgh of *An Analysis of the Moral and Religious Sentiments Contained in the Writings of Sopho [Kames], and David Hume, Esq.,* which is usually attributed to Rev. John Bonar of Cockpen. Addressed specifically to the members of the current assembly, this pamphlet listed a series of heretical propositions said to be explicitly or implicitly endorsed by these "infidel" philosophers. The charges against Hume included denying Christian revelation, preferring "Popery" to Protestantism, throwing doubt on the reality of virtue and justice, and portraying religion and its ministers as "prejudicial to mankind"; those against Kames centered on his apparent denial of free will in his *Essays on the Principles of Morality and Natural Religion* (1751).[65] Thanks to the philosophers' friends,

[64] For a fuller account of this campaign, with special attention to Hume, see Mossner, chap. 25.

[65] Excerpts from Bonar's charges are printed in Jane Rendall, *The Origins of the Scottish Enlightenment, 1707–1776* (London, 1978), 215–16. Ironically, a prime objective of Kames's *Essays* was to refute Hume's skepticism.

these charges were transformed into an impersonal and unobjectionable resolution against impiety and immorality that was passed unanimously by the general assembly.[66] It was understood, however, that the matter was not yet resolved. "My damnation is postponed for a twelvemonth," Hume wrote to Allan Ramsay with a mixture of relief and apprehension. "But next Assembly will surely be upon me."[67]

In light of Hume's long record as a notorious skeptic, why did orthodox Presbyterians choose the mid-1750s to begin a serious ecclesiastical campaign against him? Part of the explanation concerns the growing accessibility and sometimes audacity of Hume's skeptical writings in the relatively liberal intellectual climate of the post-'45 era. The anonymous and abstruse *Treatise of Human Nature* of 1739–1740 had fallen, in Hume's words, *"dead-born from the Press*; without reaching such distinction as even to excite a Murmur among the Zealots."[68] By contrast, some of Hume's publications from the late 1740s and early 1750s—including the two *Enquiries* (1748 and 1751); *Three Essays* (1748), with its pointed criticisms of the clergy in "Of National Characters" and of Whig ideology in "Of the Original Contract"; the essay "Of the Protestant Succession" in *Political Discourses* (1752); and the first volume of the *History of England* (1754)—either put forward new and more threatening skeptical arguments or restated old ones in more readable formats. Hume's moral and political thought may now seem moderate and impartial, as it did to Hume himself, but from the Scottish Presbyterian viewpoint of his own day it looked very much like a series of potshots at cherished principles. Matters came to a head with the *History*, which indirectly undermined the historical foundations of the Presbyterian establishment in Scotland and boldly proclaimed the "enthusiasm" and "fanaticism" of the Scottish Reformation to be worse than anything that occurred "during the darkest night of papal superstition."[69] Similarly, Kames's great crime in upholding the doctrine of necessity was to pass judgment, with naive imprudence that was easily mistaken for arrogance, on an issue of

---

[66] The resolution is printed in Mossner, 343.

[67] Hume to Allan Ramsay, [June 1755], *HL*, 1:224.

[68] David Hume, "My Own Life" (1776), in Mossner, app. A.

[69] David Hume, *The History of Great Britain: The Reigns of James I and Charles I*, ed. Duncan Forbes (Harmondsworth, 1970), 71–72, 145–49. In a letter to Dr. John Clephane of 18 February 1755, newly published in J. C. A. Gaskin, "Hume's Attenuated Deism," *Archiv für Geschichte der Philosophie* 65 (1983): 166–73, Hume admitted that his treatment of religion in the first volume of his history was generally "indiscreet" and "should have received some more Softenings." But his regrets at this time had less to do with the book's "passionate Enemies" in Scotland than with its poor sales in London.

the utmost sensitivity and importance to strict Calvinists.[70] Thus, general fears about the growth of infidelity and skepticism were compounded by specific fears about challenges to the theological and historical underpinnings of Scottish Presbyterianism.

A second motive for instigating a campaign against Hume and Kames at this particular time concerns Scottish ecclesiastical politics. How could the members of the assembly fail to censure these infidel philosophers, asked John Bonar, "after the zeal you have lately shewn to support the authority of your own sentences?" How could you depose "a minister who disowned your authority" (Thomas Gillespie) while making Kames an honorary elder of the commission and tolerating some churchmen living "in the greatest intimacy with one who represents the blessed Saviour as an impostor, and his religion as a cunningly devised fable"?[71] Bonar and his associates were seeking revenge against the men deemed responsible for deposing Thomas Gillespie in 1752 and blocking his reinstatement the following year. In this sense the primary targets of the infidelity campaign of 1755–1756 were not Hume and Kames but their best friends among the Presbyterian clergy—the Moderate literati of Edinburgh.

Both these reasons for attempting to censure Hume and Kames in the mid-1750s—one centering on their ideas, the other on their ecclesiastical friends—were addressed by Hugh Blair in his anonymous pamphlet of 1755, *Observations upon a pamphlet intitled An Analysis of the Moral and Religious Sentiments Contained in the Writings of Sopho and David Hume, Esq.* In addition to showing how the author of the *Analysis* "misrepresented the meaning, and quoted unfairly the words of those books he would expose to censure," Blair presented two general arguments basic to the philosophy of Moderatism. The first is that "the freedom of inquiry and debate, tho' it may have published some errors to the world, has undoubtedly been the source from whence many blessings have flowed upon mankind."[72] Specifically, this "noble

---

[70] "The Clergy . . . say he is as bad as me," Hume commented shortly after the publication of Kames's *Essays.* "Nay some affirm him to be worse, as much as a treacherous friend is worse than an open Enemy" (Hume to Michael Ramsay, 22 June 1751, *HL,* 1:162). The charge of necessitarianism was first brought against Kames in an anonymous article of August 1752 (*SM* 14:399–402), followed the next year by George Anderson's *Estimate of the Profit and Loss of Religion,* chap. 2, and an article by J[ohn] W[itherspoon] in *SM* 15 (April 1753): 165–70, which is reproduced and analyzed in George Eugene Rich, "John Witherspoon: His Scottish Intellectual Background" (Ph.D. diss., Syracuse University, 1964), 60–67, 169–84. See also Ian Simpson Ross, *Lord Kames and the Scotland of His Day* (London, 1972), chap. 6.

[71] Bonar, *Analysis,* 49. Kames had been an honorary elder in the general assembly's commission in 1753 and 1754, though his name was discreetly dropped from the list of such elders in 1755. *Annals,* 2:58n.

[72] Hugh Blair, *Observations* (Edinburgh, 1755), 1–2.

principle" of intellectual freedom was seen as the force behind the rise of Christianity, the Reformation, and even the Church of Scotland itself. In invoking the principle of intellectual freedom in this way, Blair provided a blanket defense against any erroneous or dangerous ideas in the works of Hume and Kames. But how could he then defend the Moderates against charges of inconsistency for supporting the right of philosophers to write what they please while denying clergymen the right to follow their consciences in church settlement disputes? Blair's defense rested on a critical distinction between freedom of expression and freedom of action. This distinction led to the second general point of Blair's pamphlet, that "the proper objects of censure and reproof are not freedom of thought, but licentiousness of action; not erroneous speculations, but crimes pernicious to society."[73] Here was the Moderates' answer to charges of inconsistency for censuring Gillespie while exonerating Hume and Kames. For Blair and the other Moderate literati, *actions* harmful to society must be punished, but erroneous *ideas*, whether religious or secular, should be tolerated. According to this view, which was implicit in Robertson's "Reasons of Dissent" of 1752, a Gillespie was far more culpable than a Hume or Kames even if the latter were actually guilty of infidelity. Convinced that a majority of Scottish churchmen now believed that "the perfection of religion is the spirit of moderation," Blair confidently predicted that these arguments would prevail over "the counsels of a violent and unchristian zeal."[74]

Before Blair's optimism could be put to the test at the general assembly of 1756, the Moderate literati and some of their close friends initiated a new project that joined their intellectual inclinations with party propaganda. This was the *Edinburgh Review*, produced anonymously by Robertson, Blair, Jardine, Alexander Wedderburn, James Russel, and Adam Smith.[75] As stated in Wedderburn's preface to the first issue, which appeared during the summer of 1755, the primary purpose of this journal was to demonstrate "the progressive state of learning in this country" by giving "*a full account* of all books published in Scotland within the compass of half a year." Admitting that Scottish letters had fared poorly during the stormy days of the seventeenth century, Wedderburn contended that all obstacles to a Scottish literary revival had since been removed. The Revolution of

---

[73] Ibid. The same point is made by Robert Wallace in his unpublished essay of 1755, "Irenicum," quoted in Sefton, "Robert Wallace," 15.

[74] Blair, *Observations*, 14–15.

[75] "Preface to the Reprint of *The Edinburgh Review* of 1755," in *The Miscellaneous Works of Sir James Mackintosh*, 3 vols. (London, 1854), 2:466–75, where the authors of most reviews are identified.

1688–1689 and the Union of 1707 had brought improvements in industry, laws, government, and manners, and two serious drawbacks for the advancement of learning—the absence of any "standard of language" and backwardness in the art of printing—had recently been remedied. Under these circumstances, it was decided that "shewing men the gradual advances of science, would be a means of inciting them to a more eager pursuit of learning, to distinguish themselves, and to do honour to their country; With this view, the present work was undertaken."[76] This endeavor to exhibit and at the same time stimulate Scottish literary accomplishments reflected the Moderates' love of letters and desire to lead their native land toward politeness and enlightenment.

The second, unstated function of the *Edinburgh Review* was to serve the interests of Moderatism and the Moderate party. Blair set the tone with his review of Francis Hutcheson's posthumous *System of Moral Philosophy*.[77] Although never technically a Moderate in a party sense, Hutcheson had exemplified the Moderate ideal of an enlightened Presbyterian clergyman-academic, and Blair's glowing description of his character provided a model for Moderate ministers to emulate: "a superior genius, joined with disinterested views and public spirit; a great fund of knowledge, and a remarkable facility in communicating it to others; an uncommon zeal, even to a degree of enthusiasm, for the interests of learning, liberty, and virtue." One of the few criticisms of Hutcheson concerned his "stile," which Blair considered "careless and neglected." But this fault, as Wedderburn's preface implied, would soon be set right by the rising generation of Scottish literati.

The Moderate thrust in the first issue of the *Edinburgh Review* was most evident in the treatment of religious works. Immediately following his harsh attack on the crude, pious sermons of Ebenezer Erskine, for example, John Jardine praised William Robertson's recently published s.p.c.k. sermon as representative of a general improvement in Scottish preaching.[78] This approach was continued in the next issue, published early in 1756. Blair extolled the polite sermons of the Anglican bishop Thomas Sherlock for being "free from low metaphors and false tinsel"[79] while Jardine criticized those of the Scottish evangelical Thomas Boston for their vulgarity. "There are

---

[76] *Edinburgh Review* 1 (August 1755): i–iv. Wedderburn's words negate the common charge that the reviewers were afraid to touch Hume's history of the early Stuarts, which appeared more than six months before their first issue.

[77] *Edinburgh Review* 1:9–23.

[78] Ibid., 42–43.

[79] Ibid., 2 (March 1756): 32.

some expressions and allusions in these sermons," Jardine quipped, "which, however acceptable they may be to the *lowest* class of readers, yet to every person of judgment, and who has any regard for religion, . . . must appear to be mean and unworthy of the dignity of the subject."[80]

The second issue of the *Edinburgh Review* was also the last. One probable reason for its demise was the paucity of first-rate books appearing in Scotland at this time. Since Hutcheson's *System of Moral Philosophy* was the only major Scottish book published in 1755, the ambitious editors were compelled to review obscure books and pamphlets that did nothing to enhance the reputation of Scottish letters. They were also compelled "to take some notice of such books published elsewhere, as are most read in this country, or seem to have any title to draw the public attention."[81] In practice "elsewhere" meant England.[82] Although there is evidence that works by French writers such as d'Alembert and Rousseau might have been reviewed if a third issue of the journal had been published,[83] substitution of French books for English ones could not have hidden the fact that the Scottish literati and the Scottish presses simply were not producing enough good books to support an avowedly nationalist literary journal.

If the stated objective of the *Edinburgh Review* failed, the unstated, sectarian objective succeeded all too well. It was plain to every informed reader that the Moderate party was the real power behind the new journalistic enterprise. At times a show of impartiality was affected, as in the reviews of Bonar's *Analysis* and Blair's *Observations*, which were briefly acknowledged and described without editorial comment.[84] But this facade of objectivity fooled few, and it was not long before orthodox Presbyterians were hammering away at the *Edinburgh Review* in pamphlets and letters to newspapers.[85] According to Lord Kames, this public outcry by religious zealots did more than anything else to convince the editors that for the sake of "the public tranquility and their own" their journalistic enterprise should be terminated.[86]

---

[80] Ibid., 26.

[81] Ibid., 1:iii.

[82] Approximately twenty-five percent of the books reviewed in the first two issues of the *Edinburgh Review* were written by Englishmen and published at London.

[83] Adam Smith, "Letter to the *Edinburgh Review*," *Edinburgh Review* 2:63–79, reprinted in Smith, *Essays on Philosophical Subjects*, ed. W. P. D. Wightman and J. C. Bryce (Oxford, 1980), 242–54, esp. 242.

[84] *Edinburgh Review*, vol. 1, reviews 14 and 15.

[85] Mossner, 339.

[86] Quoted in John Campbell, *Lives of the Lord Chancellors*, 5th ed., 10 vols. (London, 1868), 7:368.

Considering the antagonistic mood of orthodox churchmen toward Hume, Kames, and their clerical friends, this decision was unquestionably a wise one. The *Scots Magazine* of September 1755 carried a hostile front-page critique of Kames's necessitarianism by George Anderson, the relentless leader of the infidelity cause.[87] This was followed in January 1756 by John Erskine's strictures on Hume in a sermon preached before the s.p.c.k. and by Rev. Daniel MacQueen's *Letters on Mr Hume's History of Great Britain*—a lengthy critique of Hume's treatment of seventeenth-century religion to which the author appended a doctrinaire Calvinist sermon on "true piety."[88] As the general assembly of 1756 drew near, Anderson and his allies intensified their attack. Five days before the opening of the assembly in May, Anderson published at Glasgow a short pamphlet with a long and informative title: *Infidelity a Proper Object of Censure. Wherein is shewn, The indispensible Obligation that lies upon Church-rulers to exercise the Discipline instituted by Christ, upon such avowed Infidels as have been solemnly initiated Members of the Christian Church by Baptism; and, if irreclaimable, to cast them out of Christian Society.* His target was the liberal philosophy of church censorship in Hugh Blair's *Observations.* To Anderson, Blair's cherished principle of "freedom of thought" might be admitted in regard to secondary issues but could not be allowed in regard to the absolute truths of salvation. Since God has provided enough evidence of religious truth "to satisfy any reasonable man, any fair and serious inquirer," it follows that nothing "can hinder a diligent inquirer from obtaining the possession of it, but some criminal bias that turns him out of his road." Infidelity, then, constitutes not a mere error of the intellect but a crime, indeed a sin, indeed "the chief sin," because it is "the source of all others." "How then," Anderson asked, "can a Christian clergyman receive it as a certain truth (which undoubtedly he must) that *he who believeth not shall be damned,* and yet be persuaded, at the same time, that he who believeth not, may, for all that, be an honest, unprejudiced, or *free inquirer?*"[89] Such reasoning led him to conclude that excommunication of infidel writers was the only proper course for the Church of Scotland to pursue.

[87] *SM* 17 (September 1755): 417–25.

[88] John Erskine, "The Influence of Religion on National Happiness," in *Discourses Preached on Several Occasions,* 2d ed., 2 vols. (Edinburgh, 1801–1804), 2:325–61, esp. 349n., where Erskine notes "the uncommon freedom with which Mr. Hume has insulted the religion of his country"; Daniel MacQueen, *Letters on Mr Hume's History of Great Britain* (Edinburgh, 1756).

[89] George Anderson, *Infidelity a Proper Object of Censure* (Glasgow, 1756), 9–11, 14, 21–22. An abstract of this pamphlet appeared in *SM* 18 (May 1756): 223–27.

On 20 May the general assembly met in Edinburgh amid news of the outbreak of war with France. Tensions were kept high by new pamphlets from the Moderates' opponents, including *A View of the Edinburgh Review.* It was the work of Rev. Edward Johnston, whose published sermon had been unfavorably reviewed by Jardine in the second number of the *Edinburgh Review.* Johnston's chief point was that the editors of that journal had set themselves up as an intellectual elite to pass judgments on the writings of others. In so doing, they had, "like vinegar upon polished steel . . . attempted to sully the lustre of the brightest performances; of every performance, excepting those that have passed through their own channel, and to which they have given the mighty sanction of their all-controlling Imprimatur."[90] The strategic publication date of Johnston's pamphlet suggests that it was part of a general plan to discredit the Moderate literati and decrease their effectiveness as defenders of Hume and Kames.

Meanwhile, Robertson, Carlyle, Home, Jardine, Ferguson, Wilkie, Gilbert Elliot, Lord Elibank, and Hume himself were among those who gathered at a little-known tavern called Carriers' Inn to discuss party strategy for the defense of the "infidel" philosophers over a dozen cases of claret specially ordered for the occasion.[91] Their success in the general assembly was impressive. Though the overture against Hume called only for an investigation and did not mention excommunication or any other censure, it was defeated in the committee of overtures after two days of debate by the overwhelming margin of fifty to seventeen.[92] It never came close to reaching the floor of the assembly, let alone to getting enacted. Among the many factors that contributed to this outcome were the political and oratorical skill of the Moderates and the effectiveness of Hugh Blair's published arguments on behalf of the "spirit of moderation."

When George Anderson made a last desperate attempt to punish infidelity by registering a formal complaint in the Presbytery of Edinburgh against the printers of Kames's *Essays,* the latter's lawyers echoed Blair's *Observations* by adopting the principle of "freedom of inquiry and reasoning" as a primary ground of defense.[93] Blair, assisted by three other Select Society clergymen, produced a new pam-

---

[90] Edward Johnston, *A View of the Edinburgh Review, Pointing Out the Spirit and Tendency of that Paper* (Edinburgh, 1756), 7.

[91] *Auto.,* 323–24.

[92] *SM* 18 (June 1756): 280–84.

[93] George Anderson, *The Complaint made to the Presbytery of Edinburgh, Verified* (Edinburgh, 1756), summarized in *SM* 18 (October 1756): 528; *SM* 18 (December 1756): 589.

phlet intended to demonstrate that, as Kames himself later put it, "my doctrine of necessity coincides precisely with that which is taught by Calvin."[94] They argued that determinism had always been insisted on by true Calvinists against the blind chance of the Stoics and the "liberty of indifference" of the Arminians. In order to substantiate this claim, necessitarian passages were cited from the writings of such impeccable Calvinists as Francis Turrettini, Theodore Beza, John Knox, Samuel Rutherford, Jonathan Edwards, and Calvin himself.[95] As the only living member of this group, Edwards was distressed by this ex-post facto attempt to transform Kames into a faithful Calvinist.[96] But Edwards lived in distant America, and it was over a year before his disclaimer appeared in Edinburgh.[97] In the meantime Kames's supporters saw to it that copies of Blair's pamphlet were sent to all the members of the Presbytery of Edinburgh, who were led to believe that Kames himself was the author.[98] At its meeting of 26 January 1757 the presbytery decided to dismiss the case because, despite some questionable ideas and "unguarded expressions" in the *Essays*, Kames had obviously meant no harm to religion and subsequently had "disavowed and disclaimed" his errors in the pamphlet he was thought to have written.[99]

By this time the man who had brought the complaint against the printers of Kames's *Essays* was as dead as the infidelity cause he had so fervently led. The death of George Anderson in December 1756 symbolized the end of an era in the Church of Scotland, for Anderson was the last major voice of the narrow, intolerant, scholastic, theocratic style of Scottish Presbyterianism that had flourished in the seventeenth century. The fact that he was a marginal ecclesiastical figure whose campaign against Hume and Kames had made much noise but attracted little firm support indicates that growing numbers of Scottish churchmen were coming to regard the old policy of persecuting infidels and heretics as out of step with the times. Younger opponents of the Moderates may have felt uncomfortable with An-

[94] Kames to Elliot, 14 June 1758, NLS, 11014:115–16.

[95] Hugh Blair (assisted by Robert Hamilton, George Wishart, Robert Wallace, and presumably Kames himself), *Objections against the Essays on Morality and Natural Religion Examined* (Edinburgh, 1756).

[96] Sir Henry Moncreiff Wellwood, *Account of the Life and Writings of John Erskine* (Edinburgh, 1818), 207–17.

[97] Jonathan Edwards, *Remarks on the Essays on the Principles of Morality and Natural Religion* (Edinburgh, 1758).

[98] *SM* 18 (December 1756): 589 and 19 (February 1757): 108–109. On authorship of the *Objections*, see Samuel Halkett and John Laing, *Dictionary of Anonymous and Pseudonymous English Literature*, 7 vols. (New York, 1971), 4:211.

[99] *SM* 19 (February 1757): 108–109.

derson's harsh rhetoric of excommunication and old-fashioned preoccupation with abstract and subtle philosophical and theological points. They were concerned less with "infidels" outside the kirk than with "backsliders" within it. Even John Witherspoon, who had published a letter against Kames's necessitarianism in 1753,[100] soon came to believe that philosophical deviations of that sort were relatively harmless. The false teachings of Hume and Kames would be "retailed in conversation," Witherspoon conceded in his s.p.c.k. sermon of 1758, but "only by way of amusement, on account of their boldness or novelty, not one in an hundred appearing to have any serious conviction of their truth." Far more dangerous were "nominal Christians" who "disguise or alter the gospel, in order to defend it," who "endeavour to give such views of Christianity, as will render it palatable to a corrupt worldly mind," and who speak of Christ not as a savior but as a moral teacher "excellently qualified to reform the abuses that had some how or other crept into the world."[101]

Here, as in his *Ecclesiastical Characteristics*, Witherspoon was thinking chiefly of his arch opponents in the kirk, the Moderate literati of Edinburgh.[102] The campaign against Hume and Kames had placed the Moderate literati in the awkward position of having both to defend "infidel" philosophers and to justify that policy in light of their own harsh treatment of the devout Thomas Gillespie in 1752–1753; but the attack on them had been indirect on this occasion, and it had failed completely. Even before George Anderson was in his grave, however, the infidelity issue was giving way to a different sort of ecclesiastical controversy. This time the parties would be more evenly balanced and the possible consequences of defeat more serious for "enlightened" clergymen. And this time the Moderate literati of Edinburgh would occupy center stage from start to finish.

The new controversy concerned the Scottish theater and that aspiring Moderate tragedian John Home. While struggling unsuccessfully to arrange a local stage production of *Agis* during the early 1750s, Home had begun writing a second dramatic work, the tragedy of *Douglas*. Once again his theme was virtue, with emphasis on the heroic values of patriotism and military valor associated chiefly with ancient Greece and Rome.[103] But now the scene had shifted from Sparta

---

[100] See n. 70 above.

[101] John Witherspoon, *The Absolute Necessity of Salvation through Christ* (Edinburgh, 1758), 4–5.

[102] The last charge was probably an allusion to William Robertson's s.p.c.k. sermon of 1755.

[103] Home, *Douglas*, act 4, lines 125–36; "To Mr H[ome]," *SM* 18 (December 1756): 609.

to Scotland, and the protagonist had become a virtuous young shepherd named Norval, who was really the secret son of the late Lord Douglas and Lady Randolph. "Rude . . . in speech and manners," yet brave and virtuous in his deeds, young Norval was meant to represent the idealized fusion of bucolic simplicity and noble greatness—a model, incidentally, for the playwright's own highly idealized self-image.[104] The sentimental reunion of mother and son in the fourth act was typical of the play's attempt to arouse the emotions on behalf of virtuous sentiments in a manner characteristic of mid-eighteenth-century "pathetic," neoclassical drama.[105] The Scottish setting added a nationalist element that the author exploited fully in the prologue spoken before Edinburgh performances:

> Often has this audience soft compassion shown
> To woes of heroes, heroes not their own.
> This night our scenes no common tear demand,
> He comes, the hero of your native land.[106]

Douglas was indeed coming, but it remained to be seen exactly what sort of reception he would receive in his native land.

By the autumn of 1754 a manuscript of *Douglas* was circulating among Home's friends in the Edinburgh area. Corrections and revisions were supplied by Robertson, Blair, Carlyle, Lord Elibank, Gilbert Elliot, and other friendly critics.[107] In January 1755 Elliot was optimistic that the play could be produced in London the next winter.[108] The following month Home confidently set out for London to arrange a production by David Garrick of Drury Lane—only to discover that Garrick thought as little of *Douglas* as he had of *Agis*. Home seems to have been deeply depressed for some time after this second rejection by Britain's greatest actor and theatrical manager.[109] His trip to London was not entirely in vain, however, for it was probably during this visit that Elliot or the duke of Argyll introduced him to the man who would soon become his most devoted patron, John Stuart, third earl of Bute.[110]

---

[104] Home, *Douglas*, act 2, lines 106–107; Mackenzie, 6–7. For the deeper roots of young Norval's character, cf. Allan Ramsay, *The Gentle Shepherd* (Edinburgh, 1725).

[105] Home, *Douglas*, act 4, lines 137–265, and Gerald D. Parker's remarks on page 5 of his edition (Edinburgh, 1972); Clarence C. Green, *The Neo-Classic Theory of Tragedy in England during the Eighteenth Century* (Cambridge, Mass., 1934).

[106] Home, *Douglas*, lines 19–22. The Edinburgh Prologue was published separately in *SM* 19 (February 1757): 76.

[107] *Auto.*, 244, 316.

[108] Gilbert Elliot to Lady Elliot, 17 January 1755, NLS, 11006:100–101.

[109] Elliot to Dr. John Clephane, June 1755, quoted in Mossner, 357.

[110] Even if Home's formal introduction to Bute came from Argyll, as Henry Mackenzie later claimed (Mackenzie, 33), it was Elliot who cemented their relationship (*Auto.*,

Once over his depression, Home began to revise his tragedy in hopes of satisfying Garrick's objections. By April 1756 the new version of *Douglas* was complete, and the author enthusiastically sent the fourth act to Lord Bute with a promise of the remaining four acts by the next post.[111] The earl must have been pleased with this revised version, for in the months to come he exerted his personal influence in an effort to make Garrick change his mind about *Douglas*. Garrick was apologetic but firm; in July he sent Bute a long and detailed account of the "insurmountable Objections, which in my Opinion, will Ever make *Douglas* unfit for ye Stage."[112] At Garrick's request Bute then passed on the bad tidings to Home by way of Elliot. "Don't show Hume [Home] Garricks letter abruptly," he warned, "but break it to him first, for I declare I feel extremely for Him."[113]

It was shortly after Garrick's second rejection of *Douglas* that Home and his friends decided to stage the play in Edinburgh, reasoning that "if it succeeded in the Edinburgh theatre, then Garrick could resist no longer."[114] Their plan was controversial for two reasons. First, mid-eighteenth-century British law prohibited professional theatrical performances without a special license that was impossible to procure in Presbyterian Scotland. Two decades earlier George Anderson and other zealous Presbyterians had forced the closure of Allan Ramsay's Edinburgh playhouse, which they had condemned as a den of iniquity.[115] Since that time some professional theater had returned to Edinburgh by means of English actors and a legal technicality,[116] but it was still considered sinful by many churchmen. The fact that the author of *Douglas* was an ordained minister in the Church

---

353). Bute's letter to Home of 20 September 1755 (Mackenzie, 143–45) shows that the earl was already serving as Home's patron at that early date.

[111] Home to Bute, 27 April [1756], Bute, box 1 (1755), no. 38.

[112] Garrick to Bute, 10 July 1756, in *The Letters of David Garrick*, ed. David N. Little and George M. Kahrl, 3 vols. (Cambridge, Mass., 1963), 1:246. Home's friends and enemies never let this rejection be forgotten. "How shall the English curse their Garrick's name / Who banished Douglas far from Drury Lane," wrote the ironical author of "A Prologue to the Long Expected Tragedy of Douglas" (St. Andrews University Library, 5BR55.C62). Cf. the criticism of Garrick in *The Tragedy of Douglas Analysed* (London, 1757).

[113] Bute to Elliot, 16 August 1756, NLS, 11014:21–22. Elliot eventually showed Garrick's letter to Home, whose reply to Garrick of 3 November 1756 (Hyde Collection, Somerville, N.J.) betrays his anger and frustration.

[114] *Auto.*, 325.

[115] George Anderson, *The Use and Abuse of Diversions* (Edinburgh, 1733) and *A Reinforcement of the Reasons proving that the Stage is an Unchristian Diversion* (Edinburgh, 1733).

[116] William Law Mathieson, *The Awakening of Scotland: A History from 1747 to 1797* (Glasgow, 1910), 159–60.

of Scotland further complicated matters. Orthodox clergymen might grudgingly endure a certain amount of Shakespeare and Otway in their midst, but they could scarely be expected to tolerate the production of a stage play written by a member of their own order.

Considering these circumstances, it is unlikely that the friends of *Douglas* would have risked producing the play in Edinburgh without support from the local political establishment. The approbation of Lord Milton was particularly important since his patron the duke of Argyll controlled Edinburgh politics at this time. Fortunately for Home, Milton was kept loyal to the *Douglas* scheme by the combined influence of his daughter Elizabeth and his trusted assistant Adam Ferguson.[117] Home was also fortunate that the duke of Argyll was a man of learning and taste who detested religious fanaticism. In the autumn of 1756, while Ferguson was entrusted with the delicate task of accompanying Milton's severely depressed son on a trip to the Continent,[118] Milton took Home on a visit to Inverary, where the playwright impressed Argyll and obtained his approval for an Edinburgh production of *Douglas*.[119] "The Duke's good opinion," Carlyle wrote, "made Milton adhere more firmly to him, and assist in bringing on his play in the end of that season."[120]

The plan called for *Douglas* to be staged at the Canongate Theatre by an English acting company featuring West Digges and Sarah Ward in the leading roles. In late November or early December Home and his friends held a reading in order to help Mrs. Ward understand the full meaning of the play. The audience at this reading included Milton, Elibank, Wedderburn, and Kames. The cast of characters was equally distinguished, featuring Robertson and Ferguson as Lord and Lady Randolph, Carlyle as the hero's shepherd "father" Norval, Hume as the villain Glenalvon, Blair as the maid, and the playwright himself as young Douglas.[121] The first professional performance of *Douglas* on 14 December 1756 created "an uproar of exultation that a Scotchman had written a tragedy of the first rate, and that its merit was first submitted to their judgment."[122] A contemporary magazine account described large crowds being turned away at the door and

---

[117] *Auto.*, 345–46.

[118] Fagg, 36–38.

[119] Home to Elliot, 5 November 1756, NLS, 11008:17–18; *Auto.*, 325.

[120] *Auto.*, 325.

[121] The source for this story is a letter by Alexander Carlyle in *The Life and Times of Henry, Lord Brougham*, 2d ed., 3 vols. (Edinburgh, 1871), 1:540–42. Ernest Mossner errs both in doubting the story's authenticity and in casting Hume as the "young hero." Mossner, 358.

[122] *Auto.*, 327; MacDonald Emslie, "Home's *Douglas* and Wully Shakespeare," *Studies in Scottish Literature* 2 (1964): 128–29.

observed that "there never was so great a run on a play in this country."[123] Tears flowed generously, both in the playhouse and at private tea-party readings by Edinburgh ladies.[124] Thrilled by his Edinburgh triumph, Home made preparations for yet another London jaunt to arrange a production of *Douglas* in the capital. This time, with help from Bute and William Pitt, he succeeded, and *Douglas* opened at Covent Gardens on 14 March 1757, exactly three months after its Edinburgh debut. Pitt and Gilbert Elliot went together to the opening-night performance along with Lady Bute and several other ladies who had been busily disposing of tickets for several days.[125] Such party enthusiasm compensated for the Scottish nationalist fervor that had been present at the Edinburgh performances and helped to make *Douglas* a tremendous success on the London stage.[126]

Back in Edinburgh ecclesiastical opposition to *Douglas* was mounting. The Presbytery of Edinburgh took the lead with its "Admonition and Exhortation" of 5 January 1757,[127] which it ordered read from every pulpit within the presbytery on the last Sabbath of the month. Without referring directly to *Douglas* or its author, this statement condemned stage plays as illegal and "prejudicial to the Interests of Religion and Morality." It further criticized the theater for being a superfluous upper class luxury, particularly odious during a period of foreign war and scarcity. Similar ideas had already been expressed by the Presbytery of Edinburgh in a letter to the other presbyteries calling for strong disciplinary action against ministers who had attended performances of *Douglas*.[128] On 12 January the Presbytery of Edinburgh tried to set an example by suspending one of the offenders, Rev. Thomas Whyte of Liberton, for three weeks.[129] Most of the other presbyteries were content to let off offenders with a mild rebuke, however, and one of them, Dunse, even charged the Presbytery of Edinburgh with unwarranted "intermingling" in its affairs.[130] In Home's own Presbytery of Haddington, Robertson, Hugh Bannatine, and other Moderates were strong enough to prevent disciplinary action against their friend for many months.[131] Only Alex-

---

[123] *SM* 18 (December 1756): 623–24.

[124] Mackenzie, 38; Mossner, 259–60.

[125] Elliot, *Border Elliots*, 348.

[126] Home to Milton, 15 and 17 March 1757, NLS, 16700:192–94; Elliot to Lady Elliot, 15 March 1757, NLS, 11007:18–19.

[127] Printed in Alice Edna Gipson, *John Home: A Study of His Life and Works* (Caldwell, Idaho, [1917]), 72–73. The Presbytery of Glasgow endorsed this statement and added one of its own on 14 February. Ibid., 74–76.

[128] Ibid., 76–77. The letter is dated 29 December 1756.

[129] *SM* 19 (April 1757): 264.

[130] Ibid., 216.   [131] *Auto.*, 341.

ander Carlyle had the misfortune to belong to a presbytery that not only heeded but far outdid the Presbytery of Edinburgh in the severity of its disciplinary measures.

While the presbyteries were deciding how to discipline playgoing clergymen Edinburgh was torn by a major pamphlet war. The primary issue was the alleged immorality of theater per se, but this matter soon became inseparable from the question of the alleged immorality of *Douglas* in particular. Ecclesiastical politics was also at issue. Many anti-*Douglas* pamphlets were really anti-Moderate tracts, filled with references to the Inverkeithing affair of 1752 and the close association of Home and his Moderate friends with David Hume and the Select Society. Pro-*Douglas* pamphlets often ridiculed Popular party leaders such as Alexander Webster, whose self-righteous opposition to *Douglas* was considered hypocritical in light of his own reputation as a heavy drinker. Moderate pamphleteers were especially upset about the defections of Patrick Cuming and his assistant John Hyndman. The former was promptly dubbed "Dr Patrick Turnstyle," and the latter was sarcastically excused for his "sin" because "he follows his Peter [Cuming] thro' thick and thro' thin."[132] An Edinburgh university professor accurately summed up the situation in February 1757 when he wrote to a correspondent in London: "There is nothing going on here except the wit on *Douglas*, which is very scurrilous on both sides."[133]

In the early going Home's friends held the upper hand. Carlyle, who had already composed an effective broadside to attract "the lower orders of tradesmen and apprentices" to the playhouse, published in January 1757 his ironical *An Argument to Prove that the Tragedy of Douglas Ought to be Publickly burnt by the Hands of the Hangman*.[134] This was soon followed by the most important of the pro-*Douglas* pamphlets, Adam Ferguson's *The Morality of Stage Plays Seriously Considered*. Ferguson tried to show that there is no basis either in scripture or Scottish ecclesiastical law for the belief that stage plays are by definition "offensive and pernicious." He proceeded to argue that *Douglas*, like the biblical story of Joseph and his brothers, is a profoundly moral tale that teaches such praiseworthy values as "admiration of virtue, compassion to the distressed, and indignation against the wicked cause of their suffering."[135] Turning from moral to social and economic considerations, he challenged the Presbytery of Edin-

---

[132] George Bannatine, *The Admonition: An Execrable New Ballad* (Edinburgh, 1757).

[133] George Stuart to Gilbert Elliot, 17 February 1757, NLS, 11014:45.

[134] Printed in Gipson, *John Home*, app. A; Alexander Carlyle, *A Full and True History of the Bloody Tragedy of Douglas* (Edinburgh, 1756).

[135] Adam Ferguson, *The Morality of Stage Plays Seriously Considered* (Edinburgh, 1757), 10.

burgh's depiction of theater as a wasteful, decadent pastime. Part of his case rested on the common economic defense of upper class diversions like theater on grounds that they ultimately benefit the poor by providing various types of employment, such as costume making. A more significant line of defense was put forward in the following passage:

> It has pleased Providence, for wise purposes, to place men in different stations, and to bestow upon them different degrees of wealth. Without this circumstance there could be no subordination, no government, no order, no industry. Every person does good, and promotes the happiness of society, by living agreeable to the rank in which Providence has placed him.[136]

Such Christian-Stoic notions of social conservatism would continue to play a major role in the ideology of the Moderate literati of Edinburgh.

Another early defense of *Douglas* and its author came from the pen of David Hume. At the beginning of 1757 the philosopher composed an open letter to John Home in which *Douglas* was called "one of the most interesting and pathetic pieces, that was ever exhibited on any theatre."[137] While praising his friend's theatrical genius and character Hume was careful to acknowledge "the opposition, which prevails between us, with regard to many of our speculative tenets." This qualification not only protected Home from charges of impiety but also provided a pretense for exalting the principle of "liberty of thought." Hume conjured up a vision of an idealized ancient world in which all men of letters maintained "a mutual friendship and regard" despite their differences of opinion—a situation that he obviously wished for in his own day. The Moderate literati of Edinburgh shared Hume's vision but disputed his tactics. On 20 January Hume informed his publisher in London that the open letter on *Douglas* should be temporarily suppressed as the dedication to his forthcoming book *Four Dissertations* because some of Home's friends "were seiz'd with an Apprehension, that it wou'd hurt that Party in the Church with which he had always been connected, and wou'd involve him, and them of Consequence, in the Suspicion of Infidelity."[138] The cautious Moderates apparently felt that praise from the infamous David Hume, prefixed to a book that included the skeptical essay "The Natural History of Religion," would be more of a

---

[136] Ibid., 24.

[137] David Hume, "To the Reverend Mr. Hume, Author of *Douglas*, a Tragedy," in Gipson, *John Home*, 88–89.

[138] Hume to Andrew Millar, 20 January 1757, *HL*, 1:239–40.

hindrance than an asset to their colleague and their cause. Subsequent developments proved them right. After the controversial open letter to Home finally began to appear in copies of *Four Dissertations* published early in February, the enemies of *Douglas* took delight in citing this dedication "which *dainty Davie* has thought fit to write to *jumping John.*"[139]

By late March momentum had begun to swing to the critics of *Douglas*. Publication of the play in London (17 March) and Edinburgh (29 March), while greatly increasing its fame,[140] provided its enemies with ammunition for further attacks. Anticipating this response, Home had omitted from the published editions certain phrases likely to give offense, such as a dying character's exclaiming, "I'll risk eternal fire."[141] But pious opponents of *Douglas* could still point to "Despiteful Fate," "O God of heaven," and similar phrases in the printed text to support their contention that *Douglas* was immoral and used the name of the Lord in vain. Rev. Archibald Walker of Temple testified that after reading some lines like these "I threw the Book from me to the Ground" in horror.[142] Such critics also complained that the self-inflicted death of Lady Randolph following the murder of her son appeared to provide justification for that "monstrous and unnatural Crime of Suicide."[143] From Glasgow came John Witherspoon's *A Serious Inquiry into the Nature and Effects of Stage Plays*, the best statement of the antitheater position. Adam Ferguson's defense of *Douglas* and the theater was attacked by a certain Rev. Harper in *Some Serious Remarks on a Late Pamphlet entitled the Morality of Stage-Plays Seriously Considered*. One of several pamphlets and squibs by John Maclaurin (later Lord Dreghorn) assailed Home's poetry and attributed the success of his play to the connivance of his "dictatorial club," the Select Society.[144] "They indeed have thought proper to style themselves *select*," quipped the anonymous author of *Douglasiana*, "But, alas! 'tis too plain they're none of the *elect*." Another of Maclaurin's pamphlets, *The Deposition, or Fatal Miscarriage: A Tragedy*, suggested that Home should be deposed since he had been among those who

---

[139] *The Stage or the Pulpit*, part 3 (Edinburgh, 1757). Hume's dedication was reprinted in several British newspapers and in *SM* 19 (June 1757): 293–94. On Hume's role in the *Douglas* controversy, see Ernest Mossner, *The Forgotten Hume: Le Bon David* (New York, 1943), 38–66, and Mossner, chap. 26.

[140] Home to Milton, 17 March 1757, NLS, 16700:194.

[141] Gipson, *John Home*, 116–17n.

[142] Carlyle's account of the meeting of the Presbytery of Dalkeith, 19 April 1757, NLS, 17601:68.

[143] Ibid., David Plenderleath's speech; *Douglas, A Tragedy, weighed in the Balance and Found Wanting* (Edinburgh, 1757).

[144] *Apology for the Writers against the Tragedy of Douglas* (Edinburgh, 1757).

had instigated the deposition of Thomas Gillespie in 1752. Faced with this barrage of hostile criticism, the friends of *Douglas* fell silent.

More serious than these paper bullets was the prosecution of Alexander Carlyle by the Presbytery of Dalkeith. When first summoned before that body in February 1757, Carlyle canvassed his fellow presbyters and determined that they were dead set against him. This situation, he later remarked, "confirmed my resolution not to yield, but to run every risk" rather than submit tamely to a "fanatical" exercise of power that would have "stamped disgrace on the Church of Scotland" and discouraged enlightened young men from entering the ministry.[145] Carlyle therefore acted rather arrogantly at his first appearance before the presbytery on 1 March, even daring to conclude his prepared remarks with a boastful statement about his achievements as a parish minister.[146] At his second appearance on 15 March he was a little more humble, though not enough to satisfy his enemies, who were preparing a serious formal accusation or "libel" against him. Ten days later the libel was issued, listing three major charges:

> 1. His associating himself or familiarly keeping company with the players, persons who by their profession, and in the eye of the law, are of bad fame. 2. His attending the rehearsal of the tragedy of *Douglas*, and assisting or directing the players on that occasion. 3. His appearing openly in the playhouse in the Canongate, within a few miles of his own parish, near to an university-seat, and hard by the city of Edinburgh, where he was well known.[147]

The defendant was ordered to present his answers to these and other charges on 5 April.

Concerned about his personal reputation as well as the principle at stake, Carlyle was deeply vexed when Lord Milton, under the influence of Patrick Cuming, expressed displeasure at his obstinacy before the presbytery. "Supported by your Lordship," Carlyle replied, "I had hopes to come off with some degree of honour, and in a manner that would convince the World that I am neither so insignificant in the Church, nor so worthless in point of Morals as some

---

[145] *Auto.*, 331–32.

[146] Papers Relating to Libell against A. Carlyle for attending Douglas, EUL, La. 2/483, no. 4.

[147] *SM* 19 (March 1757): 159. On the same day (25 March 1757), Rev. Ebenezer Brown of Dalkeith wrote to the moderator of the Presbytery of Edinburgh seeking assistance in the prosecution of Carlyle and recommending disciplinary action against Adam Ferguson for continually and defiantly attending the theater. *Historical Manuscripts Commission Report on the Laing Manuscripts Preserved in the University of Edinburgh* (London, 1925), 2:416–18.

people have secretly misrepresented me."[148] These differences seem to have been patched up very soon, for two drafts of Carlyle's presbytery speech of 5 April are among Milton's private papers.[149] In this speech Carlyle first described his role in the production of *Douglas* and defended the play against charges of immorality. He then apologized for his offensive conduct and promised not to repeat it. A concluding passage, added to the final draft of the speech, contended that the offense deserved only a privy censure and that the libel should be dropped. The presbytery was unwilling to comply but agreed to continue debate at its next meeting on 19 April.

With Home lying low in London, the Carlyle case now became the rallying point for the anti-*Douglas* and anti-Moderate forces in the Church of Scotland. Home himself had mixed feelings about the affair, as he indicated to Lord Milton on 9 April:

> I Dont know whether or no I am sorry for Carlyles having got a Libel. I wish indeed that they had given it to me, but I cannot help thinking that it is the interest of the Publique & of every Gentleman & Scholar in Scotland that the Church should come to a decision, & wipe away as I am sure they will the reproach of our Country.[150]

After noting that the duke of Argyll and almost all the Scottish members of Parliament would "give their interest in the right way" when the matter came before the general assembly,[151] Home concluded with an appeal for Milton's continued support for his friend, adding, "I really think that he can not make the confession & recantation they would have him to do without dishonouring himself for ever."

On 19 April Carlyle made another unsuccessful attempt to overturn the libel against him. Led by Archibald Walker of Temple, David Plenderleath of Dalkeith, and Charles Primrose of Creighton, the majority of the presbyters sought to humiliate Carlyle and his ecclesiastical party. They were assisted in this endeavor by Robert Dundas of Arniston, then lord advocate and a powerful force within the presbytery. Carlyle believed that Dundas could have easily silenced the proceedings against him but chose not to do so largely because

---

[148] Carlyle to Milton, 28 March 1757, NLS, 16699:132.

[149] NLS, 17601:64, 66; also EUL, La. 2/483, no. 12; summarized in *SM* 19 (March 1757):160.

[150] Home to Milton, 9 April 1757, NLS, 16700:196–97.

[151] According to Milton's son, Argyll intervened in "Parson Home's affair" as early as 21 April, when he instructed Lord Cathcart to "moderate the zeal of Hyndman & C[uming]." Andrew Fletcher to Milton, 21 April 1757, NLS, 16519:96.

of personal and political rivalries with Lord Milton and other patrons of *Douglas*.[152] Several ministers in the presbytery supported Carlyle, though only one of them, Thomas Turnbull of Borthwick, spoke effectively on his behalf. He also had the backing of the town council of Inveresk, the elders of his church, and more than a hundred parishioners, who submitted petitions in his favor.[153] But all this was to no avail in the face of his opponents' contention that Carlyle had not truly repented. "No, Moderator, he is not humble enough," proclaimed Archibald Walker, whom Carlyle later described as "a rank enthusiast, with nothing but heat without light."[154] "He is not yet humble enough, Moderator. Moderator he is not so humble as I would have him. Yea, Moderator, he is not so humble as I aim to make him if I can get my will."[155] When the presbytery voted to retain the libel, Carlyle immediately appealed the case to the Synod of Lothian and Tweeddale.

The night before the opening of the synod, Carlyle's supporters met to plan their strategy. Carlyle proposed that his friend Robert Dick be elected moderator, partly in order to bring Dick into the Moderate inner circle and partly in order to "exclude Robertson, whose speaking would be of more consequence if not in the [moderator's] chair."[156] The following day (10 May) Dick was elected as planned, giving the Moderates an important procedural advantage over their opponents. Carlyle's affair was considered on the eleventh. The defendant opened with a remonstrance, followed by eloquent supporting speeches from Robertson, Andrew Pringle, and John Dalrymple of Cranston. At one point the debate began to grow ugly as John Hyndman hurled personal abuse at Carlyle and Home for associating "with an avowed Infidel who in his late *natural history of Religion* says that Religion is all an Enigma, a Riddle, an uncertainty."[157] Without actually mentioning David Hume's name, Hyndman insisted that the author of *Douglas* renounce and disclaim all connection with this infidel writer. John Home, who had returned to Scotland in time for the synod meeting, promptly called Hyndman to order. Robert Dick then justified Carlyle's confidence in him by severely rebuking Hyndman from the chair. The Moderates took advantage of this opportunity to propose an overture censuring the

---

[152] *Auto.*, 333–35.

[153] EUL, La. 2/483, nos. 2, 3, 6, 7, 9.

[154] *Auto.*, 247.

[155] Carlyle's account of the meeting of the Presbytery of Dalkeith, 19 April 1757, NLS, 17601:68.

[156] *Auto.*, 336.

[157] Carlyle's account of the synod debate, 12 May 1757, NLS, 17601:74.

Presbytery of Dalkeith for its vague and inexpedient libel and adding, almost as an afterthought, its "displeasure" with Carlyle's theater-going and its wish that he abstain from such activity in the future. When put to the test, the overture carried by three votes, despite the protests of Alexander Webster and the majority of the Presbytery of Dalkeith.[158] Now it was their turn to appeal the matter to a higher ecclesiastical court, in this case the general assembly, which was to meet at Edinburgh one week later.

The final debate on the Carlyle affair occurred in the assembly on 24 May 1757. Many of the Moderates' foremost opponents were members, including Plenderleath and Walker from the Presbytery of Dalkeith, John Witherspoon, John Erskine, and the Moderate literati's newest foe, Patrick Cuming. George Whitefield himself was in the gallery, "as if," one observer remarked in his diary, "people's passions were not sufficiently inflamed already."[159] Carlyle was ably defended by Robertson, Gilbert Hamilton, and, according to one account, John Home, who nobly declared that he rather than Carlyle was responsible for any harm done.[160] At the end of the day the Moderates were rewarded for their efforts with a vote of 117 to 39 to affirm the lenient sentence of the synod.[161] To the relieved defendant the vast majority in his favor demonstrated conclusively "that the heat and animosity raised against the tragedy of *Douglas* and its supporters was artificial and local"—which is to say, political and personal.[162]

The matter of formulating a general policy regarding theater attendance by church members was taken up in the assembly three days after the settlement of the Carlyle case. Extremists in the Popular party first proposed a severe act prohibiting any future attendance by laymen as well as clergymen within the church. The Moderates successfully defeated this proposal, but they were caught off guard when Robert Dundas pulled from his pocket a much milder statement strongly recommending that presbyteries "take care that none of the ministers of this church do upon any occasion attend the theatre." Lacking a clear plan of action, the Moderates acquiesced in the unanimous passage of Dundas's statement by voice vote.[163] But this mild measure was scarcely a defeat for the theater. On the contrary,

---

[158] *SM* 19 (April 1757): 217.
[159] *The Diary of George Ridpath*, ed. Sir James Balfour Paul (Edinburgh, 1922), 136.
[160] Ibid., 138–39; John Jackson, *The History of the Scottish Stage* (Edinburgh, 1793), 317; "An Essay on the Life and Writings of William Robertson," in *WWR*, 1:x.
[161] *SM* 19 (May 1757): 263–64.
[162] *Auto.*, 338.
[163] *SM* 19 (May 1757): 264; Home to Elliot, 1 June [1757], NLS, 11009:141–42.

it was, as John Witherspoon noted bitterly in 1763, "so gentle, that it was then the opinion of many, it would have a greater tendency to encourage, than to prevent the repetition of the offence. *It now appears they judged right.*"[164] After *Douglas*, the Edinburgh theater rapidly improved its social and legal status. In 1776 half of the general assembly went to the theater to see Mrs. Barry, and eight years later the most important business of the assembly was specially scheduled so that members could conveniently attend performances by the renowned Sarah Siddons at the Royalty Theatre![165]

Coming on the heels of the unsuccessful infidelity campaigns against Hume and Kames, the *Douglas* affair of 1756–1757 established that the future direction of the Church of Scotland and of Scottish society as a whole would be toward cultural and intellectual freedom, religious moderation, and respect for serious endeavors in all branches of the arts and sciences. It signified, in short, the triumph of the Moderate ideal of a polite ministry leading Scotland down the path to enlightenment. *Douglas* was considered enlightened entertainment not only because theater as such symbolized civilization and refinement but also because this particular play inspired its audiences with moral principles such as military valor and maternal love. As Hugh Blair would later declare from his university lectern, "the end of tragedy is, to improve virtuous sensibility."[166] The victory of *Douglas* was the victory of the theater of virtue as much as it was the victory of theater itself.

The issue of the theater as a force for virtue and enlightenment was by no means restricted to the literati of Scotland. In the seventh volume of the *Encyclopedia*, published in 1757, d'Alembert suggested that Geneva would do well to establish a theater while enacting strict laws to guard against moral degeneration. "With these measures," he speculated,

> Geneva would have plays and good morals and enjoy the advantages of both. Theatrical performances would form the taste of citizens and give them a delicate sense of tact, a refinement of feeling that is very difficult to acquire without this assistance. Literature would profit from it without libertinage making any

[164] Witherspoon, *Serious Apology*, in *Works*, 6:270–71. Emphasis added.

[165] Blair to Hume, [May–June 1776], RSE, 3/63; Andrew Dalzel to Sir Robert Liston, 17 June 1784, in Dalzel, *History of the University of Edinburgh*, 2 vols. (Edinburgh, 1862), 1:44–45; James C. Dibden, *The Annals of the Edinburgh Stage* (Edinburgh, 1888), 186–90.

[166] Hugh Blair, *Heads of Lectures on Rhetorick and Belles Lettres, in the University of Edinburgh* (Edinburgh, 1771), 45.

progress, and *Geneva* would join the wisdom of Sparta with the refinement of Athens.[167]

These were precisely the sentiments of the Moderate literati of Edinburgh. Upon receiving a copy of Rousseau's pamphlet of 1758 attacking d'Alembert's views on the theater, John Home expressed the indignation of *philosophes* everywhere that "he who has libelled society itself" should now attack "the most refined entertainment of social life."[168] Two years later Voltaire, whose *Mérope* had been a source for *Douglas,* paid tribute to John Home and his namesake David in the preface to his comedy *Le Caffé, ou l'Écossaise.*[169] By this time the *Douglas* affair had attained international recognition among *philosophes* as an important provincial skirmish between the forces of "light" and "darkness."

Within Scotland it represented much more. For the literati of Edinburgh the *Douglas* affair had a liberating effect on their hopes and aspirations for the future of Scottish letters. If an obscure parish minister could produce a first-rate tragedy, then why should the Scots not distinguish themselves in other branches of polite literature as well? Even as the general assembly was deliberating about *Douglas* in May 1757, Scotland was "in raptures" (as John Home put it) over a new epic poem, *The Epigoniad,* by William Wilkie, the clergyman-farmer whose manners were so rough that Charles Townshend is said to have called him the nearest thing to "the two extremes of a god and a brute."[170] David Hume was much taken with Wilkie's peculiar mixture of vulgarity and genius; indeed, it was the *Epigoniad,* along with *Douglas* and the unfinished manuscript of Robertson's *History of Scotland,* that brought forth Hume's celebrated outburst of cultural chauvinism in a letter to Gilbert Elliot of 2 July 1757:

> Really it is admirable how many Men of Genius this Country produces at present. Is it not strange that, at a time when we have lost our Princes, our Parliaments, our independent Government, even the Presence of our chief Nobility, are unhappy, in our Accent & Pronunciation, speak a very corrupt Dialect of

[167] "Geneva," in Denis Diderot, *The Encyclopedia: Selections,* ed. and trans. Stephen J. Gendzier (New York, 1967), 114.

[168] Home to Bute, 12 December 1758, Bute, box 1 (1758), no. 192; Jean-Jacques Rousseau, *Politics and the Arts: Letter to M. d'Alembert on the Theatre,* ed. and trans. Allan Bloom (Glencoe, Ill., 1960).

[169] *Le Caffé, ou l'Écossaise, Comedie, par Mr. Hume [Home], traduite en français* (The Hague, 1760), 3. "These two philosophers do equal honor to Scotland, their native country," Voltaire added in a commentary on this play. *The Works of Voltaire,* ed. and trans. William F. Fleming, 22 vols. (New York, 1901), 19, pt. 2:70.

[170] *Auto.,* 413; Home to Elliot, 10 July [1757], NLS, 11009:143–44.

the Tongue which we make use of; is it not strange, I say, that, in these Circumstances, we shou'd really be the People most distinguish'd for Literature in Europe?[171]

On the very same day this letter was written, Alexander Wedderburn sent Elliot a letter containing similar views. As indicated earlier Wedderburn's expectations of a rebirth of Scottish letters in 1755 had been disappointed by the paucity of first-rate Scottish books published at that time. In the summer of 1757, however, Wedderburn's claims seemed justified by the impressive list of recent and forthcoming Scottish publications that he proudly enumerated for the benefit of his friend in London:

> The most agreable prospect in this Country arises from the Men of Letters. Robertson has almost finished a History, which will do honour to any age & bids fair to dispute the prize w^t Dav^d Hume. John Hume has finished [i.e. rewritten] the first act of Agis & applies in earnest. Ferguson is writing a very ingenious System of Eloquence or Composition in general. Wilkie['s] Epick poem you have certainly seen. [Adam] Smith has a vast work upon the arrival. It discloses the deepest principles of philosophy, but I forgot that you have seen the plan. Ld Kaims has a book upon Law ready to appear. Dav: Hume is well advanced in the reign of Henry ye 7th. You see how we endeavour to fill up some part of the System here.[172]

Of the seven authors mentioned by Wedderburn, Hume and Kames were by this time familiar names. It was the addition of five newcomers that created the sensation of a sudden awakening of polite literature in Scotland. All five had been born between 1721 and 1723, and four were ordained ministers in the Church of Scotland. In this sense the *Douglas* affair marked the emergence of a new literary generation—dominated by Moderate clergymen—that would subsequently constitute the driving force behind the Scottish Enlightenment.

Apart from its intellectual and cultural significance, the *Douglas* affair had important political ramifications for the Moderate literati of Edinburgh. Within the Church of Scotland it spelled the end of their uneasy alliance with the old Argathelian interest headed by Patrick

---

[171] Hume to Elliot, 2 July 1757, *HL*, 1:255.

[172] Wedderburn to Elliot, 2 July 1757, NLS, 11008:58–59. The works in question were William Robertson, *The History of Scotland* (1759); John Home, *Agis* (1758); William Wilkie, *The Epigoniad* (1757); Adam Smith, *The Theory of Moral Sentiments* (1759); Lord Kames, *Historical Law Tracts* (1758); and David Hume, *The History of England under the House of Tudor* (1759). Adam Ferguson never published the book on "Eloquence or Composition" mentioned by Wedderburn.

Cuming. This coalition had functioned smoothly only during the Inverkeithing controversy of 1752–1753, when the Moderate literati had been too young, too inexperienced, and too little known to proceed without Cuming's assistance. Since then there had been little cooperation between the two factions. Carlyle believed that Cuming's zealous opposition to *Douglas* derived from his jealousy about the growing intimacy of Robertson, Home, and himself with Lord Milton.[173] Whatever the reasons for it, Cuming's course of action left the Moderate literati on their own in the church courts. Their success there, especially in the crucial Carlyle libel case, signaled the beginning of Cuming's decline as an ecclesiastical leader. It was also an indication that the Moderate party would be more independent, which is to say less slavishly tied to the duke of Argyll, than would have been possible if Cuming had remained affiliated with it.

One reason for this new-found independence was the Moderates' belief that ecclesiastical parties should be guided by firm ideological principles rather than by the dictates of some "great man."[174] Political patrons were to be courted of course, but party policy was to emanate from within the church along relatively consistent lines. Throughout their careers the Moderate literati always maintained the basic principles of patronage and order, politeness and enlightenment, for which they had fought so effectively in the ecclesiastical struggles of the 1750s. By giving their own party a distinct ideological identity, they inadvertently helped to provide a clearer identity for those churchmen who agreed on little else except their opposition to the principles of Moderatism. Thus, the split between Cuming and the Moderate literati over *Douglas* constituted another step toward the establishment of two ideologically and politically autonomous church parties in place of the old political interest groups that had dominated Scottish ecclesiastical politics before the Moderate Revolution.

A second reason for the Moderates' increased independence is less idealistic. After *Douglas* the Moderate literati could afford to be less subservient to the duke of Argyll than Cuming had ever been because they were cultivating a second set of powerful political connections. In addition to their close ties with the Drummond-Milton-Argyll axis in Scotland, they also enjoyed the patronage of the Pitt-Bute-Leicester House party in London. It was Pitt who had arranged the production of *Douglas* at Covent Gardens while Bute had, as Home remarked to Milton, "taken the same charge of Douglas in England

---

[173] *Auto.*, 330.
[174] Clark diss., 46–48.

that your Lordship did in Scotland."[175] The appearance at the theater of the Prince and Princess of Wales and the generous pension of £100 per annum that they bestowed on the playwright can almost certainly be attributed to Bute's pervasive influence at Leicester House.[176] When Home resigned his parish charge in June 1757, he did so with the knowledge that he would be well provided for by Bute, who soon made him his secretary while continuing to patronize his theatrical pursuits.

Why did Pitt and above all Bute champion Home and *Douglas* so enthusiastically in 1757? The explanation would seem to be partly ideological, partly personal and political. The heroic values of *Douglas* were similar to the "patriot" principles that Bute was then seeking to instill in the young Prince of Wales.[177] They were also supportive of Pitt's militia scheme and the spirit of public virtue that was hailed by Pittites and Moderates alike as a prerequisite to victory in the war with France and Austria. Home's *Agis*, which finally reached Garrick's Drury Lane Theatre in late February 1758, was still more emphatic in its endorsement of these heroic values. Bute himself participated in the revision of *Agis*, and Sir Harry Erskine, a Scottish M.P. and Bute supporter, penned the prologue that spelled out the lesson to be learned from the performance to follow:

> May this sad scene improve each Briton's heart:
> Rouse him with warmth to act a Briton's part!
> Prompt him with Sparta's noblest sons to vie;
> To live in glory; and in freedom die![178]

Indeed, *Agis* was so closely tied to Pitt, Bute, and Leicester House that political opponents branded it a "rank Party-Piece,"[179] and

[175] Home to Milton, [February 1757] and 17 March 1757, NLS, 16700:190, 194.

[176] *The Story of the Tragedy of Agis, with Observations on the Play, the Performance, and the Reception* (London, 1758), 6.

[177] James Lee McKelvey, *George III and Lord Bute: The Leicester House Years* (Durham, N.C., 1973), 82–89; John Brooke, *King George III* (New York, 1972), 64–66. The heart of Bute's "patriot" ideology was the belief that Britain was on the verge of ruin due to the prevalence of factionalism and disunity. Bute convinced the young prince that his mission as a British sovereign was to lead his country out of crisis by rising above party differences and reviving a bipartisan spirit of moral commitment and religious piety.

[178] *WJH*, 1:191; Home to Bute, 17 August 1757, Bute, box 1 (1757), no. 107; *Story of Agis*, 2–9.

[179] *The Dramatic Execution of Agis* (London, 1758). According to this virulent pamphlet, at the first performance of *Agis* "it is certain there was not a Clap throughout, but at Party-Strokes." The opening night audience was said to have been divided into a camp that gave "riotous Applause" upon the pronouncement of lines that could be interpreted as calls for patriotic virtue in the war, such as "All necessary Danger must

Alexander Carlyle felt obliged to declare that it was not a work of "faction and party." "Surely it can forbode nothing but good to Britain," Carlyle asserted in the conclusion of his review of *Agis* in the *Critical Review,* "that a play full of the highest spirit of patriotism and heroic virtue, drew the attention of her princes, and received the most distinguishing marks of their approbation."[180] Home's Scottishness added to these heroic and patriotic values a sense of Scottish national loyalty to the Hanoverian establishment that may have been considered politically useful by Bute and Pitt as an antidote to charges that the Scots were potential rebels who should not be allowed their own militia under any circumstances.

On a personal level, the enthusiasm of Bute and Pitt for Home's early plays can be traced to Gilbert Elliot, who joined together many disparate strands of ideology, political allegiance, and personal friendship. As a Pittite M.P. and a close friend of Bute, Elliot was the chief bridge between the two poles of the Bute-Pitt alliance that came into existence in May 1755.[181] As a Scotsman, a respected literary critic, a former classmate of Home and his friends at Edinburgh University, a lay Moderate, and a strong advocate of militia and martial spirit, Elliot naturally did all he could to advance Home's theatrical career by means of his political connections in London. The Moderate literati considered Elliot their man in London, and they rejoiced at his political ascendancy in the Pitt-Newcastle coalition government of June 1757.[182] In terms of political connections, Elliot was at this time the London equivalent of Lord Milton in Edinburgh—a vital link between the Moderate literati of Edinburgh and the "great men" who could exert the most influence on their behalf.

After *Douglas,* then, the Moderate literati of Edinburgh had friends in high places. Yet their situation remained precarious. For one thing, there was always the possibility that their political friends might lose power and influence as a result of death or political defeat. Furthermore, although a policy of divided political loyalties might provide a greater degree of independence, it could also create problems in the event of a rift between patrons, such as actually occurred between

---

be risk'd," and a camp that regarded the play with "just Contempt" that later became "national Resentment, on seeing what extraordinary Methods (unprecedented in this Kingdom) were taken to support it." It is significant, in light of the shady dealings of Pitt and Bute's arch foe Henry Fox, that the author of this pamphlet particularly resented the play's "sarcastic Innuendos of Corruption, Bribery, Degeneracy, Cowardice, Venality, etc." in government. Cf. the strongly partisan account of the play and its supporters in *Story of Agis.*

[180] *Critical Review* 5 (January–June 1758): 242.
[181] McKelvey, *George III and Lord Bute,* 20, 117–18; Elliot, *Border Elliots,* 342.
[182] Home to Elliot, 10 July [1757], NLS, 11009:143–44.

Bute and Argyll and between Bute and Pitt in the late 1750s.[183] For the Moderate literati to become truly independent, it would be necessary for them to overcome these contingencies and consolidate their gains by obtaining permanent positions of prestige and authority within the institutional framework of Scotland. At the time of the *Douglas* affair this was merely a dream. In the decade that followed it became a reality.

[183] On the Argyll-Bute feud, see Alexander Murdoch, *"The People Above": Politics and Administration in Mid-Eighteenth-Century Scotland* (Edinburgh, 1980), chap. 4. On the rift between Bute and Pitt, see Romney Sedgwick, "William Pitt and Lord Bute: An Intrigue of 1755–58," *History Today* 6 (1956): 647–54, and McKelvey, *George III and Lord Bute,* chap. 5.

CHAPTER THREE

The Institutionalization
of Moderate Authority

❀

POSITIONS OF PRESTIGE,
POWER, AND PECUNIARY GAIN

A subsistence altogether precarious, however honourable for the
present or big with hopes, was never to my mind. Every man of
worth shoud have a firm bottom on which he may stand however narrow it is. . . . I never coud love a man entirely whilst I
remain in absolute dependance on him or at least . . . I never
coud act as if I did love him so. Give me ground enough to stand
on as my Predecessor Archimedes said & then I will show you
what kind of Mechanic I am.

Adam Ferguson,
Letter to Gilbert Elliot, 1760

The Moderate literati of Edinburgh had now emerged as the leading
ecclesiastical exponents of order and enlightenment in Scotland, but
their struggles had not brought them any significant increases in status, income, or institutional authority. When the smoke cleared after
the battle over *Douglas* in 1757, none of them had yet received a mark
of official distinction within the kirk, such as a royal chaplaincy; none
was affiliated with the University of Edinburgh; and none earned
more, and most earned considerably less, than the £139 stipend that
Hugh Blair received in his capacity as minister of an Edinburgh
church. Within a few years, however, the Moderate literati of Edinburgh would be well off financially and extremely powerful in the
Church of Scotland and University of Edinburgh. How they accomplished this rapid ascent and subsequently secured their places at the
academic and ecclesiastical summit of Scotland is the subject of this
chapter.

Since returning to Edinburgh in the mid-1750s, Adam Ferguson had
been searching for an academic position that would allow him to re-

sign his military chaplaincy and give up the "character" of a Presbyterian clergyman. His ultimate goal was the chair of moral philosophy at the University of Edinburgh, for which he is supposed to have
been recommended in 1754 by the dying incumbent, William Cleghorn.[1] Ferguson had lost that chair to James Balfour of Pilrig, a lawyer, landowner, and author of a timely attack on the moral philosophy of David Hume.[2] Two years later John Home had initiated an
unsuccessful scheme to create an unsalaried rhetoric chair for him
at the University of Edinburgh.[3] Forced to lower his sights somewhat, Ferguson had then followed the course of another frustrated
Scottish academic, David Hume, by becoming keeper of the Advocates Library in Edinburgh at a meager salary of £40 per annum.[4]
There he had remained for several months, until negotiations began
in the summer of 1757 for a more lucrative position as tutor to the
earl of Bute's eldest son, John, Viscount Mountstuart.

These negotiations were carried out primarily by Gilbert Elliot and
John Home, who had originally recommended Ferguson for the post.
At the outset Ferguson was reluctant to agree to terms, in part because Bute wanted someone to serve as tutor to his second son as
well as to Lord Mountstuart.[5] Ferguson's friends insisted that he was
worth employing for one boy alone if Bute "wants to have a Man of
Sense, Knowlege, Taste, Elegance, & Morals, for a Tutor to his Son."[6]
The earl was finally won over by Home's glowing description of his
friend.[7] "A person acting up to the character you draw of Mr. Ferguson would be a treasure to me, and deserve my warmest protection," he informed Home. "It is not Greek and Latin that I am most
anxious about, 'tis the formation of the heart—the instilling into the
tender ductile plant, noble, generous sentiments, real religion, moral
virtue, enthusiasm for our country, its laws and liberties."[8] For his
part, Ferguson was impressed by Bute's commitment to the same ideals
of virtue, piety, and patriotism that he also held dear.[9] By October
1757 he was preparing to resign his positions as keeper of the Ad-

[1] John Lee, "Adam Ferguson," *EBS*, 4:241.

[2] *A Delineation of the Nature and Obligation of Morality, With Reflexions on Mr. Hume's
Book, intitled, An Inquiry concerning the Principles of Morals* (Edinburgh, 1753).

[3] Home to Milton, August 1756, NLS, 16696:74.

[4] Mossner, 251–55.

[5] Home to Elliot, 11 August [1757], NLS, 11008:103–104. Ferguson added other
reasons, such as his desire to remain in Edinburgh "after some years of wandering &
uncertainty," in his letter to Elliot cited in note 10 below.

[6] Hume to Elliot, 9 August 1757, *HL*, 1:263.

[7] Home to Elliot, 10 July [1757], NLS, 11009:143–44.

[8] Bute to Home, 7 August 1757, in Mackenzie, 145.

[9] Home to Bute, 17 August 1757, Bute, box 1 (1757), no. 107.

vocates Library and chaplain of the Black Watch in order to join young Mountstuart at Harrow.[10]

Early in 1758 several of Ferguson's Moderate friends also had occasion to spend time in the London vicinity. John Home came to arrange the stage production of *Agis* and to enter Lord Bute's employ as personal secretary. William Robertson, making his first visit to the capital at age thirty-six, came to peddle the manuscript of his history of Scotland. Alexander Carlyle came to lobby for exempting the Scottish clergy from the tax on windows. Of the three, Carlyle was the only one who did not immediately accomplish his goal, though his ardent exertions on the clergy's behalf did help to improve his standing within the church.[11] Home was soon basking in the glory that fell to him after the successful run of *Agis* at Drury Lane. The opening-night performance prompted Robertson, a self-proclaimed "novice" in such matters, to write that he had previously "had no conception of such admirable power of expressing the strong passions. . . . The applauses of the audience were as great as any of Homes friends could wish."[12] After the usual run of nine nights, the play was performed two additional times "with as full applause as formerly."[13] Home, now constantly at Bute's side, received several hundred pounds and a degree of public acclaim that he described as "beyond my own expectations."[14] Robertson's London mission of 1758 was also an unqualified success. For several weeks a handwritten copy of his history circulated among some of London's greatest literary patrons, including Bute, Argyll, and Horace Walpole, while the author himself made use of manuscripts in the new British Museum. The enthusiastic praise of these critics and his friend David Hume enabled Robertson to sell his history to Andrew Millar in April for the handsome sum of £600, "more than was ever given for any book except David Hume's."[15]

[10] Ferguson to Elliot, 4 October 1757, NLS, 11014:71. This letter nullifies previous speculation that Ferguson resigned his chaplaincy in 1754.

[11] "You will be surpriz'd to find me a Leader of the Kirk so soon again, after the Bloody Tragedy of Douglas," Carlyle told Gilbert Elliot (19 November 1757, NLS, 11014:100–101). "I should say you will not be surpriz'd, as you know the Nature of faction much better than I do." Carlyle remained the ecclesiastical spokesman for the window tax relief campaign until an exemption was finally obtained in 1782.

[12] Robertson to Milton, 22 February 1758, NLS, 16707:92–95. The openness and frequency of Robertson's visits to the theater at this time suggest that the deathbed promise he made to his father never to go to the theater (Brougham, 257) pertained only to the *Edinburgh* theater, which he never did attend. *Auto.*, 339.

[13] Robertson to Milton, [mid-March 1758], NLS, 16707:96.

[14] Home to Milton, 10 May 1759, NLS, 16710:189; *Auto.*, 375.

[15] Robertson to Jardine, 20 April 1758 (incorrectly dated 1759), in Brougham, 278–79; Robertson to Milton, 10 April 1758, NLS, 16707:98.

When not occupied with personal business, the Moderate literati enjoyed as full a social life in London as their modest incomes would allow. In addition to the theater, they frequented the duke of Argyll's private parties; the meeting house of a congregation of Presbyterian dissenters; numerous services at Anglican churches; the House of Commons, where they heard their beloved William Pitt; and the British Coffee House, where they mingled with the many transplanted Scotsmen who gravitated there. Through Home they met David Garrick, Lord Bute, and Charles Townshend, and they renewed old acquaintances with Gilbert Elliot, Tobias Smollett, and their former college friend John Blair. But their most intimate social gatherings took place each Wednesday, when Ferguson rode in from Harrow on his day off to join Robertson, Carlyle, Home, John Dalrymple, Robert Adam, and Alexander Wedderburn for a five-shilling dinner at a London tavern.[16]

While the Moderate literati were enjoying the social and cultural highlights of London ecclesiastical trouble was brewing back in Edinburgh. In mid-April Robertson learned from John Jardine that Patrick Cuming was actively seeking the moderator's chair at the next general assembly. Jardine suggested that Robertson obtain the support of important lay elders residing in London in order to ensure Cuming's defeat. Robertson replied that he was "as much interested as you can possibly be in preventing the intended elevation of Turnstill [Cuming] to the Moderator's chair"—but not by means of lay influence. "If we can discomfort him by our own strength, this will render him inconsiderable: all other methods of doing so would be ineffectual," he warned. Jardine was advised to select some "grave, inoffensive ecclesiastical personage" to oppose Cuming, who would be vulnerable to charges of being a "perpetual moderator" because he had already served in that capacity on three previous occasions.[17]

The moderator's chair at the general assembly was a matter of urgency to Robertson and Jardine because Cuming and his associate John Hyndman, still smarting from their humiliating defeat over *Douglas*, were scheming to deprive Hugh Blair of his expected transfer or "translation" to Edinburgh's most prestigious church—the portion of St. Giles Cathedral known as the New or High Kirk. As early as February 1757 the town council of Edinburgh, apparently acting in accordance with the wishes of leading members of the Edinburgh legal community, had requested that the Presbytery of Edinburgh translate Blair to the New Kirk because that church "is

---

[16]*Auto.*, 347–78.
[17]Robertson to Jardine, 20 April 1758, in Brougham, 278–79.

frequented by persons of the most distinguished Character and eminent rank in this Country," to whom Blair would be most desirable.[18] Shortly thereafter the presbytery had complied with the council's request by a unanimous vote, with the customary stipulation that no action be taken until after the induction of Blair's replacement at his current church, Lady Yester's. Unfortunately for Blair, the deaths of four of Edinburgh's sixteen ministers in the mid-1750s had created much confusion about the proper order of translations and delayed implementation of the presbytery's ruling for more than a year. This situation was also unfortunate for William Robertson, who happened to be the minister slated to replace his friend at Lady Yester's once Blair's next church had been determined.[19]

It was during this period of confusion and delay that Cuming and Hyndman decided to take revenge against the Moderates. Their first objective was to see to it that the vacancy in Cuming's own church, the Old or Southeast Kirk, would be filled by their friend Daniel MacQueen rather than by Robert Dick, who had publicly rebuked Hyndman during the *Douglas* case.[20] After winning this point at a meeting of the Presbytery of Edinburgh in late April 1758, they set out to do more damage to the Moderates by persuading the lord provost and others of the desirability of sending Henry Lundie to the New Kirk in place of Hugh Blair. With Robertson and Carlyle in London, they were able to push this measure through the Synod of Lothian and Tweeddale in mid-May by a scant margin of two votes. Blair's friends were "incensed" at Hyndman's "lyes" and Provost Montgomery's apparent duplicity on behalf of Cuming's "dirty jobb." Letters were written to important people in an effort to "sett it to rights" at the approaching general assembly.[21] Blair, supported by George Wishart, Robert Hamilton, John Jardine, and several other Edinburgh ministers, formally appealed to the assembly. So did the town council of Edinburgh, despite the objections of Provost Montgomery and at least ten other members.[22] Cuming and Hyndman tried

---

[18] Case for Hugh Blair, NLS, 17601:76; Baron Maule to Milton, 27 May 1758, NLS, 16706:247 (courtesy of Alexander Murdoch); Robertson to Milton, 14 May 1758, NLS, 16707:100; Home to Milton, May 1758, NLS, 16705:229.

[19] Robertson had been called to Edinburgh in 1756, chiefly by means of the influence of his cousin John Nisbet. See Robertson to Elliot, 22 January 1766, NLS, 11010:32–33, and George Drummond's letters to Milton of 14 and 18 October 1755, NLS, 16691:216, 219.

[20] Cuming to Milton, 25 April 1758, and Dick to Milton, 13 April 1758, NLS, 16704:169, 221.

[21] Baron Maule to Milton, 27 May 1758, NLS, 16706:247.

[22] Montgomery to Milton, 24 May 1758, NLS, 16707:24 (courtesy of Alexander Murdoch).

to convince Lord Milton that George Drummond's faction had sponsored the town council's appeal in order to overturn the Argathelian interest.[23] At about the same time Robertson wrote imploringly to Milton in favor of Blair, "whom I have known more intimately, and love better than most men," and Home informed him that "the principal affair, which is the support of Blairs settlement requires it seems a little of your Lordships immediate interposition, as it is to be determined on Wednesday next in the town council, whether the town shall drop this appeal or not."[24] Although Milton was apparently not persuaded by Robertson and Home's remonstrances, the majority of the town council defied both Milton's agent William Alston and Provost Montgomery by voting to retain the appeal to the general assembly on Blair's behalf.[25]

Robertson and Carlyle returned from London prepared for a major confrontation in the general assembly. The first order of assembly business showed the strength of the Moderates, who managed to secure the election of their candidate for moderator, Thomas Turnbull. After a special committee established to review the New Kirk case recommended that the sentence of the Synod of Lothian and Tweeddale be reversed, the main body of the assembly concurred by a vote of 64 to 54.[26] The Moderates tasted the fruits of their latest ecclesiastical triumph several days later, when Hugh Blair moved to the New Kirk in majestic St. Giles and William Robertson went to Edinburgh as Blair's replacement at Lady Yester's.

Following his settlement in Edinburgh, Robertson wrote to Gilbert Elliot to justify the tardiness of the revisions he was making in the manuscript of his history of Scotland. Immediately after returning to Scotland from London, he explained,

> I was plunged . . . into the depths of Kirk politics. The Edinburgh Clergy, who for the sake of trifles, are guilty of all the vices imputed to the great, had by a most wanton piece of injustice deprived Blair of the new Kirk, & it cost us no small difficulty to overturn that deed; but I hope that, added to the play house folly last year, will make it easy for us [to] defeat all Cum-

[23] Cuming to Milton, 18 and 23 May 1758, NLS, 16704:167–69; Hyndman to Milton, 18 and 24 May 1758, NLS, 16705:244–45.

[24] Home to Milton, May 1758, NLS, 16705:229; Robertson to Milton, 14 May 1758, NLS, 16707:100.

[25] Milton to Montgomery, May 1758 (draft), NLS, 16707:269; William Alston to Milton, 25 April 1758, NLS, 16703:32–33. The draft of Milton's reply to Alston of 31 May 1758 (NLS, 16703:39) takes this defeat lightly. These letters courtesy of Alexander Murdoch.

[26] *SM* 20 (May 1758): 268.

ming & Highdmans projects in time to come. This together with my own translation, which has now taken place, had kept me very busy.

Sensing that his star was rising, Robertson went on to assure Elliot of his determination not to become ensnarled in the web of secular politics he had witnessed in London. "I grow every day more confirmed in the resolution of keeping my hands clean of all the dirty work which in this country goes by the name of politics," he remarked. "I see nothing a Clergyman can gain, but much that he must necessarily lose by meddling with them."[27] True to his resolution, Robertson always maintained the dignified air of a clergyman untouched by the petty squabbles of secular politics, even though the outcome of those squabbles was often of considerable importance to his party and his personal career. What made Robertson's aloofness feasible was the fact that several of his Moderate friends were happy to handle the party's "dirty work" for him. Time and again Adam Ferguson and Alexander Carlyle drew the invective of the Moderates' enemies and the praise of their friends with pamphlets on controversial topics such as *Douglas*, the militia, the window tax, and the American war, while Robertson, who shared their views on all these subjects, appeared to remain above the fray.

Robertson's literary energy was wholly reserved for his forthcoming history, which he continued to revise and correct for many months after coming to terms with Andrew Millar. By January 1759 the manuscript was finally deemed ready for the press, though the author remained apprehensive. "I feel at present the utmost anxiety about the reception I shall meet with," he confided to his childhood friend Gilbert Elliot, "but, like a true desperado, I shut my eyes, think as little as I can, & rush forward."[28] Publication of the book in late January quickly put his fears to rest, for the *History of Scotland* was a spectacular triumph. In March Robertson happily informed Elliot that he was "overwhelmed" by praise and "perfectly astonished at my own success."[29] Before the end of April a second edition had been rushed into print and the author granted a modest crown sinecure as chaplain of Stirling Castle, with talk of better things to come.[30] Twenty years later Robertson could boast that the book had earned its pub-

[27] Robertson to Elliot, 24 June 1758, NLS, 11009:58–59.
[28] Robertson to Elliot, 4 January 1759, NLS, 11008:80–81.
[29] Robertson to Elliot, March 1759, NLS, 11008:92–93.
[30] John Blair to Robertson, 27 February 1759, and Elliot to Robertson, 23 March 1759, NLS, 3942:21–22, 29–30; Hume to Robertson, 7 April 1759, *New Letters of David Hume*, ed. Raymond Klibansky and Ernest C. Mossner (Oxford, 1954), 50.

lishers £6000—ten times more than the author had been paid for it.[31]

To understand the enormous appeal of Robertson's *History of Scotland*, as well as the reasons for the author's anxiety concerning its reception, it is necessary to know something about the form, content, and background of the work. Except for a brief introductory essay and a few concluding paragraphs, the *History of Scotland* deals exclusively with the critical period from the middle of the sixteenth century to the union of English and Scottish crowns under James I in 1603. The central themes of those years—the Reformation, Anglo-Scottish relations, and above all the tale of Mary Queen of Scots—were highly controversial matters in the eighteenth century, and a delicate touch was required to avoid giving offense. The situation was further complicated by the fact that Robertson's good friend David Hume was about to publish the volume of his *History of England* covering roughly the same years and topics. Furthermore, Robertson, who spoke with a strong Scottish accent, was worried about whether his style would be considered "pure" by English critics.

The "polite" history of Hume and especially Robertson represented a distinct departure from the antiquarian and controversial traditions that had dominated Scottish historical composition before the 1750s.[32] In addition to being less dull than the work of antiquarian chroniclers and annalists, it strove to be scholarly and instructive and to avoid interpreting the past along party lines in the manner of the controversialists. To "Whig" historians like George Buchanan, Mary was a thoroughly evil woman who had participated in the murder of her husband, Lord Darnley, and had attempted to restore "Popery" to Scotland. To Tories and Jacobites, on the other hand, she was the unfortunate victim of the unrestrained zeal of the Protestant reformers and the unjustified jealousy of her unscrupulous English rival, Elizabeth. In referring to these contrary assessments of Mary by Whigs and Tories, Robertson characteristically asserted that "she neither merited the exaggerated praises of the one, nor the undistinguished censure of the other."[33] Mary, he believed, was an "agreeable" though "often imprudent" woman, guilty, it would seem,

---

[31] James Boswell, *The Life of Samuel Johnson*, ed. George Birkbeck Hill and L. F. Powell, 6 vols. (Oxford, 1934–1940), 4:334.

[32] Douglas Duncan, *Thomas Ruddiman* (Edinburgh, 1965), chap. 8; Thomas Preston Peardon, *The Transition in English Historical Writing, 1760–1830* (New York, 1933), 10–11. The essential traits of polite history were laid down by Hugh Blair in *Lects.*, 2:259–60.

[33] *WWR*, 2:141, and the preface to the first edition of the *History of Scotland*. Cf. Robertson's remarks about the Marian controversy in *The Anecdotes and Egotisms of Henry Mackenzie, 1745–1831*, ed. William Thompson (London, 1927), 171–72, and in a letter to the earl of Hardwicke, 30 January 1786, BL, Add. 35350:72–73.

of complicity in the murder of Darnley but innocent of collusion in the Babington conspiracy against Elizabeth. Of course, Robertson's cautious, moderately critical attitude toward Mary did not satisfy extremists in either party, but it did satisfy the great number of British and European readers who desired a more dispassionate account of Mary's story than had previously been available. "Impartiality," "prudence," "candour," and "moderation" were among the words most commonly used by contemporaries to describe Robertson's position.[34]

This point must be seen in the broader political context suggested by Alexander Murdoch's remarks about the surprisingly conciliatory policy adopted by the duke of Argyll and Lord Milton during and immediately after the '45.[35] Like Argyll and Milton, Robertson and his Moderate friends were willing to risk the wrath of less tolerant Scottish Whigs (such as the remnants of the Squadrone party) and unsympathetic Englishmen (such as the dukes of Newcastle and Cumberland) in order to unify Scotland and make the Union work. As a Scottish Presbyterian minister who had borne arms against the Jacobites in 1745 and subsequently joined the ultra-Whig Revolution Club,[36] Robertson would have been expected to show Mary no mercy; instead he deliberately tried to produce a balanced assessment of her character and policies. The effect was comparable to that of an earlier incident related by Lord Elibank, who recalled that Robertson had first earned his admiration when he had asserted in the Select Society, at a time when Whigs and Jacobites "had a detestation of each other," that he "did not think worse of a man's moral character for his having been in rebellion."[37]

Robertson's handling of zealous Protestant reformers like John Knox was equally attractive to the polite reading public of his day. Although critical of the religious intolerance of the sixteenth century, Robertson made it clear that his sympathies lay with the advocates of Reformation rather than with the supporters of "Romish superstition."[38] The "moderation of those who favoured the Reformation"

---

[34] Horace Walpole to Robertson, 4 February 1759, *Yale Edition of Horace Walpole's Correspondence*, ed. W. S. Lewis (New Haven, 1951), 15:43–45; Thomas Birch to Robertson, 8 February 1759, NLS, 3942:17–18; Hume to Robertson, 20 [February] 1759, *HL*, 1:299; "A Character of Dr Robertson's *History of Scotland*," *SM* 21 (February 1759): 77–81.

[35] Alexander Murdoch, *"The People Above": Politics and Administration in Mid-Eighteenth-Century Scotland* (Edinburgh, 1980), 33–39.

[36] List of the Members of the Revolution Club at Edinburgh, EUL, Dc. 8.37.

[37] *Tour*, 384.

[38] *WWR*, 1:140–41, 148–49; J. H. S. Burleigh, "The Scottish Reformation as Seen in 1660 and 1760," *RSCHS* 13 (1959): 241–56.

was continually stressed; and even when forced to concede that the character of the redoubtable John Knox might seem overly severe by modern standards, Robertson could exonerate Knox on the grounds that "those very qualities . . . which now render his character less amiable, fitted him to be the instrument of Providence for advancing the Reformation among a fierce people."[39] This willingness to excuse the excesses of the Reformation in the context of an uncivilized age while implying that such excesses would be thoroughly unacceptable in the present, enlightened era was a good deal more palatable to polite eighteenth-century Presbyterians and Anglicans alike than the pointed attacks on the Protestant reformers in Hume's recently published history of the Stuarts.

In his treatment of Scotland's relations with England, similarly, Robertson gave his polite audience exactly what it wanted. The union of the crowns and its implications were described in glowing terms.[40] Robertson admitted that the loss of a national court and the difficulty of adapting to English political and cultural ways had made the seventeenth century a painful time for many Scots. But he claimed that the parliamentary Union of 1707 had eradicated most national "distinctions" and "peculiarities" and forged "one people" with almost identical tastes and interests.[41] Like the religious enthusiasm and intolerance of the Reformation era, Anglo-Scottish tension was acknowledged but rendered harmless by means of relegation to an uncivil historical past. As Scotsmen had come to share the same manners, literature, and culture as their southern brothers, Robertson argued, "every obstruction that had retarded their pursuit, or prevented their acquisition of literary fame, was totally removed."[42] It was on this note of cultural and, one suspects, personal optimism— of faith in the Union as the source of equality of opportunity for all the inhabitants of Great Britain, not least of all men of letters—that the *History of Scotland* concluded. Such optimism seems ironic in view of the increase in Anglo-Scottish tension that was actually taking place at this time. In this sense, Robertson's achievement was to portray Anglo-Scottish relations not as they were but as polite society might wish them to be.[43]

[39] *WWR*, 1:133, 2:34–35.

[40] Ibid., 2:235.

[41] Ibid., 246.

[42] Ibid.

[43] Cf. the similar glorification of the Union in the unsigned article on that subject in volume 17 of Diderot's *Encyclopédie* (1765), as discussed in Leonard Adams, "Scotland in the *Encyclopédie*," *Scottish Tradition* 9/10 (1980): 49–63. To the extent that his book was responsible for spreading this interpretation, Robertson played a role in transforming the international image of Scotland from one of backwardness and belligerence to one of peaceful cooperation and harmony.

Just as Robertson's discussions of controversial topics such as Mary Queen of Scots, the Reformation, and the Union were calculated to appeal to his readers' sense of moderation and politeness, so was his writing style designed to conform to accepted standards of polite historical composition. As expressed in the lectures of Adam Smith and Hugh Blair, the prevailing rhetorical theory of Robertson's time stressed simplicity and clarity of expression. Prose was to be free of the "ornaments" and "tropes" of classical rhetoric; "perspicuity" was to be valued above embellishment; Swift, Defoe, and Addison were to be preferred to more ornate stylists.[44] History in particular was considered a predominantly narrative art, with emphasis on "Clearness, Order, and due Connection" and a high degree of "gravity."[45] Robertson's prose was perfectly suited to meet these criteria. It was, with few carefully segregated exceptions, an essentially narrative style,[46] characterized by its clarity; by its lack of similes, metaphors, and similar rhetorical devices; by its formality, or freedom from idiomatic expressions; by its heavy reliance on nouns and complex nominal constructions that convey a sense of specificity or "thingness" considered appropriate to the narration of facts and events;[47] and by its effective utilization of "binary opposition" or "patterns of contrast" to sustain interest and achieve credibility and coherence.[48] These traits are not likely to impress the twentieth-century reader, who is apt to find Robertson's narrative prose dry and prosaic, but in the eighteenth century the *History of Scotland* drew high praise for its style. English critics like Horace Walpole were astonished that an untraveled Scottish minister "whose dialect I scarce understand" could write English in a style so "pure" and "proper," and to account for this paradox a rumor soon spread through London that Robertson had been educated at Oxford.[49]

[44] Wilbur Samuel Howell, *Eighteenth-Century British Logic and Rhetoric* (Princeton, 1971), 536–76, 647–71.

[45] *Lects.*, 2:272–73. Cf. Adam Ferguson's comment on the proper style of historical composition in Mackenzie, 69: "The narrative should be plain and simple, without embellishment."

[46] Robertson is best known today, however, for his "conjectural" and analytical digressions from the narrative, such as the famous introduction to the *History of Charles V* (published separately as *The Progress of Society in Europe*, ed. Felix Gilbert [Chicago, 1972]) and book 4 of the *History of America*. Blair approved of digressions like these in works of history if they were employed sparingly. *Lects.*, 2:270–71.

[47] Thomas R. Brooks, "Transformations of Word and Man: The Prose Style of William Robertson" (Ph.D. diss., University of Indiana, 1967), esp. chap. 2, 190–91, and app. 2.

[48] Jeffrey Smitten, "Robertson's *History of Scotland*: Narrative Structure and the Sense of Reality," *Clio* 11 (1981): 29–47.

[49] Walpole to Robertson, 4 February and 4 March 1759, *Walpole Correspondence*, 15:43–45, 48–52; John Blair to Robertson, 25 January 1759, NLS, 3942:1–8; Hume to Rob-

The final cause of Robertson's anxiety was his fear that his achievement would be eclipsed by that of his countryman David Hume. So great was this fear that Robertson had once asked Hume to exclude the sixteenth century from his projected history of England—an unreasonable request that his friend had been obliged to refuse.[50] With characteristic openness and magnanimity, Hume proposed that he and Robertson cooperate by frankly discussing their views and criticizing each other's work before publication. But Robertson, commenting (in Hume's words) that he "woud rather be taken for an indifferent Writer than a Plagiary," kept his distance.[51] Hume did everything in his power to ensure the success of Robertson's book, and he continually softened the competitive element with a joke or a kind word. "All the people whose Friendship or Judgement either of us value," he wrote to Robertson shortly after the publication of the *History of Scotland*, "are Friends to both, & will be pleas'd with the Success of both; as we will be with that of each other."[52] Robertson was not unappreciative of Hume's generosity. "What think you of that virtuous Heathen David Hume," he wrote to a friend after the early popularity of his book had begun to wear away his initial fears. "Instead of feeling any emotion of envy on account of the success of an Author, who had intruded into the province of History, of which he was formerly in possession, & who by writing on the same subject, was brought into direct competition with himself, instead of this, he runs about praising my work, & enjoys the applause it meets with, as if it were bestowed on himself."[53]

Hume was aware that publication of his volume on the Tudors would touch off "a constant comparison" with Robertson over the Marian question, and he fully expected his enemies to use Robertson's work as a stick with which to beat down his own.[54] Nevertheless, even Hume must have been surprised at the extent to which Robertson was raised above him by contemporary critics.[55] Both his-

ertson, 8 February 1759, *New Hume Letters*, 45; Robertson to Miss Hepburn, 20 February 1759, NLS, 16711:234.

[50] Hume to Robertson, 25 January 1759, *HL*, 1:294.

[51] Hume to Sir Alexander Dick, November 1760, in Lawrence L. Bongie, "The Eighteenth-Century Marian Controversy and an Unpublished Letter by David Hume," *Studies in Scottish Literature* 1 (1964): 248.

[52] Hume to Robertson, 8 February 1759, *New Hume Letters*, 46.

[53] Robertson to Miss Hepburn, 20 February 1759, NLS, 16711:234.

[54] Hume to Robertson, 8 February and March 1759, *New Hume Letters*, 46, and *HL*, 1:300.

[55] Mossner, 398; Carlo Denina, *An Essay on the Revolutions of Literature* (1763), trans. John Murdoch (London, 1771), 280–81; Gilbert Stuart, *Critical Observations concerning the Scottish Historians: Hume, Stuart, and Robertson* (London, 1782), 45.

torians angered Tory and Jacobite writers like William Tytler and Samuel Johnson by asserting the authenticity of the controversial Casket Letters that implicated Mary in the murder of Darnley.[56] But Robertson alone declared Mary innocent of the Babington conspiracy and waxed indignant when discussing her mistreatment by Elizabeth.[57] As a result, most Jacobites and Tories were apt to find Robertson's book less odious than Hume's, and some English Whigs, ironically, thought that occasional concessions to Mary increased Robertson's credibility.[58] In addition to appearing more impartial in regard to Mary, Robertson was widely believed to be a better writer and more thorough researcher than his rival.[59] The *History of Scotland*, in short, was thought to come closer than Hume's work to the contemporary ideal of polite history, and its author was transformed almost overnight from a little-known provincial pastor into an international literary celebrity.[60]

It would be difficult to exaggerate the importance of Robertson's book for advancing the cause of Moderatism and the Enlightenment in Scotland. Here was proof that a Scottish clergyman could make a name for himself in the republic of letters without compromising his church or his calling. The Moderates' opponents in the kirk had long been identified with the view that polite literature was by definition profane and dangerous to the interests of true religion. Kames's *Essays*, Home's *Douglas*, the *Edinburgh Review*, Hume's works, and even the writings of Francis Hutcheson had all been used by John Witherspoon and his party to support that position. The *History of Scot-*

---

[56] Bongie, "Marian Controversy," 236–52.

[57] *WWR*, 2:127–28, 231–32.

[58] "It is plain that you wish to excuse Mary," Horace Walpole wrote to Robertson on 4 February 1759; "and yet it is so plain that you never violate truth in her favour, that I own I think still worse of her than I did, since I read your history." *Walpole Correspondence*, 15:43–45.

[59] In *David Hume and the History of England* (Philadelphia, 1979), 62–65, Victor G. Wexler has shown that in the case of the Babington conspiracy it was Hume rather than Robertson who took full advantage of available manuscript sources, despite their reputations to the contrary. In his eagerness to demonstrate that Hume was joined in a polemical "partnership with Robertson" to denigrate Mary (49–54, 98), however, Wexler may have missed the significance of this matter, namely, that Robertson was so committed to the appearance of impartiality where Mary was concerned that he chose to ignore certain documentary evidence brought to his attention by Hume rather than adopt the radically anti-Marian position that the evidence might have necessitated.

[60] Robertson's stature after the *History of Scotland* is clear from the fact that his second historical work, the *History of Charles V*, earned him the staggering sum of £4000 (some accounts say £4500), by far "the greatest price that was ever known to be given for any book." David Hume to the Abbé Morellet, 10 July 1769, *HL*, 2:203.

land, however, provoked no criticism of this sort because it contained nothing that could be held against Robertson and the Moderates by orthodox churchmen. In applying the principles of polite history to Scotland's most controversial age, Robertson had shown the way to a solid middle ground between skepticism or impiety and religious enthusiasm. Publication of the *History of Scotland* marked another critical stage in the process of reconciling the principles of the Enlightenment with those of the Scottish Presbyterian heritage. Moreover, the book's extraordinary success brought its author and his party fame and glory that opened doors to higher ecclesiastical and academic honors and offices.

The year of Robertson's *History of Scotland* was also the year in which the Moderate literati of Edinburgh became involved with the Ossian and Scots militia controversies, which merit detailed examination in a later chapter. Another event of 1759, the election of Adam Ferguson to an Edinburgh professorship, is more germane to the topic at hand. Several earlier schemes to obtain a Scottish chair for Ferguson had failed, including an attempt by John Home and Lord Milton to arrange the purchase of the Edinburgh public law chair for their friend during the spring and summer of 1758[61] and a plan to place Ferguson in the church history chair at Glasgow in the spring of 1759.[62] It was while the latter scheme was foundering that Ferguson and his friends turned their attention to a new vacancy created by the death in mid-May 1759 of the Edinburgh professor of natural philosophy, John Stewart.

One problem with this plan was that Ferguson had no special training or experience in natural science, whereas his chief rival for the chair—his cousin and close friend James Russel—was highly regarded as a surgeon and scientist. Another difficulty arose from the feud then in progress between the earl of Bute and his uncle the duke of Argyll.[63] As John Home sadly informed Lord Milton, Bute's latest applications to Argyll had been so coldly received that the earl, notwithstanding his full support for Ferguson, would not apply to his uncle on Ferguson's behalf. There was every chance that Ferguson "should fall betwixt the arms of the great," Home warned, unless Milton exerted his influence.[64] Two days later Home wrote again to

[61] Fagg, 51–55. A variation on this scheme was David Hume's idea of putting Adam Smith in the Edinburgh public law chair and Ferguson in Smith's moral philosophy chair at Glasgow. Hume to Smith, 8 June 1758, *HL*, 1:279–80; Home to Elliot, [late June 1758], NLS, 11017:54–55.

[62] Fagg, 55–58.

[63] Murdoch, *"People Above,"* chap. 4.

[64] Home to Milton, 10 May 1759, NLS 16710:189.

remind Milton of Ferguson's unshakable ties to his lordship and his family and to ask that immediate action be taken to settle him in the natural philosophy chair.[65]

Milton did not disappoint his Moderate friends. On 5 June Home, Ferguson, and Bute celebrated the earl's birthday together in London secure in the knowledge that Milton was preparing to arrange Ferguson's election by the town council of Edinburgh.[66] The main source of delay was an ambitious "double scheme" to obtain James Balfour's moral philosophy chair for Ferguson and the natural philosophy chair for Russel, thereby placing each man in his area of expertise. That scheme, so desirable to both Ferguson and Russel, would become practicable at a later time, but for the moment it was, as David Hume put it, "quite wild & chimerical." Hume urged that Ferguson, the needier candidate, be given the natural philosophy chair as soon as possible.[67] When Russel's supporters in the town council tried to postpone Ferguson's election until a definite deal could be concluded with Balfour, Milton's ally George Drummond convinced them "that the way to do good to the college & to get Russell, was, in the first place, to posess ourselves of Ferguson with unanimity and dispatch."[68]

Three days later the clergy of Edinburgh met to pronounce their judgment or "avisamentum" on Ferguson. William Robertson and John Jardine, who could not be present, submitted letters "heartily approving" of their friend. Hugh Blair, Robert Wallace, George Kay, and George Wishart spoke in favor of Ferguson "from their personal knowledge of the man," and the other ministers in attendance concurred "on the faith of what they had heard."[69] Significantly, Patrick Cuming, Alexander Webster, and John Erskine, the three leading opponents of the Moderate literati among the ministers of Edinburgh, all stayed away from the meeting at which the avisamentum was given. Finally, on 4 July 1759 Adam Ferguson was unanimously elected professor of natural philosophy by the town council of Edinburgh. Upon learning of his appointment, he immediately expressed his thanks to Lord Milton, "to whose friendship alone I owe that piece of good fortune,"[70] and began an intensive course of study to prepare lectures for the autumn term.

Ferguson's diligence and ability enabled him to become an ex-

---

[65] Home to Milton, 12 May 1759, NLS, 16710:191.
[66] Home to Milton, 5 June 1759, NLS, 16710:193.
[67] Hume to Robertson, 29 May 1759, *New Hume Letters*, 56–58.
[68] Drummond to Milton, 26 June 1759, NLS, 16709:252.
[69] Drummond to Milton, 5 July 1759, NLS, 16709:254.
[70] Ferguson to Milton, 12 July 1759, NLS, 16710:20.

tremely popular teacher of this formerly unfamiliar subject.[71] Yet he always regarded the chair of natural philosophy as a stepping stone to his real objective, the chair of moral philosophy. In September 1759 he wrote to Gilbert Elliot: "I like my situation very well, & begin to admire S[i]r Isaac Newton as I did Homer & Montesquieu, but it is on Condition that he will let me go as soon as I become a tolerable Professor of Natural Philosophy." In the same letter Ferguson briefly discussed the latest literary endeavors of his friends Home and Robertson and presented an assessment of Edinburgh as an emerging intellectual center. "The wit & ingenuity of this place is still in a flourishing way," he commented, "& with a few corrections, which however it is difficult to make, [it] is probably the best place for Education in the Island."[72]

One of the "corrections" that Ferguson probably had in mind concerned the matter of rhetoric. When campaigning for the establishment of a chair of rhetoric for Ferguson in 1756, John Home had pointed out that "Eloquence in the Art of speaking is more necessary for a Scotchman than any body else as he lies under some disadvantages which Art must remove."[73] The problem, as Alexander Carlyle later explained it, was that "to every man bred in Scotland the English language was in some respects a foreign tongue."[74] Although Professor John Stevenson included some discussion of rhetoric in his logic class at the University of Edinburgh, his lectures on that subject did not satisfy the growing need of his countrymen for a comprehensive, thoroughly modern treatment of the English language and its uses. It was in response to this need that Adam Smith had begun to offer a private course of public lectures on language and rhetoric in the winter of 1748–1749.[75] These lectures were the first of their

[71] The substance of Ferguson's course is sketched in the outline *Of Natural Philosophy* that the professor published for the benefit of his students around 1760. An American medical student who attended the course during the 1762–1763 term has left a first-hand account of Ferguson's teaching skill and Newtonian emphasis: "Professor Ferguson has now gone through his doctrine of attraction and repulsion, which he finished yesterday with an account of the magnet. He illustrates his lectures with a variety of very entertaining experiments; they are very agreeable, and with him we read the Newtonian philosophy." Quoted in John Brett Langstaff, *Doctor Bard of Hyde Park* (New York, 1942), 66.

[72] Ferguson to Elliot, 14 September 1759, NLS, 11015:9–10.

[73] Home to Milton, August 1756, NLS, 16696:74.

[74] *Auto.*, 543.

[75] Adam Smith, *Lectures on Rhetoric and Belles Lettres*, ed. J. C. Bryce (Oxford, 1983); Howell, *British Logic and Rhetoric*, 536–76. In his letter to Milton cited in note 73 John Home commented: "There is no Professor of teacher of Eloquence in any of our universities. Some years ago one Smith a man of parts educated in England attempted to teach the art of speaking, & was succesful (Wedderburn & Jack Dalrymple were

kind in Great Britain and attracted the leading literati, lawyers, and gentlemen of Edinburgh for three years, until Smith's appointment as professor of moral philosophy at Glasgow University took him away from Edinburgh. In the 1750s Smith's place was taken by Rev. Robert Watson, who gave up the enterprise after being called to the chair of logic and rhetoric at St. Andrews University in 1758.[76]

Late in 1759 the tradition of private rhetoric lectures in Edinburgh was carried on by Watson's relation and Smith's self-professed disciple, Hugh Blair.[77] Like Smith, Blair defined rhetoric as the theory of all forms of verbal communication—written as well as spoken—and located the key to rhetorical success in the clarity, simplicity, perspicuity, and naturalness of one's expression.[78] Dividing his course into five parts—taste, language, style, eloquence, and literature—he presented his listeners with the most systematic treatment of rhetoric and belles lettres yet formulated in the English language. Blair's success as a rhetoric teacher was formally recognized in the summer of 1760, when the town council created an unsalaried university chair specially for him. Even after coming under the auspices of the university, Blair's lectures continued to attract numerous men of rank and esteem seeking instruction in this important new discipline.[79]

Shortly after Blair's university appointment, there occurred an event that profoundly altered the political situation in Great Britain and vastly improved the position of the Moderate literati of Edinburgh. The accession of George III to the British throne on 25 October 1760 transformed the young king's friend and adviser, the earl of Bute, from a courtier at Leicester House into the prime mover behind the crown. Lacking political experience and parliamentary standing, Bute was not rash enough to accept an official position at the head of government immediately after the accession, but the fact that such a position was apparently offered to him indicates the extent of his influence over the young king.[80] Well before he acquired formal ministerial status as secretary of state for the Northern Department (March 1761)

his disciples) but he was quickly called to be Professor of moral Philosophy in Glasgow."

[76] Robert Morrell Schmitz, *Hugh Blair* (New York, 1948), 62.

[77] *Lects.*, 1:3n.; Blair to Boswell, 16 June [1779], YUL, C159.

[78] Howell, *British Logic and Rhetoric*, 547, 670; *Lects.*, introduction; Douglas Ehninger and James Golden, "The Intrinsic Sources of Blair's Popularity," *Southern Speech Journal* 21/22 (1955–1957): 27–30.

[79] Robert Orde to Elliot, 3 September 1761, Bute, uncatalogued; *SM* 21 (December 1759): 660–61.

[80] Richard Pares, *King George III and the Politicians* (London, 1970), 100–102; John Brooke, *King George III* (New York, 1972), 87.

and first lord of the Treasury (May 1762), Bute was in reality the new regime's prime minister; and well after his retirement from office in April 1763 he continued to influence affairs in Scotland from "behind the curtain"—at least until the forced resignation of his brother James Stuart Mackenzie as lord privy seal and manager of Scottish business in May 1765.

Although the ascent of Bute came as welcome news to all his friends and political supporters, no one in Great Britain benefited more from it than the earl's secretary, John Home. Home's close ties with Bute and public flattery of the former Prince of Wales[81] now paid off handsomely, for the playwright's annual pension was immediately raised from £100 to £300. Perhaps Carlyle exaggerated when he remarked that Home "might really have been said to have been the second man in the kingdom while Bute remained in power."[82] But there can be no doubt that "the favourite of the favourite," as Sir Walter Scott called him,[83] was able to affect the earl's decisions in many instances involving the dispensation of patronage in Scotland. Though hesitant to ask favors for himself, Home was by all accounts "warm and active at all times for the interest of his friends."[84] It was chiefly by means of his intervention, and that of Gilbert Elliot, that the abilities and accomplishments of Robertson, Ferguson, Carlyle, and Blair first came to the attention of Bute, who prided himself on his skill at recognizing and rewarding "merit and efficiency."[85]

In regard to the political management of Scotland, the most important consequence of Home's personal influence concerned Bute's relations with the duke of Argyll and Lord Milton. Feuding between Argyll and Bute had been a source of distress to Home and the other Moderate literati. It was clear to them that this feud would not last long beyond the accession of George III because Argyll would have need of Bute's influence at court just as Bute would have need of Argyll's extensive Scottish power base.[86] By the winter of 1760–1761

[81] John Home, "Prologue on the Birthday of the Prince of Wales, 1759," in *A Collection of Original Poems by Scotch Gentlemen*, ed. Thomas Blacklock, 2 vols. (Edinburgh, 1760–1762), 2:165–67; Home's dedication to the Prince of Wales, 1760, in *WJH*, 185–87.

[82] *Auto.*, 427–28.

[83] *The Miscellaneous Prose Works of Sir Walter Scott*, 28 vols. (Edinburgh, 1834–1835), 19:316.

[84] *Auto.*, 378; Ferguson to Elliot, 6 November 1760, NLS, 11015:67–68.

[85] Bute to Mure, 2 July 1761, in *Selections from the Family Papers Preserved at Caldwell*, 2 vols. (Paisley, 1883–1885), 1, pt. 2:128.

[86] "They will be glad to become friends again," Alexander Carlyle speculated in the autumn of 1759. "And He who can help them to come together, will be a favourite of both." Carlyle to Charles Townshend, [early November 1759], WLCL, Townshend Papers.

a reconciliation had in fact occurred, and relations remained cordial between Bute and Argyll during the last months of the latter's life.[87] John Home, who had encouraged this reconciliation, appears to have also advised Bute to employ Lord Milton as his Edinburgh manager in the event the aged duke should die.

Home's advice was evidently agreeable to Bute, for shortly after Argyll's death in April 1761 Milton received a letter from Bute "expressing in the strongest manner, his resolution to assist and support, all those who stood connected with his late uncle" and requesting Milton's continued participation in the management of Scottish business.[88] Milton was so touched that he burst into tears trying to read Bute's letter aloud to his family and Adam Ferguson, who happened to be present when it arrived.[89] Two days later Home wrote to Bute from Edinburgh to congratulate him on the wisdom of his conciliatory policy toward Argyll and Milton:

> The first thought that struck me when I heard of the Duke of Argyle's death, was, what satisfaction and comfort, would arise in your mind from the reflection upon your behaviour to him last winter. I imagine that I seldom err in judging of Lord Bute's heart, and when I arrived at Lord Milton's from a considerable distance: your letter to him satisfied me that *I was in the right in all respects* and that you had done in an instant every thing that generosity and wisdom could suggest.[90]

Home had good reason to be pleased. Bute's decision to employ Milton not only ensured a smooth transition of authority in Edinburgh politics but also brought together the three Scottish politicians most intimately connected with the Moderate literati of Edinburgh: Bute, Milton, and Elliot. Not surprisingly, the Moderate literati made their most impressive advances within the Church of Scotland and University of Edinburgh during the period of approximately two years when this political coalition was at its height.

The Moderate who gained the most during the Bute years was undoubtedly William Robertson. At the general assembly of 1761 Robertson easily overcame an attempt to block his translation to Old Greyfriars Church, where his father had served in the 1730s and 1740s.[91] The case is significant because it was the first time that Pa-

---

[87] Ian G. Lindsay and Mary Cosh, *Inveraray and the Dukes of Argyll* (Edinburgh, 1973), 376–77n.; Murdoch, *"People Above,"* 94–99.

[88] Milton to Campbell of Shawfield, 20 April 1761, NLS, 16718:218. Alexander Carlyle has caused much confusion by incorrectly reporting that Milton declined Bute's offer. *Auto.*, 434; Murdoch, *"People Above,"* 99–109.

[89] Home to Bute, 22 April 1761, Bute, box 3 (1761), no. 300.

[90] Ibid. Emphasis added.

[91] *Annals*, 2:236–41.

trick Cuming's former assistant John Hyndman appeared publicly on Robertson's side. The Moderates had engineered Hyndman's unanimous election as moderator, and in his closing address Hyndman delivered what amounted to a public apology for his unprincipled behavior during the *Douglas* and New Kirk affairs of 1757–1758.[92] Hyndman was apparently shrewd enough to realize that the death of Argyll, followed by Milton's shift to the Bute camp, spelled the political end for Cuming, who had pinned all his hopes on his slavish devotion to the old duke while his Moderate opponents had prepared themselves for a wide range of political eventualities.

While awaiting translation to Old Greyfriars, Robertson began to explore various avenues to preferment. His initial plan was to convince Bute via Gilbert Elliot to establish a chair of history for him at the University of Edinburgh.[93] When this scheme met with obstacles, he requested for the time being a recently vacated deanery of the Chapel Royal.[94] In July 1761 Robertson learned from Elliot that Bute had decided to promote John Jardine to the deanery while granting him Jardine's former position as one of His Majesty's chaplains-in-ordinary.[95] The latter office constituted only a slight increase in status and income over the chaplaincy of Stirling Castle that Robertson already possessed, but more important than the promotion itself was the understanding that accompanied it. Using Lord Cathcart as an intermediary, Bute praised the *History of Scotland* and offered its author an unofficial commission to write a history of England after completion of his next book.[96] Robertson had refused similar offers in 1759 primarily because he had not wanted to infringe on his friend David Hume's work on that subject. But now that Hume's history of England was complete, Robertson felt free to enter into serious negotiations.[97] At first there was some confusion about whether he would be required to give up his clerical status and reside in London while

[92] "The heat of youth, inexperience, and rashness, may have led me, in some parts of my former public conduct, to engage in measures which a wiser, which a cooler man than I, would have guarded against," Hyndman told the assembly (ibid., 2:244). The editor of the *Annals* erroneously assumed that these remarks referred only to Hyndman's pamphlet of 1753, *A Just View of the Constitution of the Church of Scotland*.

[93] Robertson to Elliot, 7 February 1761, NLS, 11009:79–80; Elliot to Robertson, 3 March 1761, NLS, 3942:42–43.

[94] Robertson to Elliot, 25 June 1761, NLS, 11009:81–82.

[95] Elliot to Robertson, 2 July 1761, NLS, 3942:44–45.

[96] Cathcart to Robertson, 20 July 1761, NLS, 3942:40–41. For more extensive treatments of this affair, see James L. McKelvey, "William Robertson and Lord Bute," *Studies in Scottish Literature* 6 (1969): 238–47, and Jeremy J. Cater, "The Making of Principal Robertson in 1762: Politics and the University of Edinburgh in the Second Half of the Eighteenth Century," *SHR* 49 (1970): 60–84, esp. 63–64.

[97] Robertson to Cathcart, 27 July 1761, Bute, uncatalogued; Stewart, xix.

executing his task. In a long letter to William Mure of Caldwell, Bute's personal agent in Scotland, Robertson expressed his wish to remain in Edinburgh, retain both his "character as a Scottish Clergyman" and his chaplaincy, and resign his parish charge in exchange for a lifetime government pension or sinecure.[98] After meeting with Robertson in Edinburgh, Mure proposed an exceedingly generous arrangement to Bute: Robertson should live in Scotland most of the year, keep his clerical status and chaplaincy, resign his parish charge, and receive a sinecure or pension worth about £200 per annum *plus* a promise of "the first Principal's Chair that might fall vacant in this University, or that of Glasgow."[99]

The next principal's chair to fall vacant was that of John Gowdie of Edinburgh University, who died on 19 February 1762. Even before Gowdie was dead, Robertson had set the wheels of his candidacy in motion by writing letters of intent to Lord Cathcart and Gilbert Elliot while Mure wrote on his behalf to James Stuart Mackenzie. "The office is in the gift of the Town Council, but that you know alters the matter only one remove," Robertson told Elliot.[100] Another letter to Elliot, written the day after Gowdie's death, was more explicit: "I need not say to you, that a letter from Ld Bute to Baron Mure or Ld Milton fixes the Election infallibly."[101] In both letters Robertson stressed the fact that he "would chuse the station of Principal preferably to any that can occur," even though the salary of that office (£111) was considerably less than the provision of £200 originally promised to him by Bute's agents. "It is the situation rather than any increase of Salary that is my object," he informed Elliot.

Among the early candidates for Gowdie's position were two ecclesiastical opponents of the Moderates—Daniel MacQueen and Patrick Cuming—and several of Robertson's "best friends," including Hugh Blair, John Jardine, George Wishart, and Adam Ferguson. Since MacQueen and Cuming lacked the necessary political connections for securing the principalship at this time, the competition was mainly among the Moderates themselves. "But you know us well enough to believe that the opposition will be conducted with candour, & the decision occasion no grudge nor ill will among us," Robertson assured Elliot.[102] In fact, Wishart's lack of support, Jardine's early with-

---

[98] Robertson to Mure, 25 November 1761, Bute, uncatalogued.

[99] Mure to Bute, 30 November 1761, Bute, box 3 (1761), no. 66.

[100] Robertson to Elliot, 15 February 1762, NLS, 11009:105–106.

[101] Robertson to Elliot, [20] February 1762, NLS, 11009:109–10. In his pioneering article on Robertson's election as principal, cited in note 96 above, Jeremy Cater seriously underestimates Bute and Milton's influence over the town council at this time.

[102] Robertson to Elliot, [20] February 1762, NLS, 11009:109–10.

drawal in favor of Robertson, and Blair's halfhearted candidacy soon resulted in a two-man race between Robertson and Ferguson. Robertson himself acknowledged Ferguson's "extraordinary merit of every kind" but warned that it would be a mistake to appoint a man who had given up the clerical profession to one of the few offices in Scotland still traditionally restricted to practicing clergymen.[103] He also pointed out that his own success as an author would lend prestige to the university.[104] Although Ferguson was at a disadvantage in regard to these points, he possessed an outstanding academic reputation, had been in Bute's service during his days as a tutor, and enjoyed the enthusiastic support of John Home and Lord Milton, who wrote on his behalf to James Stuart Mackenzie.[105]

By the time he received Stuart Mackenzie's reply indicating that Bute would be handling this matter personally,[106] Milton already knew that Ferguson had no chance for the principalship. For several days earlier Milton and Mure had both received letters from Bute himself informing them that William Robertson was his choice. "From the minute I first fixed on him for our great undertaking, I determined to assist him in obtaining the Principal's chair either in Edinburgh or Glasgow," Bute told Mure, "for that being *otium cum dignitate*, suited extremely to my views."[107] To Milton he explained that Robertson was about to engage in a "great & publick work" for which the principalship was to be partial payment. "I wish therefore your Lordship would signify to our Friends, that Dr Robertson is the Person, I wish may succeed to the Vacancy; Your influence joined to His establish'd Character, must make His nomination easy."[108] Upon receiving Bute's letter, Milton immediately informed the acting provost of the town council that "our friends" in London had selected Robertson, who received the "avisamentum" of the Edinburgh clergy on 9 March and was unanimously elected by the council the following day.[109]

For the institutionalization of Moderate authority and Enlightenment values in Scotland, the election of William Robertson as prin-

---

[103] Ibid.; Robertson to Elliot, 8 March 1762, In R. B. Sher and M. A. Stewart, "William Robertson and David Hume: Three Letters," *Hume Studies* (1985). Ferguson's supporters replied that their candidate was still technically a minister and that, in any case, there were precedents for selecting a layman as principal of a Scottish university.

[104] Robertson to Milton, 23 February 1762, NLS, 16726:98–99.

[105] Milton to [Stuart Mackenzie], February 1762 (draft), NLS, 16725:128–29.

[106] Stuart Mackenzie to Milton, 4 March 1762, NLS, 16725:133.

[107] Bute to Mure, 27 February 1762, *Caldwell Papers*, 1, pt. 2:146.

[108] Bute to Milton, 27 February 1762, NLS, 16726:129–30.

[109] Milton to Bailie James Stewart, 4 March 1762 (draft), NLS, 16726:126–27; Milton to Bute, 5 [March] 1762, Bute, Cdf. 2/220/1.

cipal of the University of Edinburgh was probably the most important single event of the eighteenth century. John Gowdie had treated this office as a sinecure, and Robertson quickly discovered that he had become the leader of "a College which has been several years without a Head, & has not had one who attended to its affairs of a very long time."[110] In his decade as principal, the aged and infirm Gowdie had scarcely ever presided over the senatus academicus and had never once used the prerogative of his office to attend the general assembly.[111] In addition to weakening the university administratively and perhaps academically, his incompetence had strengthened the position of the professor of ecclesiastical history, Patrick Cuming. Within weeks of Robertson's election as principal, however, Cuming arranged to transfer his chair to his son rather than serve under his younger rival.[112] Thus, the most dangerous opponent of the Moderate literati was deprived of virtually all authority within the church and university while their most effective ecclesiastical leader and administrator acquired the most prestigious office in both institutions.

The same letter from Bute to Milton that carried the order for Robertson's election as principal also brought final word of a new preferment for Hugh Blair. In August 1761 Gilbert Elliot had first informed Milton of a scheme to grant Blair a salary as Regius professor of rhetoric because "Lord Bute believes his lectures have been of service to the University."[113] Milton, praising the scheme as likely to "bring additional numbers of Schollars to the College," had suggested a salary of £100 if no class fees were to be allowed, as was customary with Regius chairs.[114] Robert Orde, chief baron of the Scottish exchequer, had approved of Milton's figure but had argued that Blair should be allowed to collect class fees in order to encourage a serious commitment by the professor and his students.[115] Blair himself employed the same logic when he warned Elliot of the danger of "free" or "open" chairs "degenerating into mere Sinecures." "In a word," he continued, "you can never have any Security for a Professor's exerting himself, without some Spurr from Interest; nor any Prospect of Students applying with care, where the doors are open att all times to all."[116]

[110] Robertson to Elliot, 7 August 1762, NLS, 11009:149–52.
[111] Minutes of the Senatus Academicus, EUL, vol. 1.
[112] Cuming to Milton, 22 April 1762, NLS, 16723:206.
[113] Elliot to Milton, 2 August 1761, NLS, 16720:88.
[114] Milton to Elliot, 8 August 1761 (draft), NLS, 16720:91.
[115] Orde to Elliot, 3 September 1761, Bute, uncatalogued.
[116] Blair to Elliot, 3 September 1761, NLS, 11009:87–88.

When the principalship at Edinburgh University became vacant in February 1762, Blair seems to have offered himself as a candidate solely in order to revive interest in his own scheme, which had lain dormant for five or six months.[117] His strategy was successful, for Bute's decisive letter to Milton on the principalship added that the king had approved a salary of £70 per annum for Blair's Regius professorship.[118] One week later Blair wrote to Elliot thanking him for his efforts in this affair, praising Robertson as "the fittest man for the office of principal which you could have found in the whole Country," requesting that the term "Belles Lettres" be added to the title of his rhetoric chair "to give it a more modern air," and reiterating his fears about "open" classes.[119] In the end Blair got his way. On 4 August 1762 he was admitted by the town council as Regius professor of rhetoric and belles lettres, with a salary of £70 on the exchequer plus the right to collect class fees. His obstinacy concerning the latter point had cost him some £30 in salary out of the £100 originally offered to him.

Commenting on this affair several years later, David Hume expressed astonishment at Blair's actions. "Why, the Devil, would you not take 100 pounds Sallary, when you might have had it?" he asked his friend.[120] Blair's response shows that five years as Regius professor had not altered his principles: "The £100 Salary was offer'd to me only on Condition of its being an open Class; which I absolutely rejected, as not only less profitable to my Self, but ruinous to Education, and accepted the alternative of a Smaller Salary."[121] Blair charged his students the minimum fee of two guineas and welcomed poor but deserving pupils who attended without payment.[122] Despite these circumstances, and the fact that his course was not part of the standard arts curriculum, he remained convinced that hard work and good teaching would not go unrewarded. His experience as Regius professor proved him correct. Throughout the 1760s, 1770s, and early 1780s Blair's rhetoric course was widely praised and well attended, and the publication of his lectures by a London publisher in 1783 brought him the additional sum of £1500.[123]

---

[117] "I was not a Candidate for the Principality," Blair later remarked. "I had the Promise of the other some time before; which is to me on many accounts more Eligible. They have given the Principality to the fittest man for the office amongst us." Blair to ———, [1762], NLS, 3219:1.

[118] Bute to Milton, 27 February 1762, NLS, 16726:129–30.

[119] Blair to Elliot, 4 March 1762, NLS, 11009:111–12.

[120] Hume to Blair, 20 May 1767, *HL*, 2:135.

[121] Blair to Hume, 4 June [1767], RSE, 3/61.

[122] Blair to Elliot, 3 September 1761, NLS, 11009:87–88.

[123] Alexander Bower, *The History of the University of Edinburgh*, 3 vols. (Edinburgh,

The period from May 1762 to April 1763 marked the high point of power for the earl of Bute, who continued to shower patronage on the Moderate literati and their friends. In filling the chair of ecclesiastical history at Glasgow University in May 1762, Bute passed over the faculty's own choice, Rev. James Oswald of Methven, in favor of Alexander Carlyle's cousin and intimate friend, Rev. William Wight.[124] The following September he heeded numerous requests to grant Carlyle himself the sinecure office of His Majesty's almoner that had become vacant at the death of John Hyndman.[125] It may be presumed that Bute was behind the appointment of John Jardine as dean of the Order of the Thistle in January 1763. It is certain that he was responsible for two other appointments of Moderates in the same year: that of John Home to the office of conservator of Scots privileges at Campvere—a crown sinecure that Home had long coveted both for the handsome stipend and for "the pleasure of sitting in the Ecclesiastical courts, by the title of Lord Conservator, to please & assist my old friends, & plague & mortify my antient foes"—and that of William Robertson to the £200 a year sinecure as historiographer royal for Scotland.[126] By this time Robertson had received from Bute two sinecures and a principalship worth a total surpassing £360 per annum—in exchange for which, it must be said, he neither honored his promise to resign his parish charge nor produced the history of England that the new preferments were supposed to subsidize.

Meanwhile the Moderate literati continued their scheming to transfer Adam Ferguson to the moral philosophy chair and place James Russel in the chair of natural philosophy.[127] The chief obsta-

---

1817), 3:17; "Dr. Hugh Blair," *Public Characters of 1800–1801* (Dublin, 1801), 237; Schmitz, *Hugh Blair*, 63; William Adam, *Sequel to the Gift of a Grandfather* (1839), 55.

[124] James Coutts, *A History of the University of Glasgow* (Glasgow, 1909), 324; *Auto.*, 445, where Carlyle claims to have had "a chief hand" in Wight's appointment. The ecclesiastical history chair included a supplemental appointment in civil history that Wight took seriously, judging from his impressive *Heads of a Course of Lectures on the Study of History* (Glasgow, 1768).

[125] Robertson to Elliot, 12 August 1762, NLS, 11009:153–54; Elliot to Bute, 17 August 1762, Bute, box 4 (1762), no. 317; Townshend to Carlyle, 4 September 1762 (copy), NLS, 3464:4; *Auto.*, 449.

[126] For details on Robertson's appointment, see McKelvey, "Robertson and Bute," 244–47. For Home's appointment, see Home to Elliot, 14 December 1761, NLS, 11015:131–33; Home to Bute, 13 December 1761, Bute, box 3 (1761), no. 698; Home to Milton, [mid] February 1763, NLS, 16728:22 (also fols. 96 and 108); *Auto.*, 378. The office of conservator conferred automatic membership in the general assembly.

[127] I have discussed the details and significance of Ferguson's appointment to the moral philosophy chair in an unpublished paper titled "Ideology, Incentive, and the Edinburgh Chair of Moral Philosophy, 1708–1764," which was originally read at the 1979 meeting of the American Society for Eighteenth-Century Studies in Atlanta.

cle to their plan was the incumbent professor of moral philosophy, James Balfour, who refused to resign his chair even though he was Russel's brother-in-law and quite unsuccessful as a teacher. In 1761 Lord Provost George Lind, citing Balfour's mediocrity, suggested to Lord Milton that Balfour be made commissary clerk in exchange for his resignation from the university.[128] Two years later William Robertson proposed a similar plan for making Balfour sheriff depute. "You know of how much importance the Class of Moral Philosophy is in a Scotch College," he told Gilbert Elliot. Since the moral philosophy class had "dwindled to nothing" during Balfour's tenure, Robertson hoped that Elliot would use his influence to remedy this situation, which he called "a cruel circumstance to the College, & a real & essential loss to the country."[129]

Neither Lind nor Robertson's schemes met with success, but early in 1764 a new plan was devised to clear the moral philosophy chair for Ferguson by promoting Balfour to the chair of public law, a lucrative sinecure in the gift of the crown. On 22 February the town council approved this plan at the personal request of Principal Robertson. At the same time they voted, again at Robertson's request, to convert the chair of moral philosophy from an "open" to a fee-paying class since past experience had shown that student attendance and teaching quality both suffered without the extra incentive provided by class fees.[130] On the following day Lord Milton wrote to James Stuart Mackenzie to seek government cooperation in the matter. Stuart Mackenzie replied that he was "most willing and ready" to facilitate any scheme beneficial to the university, the town of Edinburgh, and "the Publick in general."[131] Balfour accordingly resigned his chair at the close of the academic session, and on 23 May 1764 the town council elected Adam Ferguson professor of moral philosophy with the regular salary of £102 as well as the right to collect class fees.[132] On the same day the magistrates named James Russel as Ferguson's successor in the chair of natural philosophy and confirmed Balfour's appointment as professor of public law.

While the Ferguson-Russel scheme was being implemented Hugh Blair wrote to David Hume in Paris to acquaint him with this "great

---

[128] Lind to Milton, 19 March 1761, NLS, 16721:108.

[129] Robertson to Elliot, 8 January 1763, NLS, 11009:163–64.

[130] Transcriptions of Edinburgh Town Council Minutes, 22 February 1764, EUL, Horn Papers, Gen. 1824.

[131] Milton to Stuart Mackenzie, 23 February 1764 (draft), and Stuart Mackenzie to Milton, 5 March 1764, NLS, 16731:95, 105.

[132] Town council minutes of 23 May 1764, in Andrew Dalzel, *History of the University of Edinburgh*, 2 vols. (Edinburgh, 1862), 2:433.

improvement" being made in the University of Edinburgh.[133] By November 1764 Blair could report that "Ferguson and Russell are both beginning their new Courses with much applause."[134] The following year Ferguson's counterpart at Glasgow University, Thomas Reid, informed a friend that the moral philosophy class at Edinburgh "is more than double ours" after Ferguson's appointment.[135] He "has won the lead in the university," commented one of Ferguson's disciples in 1767, when the moral philosophy class swelled with more than one hundred matriculated pupils.[136] Students overflowed into the gallery and were frequently joined by "gentlemen of rank."[137] With the publication in 1767 of the celebrated *Essay on the History of Civil Society*, followed in 1769 by the pedagogical *Institutes of Moral Philosophy*, Ferguson acquired an international reputation that secured his place as one of the foremost moral philosophers of the eighteenth century.

[133] Blair to Hume, 6 April 1764, RSE, 3/52.

[134] Blair to Hume, 15 November 1764, RSE, 3/54.

[135] Reid to David Skene, 20 December 1765, in Reid, *Philosophical Works*, ed. Sir William Hamilton, 2 vols. (1895; reprint, Hildesheim, 1967), 1:42–43.

[136] John Macpherson to James Macpherson, 1 January 1767, quoted in Horn Papers, EUL, Gen. 1824; "Lists of Students in Arts, Law, and Medicine by Year and Subject," EUL, Da. 1.39–45.

[137] Andrew Dalzel to Sir Robert Liston, 30 November 1782, in Dalzel, *University of Edinburgh*, 1:39; Lee, "Adam Ferguson," 241; [Robert Bisset], "Dr. Adam Fergusson," *Public Characters of 1799–1800* (London, 1799), 447.

THE MODERATE REGIME, OR
"DR. ROBERTSON'S ADMINISTRATION"

> He had the happiness . . . of being warmly supported by most
> of the friends who joined him in the [General] Assembly 1751;
> and who, without any jealousy of the ascendant which he pos-
> sessed, arranged themselves with cordiality under his standard.
> The period from his appointment as Principal of the University
> till his retreat from public life, came, accordingly, to be distin-
> guished by the name of Dr. Robertson's *administration*.
>
> Dugald Stewart,
> "Life and Writings of William Robertson," 1801

The rapid ascent of the Moderate literati of Edinburgh after the
Douglas controversy of 1757 is summarized in Table 2. During the
next seven years each member of the group obtained at least one new
academic or ecclesiastical office from the town council of Edinburgh
or the crown. These offices brought them significant increases both
in status and in income—from an average well under £100 per annum in 1757 to more than £350 per annum in 1764. Other, less regular forms of income supplemented these salaried offices. Blair, Ferguson, and Robertson received substantial sums for occasionally
boarding the sons of English peers and gentlemen attending Edinburgh University.[138] They also received hundreds, in some cases
thousands, of pounds from sales of their books, as did John Home
from sales and productions of his plays. The one member of the group
who did not share in these supplementary forms of income, and whose
regular stipend remained relatively low, was Alexander Carlyle. But
Carlyle compensated for his lower income in 1760 by marrying a
Northumberland girl worth between £3000 and £4000—an amount
that he well knew "seldom falls to the share of a Parson in this Country."[139]

Increased wealth and status made it possible for the Moderate literati to integrate themselves into the social elite of Scotland, where
few Presbyterian clergymen had previously ventured. Henceforth they
moved easily in polite society as men of distinction in their own right.

---

[138] Blair and Robertson charged such students £300 a year during the 1760s and
1770s; Ferguson's rate was £240. See Blair to Elizabeth Montagu, 14 October 1773,
Huntington Library, MO 484.

[139] Carlyle to Charles Townshend, 16 October 1760, WLCL, Townshend Papers.

They visited London more frequently and more stylishly, relaxed from time to time at such fashionable English "watering places" as Bath, Harrogate, and Buxton, and associated with members of the nobility, gentry, and the liberal professions at social gatherings and in clubs like the Poker. Robertson and Blair became the first clergymen in their church to maintain their own carriages[140]—a status symbol of considerable significance in a ministry that was theoretically unstratified and perpetually impoverished.

Increased wealth and status were not the only benefits of the academic and ecclesiastical offices secured by the Moderate literati. Equally important was the acquisition of authority within the University of Edinburgh and Church of Scotland. In regard to the latter institution, it was not, as is commonly thought, by means of numerical superiority among the clergy that the Moderates came to dominate Scottish ecclesiastical affairs; for as Ian D. L. Clark has demonstrated, at no time during the eighteenth century could Moderate ministers claim a clear majority over Popular party clerics.[141] The keys to the remarkable ecclesiastical hegemony achieved by the Moderates were skillful management and organization, superior oratory, and the effective utilization of a relatively small number of prestigious positions that provided opportunities for exerting a disproportionately large amount of influence in the general assembly. As will be shown, the Moderates' victory in the critical schism overture affair of 1765–1766 proved that they were capable of controlling the assembly and the church as a whole despite the fact that Drummond, Milton, Bute, Stuart Mackenzie, and most of their other patrons had ceased to wield political power. It was chiefly by controlling the general assembly in this manner that the Moderate literati of Edinburgh dominated the kirk during the 1760s, 1770s, and early 1780s—the prime years of the Moderate Regime and the Scottish Enlightenment.

The first step toward establishing control of the general assembly was to make certain that party supporters constituted a large percentage of the assembly's membership each year and that party leaders in particular attended as often as possible. This task was made difficult by the large size of the assembly and the common practice

---

[140] Schmitz, *Hugh Blair*, 84; Henry Grey Graham, *Scottish Men of Letters in the Eighteenth Century* (London, 1908), 92; William Creech, *Letters Addressed to Sir John Sinclair* (Edinburgh, 1793), 11.

[141] Ian D. L. Clark, "From Protest to Reaction: The Moderate Regime in the Church of Scotland, 1752–1804," in *SAI*, 213, and Clark diss., 182–84. The discussion that follows derives much of its inspiration from the fifth chapter of Clark's outstanding thesis.

TABLE 2
Positions and Salaries Acquired by the
Moderate Literati of Edinburgh, 1757–1764

| | Summer 1757 | |
Name	Position	Salary (in pounds sterling)
Hugh Blair	Minister of Lady Yester's Church, Edinburgh	139
Alexander Carlyle	Minister of Inveresk	94
Adam Ferguson	Keeper of the Advocates Library, Edinburgh	40
John Home	Government Pension	100
William Robertson	Minister of Gladsmuir	75

NOTE. All figures have been rounded off to the nearest pound, with approximations in brackets. Income figures cited here do not include perquisites such as the house and orchard provided for the principal of Edinburgh University and the manse granted to country pastors. I have been unable to determine whether

| | Summer 1764 | |
Name	Position	Salary (in pounds sterling)
Hugh Blair	Minister of St. Giles Church, Edinburgh (New Kirk)	139
	Regius Professor of Rhetoric, Edinburgh University	70*
		[280–350]
Alexander Carlyle	Minister of Inveresk	94
	His Majesty's Almoner	42
		136
Adam Ferguson	Professor of Moral Philosophy, Edinburgh University	102*
		[200–300]
John Home	Government Pension	300
	Conservator of Scots Privileges at Campvere	300
		600
William Robertson	Minister of Old Greyfriars Church, Edinburgh	139
	One of His Majesty's Chaplains-in-Ordinary	50
	Principal, Edinburgh University	111
	Historiographer Royal	200
		500

Ferguson still received a salary as inactive chaplain of the Black Watch in 1757.

*Plus class fees, estimated at £70–140 for Blair and £100–200 for Ferguson.

of selecting clerical representatives by means of fixed rotations in each presbytery. Yet the Moderates were able to overcome these obstacles and to secure representation at the general assembly far in excess of their numerical strength within the clergy.

In order to understand how they accomplished this feat, it should first be noted that actual attendance at the general assembly often fell below 150, rarely reached 200, and apparently never exceeded 300 during the course of the eighteenth century, despite the fact that the official membership total was approximately 360 each year. Thus, important contests like the Carlyle libel case of 1757 and the schism overture affair of 1766 attracted only 156 and 184 votes, respectively, and the 287 votes cast in the clerkship election of 1789 are said to have been the largest number up to that time.[142] Since many churchmen were not affiliated with either ecclesiastical party, control of the assembly depended first and foremost on a party's ability to command a relatively small number of committed followers. Although some of those followers would of course be clergymen representing their presbyteries in strict rotation, a more manageable source of support came from the church elders. Lay or "ruling" elders representing the royal burghs and presbyteries, universities, and Scots Church at Campvere, Holland, constituted more than forty percent of the official membership of each general assembly, where they enjoyed virtually the same speaking and voting privileges as ministers. Unlike the latter, however, most ruling elders were selected for assembly membership by annual elections in the bodies they represented rather than by rotation, and for this reason they could more easily be returned to the assembly year after year.

Both ecclesiastical parties viewed the annual process of electing ruling elders for the next general assembly as a critical test of political strength, and neither was unwilling to secure assembly seats for lay supporters as ruling elders from distant presbyteries and burghs where they did not actually reside. Andrew Crosbie, a lay leader of the Popular party, attended five consecutive assemblies as ruling elder from the Presbytery of Skye in the Hebrides, just as William Robertson's eldest son was a regular member of the assembly after 1775 as an elder from the Hebridean Presbytery of Lewis.[143] The Moderates won the struggle for assembly elders not because they were more unprincipled than their opponents but because they were better or-

---

[142] Hew Scott, ed., *Fasti Ecclesiæ Scoticanæ: The Succession of Ministers in the Church of Scotland*, new ed., 7 vols. (Edinburgh, 1915–1928), 1:327.

[143] These and the following data concerning general assembly membership have been gathered from the unpublished registers of the assembly (SRO, CH1/18–73), a microfilm copy of which was kindly lent to me by Roger Emerson.

ganized and better connected with the lawyers, professors, and other professional men who constituted the bulk of the assembly eldership. A Popular party pamphlet of 1770 warned presbyters to be especially wary of "persons of quality, or high rank" when electing elders to represent them in the assembly.[144] But such a policy was nearly impossible to implement, particularly because persons of "quality" and "high rank" were often the only laymen in a position to go to Edinburgh for the ten days each spring when the general assembly was in session.

The ecclesiastical careers of Adam Ferguson and John Home illustrate the success of the Moderates at regularly getting key party members into the general assembly as ruling elders. The fact that Ferguson left the ministry in the 1750s has led scholars unfamiliar with the intricacies of Scottish ecclesiastical affairs to assume that he was a "lapsed Christian"[145] who ceased to have any further connection with the Church of Scotland after that time. Actually, Ferguson's prestige as a university professor and intimacy with the clerical leaders of the Moderate party made it possible for him to play a greater role in church politics as a lay elder than did most ministers. He first sat in the general assembly in 1762 as an elder from the far-off Presbytery of Cairston in the Orkneys. In 1763, while the Moderates were fighting an unpopular battle to uphold the town council's presentation of Rev. John Drysdale to an Edinburgh church, Ferguson served the Moderate cause in the Edinburgh general sessions as an elder from Lady Yester's Church.[146] In 1765 he returned to the general assembly as an elder from North Isles in the Orkneys. After visiting his birthplace near Dunkeld the following year, he became virtually a standing member of the assembly as a ruling elder from that presbytery. By the time of his academic retirement in the mid-1780s, Ferguson had acquired a reputation as one of the managers of the Moderate interest in the church.[147] The case of John Home is similar to that of Ferguson. As the minister of Athelstane-

[144] John Snodgrass, *An Effectual Method for Recovering our Religious Liberties* (Glasgow, 1770).

[145] Peter Gay, *The Enlightenment: An Interpretation*, 2 vols. (New York, 1966–1969), 2:336.

[146] *Minutes of the General Kirk Sessions of Edinburgh at their several Sederunts* (Edinburgh, 1763). On the Drysdale affair of 1762–1764, see Richard B. Sher, "Moderates, Managers and Popular Politics in Mid-Eighteenth-Century Edinburgh: The Drysdale 'Bustle' of the 1760s," in *NP*, 179–209.

[147] Alexander Carlyle, "A Comparison of Two Eminent Characters Attempted after the Manner of Plutarch," in *AC*, 280; Sir Thomas Dundas to Lord North, October 1783, cited by Henry W. Meikle, *Scotland and the French Revolution* (1912; reprint, London, 1969), 26 n. 2.

ford from 1747 to 1757, Home was a member of the general assembly only three times. After his appointment in 1763 as conservator of Scots privileges at Campvere, however, regular assembly membership was assured. Home's abilities as an ecclesiastical politician and orator were not exceptional, and his highhanded manner sometimes generated resentment, but Carlyle observed that "he now and then spoke with some energy and success in the General Assembly."[148]

Perhaps the most important means of access to the general assembly by Moderate leaders derived from their affiliations with the five universities of Scotland, each of which was empowered to send a delegate to the assembly every year.[149] It was his appointment as principal of Edinburgh University that enabled William Robertson to attend the assembly on an annual basis after 1762—a factor that must be considered as significant as his expertise in organization and debate in accounting for Robertson's preeminence in the assembly during the 1760s and 1770s. If the other universities tended to vary their representatives more than the University of Edinburgh, their selection processes did not preclude frequent assembly attendance by "provincial" clergymen-academics with Moderate inclinations, such as George Campbell and Alexander Gerard of Marischal and King's Colleges, Aberdeen, and Thomas Tullidelph, James Murison, and George Hill of St. Andrews University. In Moderate strongholds like Aberdeen and St. Andrews, it was often possible to select one Moderate faculty member to attend the general assembly as a ruling elder representing the burgh or presbytery and another as the delegate from the university itself. On one occasion (1767) St. Andrews University even sent Alexander Carlyle to the general assembly as its representative.

Besides diligently managing the elections of ruling elders, the Moderates sometimes used their influence in particular presbyteries to return key ministers with unusual frequency. The most dramatic example is that of Alexander Carlyle. During his first dozen years as minister of Inveresk in the hostile Presbytery of Dalkeith, Carlyle was a member of only two general assemblies. After the Moderates gained a majority at Dalkeith, however, Carlyle's fortunes improved, and the same presbytery that had persecuted him so tenaciously during the playhouse controversy of 1757 returned him to the general assembly two out of every three years between 1760 and 1805, when he died. Yet Carlyle's experience at Dalkeith was far from typical. The great majority of Moderate ministers who did not hold academic office

---

[148] *Auto.*, 310.
[149] Clark diss., 147.

continued to attend the general assembly in strict rotation with the other ministers in their presbyteries. The same was true of ministers in the Popular party, of course, but it is worth noting that two of them, Colin Campbell of Renfrew and Charles Nisbet of Montrose, represented their presbyteries at the general assembly on more occasions between 1765 and 1785 than any Moderate clergyman unaffiliated with a university. If the Popular party consistently failed to control the assembly, it was evidently not because of their scruples about returning party leaders on an almost annual basis when conditions permitted it.

The matter of general assembly representation during the age of the Moderate Regime is summarized in Table 3. Note that Moderate leaders enjoyed little if any advantage in assembly membership during the 1750s, when they were in the process of building up their party and their individual careers; but they had an immense advantage during the 1760s, 1770s, and early 1780s, when they dominated the academic and ecclesiastical offices of Scotland. At least eleven Moderate ministers and elders—including all the Moderate literati of Edinburgh except Hugh Blair—attended the assembly ten or more times in the quarter of a century following William Robertson's election as principal of the University of Edinburgh in 1762. The opposition, by contrast, could boast only two ministers (Campbell and Nisbet) and one elder (Andrew Crosbie) who attended the general assembly with that much frequency during those years. Even ministers who were regarded as the leaders of the Popular party, such as Robert Dick, John Erskine, Alexander Webster, and John Witherspoon, were rarely members. Indeed, those four clergymen attended the assembly a combined total of only thirteen times between 1762 and 1785, whereas John Home and Adam Ferguson, who had forsaken the ministry for more secular pursuits, were members of the assembly on a total of twenty-eight occasions during the same period. Under these circumstances, how could the Popular party possibly compete on equal terms with the Moderates in the great arena of Scottish ecclesiastical politics?

Once assured of adequate representation the Moderates employed a variety of techniques to keep the general assembly on a course of their choosing. They were nearly always better organized, better managed, and more firmly united behind a clear and consistent policy than their ecclesiastical opponents. They cultivated excellent relations with the lord high commissioners who represented the government at the general assembly—including Lord Cathcart (1755–1763 and 1773–1776), the earl of Glasgow (1764–1772), and the earl of Dalhousie (1777–1782)—and there is even some evidence that

127

TABLE 3

Membership of Selected Ecclesiastical Leaders in the General
Assembly of the Church of Scotland, 1751–1785

| | Number of Times a Member of the General Assembly | |
Name and Party	1751–1761	1762–1785
MODERATE PARTY		
1. Hugh Blair	3	6
2. George Campbell	1	7
3. Alexander Carlyle	3	14*
4. Andrew Dalzel	0	7†
5. John Drysdale	2	10**
6. Henry Dundas	0	18
7. Adam Ferguson	0	13
8. Adam Fergusson of Moulin	1	11*
9. Alexander Gerard	2	12*
10. Henry Grieve	2	10*
11. George Hill	0	12
12. John Home	4	15
13. John Jardine (d. 1766)	4	2
14. John Ker (d. 1781)	4	6
15. Joseph McCormick	0	7*
16. Duncan McFarlan	4	3
17. James Murison (d. 1779)	5	6*
18. William Robertson[a]	5	16*
19. William Robertson *secundus*	0	11††
20. Thomas Tullidelph (d. 1777)	4	5
POPULAR PARTY AND PATRICK CUMING FACTION		
1. Patrick Bannerman	3	1
2. John Bonar (d. 1761)	3	0
3. Colin Campbell	2	15
4. Andrew Crosbie	4	18
5. Patrick Cuming (d. 1776)	9**	5
6. Robert Dick[b] (d. 1782)	1	4
7. John Erskine	1	4
8. John Freebairn (d. 1773)	1	8
9. John Gillies	2	4
10. John Glen (d. 1768)	3	1
11. Henry Lundie	1	6
12. Daniel MacQueen (d. 1777)	1	4
13. Charles Nisbet	0	14
14. James Oswald	2	6*
15. William Porteous	1	6
16. Archibald Stevenson (d. 1784)	2	7

Name and Party	Number of Times a Member of the General Assembly	
	1751–1761	*1762–1785*
17. Robert Walker (d. 1783)	2	5*
18. Alexander Webster (d. 1784)	3*	5
19. Sir Henry Moncreiff Wellwood	0	3*
20. John Witherspoon[c]	4	0

SOURCES: Registers of the general assembly of the Church of Scotland, SRO, CH 1/18–73, and lists of commission members printed annually in *Principal Acts of the General Assembly of the Church of Scotland.*

   [a] Retired from ecclesiastical politics in 1780.
   [b] Switched from Moderate to Popular party ca. 1760.
   [c] Emigrated to America in 1768.
   * Moderator of the general assembly.
  ** Twice moderator of the general assembly.
   † Principal clerk of the general assembly.
  †† Church procurator.

William Robertson helped to determine which peers should fill that prestigious and lucrative office.[150] They generally agreed on some well-respected Moderate minister to stand for moderator of the assembly and usually succeeded at getting him elected. They maintained a tight grip on permanent assembly offices such as principal clerk and church procurator. The former position, worth approximately £100 a year, was occupied by George Wishart from 1746 to 1778, by Wishart and John Drysdale jointly from 1778 to 1785,[151] by Drysdale alone until his death in 1788, and by his son-in-law Andrew Dalzel until 1807. In 1778 William Robertson and Henry Dundas engineered the narrow victory of Robertson's son William over the radical Whig Henry Erskine for the legal office of procurator, where young Robertson remained for almost thirty years.[152] These assembly offices helped the Moderates to maintain control of the general

[150] Ibid., chap. 5. "As you have had some share in placing me in this situation," wrote the earl of Dalhousie to Robertson upon learning of his appointment as lord high commissioner, "I assure you, I trust to your assistance and advice in enabling me to discharge the duties of the Office with any degree of propriety." 12 April 1777, NLS, 3943:7–8.
[151] *Annals*, 1:329–31, reveals how Robertson managed the joint appointment of Drysdale.
[152] Robertson to Lady Dumfries, 13 May 1776, Bute, uncatalogued; Alexander Fergusson, *The Honourable Henry Erskine* (Edinburgh, 1882), 155–56.

assembly following Principal Robertson's retirement from ecclesiastical politics in 1780.

In addition to securing representation, maintaining party discipline and organization, cooperating with government, and dominating assembly offices like principal clerk and church procurator, the Moderates kept control of the general assembly during the Robertson era by outperforming their opponents in the critical art of debate. It has often been observed that the general assembly was the great forum for eighteenth-century Scottish lawyers seeking reputations as outstanding public speakers, and the point holds true for ministers as well. The ecclesiastical career of William Robertson, for example, owed much to his debating talents, which were further enhanced by the prestige of his academic office. Led by Robertson, the impressive array of Moderate assembly orators, both lay and clerical, was always effective and sometimes, it would seem, decisive in determining the outcome of Scottish ecclesiastical affairs.[153]

In order to appreciate the Moderates' accomplishments as assembly managers and debaters, it will be useful to look closely at one of the most important contests between the two ecclesiastical parties in eighteenth-century Scotland: the schism overture affair of 1765–1766. At issue was an overture of 1765 calling for an inquiry into the alarming growth of defections from the established church, which were rumored to have reached 100,000.[154] This schism overture, as it came to be called, was said to be the work of a "certain faction" seeking to embarrass William Robertson and the Moderate party.[155] Their leader was Robertson's old enemy Patrick Cuming, who was making one last effort to attain revenge against the men who had effectively displaced him as an academic and ecclesiastical leader several years earlier.[156] Among Cuming's associates were his kinsman Rev. Patrick Bannerman of Saltoun and his friend Rev. James Oswald of Methven, the common sense philosopher who had recently lost the Glasgow chair of ecclesiastical history to Alexander Carlyle's cousin William Wight. Oswald was moderator of the general assembly of 1765, and Bannerman introduced the schism overture itself in the committee of overtures.

Although nothing in the schism overture was overtly anti-Moder-

---

[153] See esp. Erskine, 271–72. For a different view, stressing the superior eloquence of the Popular party, see James Boswell, "Sketch of the Constitution of the Church of Scotland," *London Magazine* 41 (April and May 1772): 181–87, 237–42.

[154] *SM* 27 (May 1765): 277.

[155] *Philopatris; or, the Committee of Overtures. A Dialogue* (Edinburgh, 1766), 27; *A Short History of the Late General Assembly of the Church of Scotland, shewing the Rise and Progress of the Schism Overture* (Glasgow, 1766), 9.

[156] Somerville, 85–86.

ate, it was understood that an inquiry into the causes of secession from the established church would be likely to produce a reexamination of those Moderate policies that had fostered the greatest amount of discontent and animosity, such as church patronage and polite, moral preaching. If these policies could be exposed as the chief causes of secession, the Moderates would be cast in the role of church-wreckers and forced to defend their position under highly unfavorable circumstances. The Cuming faction was undoubtedly encouraged by the dismissal of James Stuart Mackenzie as lord privy seal and manager of Scottish affairs in the Grenville ministry just as the general assembly of 1765 convened. With the Bute era finally at an end, Cuming may have assumed that the ecclesiastical reign of William Robertson and his Moderate friends was over, just as his own authority in Scottish ecclesiastical affairs had dissipated immediately after the death of his political patron, the third duke of Argyll, in 1761.

If this was in fact Cuming's strategy, it was very nearly successful. The general assembly of 1765 voted to establish a committee of twenty-three ministers and fifteen elders to study the schism question, and the following November the committee produced a report calling for an investigation by the next general assembly into the connection between patronage and secession.[157] There soon appeared several letters and pamphlets blaming the "prevailing party" in the church for alienating so many devout Presbyterians by rigidly enforcing the law of patronage.[158] Others struck at the Moderates' excessive concern with moral preaching, and John Witherspoon contributed a new satirical pamphlet that savagely ridiculed the methods allegedly employed by the Moderates to obtain preferment during the Bute-Stuart Mackenzie years.[159] As the general assembly of 1766 drew near, it became apparent that the schism overture was to serve as the pretext for a grand assault on the Moderates by a coalition of opponents driven by a variety of motives, including personal jealousy and revenge, political rivalry, and ideological and religious differences. This ominous situation, along with the illnesses then plaguing William Robertson and John Jardine, prompted Hugh Blair to inform David Hume that the church was in "a Tottering State" just nine days before the opening of the assembly.[160]

---

[157] *SM* 27 (November 1765): 613–14.

[158] *SM* 27 (November, December, and Appendix 1765):567–68, 620–23, 682–84; John Maclaurin, *Considerations on the Rights of Patronage* (Edinburgh, 1766).

[159] *The History of a Corporation of Servants* (1765), in *The Works of John Witherspoon*, 9 vols. (Edinburgh, 1804–1805), 6:342. In *The Life of the Revd John Witherspoon* (Princeton, 1973), 66–70, Ashbel Green identifies the "servant" who gets ahead by "acquiring a very great knack of story-telling" as William Robertson.

[160] Blair to Hume, 13 May [1766], RSE, 3/57.

The first session of the general assembly of 1766 appeared to confirm Blair's worst fears about the faltering strength of the Moderates. In the customary opening sermon by the moderator of the previous assembly, James Oswald made several thinly disguised criticisms of the Moderates and denounced the multiplicity of Presbyterian sects in Scotland as a serious evil that the present assembly would have the opportunity to alleviate.[161] Following Oswald's sermon the Popular party candidate for moderator defeated the Moderate candidate by a vote of 83 to 78.[162] The Moderates soon regained some ground by successfully ousting John Witherspoon and the rest of the Paisley delegation from the assembly on a procedural question.[163] When the matter of the schism overture came before the assembly several days later, the two sides seemed almost evenly matched.

The debate on the schism overture occupied one full day and featured some of the best orators in the church. The principal speakers on behalf of the overture were Oswald, Rev. Colin Campbell of Renfrew, Rev. John Freebairn (or Fairbairn) of Dumbarton, and the articulate young advocate Andrew Crosbie. Speakers against the overture included William Robertson, Principal Thomas Tullidelph of St. Andrews University, and a lawyer even younger and more persuasive than Crosbie: Henry Dundas.[164] In Tullidelph and Robertson, the Moderates had perhaps the two greatest Scottish ecclesiastical orators of the eighteenth century.[165] Their polite manner and careful reasoning formed a sharp contrast with the "rough petulant eloquence" of opponents like Campbell and Freebairn.[166] The addition of Henry Dundas clinched the Moderates' oratorical superiority over the proponents of the overture, for according to Carlyle Dundas "was himself a match for all their lay forces, as Robertson and a few friends were for all the bands of clergy."[167]

---

[161] *A Sermon Preached at the Opening of the General Assembly, May 22, 1766* (Edinburgh, 1766), 14, 30. The first volume of Oswald's *Appeal to Common Sense in Behalf of Religion* also appeared in 1766 and may be considered, inter alia, an extension of Oswald's attack on skepticism and Moderatism in the schism overture affair. Beyond the rather simplistic "appeal to common sense" that formed the heart of his reply to skeptics like Hume, Oswald blamed overly tolerant, overly polite clergymen for helping the skeptics' cause by taking them seriously instead of ignoring them as they should. See Gavin Ardley, *The Common Sense Philosophy of James Oswald* (Aberdeen, 1980), 63–64.

[162] *Annals*, 2:311.

[163] Ibid., 312; William Oliver Brackett, "John Witherspoon: His Scottish Ministry" (Ph.D. diss., Edinburgh University, 1935), 169–70.

[164] Alexander Bower, *The History of the University of Edinburgh*, 3 vols. (Edinburgh, 1817), 3:66; *SM* 28 (July 1766): 337–41.

[165] *Auto.*, 265; Somerville, 94–96; Carlyle to Bishop Douglas, 14 March 1781, BL, Egerton, 2185:103–104.

[166] Somerville, 101; *Auto.*, 453; Bower, *University of Edinburgh*, 3:66.

[167] *Auto.*, 491.

The speech delivered by William Robertson during the schism overture debate of 1766 is particularly noteworthy for two reasons. First, Robertson charged that the entire matter was the result of "envy and resentment against him in particular, and the measures he had supported." In an apparent reference to Patrick Cuming and his associates, he stated that he had a good deal of respect for churchmen who consistently disagreed with his policies but none at all for those who promoted one set of measures and then the opposite "perhaps as one ministry or another prevails at Court."[168] Robertson was apparently alluding not only to the fall of James Stuart Mackenzie but also to the fact that the duke of Grafton, secretary for the Northern Department in Rockingham's new ministry, had announced that the wishes of parishioners would be taken into consideration in the disposal of Scottish church patronage by the crown.[169] Though Robertson's insinuations were strenuously denied by members of the Cuming circle,[170] they served as a reminder that Cuming himself had spent years enforcing the law of patronage as ecclesiastical agent for the Argathelian interest. They also served to drive a wedge between the Cuming faction and the Popular party—a wedge that may account for one spectator's insight that, in contrast to the Moderates, the supporters of the schism overture "seemed to have laid down no plan of operation, nor to be in any sort of concert among themselves."[171]

The other noteworthy aspect of Robertson's speech was its straightforward defense of patronage and secession. In all previous cases, Robertson had defended patronage on grounds of law and order, both civil and ecclesiastical, rather than for its own sake. In his speech on the schism overture, however, he sketched the history of patronage in the church in order to demonstrate the great improvement it had engendered among the clergy of Scotland. Scottish Presbyterian ministers had always been pious enough, Robertson argued, but only since the institution and enforcement of lay patronage had they added secular learning and polite manners to their fundamental piety. This argument was a bold one because it marked the first occasion on which the Moderates publicly asserted that patronage by an enlightened elite was the best means of filling parish vacancies.[172] Robertson even employed the analogy of flowers coming in many

---

[168] *SM* 28 (July 1766): 337–41.

[169] *Annals*, 2:vi–vii.

[170] *SM* 28 (July 1766): 337–41; James Oswald, *Letters concerning the Present State of the Church of Scotland* (Edinburgh, 1767), 36–37. Robertson's charges were supported in *Philopatris*, 27, and Somerville, 85.

[171] *Short History of the Late General Assembly*, 15.

[172] Similar arguments had occasionally been used by Moderates before 1766, but only in anonymous works such as Alexander Carlyle's pamphlet *Faction Detected* (London, 1763), which did not press the point.

different varieties in order to portray secession as a perfectly natural phenomenon.[173] By emphasizing the positive effects of patronage and secession, Robertson showed his skill at putting opponents on the defensive rather than meekly absorbing their blows.

On this occasion, as on so many others, Robertson's talents as an assembly debater and manager helped to win the day for the Moderate party, for the assembly voted 99 to 85 to reject the schism overture committee's proposal to pursue an investigation into the connections between patronage and seccession.[174] Even if Alexander Carlyle exaggerated somewhat when he later claimed that the margin of victory had been a "great majority" and that "the Schism Overture which we defeated was the last blow that was aimed at patronage," the significance of this affair was enormous.[175] By clearly demonstrating the Moderates' ability to manage the kirk without the support of a particular faction at Westminster, the schism overture affair revealed the extent to which Moderate principles and policies had taken hold *within* the Church of Scotland. This lesson was not lost on contemporaries. One week after the Moderates' victory in the schism overture case, George Dempster wrote to Alexander Carlyle: "I congratulate you on the success of the Assembly, because it affords the most undoubted proof that good sense and moderation are now well rooted in the Church."[176]

Outside the church, meanwhile, the Rockingham government could not help but be impressed by the Moderates' show of strength in the schism overture affair. The Moderate literati had suffered a severe blow when John Jardine had collapsed and died as the votes on the schism overture report were being tallied in the general assembly of 1766, and they considered it "extremely important" for their prestige and authority that Jardine's two deaneries "do not go in a wrong channel."[177] They therefore made strong appeals to their remaining friends of influence in Scotland and London, such as Dempster, Os-

[173] Cf. the similar argument in Somerville, 85–90. Ironically, Robertson's "principle of plenitude" argument to justify schism was indirectly supported by some of the seceders themselves, who deeply resented the framers of the schism overture for characterizing secession as unequivocally reprehensible. See *SM* 27 (May 1765): 230–32, and *Animadversions on the Overture of the last General Assembly, concerning Schism* (Edinburgh, 1766).

[174] *SM* 28 (May 1766): 275–76.

[175] *Auto.*, 490–91. There were serious, though unsuccessful, antipatronage campaigns in the general assembly in 1768–1769 and 1782–1784.

[176] Dempster to Carlyle, 7 June 1766, EUL, Dc. 4.41:92.

[177] Blair to Hume, 12 June 1766, RSE, 3/58; Blair to Oswald of Dunnikier, 2 June [1766], in *Memorials of the Public Life and Character of the Right Hon. James Oswald of Dunnikier* (Edinburgh, 1825), 119. On Jardine's death, see *Auto.*, 490.

wald of Dunnikier, Robert Orde, Henry Dundas, Sir Alexander Gilmour, and David Hume. According to Blair, who was himself a candidate for one of the deaneries, Robertson went so far as to inform Gilmour and Dempster that he would "entirely withdraw from all sort of church business and management" unless "friends to government and law"—by which he meant Moderates—were selected to fill these offices.[178] Competition for Jardine's places was exceptionally keen—so much so that one month after Jardine's death Hume informed Blair that more applications had been received for "these two small Offices . . . than if Canterbury & Durham had been both vacant: a Proof what poor Prizes you in Scotland have to contend for."[179] The unusually large number of applications was also proof of general uncertainty in Scotland about how the Rockingham ministry would dispense patronage. Before the year was out, however, the government had bestowed one of Jardine's deaneries on John Drysdale "solely by the recommendation of Dr. Robertson" and the other deanery on Robertson's respected colleague in the university, Robert Hamilton, who was certainly a Moderate sympathizer if not an actual party "member."[180] After these appointments it was clear that the ecclesiastical authority of Robertson and his Moderate friends did not depend on the support of a particular "great man" or political interest in London but was rather a function of the Moderates' offices and abilities as church and university leaders. The schism overture affair demonstrated that, regardless of personal connections or ideological differences, every government was obliged to cooperate with the party of patronage, order, learning, and politeness in the Church of Scotland. Although the intimacy of the Bute-Stuart Mackenzie years had passed, the working relationship between the Moderates and government endured with very little change.[181]

The success of William Robertson and his circle in maintaining hegemony in the Church of Scotland was equaled, if not surpassed, in

---

[178] Blair to Oswald, 2 June [1766], *Oswald Memorials*, 120.

[179] Hume to Blair, 1 July 1766, *HL*, 2:57.

[180] Andrew Dalzel, "Account of the Life of Rev. John Drysdale," *TRSE* 3 (1794), app. 2:46; *Auto.*, 492.

[181] Clark, "From Protest to Reaction," 209–10. The classic testimonial to Robertson's independence is that of his ecclesiastical rival, John Erskine: "The power of others, who formerly had in some measure guided ecclesiastical affairs, was derived from ministers of state, and expired with their fall. His remained unhurt amidst frequent changes of administration. Great men in office were always ready to countenance him, to cooperate with him, and to avail themselves of his aid. But, he judged for himself, and scorned to be their slave, or to submit to receive their instructions." Erskine, 272–73.

the University of Edinburgh. Technically, administrative authority in the college lay not with the principal and professors meeting as the senatus academicus but with the town council. Ever jealous of its prerogatives, the council had been fighting since the seventeenth century against infringements on its authority by the senatus and the introduction of new terms such as "university" and "faculty," which were thought to imply corporate academic status.[182] Possessing little formal power, the senatus academicus could be no stronger than the men who headed it. Whereas strong-willed principals like William Wishart *secundus* (1737–1753) did much to extend its jurisdiction over college business, during the exceptionally weak administration of Principal John Gowdie (1754–1762) the senatus ceased to function effectively. Meetings were held infrequently, with little important business conducted. Leadership, such as it was, passed from the ailing principal to the senior divinity professor, Patrick Cuming, who lacked either the ability or the inclination to formulate a vigorous and independent policy regarding college affairs.

The situation changed radically after William Robertson assumed the duties of principal in November 1762.[183] Meetings of the senatus academicus immediately became more frequent and productive. Committees were organized to investigate vexing administrative problems, and clear-cut policies were instituted concerning a number of important academic matters, such as the procedure for granting honorary degrees. Open encouragement was shown toward any project likely to enhance the intellectual life of the college and the town—from the Speculative Society for student debate (1764) to the Royal Society of Edinburgh for formal scholarly inquiry (1783). Ambitious plans were devised for improving the library, natural history museum, and classroom buildings, which Robertson considered the chief shortcomings of the university.[184] Although construction of the new buildings was delayed until the end of the century, Robertson managed to improve the museum and reorganize the library sufficiently to impress English visitors like Edward Topham and Samuel Johnson.[185] Even in the seemingly autonomous faculty of medicine,

---

[182] D. B. Horn, *A Short History of the University of Edinburgh, 1556–1889* (Edinburgh, 1967), 74–75; Alexander Law, *Education in Edinburgh in the Eighteenth Century* (London, 1965), 22, 25.

[183] Although appointed in March 1762, Robertson did not assume office until November of that year.

[184] Robertson to Elliot, 8 January 1763, NLS, 11009:163–64; William Robertson, *Memorial Relating to the University of Edinburgh* (Edinburgh, 1768).

[185] Horn, *University of Edinburgh*, 78–90; Edward Topham, *Letters from Edinburgh* (1776; reprint, Edinburgh, 1971), 206; *Tour*, 25. On the reorganization of the library—including a new and efficient accounting system based on meticulous record keeping

Edinburgh's biggest student attraction during the second half of the eighteenth century, Robertson's administrative skill and leadership were often necessary to resolve internal and external disputes, negotiate with the town council for new facilities like the anatomy theater built for Alexander Monro *secundus* in 1764, set policy, and influence new appointments to vacant chairs.[186] In 1768 Robertson could justly boast that "the course of Academical education is now as complete in this as in any University in Europe," and an anonymous pamphlet of 1780 was not far from the mark in calling Edinburgh "the seat of perhaps the most famous university of Europe."[187]

Contemporaries tended to give much of the credit for the great improvement in the University of Edinburgh to the principal himself. In the mid-1770s Alexander Wedderburn recalled numerous defects in the Edinburgh University of his student days that had since been remedied by Robertson's efforts.[188] At the end of the century Dugald Stewart, who had taught at the university during Robertson's last two decades as principal, remarked that "if, as a seat of learning, Edinburgh has, of late more than formerly, attracted the notice of the world, much must be ascribed to the influence of his example, and to the lustre of his name."[189] Stewart added that Robertson's control of the senatus academicus was so complete that no vote was ever taken on any issue during his thirty years as principal. This remarkable record of total unanimity in the senatus, coupled with his conciliatory manner, his international literary reputation, his undisputed competence as an administrator, his preeminent position in the church, his extraordinary forensic powers, and his formidable connections with the "great," made Robertson a far more powerful figure in the university than any of his predecessors since William Carstares. The increased autonomy of the principal and professors in the Robertson era received official recognition in October 1772, when Lord Provost Gilbert Laurie broke with precedent by formally ad-

---

and systematic collection of student matriculation fees—see C. P. Finlayson and S. M. Simpson, "The History of the Library, 1710–1837," in *Edinburgh University Library, 1580–1980,* ed. Jean R. Guild and Alexander Law (Edinburgh, 1982), 55–66, esp. 56–59, and Jeremy J. Cater, "James Robertson, 1720–1795: An Anti-Enlightenment Professor in the University of Edinburgh" (Ph.D. diss., New York University, 1976), 218–43.

[186] See, for example, Rex. E. Wright-St. Clair, *Doctors Monro: A Medical Saga* (London, 1964), 78, 83.

[187] Robertson, *Memorial,* 5; *To the Inhabitants of Edinburgh* (Edinburgh, 1780), quoted courtesy of Alexander Murdoch.

[188] Wedderburn to Robertson, 31 August 1776, NLS, 3942:271–72.

[189] Stewart, xlvi.

dressing the senatus academicus by the corporate title "Faculty of the College."[190]

Not long after Laurie's concession, the town fathers would learn to their dismay just how powerful the principal and his "faculty" had become. The occasion was Adam Ferguson's acceptance in early 1774 of a lucrative position as traveling tutor to the young earl of Chesterfield. Although Ferguson arranged for a substitute (the Moderate minister Henry Grieve) to deliver his moral philosophy lectures while he was abroad, he angered members of the town council by imprudently leaving Edinburgh to join his pupil without first obtaining the council's permission for a leave of absence.[191] To make matters worse for the Moderates, such influential enemies of skepticism as Lord Hailes, Bishop Warburton, Lord Mansfield, the earl of Dartmouth, and General Oughton took this opportunity to revive a scheme to put David Hume's arch antagonist James Beattie into Ferguson's moral philosophy chair, though Beattie himself was too intimidated to carry through this challenge to Hume's Moderate friends among the Edinburgh literati.[192] The following autumn another attempt to oust the absent Ferguson was made by Beattie's allies, including Rev. John Erskine and Beattie's publisher William Creech; but Beattie's continued reluctance allowed William Robertson and his friends to foil this scheme and persuade the council to appoint the new assistant professor of logic, John Bruce, as Ferguson's substitute for the academic year.[193] At this point the matter appeared to be closed, but at the conclusion of the term the town council abruptly rescinded Ferguson's commission and declared the moral philosophy chair vacant, adding at its next meeting that it was prepared to fight strenuously to uphold its "rights" in this affair.[194] The council, however, had underestimated the Robertson Moderates, who exerted enough pressure to bring about Ferguson's reinstatement as professor of moral

[190] Sir Alexander Grant, *The Story of the University of Edinburgh*, 2 vols. (London, 1884), 2:6–7.

[191] Copy of town council minutes of 16 February 1774, NLS, 3431. By late March Ferguson was in London, preparing to go to the Continent with Chesterfield: see his letters to [John Macpherson] of 31 March (NLS, 1273:23–26) and William Creech of 1 April (SRO, Dalguise Muniments).

[192] Jeremy J. Cater, "General Oughton *versus* Edinburgh's Enlightenment," in *History and Imagination*, ed. Hugh Lloyd-Jones et al. (New York, 1981), 254–71; Margaret Forbes, *Beattie and His Friends* (Westminster, 1904), 66, 102–108; letters of Warburton and Hailes in the Newhailes Papers, NLS.

[193] Beattie to Creech, 20 October 1774, SRO, Dalguise Muniments; copy of town council minutes of 26 October 1774, NLS, 3431; Ferguson to Robertson, 9 November 1774, NLS, 3942:171–72; Blair's notes for Ferguson's defense in John Small, "Biographical Sketch of Adam Ferguson," *TRSE* 23 (1864): 616–17.

[194] Town council minutes of April 1775, in Dalzel, *University of Edinburgh*, 2:445–46.

philosophy just three weeks after his dismissal. "You may believe I was much surprised at the attempt of the Town Council to shut the door against me," the relieved professor wrote to Alexander Carlyle after hearing the happy news; "but am obliged to them for opening it again. . . . I have been much obliged to the general voice that was raised in my favour, as well as to the ardent zeal of particular friends."[195] The "particular friends" who had humbled the town council for Ferguson's sake included Robertson, Blair, political and legal allies like Lord Mountstuart, Baron Mure, and Ilay Campbell, and presumably Carlyle himself.[196]

The incident just described is useful for illustrating not only the academic strength of the Moderate literati of Edinburgh but also the closeness of the bond that existed among them. Powerful as he was in academic affairs, William Robertson was less a dictator than a party leader who considered his own interest and influence to be bound up intimately with those of like-minded friends and kin. Foremost among them within the university were Adam Ferguson and Hugh Blair. The resignation in April 1762 of Patrick Cuming, the Moderates' only notable opponent on the faculty, cleared the way for these young Moderate academics to take control of the senatus academicus without opposition. In effect, a triumvirate of Moderate literati in their early forties replaced the eighty-year-old Gowdie and the sixty-seven-year-old Cuming at the helm of the college.

Once in power, they exerted their influence to bring qualified Moderates, friends, and relations into the university. We have seen that Ferguson's cousin James Russel became professor of natural philosophy in 1764 as part of the scheme that shifted Ferguson to the chair of moral philosophy. Blair, Ferguson, and Robertson then worked to get another of Ferguson's cousins, Joseph Black, elected professor of chemistry in 1766 as part of a maneuver that moved their friend William Cullen to the institutes of medicine chair.[197] In 1772 the chair of Greek was filled by Robertson's relation by marriage, Andrew Dalzel, who regularly served the principal in the general assembly and later (1785) assumed the additional offices of college librarian (worth about £50 per annum) and secretary of the senatus academicus by means of Robertson's patronage.[198] In 1774 Robertson and Black successfully placed John Robison in the natural

---

[195] Ferguson to Carlyle, 29 April 1775, in Small, "Adam Ferguson," 620.

[196] Ibid., 616–20.

[197] Blair to Hume, 15 November 1764, RSE, 3/54; Joseph Black to John Black, 30 June 1766, cited in A. L. Donovan, *Philosophical Chemistry in the Scottish Enlightenment: The Doctrines and Discoveries of William Cullen and Joseph Black* (Edinburgh, 1975), 182.

[198] Dalzel, *University of Edinburgh*, 1:52; Grant, *University of Edinburgh*, 2:326.

philosophy chair vacated by Russel's death, and when filling the logic chair the town council deferred to Robertson and the faculty for approval of John Bruce, who quickly proved himself a good friend by covering for Ferguson during the incident discussed above.[199] The following year John Hill—future biographer of Hugh Blair and half-brother of Robertson's protégé George Hill—won the chair of humanity, and an arrangement was made to allow Ferguson's former student and Blair's relation Dugald Stewart to replace his father, Rev. Matthew Stewart, in the chair of mathematics, from which he proceeded to the chair of moral philosophy following Ferguson's retirement from active teaching in 1785. By that year the faculty was being inundated with Moderate clergymen, including John Walker of Moffat (natural history, 1779), Blair's hand-picked replacement William Greenfield (rhetoric and belles lettres, 1784), Blair's friend and admirer James Finlayson (logic and metaphysics, 1786), Robertson's family friend John Playfair (mathematics, 1785), and Moderate pamphleteer Thomas Hardy (ecclesiastical history, 1788). In 1786 Robert Blair, Hugh's second cousin, occupied the new chair of astronomy. Another notable appointment was that of Robertson's relation Allan Maconochie, later Lord Meadowbank, to the chair of public law (1779), which he secured shortly after taking a stand in the church courts in support of Robertson and Henry Dundas's liberal policy on Roman Catholic relief.[200]

The Robertson Moderates did not use their academic influence capriciously. Every one of the men just mentioned was well qualified in his field and distinguished himself to some degree in his academic office. Some, like Maconochie and Hardy, were outstanding lecturers who brought new life to dead or dying chairs. Others were better known as scholars and researchers. By using their influence to improve the faculty while promoting the careers of their friends and relations, the Moderate literati gained credibility and authority for themselves as they raised the standards and reputation of the University of Edinburgh. Of course, they were not omnipotent in university affairs. When Robertson tried to obtain salary increases for several low-paid arts professors, he soon learned the true limitations

[199] J. B. Morrell, "Professors Robison and Playfair and the *Theophobia Gallica,*" *Notes and Records of the Royal Society of London* 26 (1971): 46; town council minutes of 25 January 1774 (courtesy of Roger Emerson). Bruce was technically assistant professor until 1775, when the incumbent died.

[200] Although Maconochie was permitted to purchase the chair from Balfour of Pilrig, this transaction was subject to the veto of Robertson, who had blocked a similar sale to Gilbert Stuart a year or two earlier on grounds of licentious behavior. Robert Kerr, *Memoirs of the Life, Writings, and Correspondence of William Smellie,* 2 vols. (Edinburgh, 1811), 1:500.

of his academic authority.[201] Nor were financial matters the only ones in which the powers of the principal and professors were somewhat restricted. Robertson and his supporters in the senatus were powerless to remove an unpopular or incompetent professor and sometimes were unable to influence the outcome of a competition for a vacant university chair. For example, in 1779 the Moderate junta in the university lost a hotly disputed contest for the chair of divinity and the following year failed to place their candidate in the civil history chair. Both their choices in these cases (Rev. James McKnight and Rev. John Logan, respectively) possessed sound credentials, but in the first instance the town council elected a relation of the provost, and in the second instance the Faculty of Advocates exercised its prerogative to restrict the civil history chair to one of its own members. A few years later Robertson was unable to obtain the Scots law chair for his eldest son.[202] Yet setbacks such as these were the exception rather than the rule in the era of "Dr. Robertson's administration." In most matters Robertson and his friends had their way, and their way benefited both the university and the Moderate cause.

Though the influence of the Moderate literati of Edinburgh was naturally greatest at their own university, their connections and affiliations sometimes extended to Scotland's other academic institutions as well. This was especially true in regard to St. Andrews. In the decades preceding the '45, St. Andrews University had consisted of three small, poor, independent, and generally insignificant colleges struggling for survival. Reform came in 1747, when Principal Thomas Tullidelph of St. Leonard's engineered the amalgamation of his college with St. Salvator's to form the United College, with eight specialized arts and science chairs in place of regenting and Tullidelph himself as principal.[203] In the same year Rev. James Murison became principal of St. Andrews's remaining independent college, St. Mary's. For the next three decades Murison and Tullidelph dominated the St. Andrews academic world. Both men supported the Moderate party in ecclesiastical affairs, and Tullidelph's daughter married into the intimate circle of Adam Ferguson's family and friends in Perthshire.[204] Academic reform of United College was closely bound

---

[201] Minutes of the Senatus Academicus, 25 March 1773, EUL, vol. 1.

[202] Robertson to Henry Dundas, [1786], WLCL, Melville Papers.

[203] Ronald Gordon Cant, *The University of St. Andrews: A Short History*, new ed. (Edinburgh, 1970), pt. 4.

[204] Tullidelph's daughter was the second wife of Thomas Bisset—successor of Adam Ferguson's father as minister of Logierait and father (by his first marriage to the daughter of Rev. Adam Fergusson of Moulin) of Ferguson's own good friend Robert Bisset, the author.

Adam Ferguson by William Millar

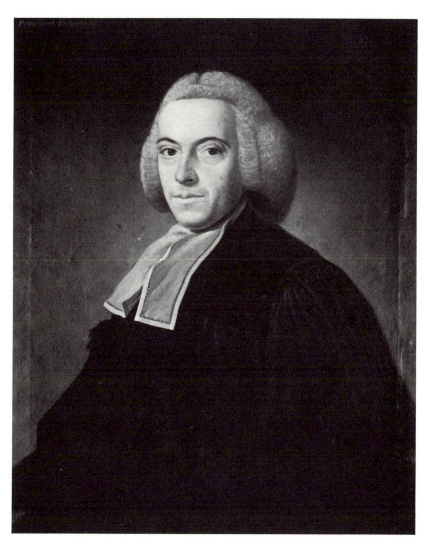

William Robertson by William Millar

John Home by Sir Henry Raeburn

Hugh Blair by Sir Henry Raeburn

Alexander Carlyle by Sir Henry Raeburn

up with the appointments of Moderate ministers such as Hugh Blair's cousin Robert Watson (logic, rhetoric, and metaphysics, 1756), William Wilkie (natural philosophy, 1759), and George Hill (Greek, 1772). After Tullidelph's death in 1777, William Robertson and his party used their influence with their friend Lord Kinnoul, the "enlightened" chancellor of St. Andrews, to place Watson (1778–1781) and subsequently Joseph McCormick (1781–1799) in the United College principalship.[205] At St. Mary's, meanwhile, they were apparently instrumental in securing the appointments of James Gillespie to the principalship left vacant by Murison's death in 1779 and Henry Spens to the divinity chair in the same year,[206] and they could take pleasure in the fact that their friend George Hill would succeed first Spens (1788) and then Gillespie (1791) through the patronage of the new chancellor, Henry Dundas.

Thus, the Moderate Regime in Scotland rested on a bifurcated institutional foundation. The kirk constituted one pillar of the Moderate system; the University of Edinburgh, and to a lesser extent the other Scottish universities, constituted the other. At the center of it all stood the imposing figure of William Robertson, who used his office as principal of Edinburgh University as a power base for managing ecclesiastical as well as academic affairs. But Robertson's effectiveness in the general assembly of the church and the senatus academicus of the university depended heavily on the able assistance that he consistently received from other members of his Moderate band. Along with their considerable abilities as debaters, managers, administrators, and authors, these Moderate men of letters owed their authority in both the church and the university to the academic and ecclesiastical offices bestowed on them in the late 1750s and early 1760s, when they enjoyed the lion's share of patronage dispensed by Argyll, Bute, Stuart Mackenzie, Milton, and their subordinates. By 1765 the Moderate literati were sufficiently entrenched in their academic and ecclesiastical positions to survive the fall of most of their early political patrons, as they demonstrated conclusively during the schism overture affair of 1765–1766 and again during the row over Adam Ferguson's unapproved leave of absence from the classroom in 1774–1775. Throughout the heyday of the Scottish Enlightenment they dominated the church and university by virtue of their collective strength within those institutions rather than the good graces of any particular patron among the "great."

---

[205] Robertson to ———, 8 March 1774, New College Library, X136, 615, box 1; Robertson's letters to McCormick of 1781, EUL, La. 2/241.

[206] Robertson to Lord ———, 15 November 1779, Public Record Office, SP 54/47:364–65.

PART II

MODERATISM AND THE SCOTTISH ENLIGHTENMENT

The Moderate Spirit
and Style

❀

THE ENLIGHTENMENT
OF THE CLERICS

There are few branches of literature in which the ministers of
this church have not excelled. There are few subjects of fine
writing in which they do not stand foremost in the rank of authors.

Alexander Carlyle,
General Assembly Speech, ca. 1793

Happily a more liberal spirit has gained ground among the Clergy
of Scotland. They think more freely than they did of old, and
consequently a spirit of inquiry and moderation seems to be on
the growing hand.

Rev. Daniel Brodie of Cawdor, 1771

Once the Moderate literati of Edinburgh had gained control of the
academic and ecclesiastical establishment, they were in a position to
provide an institutional foundation for the cultural values in which
they believed. The flowering of the Scottish Enlightenment in the third
quarter of the eighteenth century cannot be explained without reference to this fact. In no other country were the principles of the
Enlightenment so deeply rooted in the universities or so openly and
enthusiastically espoused by the leaders of the established church.
Nowhere else did clergymen and professors make up such a large
proportion of the men of letters or produce so many major works of
polite literature. If the Enlightenment in France developed outside
of, and sometimes in opposition to, the clergy and the schools, the
Enlightenment in Scotland, along with less spectacular instances in
parts of Germany and other Protestant countries, was largely an ecclesiastical and academic phenomenon. At the heart of this Enlightenment of the Scottish clerics and professors lay the Moderate

literati of Edinburgh and the intellectual and ideological program that would come to be called Moderatism.

It would be difficult to imagine a more improbable group of apostles for the Enlightenment than the Scottish Presbyterian clergy and professoriate in the years immediately following the Revolution Settlement of 1688–1690. The Scottish kirk was then as rigid and intolerant as any church in Europe, and Scottish universities were for the most part centers of straight and narrow Calvinist orthodoxy.[1] The spirit of the age manifested itself in the purges of Episcopalian ministers and professors and in the extraordinary case of Thomas Aikenhead—an eighteen-year-old Edinburgh University student executed in 1697 for having made some blasphemous remarks that he was willing to renounce.[2] Although a few Presbyterian churchmen like William Carstares struggled to reform the universities and to mitigate some of the excesses of their most fanatical brethren, the liberalization of the kirk was a slow and uneven process. Despite his modern reputation as "the first of the Moderates,"[3] Carstares himself died in 1715 still defending the severe sentence meted out to Aikenhead almost two decades earlier.[4] When Voltaire visited Britain in the late 1720s, the term "Scotch Presbyterian" was still considered synonymous with intolerance and overbearing piety.[5]

Bridging the formidable gap between the rigid Calvinism of the post-Revolution period and the polite Presbyterianism of the Moderate era were a number of learned and liberal clergymen born around the turn of the eighteenth century, such as Patrick Cuming (b. 1695), Francis Hutcheson (b. 1694), William Leechman (b. 1706), James Oswald (b. 1703), George Turnbull (b. 1698), Turnbull's brother-in-law Robert Wallace (b. 1697), and William Wishart *secundus* (b. [1692]) and his younger brother George (b. 1703). These "Neu-Lights and Preachers-Legall," as the strict Calvinist Robert Wodrow called sev-

---

[1] Calvinist orthodoxy, however, was not incompatible with "progressive" trends in certain fields of study, such as physics, where Newtonianism could take hold without a struggle because it apparently posed no more of a threat than the Aristotelian and Cartesian ideas previously in vogue. It has also been noted that the strong intellectual component in Scottish Calvinism may have encouraged a scholarly, though not necessarily liberal or enlightened, approach to many religious and philosophical questions. See the essays of Ronald G. Cant, Christine M. Shepherd, and James K. Cameron in *ONSE*, esp. 43 and 118.

[2] Thomas Howell, ed., *A Complete Collection of State Trials*, 33 vols. (London, 1816–1826), 13:917–39; James K. Cameron, "Scottish Calvinism and the Principle of Intolerance," in *Reformation Perennis*, ed. B. A. Gerrish (Pittsburgh, 1981), 113–28.

[3] Andrew L. Drummond and James Bulloch, *The Scottish Church, 1688–1843: The Age of the Moderates* (Edinburgh, 1973), 22.

[4] George E. Davie, *The Scottish Enlightenment* (London, 1981), 9.

[5] *Philosophical Letters*, trans. Ernest Dilworth (Indianapolis, 1961), 25.

eral of them who had studied divinity at Edinburgh with William Hamilton, grappled with contemporary philosophical problems at intellectual clubs like the Rankenian, served in several instances as principals and professors of moral philosophy or divinity in Scottish universities, preached and sometimes published sermons recommending moderation and reason, and generally did what they could to retard the growth of fanaticism in the kirk during the first half of the eighteenth century.[6] Together with lay contemporaries like Colin Maclaurin (b. 1698), John Stevenson (b. 1695), Alexander Monro *primus* (b. 1697), and Charles Mackie (b. 1688), they contributed to laying the philosophical, social, academic, and ecclesiastical groundwork for Moderatism and the mature Scottish Enlightenment.

All the same, the continuity between these so-called "Neu-Lights" and the subjects of the present study should not be exaggerated, as is frequently done when misleading labels like "Old Moderates" or "Early Moderates" are employed. With few exceptions, such as George Wishart and possibly William Leechman during the latter parts of their careers, the "Neu-Lights" and their friends disapproved of the Moderates' thoroughgoing support for church patronage and did not feel completely comfortable with the Moderates' ultra-liberal, elitist vision of politeness and enlightenment. In regard to the patronage question, most of them agreed with Popular party leaders of the second half of the century in favoring selection of ministers in rural parishes by heritors and elders, in accordance with the parliamentary act of 1690 and the general assembly's act of 1732—a position clearly articulated in Francis Hutcheson's pamphlet of 1735, *Considerations on Patronages*.[7] William Wishart actually headed the anti-Moderate forces in the church during the Inverkeithing affair of 1752–1753, just as Robert Wallace did during the controversy of 1762–1764 over the town council's right to present ministers to Edinburgh churches and just as Cuming, Oswald, and their friends did during the schism overture affair of 1765–1766. In regard to cultural matters, the break was less pronounced but still significant: William Wishart, apparently with the tacit support of Hutcheson and Leechman, led a less than moderate campaign to discredit Hume's candidacy for the Edinburgh chair of moral philosophy in the mid-

[6] On William Hamilton and his disciples, see Henry R. Sefton, "The Early Development of Moderation in the Church of Scotland" (Ph.D. diss., Glasgow University, 1962) and " 'Neu-lights and Preachers-Legall': Some Observations on the Beginnings of Moderatism in the Church of Scotland," in *Church, Politics and Society: Scotland 1408–1929*, ed. Norman Macdougall (Edinburgh, 1983), 186–96.

[7] See Richard Sher and Alexander Murdoch, "Patronage and Party in the Church of Scotland, 1750–1800," in Macdougall, *Church, Politics and Society*, 197–220.

1740s;[8] Patrick Cuming broke his brief alliance with the Moderates in 1756–1757 over the issue of playwriting and playgoing clergymen and afterward became one of the Moderates' most bitter foes; Cuming's friend James Oswald singled out as a major reason for his circle's disenchantment with the Moderates the latter's lenient handling of a minister brought before the church courts on charges of fornication;[9] and even the exceptionally broad-minded Robert Wallace, who was intellectually and culturally close to the Moderates in some respects, came to believe that his younger brethren had gone too far in their policy of championing cultural enlightenment.[10]

If the pioneering generation of Scottish Presbyterian divines born around 1700 initiated the cultural transformation of the kirk during the second quarter of the eighteenth century, the generation born around 1720 finished the job. The turning point was the 1750s when, as we have seen, the Moderate literati of Edinburgh and their friends distinguished themselves in the Select Society, led the successful defense of the "infidel" philosophers Hume and Kames in the general assembly, commended polite literature and polite preaching in their short-lived *Edinburgh Review,* won a victory on the issue of theater, and demonstrated, with publications like Wilkie's *Epigoniad,* Home's *Douglas,* and Robertson's *History of Scotland,* that Presbyterian ministers could produce polished and sometimes extremely profitable works of polite literature on topics that were not limited to the traditional religious and philosophical concerns of the clergy. In subsequent decades clergymen began to attend the playhouse openly and to follow Alexander Carlyle's example of "playing at cards at home with unlocked doors."[11] Hell-and-damnation sermonizing steadily lost ground to polite, moral preaching. Free intellectual inquiry and religious tolerance became, with very few exceptions, the order of the day. In short, the Church of Scotland was transformed into a stronghold of "enlightened," Moderate principles concerning manners, religion, literature, and virtually every other sphere of culture.

By the early 1770s astute observers were drawing attention to these

---

[8] See Ernest C. Mossner and John V. Price's introduction to David Hume, *A Letter from a Gentleman to his friend in Edinburgh* (1745; Edinburgh, 1967) and the valuable reassessment of this affair by M. A. Stewart, "Hume, Wishart and the Edinburgh Chair," *Journal of the History of Philosophy,* forthcoming.

[9] James Oswald, *Letters concerning the Present State of the Church of Scotland* (Edinburgh, 1767), 36–37.

[10] See, for example, Richard B. Sher, "Moderates, Managers and Popular Politics in Mid-Eighteenth-Century Edinburgh: The Drysdale 'Bustle' of the 1760s," in *NP,* 179–209, and Norah Smith, "The Literary Career and Achievement of Robert Wallace" (Ph.D. diss., Edinburgh University, 1973), 484–85.

[11] *Auto.,* 307.

changes in the prevailing mood of the Scottish clergy. The hero of Smollett's *Humphry Clinker* (1771) was surprised to discover that "even the kirk of Scotland, so long reproached with fanaticism and canting, abounds at present with ministers celebrated for their learning, and respectable for their moderation.—I have heard their sermons with equal astonishment and pleasure."[12] It was mainly the Moderate literati whom Smollett had in mind when he dubbed Edinburgh "a hot-bed of genius."[13] An equally favorable impression of the Scottish clergy was recorded in Thomas Pennant's *A Tour in Scotland, 1769,* which also appeared in 1771:

> The clergy of *Scotland,* the most decent and consistent in their conduct of any set of men I ever met with of their order, are at present much changed from the furious, illiterate, and enthusiastic teachers of the old times, and have taken up the mild method of persuasion, instead of the cruel discipline of corporal punishment. Science almost universally flourishes among them; and their discourse is not less improving than the table they entertain the stranger at is decent and hospitable.[14]

Even Edward Topham, whose anti-Presbyterian prejudices greatly distorted his opinion of the Scottish kirk, acknowledged that the clergy of Edinburgh had recently given up their persecution of stage plays and stage players, preferring instead "to leave them to their ungodliness."[15]

Few people had more reason to appreciate the new spirit in the Church of Scotland than did David Hume. It was chiefly owing to "my Protestant Pastors," as he once called Blair, Robertson, Carlyle, Ferguson, and Jardine in an amusing letter from Paris,[16] that Hume was able to escape the wrath of his enemies in the kirk and live

---

[12] Tobias Smollett, *The Expedition of Humphry Clinker*, ed. Lewis M. Knapp (London, 1966), 232.

[13] Ibid., 233. The men of "genius" cited by Smollett were Blair, Ferguson, Home, Robertson, Robert Wallace, William Wilkie, David Hume, and Adam Smith. In the next sentence he added that Alexander Carlyle "wants nothing but inclination to figure with the rest upon paper." Though Smollett's phrase is frequently quoted, its full significance has eluded most commentators. All but two of the nine men of letters to whom he was referring were Presbyterian clergymen, and all but one of the latter was a Moderate born (like Smith and Smollett himself) within three years of 1720.

[14] Thomas Pennant, *A Tour in Scotland, 1769*, 2d ed. (London, 1772), 143. An appendix to Pennant's *Tour* contained the Moderate minister Daniel Brodie's account of the Church of Scotland, quoted in one of the epigraphs at the beginning of this chapter.

[15] Edward Topham, *Letters from Edinburgh* (1776; reprint, Edinburgh, 1971), 101.

[16] Hume to Blair et al., 6 April 1765, *HL*, 1:495.

peacefully and happily in Edinburgh during the last years of his life. Hume expressed his gratitude in various ways, including his will, which singled out Blair, Ferguson, and Home for special tokens of friendship.[17] Some of his most complimentary remarks about the Moderate literati appeared in a suppressed review of the second volume of the *History of Great Britain* (1773) by Rev. Robert Henry, who was not himself a Moderate in church politics. Toward the end of this piece Hume paid tribute to the enlightened Presbyterian ministers of Edinburgh, among whom "the *celebrated* Dr. Robertson" was judged the most distinguished figure: "It is happy for the inhabitants of this metropolis, which has naturally a great influence on the country, that the same persons who can make such a figure in profane learning, are entrusted with the guidance of the people in their spiritual concerns." The concluding paragraph extolled another Moderate Edinburgh clergyman, whom we know to be Hugh Blair, for uniting "Learning and Piety, Taste and Devotion, Philosophy and Faith."[18]

Was this the same David Hume who had written about the Scottish clergy in such disparaging terms during the 1740s?[19] It was not Hume but the clergy that had changed. As Hugh Blair proudly pointed out in a sermon that echoed the sentiments of Smollett and Pennant, the "sour," "narrow," "severe," and "intolerant" Scottish Presbyterian clergy of former times had become a knowledgeable, liberal, "conciliating" body "addicted to useful literature."[20] Alexander Carlyle traced the origins of this change of spirit among the clergy to a "set of young men" who entered the ministry during the 1730s and 1740s[21]—an obvious reference to his own circle of clerical friends, with whom Hume got on so well.

Though Carlyle himself never attained the high degree of literary fame accorded to several of his colleagues in the kirk, he was regarded in his day as the leading spokesman for the ideal of a learned, enlightened Presbyterian clergy. Carlyle's chief fear was that the gradual impoverishment of Scottish clergymen would soon reduce them to the same "narrow principles and illiberal spirit" that had flourished during the 1690s, when so many of the ministers called to parish livings had been "but half educated, of low habits and vulgar

---

[17] Mossner, 591, 599.

[18] "Review of Robert Henry's *History of Great Britain*," in *David Hume: Philosophical Historian*, ed. David Fate Norton and Richard H. Popkin (Indianapolis, 1965), 388.

[19] Cf. "Of National Characters" (1748), in Hume's *Philosophical Works*, ed. T. H. Green and T. H. Grose, 4 vols. (1882; reprint, Darmstadt, 1964), 3:244–57.

[20] *Sers.*, 4:424–25.

[21] Quoted in Henry Grey Graham, *Scottish Men of Letters in the Eighteenth Century* (London, 1908), 87n.

manners."[22] In spite of his persistent attempts to ease the financial plight of the clergy—first by campaigning for stipend augmentation in the late 1740s, and then by leading a more successful movement to exempt the clergy from the window tax—Carlyle was forced to admit that the "real" income of the great majority of his fellow ministers would continue to decline as long as Scotland experienced economic growth and rising prices. Inflation had doubled and in some cases tripled the cost of living since the mid-seventeenth century, said an anonymous pamphlet of 1748 that is usually ascribed to Carlyle, yet "the clergy are the only set of men in Scotland, whose income is not increased with the expense of the times."[23] Accelerated economic growth toward the end of the eighteenth century made matters even worse, especially for urban ministers paid in cash rather than crops. Although fairly well off himself as a result of a decent stipend, a sinecure church office, and his wife's sizable dowry, Carlyle publicly sympathized with the "difficult situation" faced by those members of the ministry who were trying to maintain the dignity of a cultured elite on the scantiest of incomes.[24]

For Carlyle, the solution to the dilemma confronting the Scottish clergy lay in the cultivation of polite literature and learning, which could provide compensation for their declining economic status. In a sermon preached before the Synod of Lothian and Tweeddale on 5 May 1767, Carlyle developed his views on this matter:

> Though the provision for the clergy has fallen very much in its value: yet is not their rank, in some respect, raised; not only by the removal of certain political prejudices, which separate them from many of superior order; but also by the rise of all orders of men beneath them, through the improvements of industry, and the increase of wealth? What advantage may not be gained, from the clergy having become the chief depositories of general learning, now that the attention and efforts of almost all other men are devoted to commerce alone? Do not our universities borrow many of their fairest ornaments from the church? And what glory may not be won in that field of distinction so lately opened to the learned of this country, I mean composition and the art of writing; where the whole range of science is before them, where there are laurels enough to satisfy the most ardent

[22] Alexander Carlyle, *The Usefulness and Necessity of a Liberal Education for Clergymen* (Edinburgh, 1793), 37–38.

[23] *Reasons for applying to the King and Parliament for an Augmentation of the Stipends of the Ministers of the Church of Scotland* (Edinburgh, 1748); Alexander Carlyle, *Essay upon Taxes* (Edinburgh, 1769), 22–23.

[24] Carlyle, *Liberal Education*, 20.

ambition of literary fame? It is here, ye rising hopes of our Jerusalem! my younger friends, who are still candidates for the ministry, who have forsaken all to follow this ungainful profession; it is here that you must look for your rewards in this world.[25]

Although the rewards to which Carlyle alluded were of a psychological nature, few members of his audience would have been unaware of the substantial *material* rewards that might also accrue to a clergyman of intellectual distinction.[26] A minister in Edinburgh, earning the highest stipend in the church, would have had to labor nearly thirty years to match the £4000 that William Robertson received for his *History of Charles V* just a year or two after Carlyle's synod sermon. Though Robertson's case was unusual, it was not unique: Robert Henry, for example, was paid £3300 for his *History of Great Britain* during the 1770s and early 1780s. Moreover, ministers who demonstrated merit as men of letters could usually count on indirect rewards such as chaplaincies, pensions, university chairs, and more lucrative parish livings in addition to whatever they got from the booksellers. Literary and philosophical accomplishments were the best hope for clergymen who were not content with a life of pious provincial poverty.

Carlyle's call for a clergy of polite letters was soon challenged by one of the lay leaders of the Popular party, Andrew Crosbie. In an anonymous pamphlet of 1769 titled *Thoughts of a Layman concerning Patronage and Presentations,* Crosbie argued that even if, as the Moderates claimed, lay patronage tends to encourage "polite literature" and "elegant erudition" among the clergy, those qualities are of "no use" for the proper performance of clerical duties. According to Crosbie, the true function of a parish minister is to render pastoral services such as visiting the sick and catechizing, for which one needs not polite learning but "plain sense, a sincere heart, and a sufficient knowledge of practical divinity."[27] No sooner had Crosbie's remarks appeared in print than the Moderates set out to discredit them. They certainly did not dispute the necessity of a conscientious performance of pastoral duties by every minister, but they rejected the inference that this ideal was somehow incompatible with polite man-

[25] Alexander Carlyle, *The Tendency of the Constitution of the Church of Scotland to form the Temper, Spirit, and Character of Her Ministers* (Edinburgh, 1767), reprinted in *The Scotch Preacher*, 4 vols. (Edinburgh, 1775–1789), vol. 2 (1777): 25–26.

[26] One clergyman ordained in the year of Carlyle's sermon, Thomas Somerville, candidly admitted that his subsequent career as a historian had been inspired chiefly by "pecuniary embarrassments." Somerville, 205.

[27] Andrew Crosbie, *Thoughts of a Layman concerning Patronage and Presentations* (Edinburgh, 1769), 32–33.

ners and learning. "Every clergyman should aspire after as much polite learning as he can possibly acquire," argued Henry Grieve, "and study the decorum of manners, which consists in the due medium between a low familiarity with, and a supercilious neglect of the people under his care."[28] To Moderates like Grieve and Carlyle, the proper role of the clergy was not so much to placate popular taste as to enlighten it, not so much to serve the people as to lead them.[29] Polite learning was thought to be the key to this process insofar as it contributed to the liberalization of manners and the decline of superstition, prejudice, and vice.[30] As late as 1793 Alexander Carlyle would still be using Crosbie's remarks of 1769 as a foil for his own views on the importance of liberal education and learning for members of the clergy.[31]

The election of Carlyle as moderator of the general assembly of 1770 represented, among other things, a rejection by Scottish churchmen of the anti-intellectualism implicit in Crosbie's statements of the previous year. If strict Calvinists like Rev. Thomas Walker of Dundonald had not forgiven Carlyle for "the offensive zeal whereby he distinguished himself in countenancing and promoting the licentious entertainments of the stage" during the *Douglas* controversy,[32] most of the ministers and elders in the assembly were apparently no longer troubled by such things. What mattered most to them were Carlyle's efforts to obtain relief from the window tax (which to Walker smacked of excessive worldliness and courtly vice)[33] and to encourage politeness and learning among the Scottish clergy. To old-line Presbyterians like Walker, Carlyle symbolized everything that was wrong with the "prevailing party" in the kirk. But to a growing number of churchmen, he was revered as the embodiment of the new style of polite, enlightened Presbyterianism that so impressed Smollett, Pennant, Hume, and others.

Perhaps the most remarkable aspect of the controversy set off by Andrew Crosbie's comments on the uselessness of polite learning for

---

[28] Henry Grieve, *Observations on the Overture concerning Patronage, with Remarks on a late Pamphlet, entitled, Thoughts of a Layman concerning Patronage and Presentations* (Edinburgh, 1769), 10–11.

[29] "We prefer their interest to their approbation," wrote Rev. Thomas Hardy in *The Principles of Moderation* (Edinburgh, 1782), 14.

[30] *A Letter to the Author of a Pamphlet on Patronage and Presentations* (Edinburgh, 1769), 10. See also *A Plain Answer to Thoughts of a Layman concerning Patronage and Presentations* (Edinburgh, 1769).

[31] *Liberal Education*, 1–2.

[32] Thomas Walker, *An Alarm to the Church of Scotland, on the Apparent Prevalence of a Worldly above a Spiritual and Religious Interest in her Supreme Judicatory* (Edinburgh, 1771), 8.

[33] Ibid., 11.

clergymen is the fact that so few ministers in the Popular party came to Crosbie's defense.[34] In the 1750s Crosbie might have received support from Walker of Dundonald's nephew John Witherspoon, who had stated in a sermon of 1758 that

> a minister should be separated and set apart for his own work; he should be consecrated to his office. It is little glory to him to be eminently skilled in any other science, except such as may be handmaids to theology, and are by him habitually turned into a divine channel.[35]

But Witherspoon had left Scotland in 1768 to become president of the College of New Jersey (Princeton) and, what is far more significant, he and most of the other clerical leaders of the Popular party had steadily shifted their position on the issue of polite literature and polite manners. In the divinity lectures that he delivered at Princeton, Witherspoon insisted at length on the importance of learning for ministers and specifically recommended the study of history because "a clergyman should be a man of liberal knowledge, and fit for the conversation and society of men of rank and letters."[36] His lectures on education emphasized the compatibility of religion with "true politeness"; his lectures on eloquence praised William Robertson and David Hume as two of the greatest modern stylists of English prose; and his lectures on moral philosophy recommended (though not always without reservation) several of the same writers whom he had formerly criticized or chided the Moderates for favoring, such as Leibniz, Hutcheson, Kames, Hume, and the English deists.[37] In matters of theology and ecclesiastical politics he could be surprisingly moderate, to the dismay of the evangelical New Lights responsible for his academic appointment.[38] He even tolerated a dance master and allowed a student production of John Home's *Alonzo* to go unpunished.[39] It is ironic that Witherspoon, whose Scottish ministry was devoted so largely to combating the Moderate vision of an enlightened clergy in an enlightened society, should be remembered today as the man most responsible for transporting the ideals and

---

[34] The only explicit support for Crosbie's remarks that I have found is in the anonymous *Patronage Demolished, and the Rights of the Christian People Restored* (Edinburgh, 1769), which was apparently by a seceder.

[35] *The Works of John Witherspoon*, 9 vols. (Edinburgh, 1804–1805), 5:40.

[36] Ibid., 8:26.

[37] Ibid., 8:192–95; John Witherspoon, *An Annotated Edition of Lectures on Moral Philosophy*, ed. Jack Scott (Newark, Del., 1982), for example, 187.

[38] Henry F. May, *The Enlightenment in America* (Oxford, 1976), 62–64, 347.

[39] Andrew L. Drummond, "Witherspoon of Gifford and American Presbyterianism," *RSCHS* 12 (1958): 185–201.

philosophical principles of the Scottish Enlightenment to the colleges of colonial America.[40]

Most of Witherspoon's colleagues in the Popular party followed a similar pattern of accommodation to the cultural and intellectual values of Moderatism during the second half of the eighteenth century.[41] Differences between the two ecclesiastical parties continued to exist, of course, but they were increasingly limited to matters of ecclesiastical and secular politics.[42] Prominent clergymen in the Popular party grew noticeably more tolerant of their brethren engaging in "profane" literary pursuits. John Erskine, for example, praised William Robertson's accomplishments as a man of letters in a laudatory sermon preached on the occasion of Robertson's death in 1793.[43] When members of the "wild clergy" visited the theater to see Sarah Siddons perform in 1784, Alexander Carlyle was delighted to report that even Andrew Hunter, the pious Edinburgh professor of divinity, let the incident pass without comment.[44]

As the Popular party softened its attitude toward polite culture, Alexander Carlyle saw the realization of his dream of an enlightened Presbyterian clergy compensating for its poverty with learning. More than a quarter of a century after first expressing this dream, Carlyle returned to it with renewed vigor in a sermon preached before the Society for the Benefit of Sons of the Clergy in 1793. "What branch of literature is there, in which some of the ministers of this church have not excelled?" he asked rhetorically. "What subject of fine writing is there, in which they do not, as authors, stand in the foremost ranks, which is a prouder boast than all the wealth and splendour of a hierarchy?" Excluding sermons and other religious writings commonly expected from the clergy, Carlyle continued:

> Who are they who have wrote the most excellent histories antient and modern? They are clergymen of this church. Who have given the clearest delineation of the human understanding, and the most sublime system of ethics that the world has ever seen? They are clergymen of this church. Who has written the best

[40] Douglas Sloan, *The Scottish Enlightenment and the American College Ideal* (New York, 1971), esp. chap. 4: "The Scottish Enlightenment Comes to Princeton: John Witherspoon."

[41] This point has been made in more general terms in William Law Mathieson, *The Awakening of Scotland: A History from 1747 to 1797* (Glasgow, 1910), 229, and William Ferguson, *Scotland: 1689 to the Present* (Edinburgh, 1968), 228.

[42] Hardy, *Principles of Moderation*, 4–5.

[43] Erskine, 262–77.

[44] Carlyle to Henry Dundas, 28 May 1784, Public Record Office, Home Office Papers (courtesy of Ian D. L. Clark).

system of rhetoric in our tongue, and exemplified it by his most eloquent orations? Who have excelled in some of the highest parts of poetry? Who have been and still are the most illustrious philosophers, mathematicians, and astronomers of their times, or have excelled in natural history, or have given the most useful lessons in agriculture, the first of all necessary arts? They have been clergymen of this church.[45]

The particular ministers whom Carlyle had in mind were identified in footnotes as Hugh Blair, George Campbell, Adam Dickson, Adam Ferguson, James Finlayson, Alexander Gerard, William Greenfield, Robert Henry, John Home, William Leechman, John Playfair, Thomas Reid, William Robertson, Matthew Stewart, John Walker, Robert Watson, and William Wilkie. It is an impressive group and might easily have been more so had Carlyle not omitted David Fordyce, Francis Hutcheson, Robert Wallace, and several younger and less eminent Presbyterian clergymen of letters, such as the poets and miscellaneous writers Thomas Blacklock, William Duff, John Logan, and John Ogilvie, the common sense philosopher James Oswald, and the historians William Lothian, George Ridpath, and Thomas Somerville. Despite these omissions, an analysis of this group reveals much about the nature of the clerical enlightenment in eighteenth-century Scotland. More than half of the seventeen ministers named by Carlyle were born within three years of 1720. Nearly all of them were affiliated more or less closely with the Moderate party, whereas only one (Robert Henry) seems to have sided frequently with the Popular party in the church courts.[46] Equally revealing is the fact that fourteen of these seventeen clergymen were principals (four) or professors (ten) at one or another of Scotland's five universities—more than half at the University of Edinburgh.[47] A chronological table of the polite literature published by these Scottish ministers between 1746 and 1793 includes many of the most popular and important works of their day

---

[45] *Liberal Education*, 33–34.

[46] See "The Life of Robert Henry," in Henry, *The History of Great Britain*, 5th ed., 12 vols. (London, 1814), 1:xix, where Henry is portrayed as an ecclesiastical independent who often sided with the Popular party against the Moderates. I have been unable to discover any firm evidence of Moderate party ties in the cases of Reid and Leechman, though a tenuous connection may be established on the basis of common friends and other circumstances.

[47] Robertson (Edinburgh), Leechman (Glasgow), Campbell (Marischal), and Watson (United College, St. Andrews) were college principals (the last three were also professors before or during their tenures as principal). Ferguson, Blair, Stewart, Playfair, Finlayson, Walker, and Greenfield were professors at the University of Edinburgh. Other chairs were held by Wilkie at St. Andrews, Gerard at Marischal and King's, and Reid at King's and Glasgow.

(see Table 4). Their range of intellectual interests is remarkably broad: of the forty-two works cited, eight are best categorized as poetry or drama, eight as history, nine as philosophy (including one philosophical biography), five as literary criticism or rhetoric, and twelve as mathematics, science, or technology (though most of the entries in this last category were noticeably briefer). The data also suggest a pattern of intellectual productivity—increasing toward the end of the 1750s, reaching a peak during the 1760s and 1770s, and gradually declining (except for scientific publications) during the 1780s and 1790s—that directly corresponds to the rise and fall of the Moderate literati of Edinburgh and the mature Scottish Enlightenment.

Alexander Carlyle was justifiably proud that the accomplishments of these clergymen of letters had brought the Scottish kirk an international reputation for learning far exceeding that of much larger and wealthier churches. Although the Church of Scotland remained poor, "ours is a splendid poverty," he observed; "it is the *paupertas fecunda vivorum.*"[48] Yet for how long could the Scottish clergy continue to attract young men of learning and intellect in the face of increasing financial strain? For how long would the poverty of the kirk seem "splendid" to young men with enlightened sensibilities? Even as Carlyle addressed the sons of the clergy in May 1793, William Robertson lay on his deathbed, and what Carlyle called the "æra of ability and genius"[49] in the church had already run its course. It was a short-lived phenomenon, dominated by the remarkable generation of Scottish divines born around 1720, among whom the Moderate literati of Edinburgh were the leading figures. By the end of the eighteenth century most of the seventeen authors cited by Carlyle had either died or retired, and few younger ministers had arisen to take their place in the republic of letters.

The demise of the clerical enlightenment will receive fuller treatment in chapter 8. The present concern has been to delineate the prevailing spirit and intellectual accomplishments of the Scottish Presbyterian clergy during the 1760s, 1770s, and 1780s, when the Moderate literati of Edinburgh were at their peak of power and influence in the established church and universities of Scotland. We have seen that contemporary observers reported a dramatic transformation in the manners, values, and tastes of the clergy, and that this transformation affected even ministers in the Popular party. We have also seen that roughly a score of clergymen, most of them Moderate principals and professors, distinguished themselves during this period by publishing works in the various genres of polite literature.

[48] *Liberal Education*, 35.   [49] Ibid., 39.

In dealing a blow to the traditional conception of Presbyterian Scotland as a center of fanaticism and persecution, these developments laid to rest the ghost of poor Thomas Aikenhead. But to prevent that ghost from returning to haunt its native land would involve enlightening the populace, using the bountiful academic and ecclesiastical resources that the Moderate literati now had at their disposal.

TABLE 4

Polite Literature Published by Scottish Ministers, 1746–1793

Date	Author	Short Title	Classification
1746	Matthew Stewart	*Some General Theorums*	m/s/t
1748	Thomas Reid	"Essay on Quantity"[a]	m/s/t
1755	William Leechman	Preface to Hutcheson's *System*[b]	p
1757	John Home	*Douglas*	p/d
1757	William Wilkie	*Epigoniad*	p/d
1758	John Home	*Agis*	p/d
1759	Alexander Gerard	*Essay on Taste*	lc/r
1759	William Robertson	*History of Scotland*	h
1760	John Home	*Siege of Aquileia*	p/d
1761	Matthew Stewart	*Tracts, Physical & Mathematical*	m/s/t
1762	George Campbell	*Dissertation on Miracles*	p
1762–1770	Adam Dickson	*Treatise of Agriculture*	m/s/t
1763	Hugh Blair	*Dissertation on Ossian*	lc/r
1764	Thomas Reid	*Inquiry into the Human Mind*	p
1767	Adam Ferguson	*Essay on Civil Society*	p
1769	Adam Ferguson	*Institutes of Moral Philosophy*	p
1769	John Home	*The Fatal Discovery*	p/d
1769	William Robertson	*History of Charles V*	h
1769	William Wilkie	*Moral Fables in Verse*	p/d
1771–1785	Robert Henry	*History of Great Britain*	h
1773	John Home	*Alonzo*	p/d
1774	Alexander Gerard	*Essay on Genius*	lc/r
1774	Thomas Reid	"Account of Aristotle's Logic"[c]	p
1776	George Campbell	*Philosophy of Rhetoric*	lc/r (or p)
1777	William Robertson	*History of America*	h
1777	Robert Watson	*History of Philip II*	h
1778	John Home	*Alfred*	p/d
1779	John Playfair	"Impossible Quantities"[d]	m/s/t
1783	Hugh Blair	*Lectures on Rhetoric*	lc/r
1783	Adam Ferguson	*Roman Republic*	h
1783	Robert Watson	*History of Philip III*	h

Date	Author	Short Title	Classification
1785	Thomas Reid	*Essays on Intellectual Powers*	p
1788	Adam Dickson	*Husbandry of the Ancients*	m/s/t (or h)
1788	William Greenfield	"Negative Quantities"[e]	m/s/t
1788	John Playfair	"Barometrical Measurements"[e]	m/s/t
1788	John Playfair	"Account of Matthew Stewart"[e]	m/s/t
1788	John Walker	"Motion of Sap in Trees"[e]	m/s/t
1788	Thomas Reid	*Essays on Active Powers*	p
1790	John Playfair	"Astronomy of the Brahmins"[f]	m/s/t
1791	William Robertson	*Disquisition concerning India*	h
1792	Adam Ferguson	*Principles of Moral Science*	p
1792	John Walker	*Institutes of Natural History*	m/s/t

NOTE. This table is limited to works of polite literature and learning published between 1746 and 1793 by the seventeen ministers cited by Alexander Carlyle in *The Usefulness and Necessity of a Liberal Education for Clergymen* (1793), 33–34n. All varieties of religious writings—including Blair's celebrated *Sermons*—have been excluded in accordance with Carlyle's intentions, as have polemical pamphlets, book reviews, short poems, heads of lectures, minor articles, and posthumously published writings from this period, such as *The Rev. Dr. John Walker's Report on the Hebrides in 1764 and 1771,* ed. Margaret M. McKay (Edinburgh, 1980).

CLASSIFICATION KEY: h = history; lc/r = literary criticism/rhetoric; m/s/t = mathematics/science/technology; p = philosophy; p/d = poetry/drama.

[a] In *Philosophical Transactions of the Royal Society of London,* Vol. 45.

[b] In Francis Hutcheson, *A System of Moral Philosophy,* vol. 1.

[c] In Henry Home, Lord Kames, *Sketches of the History of Man,* appendix to book 3, pt. 1.

[d] In *Philosophical Transactions of the Royal Society of London,* vol. 68.

[e] In *TRSE,* vol. 1.

[f] In *TRSE,* vol. 2.

---- ❋ ----

THE RELIGION OF VIRTUE
AND THE VIRTUE OF RELIGION

Whatever does not have happiness and virtue as its final goal is
worth nothing.

Denis Diderot, "The Encyclopedia," 1755

If virtue be the supreme good, its best and most signal effect is,
to communicate and diffuse itself.

Adam Ferguson,
Essay on the History of Civil Society, 1767

In their capacities as parish ministers and university professors the
Moderate literati of Edinburgh functioned as ideological propagandists, striving to instill the main tenets of their moral philosophy into
their congregations and students. "The end of all preaching is, to
persuade men to become good," Hugh Blair asserted. "Every Sermon should therefore be a persuasive oration."[50] Alexander Carlyle
echoed these words when he defined "the Christian orator's voca-
tion" as "enlightning the minds, and purifying the passions of men,
to make them wise and virtuous and happy."[51] This concern with
moral preaching does not necessarily mean that the Moderate literati
were the Socinians or deists that their critics have so frequently thought
them to be. It simply means that they regarded ethical concerns as
inseparable from doctrinal ones, as Hugh Blair argued in the first of
his collected sermons, "On the Union of Piety and Morality."[52] Of
course, Blair and his Moderate colleagues did not originate the moral
sermon in the Scottish Presbyterian tradition, but they were chiefly
responsible for perfecting it as a mode of pulpit discourse and for
giving it respectability and widespread acceptance in the church.

Similarly, Adam Ferguson did not invent the normative, didactic
approach to Scottish academic moral philosophy, but he was the first
Edinburgh professor of that discipline to apply it successfully. Ferguson told his students that "Moral Philosophy is not the knowledge
of *what is,* but rather of *what ought to be*"—though he added, with no
apparent concern for Hume's warning about the danger of deriving
"ought" from "is," that "what ought to be" could be ascertained only

[50]*Lects.*, 2:105, 125.
[51]*Liberal Education*, 16.
[52]*Sers.*, vol. 1, no. 1; Clark diss., chap. 7.

on the basis of "what is."[53] On this point he was in essential agreement with the father of Scottish academic moral philosophy during the age of the Enlightenment, Francis Hutcheson, who declared that "the intention of Moral Philosophy is to direct men to that course of action which tends effectually to promote their greatest happiness and perfection; as far as it can be done by observations and conclusions discoverable from the constitution of nature."[54] Hutcheson and Ferguson were both moral Newtonians of a sort, striving to discover nature's secret laws about man and society in order to reveal the majesty of God's handiwork, but they insisted that the purely descriptive aspect of moral philosophy was subservient to its prescriptive aspect. A strictly empirical science of the moral world was impossible for them because it demanded a positivist methodology that would have left too little room for moralizing. Far from emphasizing the potential continuity between the study of the physical and moral realms, Ferguson stressed the contrast between them: "physical science" was defined as the knowledge of natural uniformities or matters of fact, "moral science" as "the knowledge of what is right and proper in the actions and characters of men."[55]

It is just this emphasis on the inculcation of moral precepts that most clearly differentiates the didactic or pedagogical tradition of Hutcheson, Ferguson, and most other eighteenth-century Scottish professors of moral philosophy from the more rigorously analytical or "scientific" approach of David Hume.[56] To be sure, Hutcheson and Ferguson did not always agree on particular ethical and political issues, but they both believed that the primary purpose of instruction in moral philosophy was to prepare young men for practicing "virtue" in all spheres of life, religious as well as secular, public as well as private. As Whig-Presbyterian moralists they felt somewhat threatened by the Humean approach to moral philosophy, both be-

---

[53] *Insts.*, 13–14; *Princs.*, 1:5; David Hume, *A Treatise of Human Nature*, 2d ed., ed. L. A. Selby-Bigge, and P. H. Nidditch (Oxford, 1978), 469.

[54] Francis Hutcheson, *A System of Moral Philosophy*, 2 vols. (London, 1755), 1:1. "The Rev. Adam Ferguson, A. M." is among the many names of subscribers prefixed to this posthumous work.

[55] *Insts.*, 4–7.

[56] On Hume, see especially Duncan Forbes, *Hume's Philosophical Politics* (Cambridge, 1975). It is, of course, an open question as to how closely Hume would have conformed to the moralizing conventions of the discipline if he had won the Edinburgh chair in 1745. The academic career of his friend Adam Smith indicates that a Scottish professor of moral philosophy could be a good deal more detached and "scientific" in the classroom than fervent moralists like Hutcheson, Ferguson, or Beattie. But for a different view of Hume and Smith, as "practical moralists," see the most recent essays by Nicholas Phillipson cited in the bibliographical essay.

cause of its ideological and religious "impartiality" and because of its tendency to transform moral philosophy from a far-reaching, didactic, character-building discipline into an abstract, descriptive, and more narrowly metaphysical and epistemological enterprise. In contrast to Hume, they were chiefly concerned with moralizing rather than analyzing. Hence Hutcheson's charge that book three of Hume's *Treatise of Human Nature* lacked "a certain Warmth in the Cause of Virtue" and his preference for a flock of bright, if philosophically unaccomplished, young men with sound Whig-Presbyterian credentials for the Edinburgh moral philosophy chair that Hume so coveted in the mid-1740s.[57] Hence also Ferguson's impatience with the common philosophical practice of confounding the terms "moral" and "mental", as a result of which, he was sorry to say, "any theoretical question relating to mind has been substituted for moral philosophy; and speculations of little moment have supplanted the study of what men ought to be, and of what they ought to wish, for themselves, for their country, and for mankind."[58] As Ferguson later put it in an unpublished dialogue directed against Hume and Smith, the only "important or Genuine Question of Moral Philosophy" is *"de finibus,* or what is the End?"[59]

The "end" was to guide people to virtue and happiness: herein lies the first point of convergence between the moral sermons of Hugh Blair and other Moderate preachers and the moral philosophy lectures of Adam Ferguson—a point about which more will be said in the next chapter. A second point of convergence concerns the rhetorical means employed to attain that end. As polite men of letters, the Moderates took it for granted that all forms of spoken discourse should be "correct," "polished," and "rational," which is to say, free from the taint of enthusiasm, provincialism, and impropriety. As moralists and ideologists, on the other hand, they were naturally drawn to a vigorous and forceful mode of address that would inspire as well

[57] Hutcheson to Sir Gilbert Elliot, Lord Minto, 4 July 1744, NLS, 11004:57; Hume to Hutcheson, 17 September 1739, *HL*, 1:32. In the same letter Hume identified himself with the "Anatomist" who probes the "most secret Springs & Principles" of the mind without attempting to pass moral or aesthetic judgments on his subject. Hutcheson's pedagogical plea that moral philosophy be "a medicine for the disorders of the soul" ("To the Students in Universities," *A Short Introduction to Moral Philosophy* [Glasgow, 1747], iv) forms an illuminating contrast, for the tension between anatomy and medicine as competing scientific models for moral philosophy goes to the root of the distinction I am making.

[58] *Insts.*, 83.

[59] Adam Ferguson, " 'Of the Principle of Moral Estimation: A Discourse between David Hume, Robert Clerk, and Adam Smith': An Unpublished MS," ed. Ernest Campbell Mossner, *JHI* 21 (1960): 232. Cf. Hutcheson, *Short Introduction*, 2.

as inform their listeners. If, as Hugh Blair claimed, true eloquence was the "Art of Persuasion,"[60] then moral preaching and teaching would have to be more than polite and correct in order to be eloquent and inspiring: they would also have to be lively and entertaining, perhaps even passionate and emotional.

The notion that the Moderates were committed to a dynamic style of pulpit rhetoric directly contradicts their traditional image as dry, philosophical, elitist preachers. Did they not read their sermons in the formal manner of the English Augustans?[61] Did they not fill them with large words and complicated, abstract ideas that lay far beyond the comprehension of ordinary people?[62] Were they not, in short, accurately described by John Witherspoon when he castigated certain unnamed preachers for resorting to "an ostentatious swell of words, or a pointed ornamented foppery of style, so ill suited to the gravity of the pulpit; an abstracted, refined, or philosophical disquisition, which, if it has any meaning at all, perhaps not three in the audience can understand"?[63] These common misconceptions about Moderate preaching can be cleared up quite simply by examining the thorough discussion of pulpit eloquence in the twenty-ninth lecture of Hugh Blair's course on rhetoric and belles lettres, which may be regarded as the bible of Moderate pulpit oratory.

According to Blair, "the chief characteristics of the Eloquence suited to the Pulpit" are "Gravity and Warmth." Too much attention to the former is likely to produce "dull uniform solemnity," whereas an overemphasis on the latter makes for sermons that are "theatrical and light."[64] The ideal sermon maintains a delicate balance between these two tendencies, which Blair later associates with English and French preaching styles, respectively.[65] Blair is especially critical of such celebrated English preachers as Samuel Clarke and Bishop Butler, whom he accuses of abstract philosophizing devoid of all warmth and passion.[66] Having emerged as part of a reaction to the religious enthusiasm that had racked England in the seventeenth century,[67] this abstract style of preaching is thought to violate Blair's fundamental canons of pulpit eloquence. "It must be remembered," he writes,

---

[60] *Lects.*, 2:3–4, 104.

[61] Charles Rogers McCain, "Preaching in Eighteenth-Century Scotland: A Comparative Study of the Extant Sermons of Ralph Erskine, John Erskine, and Hugh Blair" (Ph.D. diss., Edinburgh University, 1949), 95.

[62] Crosbie, *Thoughts of a Layman*, 34–35.

[63] *Works*, 6:265.

[64] *Lects.*, 2:107.

[65] Ibid., 119.

[66] Ibid., 123–24.

[67] Ibid., 122.

that all the Preachers instructions are to be of the practical kind; and that persuasion must ever be his ultimate object. It is not to discuss some abstruse point, that he ascends the Pulpit. It is not to illustrate some metaphysical truth, or to inform men of something. which they never heard before; but it is to make them better men; it is to give them, at once, clear views, and persuasive impressions of religious truth.

From this it follows that the eloquence of the pulpit

must be Popular Eloquence. One of the first qualities of preaching is to be popular; not in the sense of accommodation to the humours and prejudices of the people (which tends only to make a Preacher contemptible), but, in the true sense of the word, calculated to make impression on the people; to strike and to seize their hearts. I scruple not therefore to assert, that the abstract and philosophical manner of preaching, however it may have sometimes been admired, is formed upon a very faulty idea, and deviates widely from the just plan of Pulpit Eloquence.[68]

In order for a preacher to satisfy fully Blair's criteria of "Popular Eloquence," he must be "very perspicuous" in his use of language. "All unusual, swoln, or high sounding words, should be avoided," Blair argues, as should "affected smartness and quaintness of expression" likely to "give to a Preacher that air of foppishness, which he ought, above all things, to shun."[69] But simplicity of expression should not be thought incompatible with a vigorous and lively manner of delivery. On the contrary, Blair states, "the words employed may be all plain words, easily understood, and in common use; and yet the Style may be abundantly dignified, and, at the same time, very lively and animated. *For a lively and animated Style is extremely suited to the Pulpit.*"[70] In Blair's opinion, one of the greatest obstacles to eloquent preaching is the peculiarly English habit of reading sermons. The problem is that

no discourse, which is designated to be persuasive, can have the same force when read, as when spoken. The common people all feel this, and their prejudice against this practice is not without foundation in nature. What is gained hereby in point of cor-

---

[68] Ibid., 105–106. Cf. William Leechman's remarks on Francis Hutcheson's similar style of preaching in the preface to Hutcheson's *System of Moral Philosophy*, 1:xxxviii–xxxix.

[69] *Lects.*, 2:114, 116.

[70] Ibid., 115. Emphasis added.

rectness, is not equal, I apprehend, to what is lost in point of persuasion and force.[71]

Whether a sermon should be written out fully and committed to memory or delivered from "short notes" is to Blair a matter best left to the judgment and talents of each particular minister, but he is unequivocal in his opposition to the practice of reading sermons from prepared texts.[72]

Existing evidence indicates that Moderate preachers followed the rules of pulpit eloquence laid down in Blair's rhetoric lectures. Their extant sermons tend to be brief in length, clear and simple in diction, unexceptionable in doctrine, and practical rather than abstract in subject matter.[73] Blair himself privately described his first volume of sermons as being "mostly of a popular and Sentimental kind; intermixed with one or two of a more Philosophical cast"[74]—a description that applies equally well to the sermons of the other Moderates of his generation. Almost every one of Blair's sermons was a carefully structured commentary on a specific moral theme suggested by a relevant scriptural text, such as "The Duties of the Young," "The Duties and Consolations of the Aged," "The Importance of Order in Conduct," "The Compassion of Christ," "Gentleness," and "Death." That Blair did not read these sermons seems certain from the strong remarks on this topic in his rhetoric lectures, but more precise evidence exists regarding some of his Moderate colleagues. Thomas Somerville recited his sermons from memory, whereas William Robertson and John Drysdale preached exclusively, and often quite powerfully, from note cards.[75] Perhaps the most unusual style of preaching was the one employed by John Home during his brief tenure as minister of Athelstaneford. Home generally wrote out and

---

[71] Ibid., 118.

[72] Ibid., 117–18. Ironically, most of Blair's principles of pulpit eloquence were violated by the nineteenth-century Evangelical leader Thomas Chalmers, who read his sermons in a self-consciously grandiloquent manner. See Stewart J. Brown, *Thomas Chalmers and the Godly Commonwealth in Scotland* (Oxford, 1982), 58–59.

[73] James L. Golden, "Hugh Blair: Minister of St. Giles," *Quarterly Journal of Speech* 38 (1952): 155–60, except on doctrine. John Erskine said William Robertson's sermons were "so plain, that the most illiterate might easily understand them," and he praised Robertson's expository lectures for their strict Calvinist doctrine as well as their sound moral guidance. Erskine, 274.

[74] Blair to [William Strahan], 29 October 1776, NLS, 1707:4. One contemporary writer went so far as to claim that Blair's sermons were "possessed of an evangelical Spirit." Robert Alves, *Sketches of a History of Literature* (1794; reprint, Gainsville, Fla., 1967), 236.

[75] Somerville, 173; Andrew Dalzel, "Account of the Life of Rev. John Drysdale," *TRSE* 3 (1794), app. 2:40–42; Stewart, xlvii.

memorized about two-thirds of a sermon, leaving the final third to be completed extempore. According to one of his contemporary biographers, "these unpremeditated perorations, occasionally eloquent, were delivered with more than his usual vehemence of action, and are said to have been not a little admired by his rustic audience."[76] Blair, too, possessed the ability to move congregations, even if his style of preaching was somewhat stiff and formal.[77] Among the members of his congregation at St. Giles were Lord Kames, who called him "the best preacher in Britain," and James Boswell, who once remarked that Blair "would stop hounds by his eloquence."[78] At the end of his life Blair could still fill a church to capacity whenever word got out that he would be preaching the following Sunday.[79]

Blair's popularity as a moral preacher was matched by Adam Ferguson's as a moral teacher, and for similar reasons. Ferguson did not read his lectures in the manner of most other eighteenth-century professors; rather, he spoke freely from notes or outlines that were continually being revised and republished in increasingly sophisticated forms—first as the *Analysis of Pneumatics and Moral Philosophy*, then as the *Institutes of Moral Philosophy*, and finally as the two-volume *Principles of Moral and Political Science*. In the introduction to the *Principles* Ferguson explained his lecturing style in terms that are reminiscent of Blair's remarks about the proper method of delivering a sermon:

> Conceiving that discussion, and even information, might come with more effect from a person that was making his own highest efforts of disquisition and judgement, than from one that might be languishing while he read, or repeated a lecture previously composed; he [Ferguson] determined, while he bestowed his utmost diligence in studying his subject, in chusing the order in which it was to be treated, and in preparing himself for every successive step he was to make in his course, to have no more in writing than the heads, or short notes, from which he was to speak; preparing himself however very diligently for every particular day's work.[80]

Ferguson's pedagogical dedication and "uncommon flow of eloquence" produced a series of lectures that were, according to one

---

[76] John Lee, "John Home," *EBS*, 4:645.

[77] Somerville, 57; John Hill, *An Account of the Life and Writings of Hugh Blair* (Edinburgh, 1807), 191; Blair to Boswell, 19 February 1763, YUL, C156.

[78] Quoted in Golden, "Hugh Blair," 155. Cf. Robert Morrell Schmitz, *Hugh Blair* (New York, 1948), 16.

[79] "Dr. Hugh Blair," *Public Characters of 1800–1801* (Dublin, 1801), 243.

[80] *Princs.*, 1:v.

admiring student, "firm, manly, and impressive" while "mild and elegant."[81] This combination of vigor and polish helped to transform the moral philosophy professorship at Edinburgh University from a little-known and generally undistinguished chair, far below its counterpart at Glasgow in stature and popularity, into the leading chair of moral philosophy in Great Britain, and perhaps in all of Europe.

Ferguson's lively, dynamic manner of teaching moral philosophy may have been influenced by his friend William Cleghorn, whose lectures he probably attended during the early 1740s.[82] Another possible influence came from Glasgow, where Francis Hutcheson, professor of moral philosophy from 1730 until his death in 1746, lectured extemporaneously while pacing back and forth in front of the classroom.[83] This method was ideally suited to Hutcheson's fervently moralistic approach to his discipline. As William Robert Scott put it, Hutcheson was above all else "a teacher who *preached* philosophy."[84] Alexander Carlyle, who attended Hutcheson's moral philosophy class "with great satisfaction and improvement" in 1743 and 1744, recalled that the professor "raised the attention of his hearers at all times; and when the subject led him to explain and enforce the moral virtues and duties, he displayed a fervent and persuasive eloquence which was irresistible."[85] Hutcheson's innovative use of English in the classroom was also well suited to his rhetorical and pedagogical aims, for dry, scholastic Latin did not constitute a very effective medium for didactic moralizing.[86] For Hutcheson, a Presbyterian minister by training, the discipline of moral philosophy fulfilled a social and ideological function for which a vibrant mode of academic "preaching" was deemed most appropriate.

The same holds true for Adam Ferguson. Like Hutcheson, Ferguson entered academics from the ranks of the Presbyterian clergy, and his approach to moral philosophy betrayed the manner and method of a Christian preacher. In spirit and style as well as in ethical and ideological substance, his lectures were the academic equivalent of Hugh Blair's moral sermons. Blair assumed the pedagogical

[81] [Robert Bisset], "Dr. Adam Fergusson," *Public Characters of 1799–1800* (London, 1799), 448.

[82] Douglas Nobbs, "The Political Ideas of William Cleghorn, Hume's Academic Rival," *JHI* 26 (1965): 575–86.

[83] *Auto.*, 78.

[84] William Robert Scott, *Francis Hutcheson: His Life, Teaching and Position in the History of Philosophy* (Cambridge, 1900), 65.

[85] *Auto.*, 78. Cf. Leechman, preface to Hutcheson's *System of Moral Philosophy*, 1:xxxii–xxxiii.

[86] Cf. the different interpretation in Peter Jones, "The Scottish Professoriate and the Polite Academy, 1720–46," in *WV*, 108.

duties of an ethical teacher, whereas Ferguson adopted rhetorical features formerly associated with pulpit oratory. In short, Ferguson preached the "religion of virtue" in the classroom much as Blair and other Moderate ministers expounded on the "virtue of religion" from the pulpit.

CHAPTER FIVE

The Teaching and Preaching of Moderate Morality

❧

CHRISTIAN STOICISM,
OR "PRIVATE VIRTUE"

A man is not fit to live at all, far less to live so long as I have done, who does not adjust his mind to his State in the Universe with resignation to that Supreme Being who brings us forth here to act a part for a while on his Theatre, & then, according as that part has been acted, removes us into a different station.

Hugh Blair, Letter to James Boswell, 1789

The Stoic enlisted himself, as a willing instrument in the hand of God, for the good of his fellow-creatures.

Adam Ferguson,
Principles of Moral and Political Science, 1792

If the central point of Moderate moral teaching and preaching was the cultivation of polite yet impassioned eloquence in the service of virtue and happiness, it is now necessary to determine what the Moderates meant by the latter terms. A good place to begin such an investigation is with Adam Ferguson's personal avowal of Stoicism in the introduction to his *Principles of Moral and Political Science*. Although Ferguson was dismayed that Stoicism had become "in the gentility of modern times, proverbial for stupidity," he was comforted that it had continued to be "revered" by the few modern philosophers, such as Shaftesbury, Montesquieu, James Harris, and Hutcheson, who understood its "real spirit."[1] As Ferguson saw the matter, the "real spirit" of Stoicism had nothing at all to do with the vulgar concept of contemplative withdrawal from the world. Indeed, Ferguson made a point of renouncing inactivity and withdrawal and proclaiming man an active, social creature. For Ferguson, and for the

[1] *Princs.*, 2:7–8.

other Moderate literati as well, the "real spirit" of Stoicism lay in the belief that virtue must be defined primarily in terms of selfless duty or benevolence, that virtue is the sole path to true happinness, and that, as Ferguson once put it, "virtue is, in reality, a qualification of the mind."[2]

Once again the way had been paved for the Moderate literati by Francis Hutcheson. In 1725, when the Moderate literati were young children, Hutcheson's first book had appeared bearing the long and significant title *An Inquiry into the Original of Our Ideas of Beauty and Virtue: in Two Treatises. In which the Principles of the late Earl of Shaftesbury are explain'd and defended, against the Author of the Fable of the Bees: and the Ideas of Moral Good and Evil are establish'd, according to the Sentiments of the antient Moralists*. The "antient Moralists" mentioned in the title of the *Inquiry* were in fact the "Stoicks," who taught that the highest good and greatest happiness consist in the exercise of as much virtue or benevolence as possible, given one's capabilities and "Station in the World."[3] Although he sometimes confronted Mandeville on utilitarian ground, by challenging his claim that the good of society may result from the vices of individuals within it, Hutcheson mainly followed Shaftesbury and the Stoics in regarding unforeseen and unintended social consequences as entirely irrelevant to virtue and happiness. For Hutcheson, virtue or benevolence is literally its own reward, in the sense that the virtuous man attains happiness from the very state of being virtuous, regardless of the results of his action. "The reality and perfection of virtue" therefore depended not on "external success, but on the inward temper of the soul."[4]

This fundamentally Stoic edifice was buttressed by Hutcheson's Christian principles. In the preface to the second edition of the *Inquiry* (1726), Hutcheson explicitly disassociated himself from his philosophical master Shaftesbury regarding religious matters. "It is indeed to be wished," he wrote, "that [Shaftesbury] had abstained from mixing with such Noble Performances, some Prejudices he had received against Christianity; a Religion which gives us the truest Idea of Virtue, and recommends the Love of God and of Mankind, as the Sum of all true Religion."[5] In the posthumously published *System of Moral Philosophy*, he noted that the definition of virtue as benevolence was nothing more than a restatement of the sum of Christian

---

[2] *Insts.*, 239.

[3] Francis Hutcheson, *An Inquiry into the Original of Our Ideas of Beauty and Virtue*, 2d ed. (1726; reprint, New York, 1971), 187, 194–95.

[4] Francis Hutcheson, *A System of Moral Philosophy*, 2 vols. (London, 1755), 1:224.

[5] *Inquiry*, xxi. Cf. Stanley Grean, *Shaftesbury's Philosophy of Religion and Ethics* (Athens, Ohio, 1967), chap. 7.

moral law as recorded in Matthew 12:30, 31: "viz. *Loving God* and *our neighbour*."[6] Moreover, Hutcheson brought God into his essentially Stoic discussion of moral theory as a replacement for the Stoic concept of fate:

> When we despair of glory, and even of executing all the good we intend, 'tis a sublime exercise to the soul to persist in acting the rational and social part as it can; discharging its duty well, and committing the rest to *God*. Thus the most heroick excellence, and its consequent happiness and inward joy, may be attained under the worst circumstances of fortune; nor is any station of life excluded from the enjoyment of the supreme good.[7]

Since "in human affairs men must follow probabilities," they can have no certainty that even the most benign actions will not have evil consequences.[8] This being the case, they should practice virtue as best they can and leave the rest to divine Providence, comforted by the belief that "God will espouse [the virtuous person's] cause by making the virtuous happy, either in this life, or the next."[9] For Hutcheson, only the existence and perfection of God save the Stoic system from ultimate pessimism and make happiness possible "in this uncertain world."[10]

Hutcheson's brand of Christian Stoicism exerted a powerful influence on Scottish moral philosophy and religion throughout the eighteenth century.[11] It was Adam Ferguson and the Moderate literati of Edinburgh, however, who adopted Hutcheson's Christian-Stoic principles most enthusiastically and completely. For Ferguson, as for Hutcheson and the Stoics, "the qualities of man's nature are of more moment than any of the circumstances in which men are placed and . . . the first concern of a man is to consider what he himself is, not how he is situated."[12] Virtue depends not on the consequences of our actions, which lie outside our control, but on the peculiarly "human" qualities of "will, intention, and design, whether benevolent or malicious."[13] Thus, the "fundamental Law of Morality" or "greatest good competent to man's nature" is a benevolent disposition or, as Fer-

---

[6] *System of Moral Philosophy*, 1:225–26.

[7] Ibid., 245–46.

[8] Ibid.

[9] Ibid., 248.

[10] Ibid., 204, 215. Cf. David Fate Norton, *David Hume: Common-Sense Moralist, Sceptical Metaphysician* (Princeton, 1982), 87–92.

[11] See, for example, Adam Smith, *The Theory of Moral Sentiments*, ed. D. D. Raphael and A. L. Macfie (Oxford, 1976), esp. 5–10.

[12] *Insts.*, 146, 162, 172.

[13] Ibid., 177–78.

guson prefers to call it, "the love of mankind."[14] A benevolent dis-position normally manifests itself in benevolent conduct, for "the law which requires the love of mankind . . . likewise requires every ex-ternal action that is suited to this affection."[15] Conversely, actions performed without this benevolent spirit cannot be virtuous, even if they should have the most beneficial consequences.[16] Virtue, then, is "that qualification of soul which fits the individual to procure the good of mankind."[17]

In the course of everyday life, benevolence or the love of human-ity means for Ferguson the love of one's family, friends, and soci-ety.[18] The virtuous person understands that human beings are social animals whose private interests are intrinsically bound up with those of the society in which they live, and he therefore strives to carry out the duties of his social station as conscientiously as possible.[19] As for happiness, Ferguson believes that "the definitions of perfect happi-ness and perfect virtue are the same."[20] Happiness is ultimately re-ducible to a benevolent state of mind and the humane, socially con-structive conduct that normally follows from it. It does not consist "in a freedom from trouble, or in having nothing to do."[21] Nor does it depend on one's position in life, or the consequences of one's ac-tions, or "external circumstances," or any other factor beyond the agency of human control.[22] Ferguson's relentless insistence on the Stoic conception of happiness prompted one former student to complain that "he is so entirely and constantly occupied with it, as to forget every thing else."[23]

Like Hutcheson, Ferguson and the Moderate literati relied on Christian notions of the deity to ensure a meaningful and just order in human affairs. In the *Institutes* Ferguson writes:

> It is happy to have continually in view that we are members of society, and of the community of mankind; that we are instru-ments in the hand of God for the good of his creatures; that, if

---

[14] Ibid., 163.

[15] Ibid., 175–76, 254.

[16] Ibid., 175.

[17] Adam Ferguson, *Analysis of Pneumatics and Moral Philosophy. For the Use of Students in the College of Edinburgh* (Edinburgh, 1766), 33.

[18] David Kettler, *The Social and Political Thought of Adam Ferguson* (Columbus, Ohio, 1965), 150.

[19] *Insts.*, 111–12.

[20] Ibid., 166.

[21] Ibid., 169.

[22] Ibid., 172.

[23] Sir James Mackintosh's journal, 1812, in *Memoirs of the Life of the Right Honourable Sir James Mackintosh*, 2d ed., 2 vols. (London, 1836), 2:243–44.

we are ill members of society, or unwilling instruments in the hand of God, we do our utmost to counteract our nature, to quit our station, and to undo ourselves.[24]

It is no accident that the section of the *Institutes* dealing with moral laws appears immediately after the section dealing with the existence and attributes of God. Since the world is governed by a God whose chief attributes are "Unity, Power, Wisdom, Goodness, and Justice," Stoicism loses its quality of desperate inwardness or pessimism.[25] God gives moral meaning to the universe and sees to it that "every part, in the order of nature, is calculated for the preservation of the whole."[26] Hugh Blair made a similar point in a different context when he quoted Calvin to show that the Christian doctrine of "moral necessity" is distinguishable from "the fate of the Stoics" because "we place God at the head of all, as the supreme director and governor."[27]

The main conclusion to be drawn from Ferguson's lectures on ethics is that to attain true happiness people should concentrate on being benevolent in thought and deed, leaving results, outcomes, and consequences in the capable hands of the deity. "Men are charged only with the care of chusing what is good, and of doing what is right," Ferguson remarks in his earliest lecture outline. "Events are reserved to God."[28] Here is the central tenet of Christian Stoicism as formulated by the Moderate literati. It is a doctrine calculated above all else to increase "warmth for virtue" and decrease concern about worldly pleasure and success. It is also a profoundly conservative doctrine, in that it emphasizes the limited extent of human control over the world, the desirability of total resignation to the will of God, and the insignificance of one's social "station" for the attainment of true happiness.

The first of these conservative implications was made explicit in Ferguson's *Essay on the History of Civil Society:*

Every step and every movement of the multitude, even in what are termed enlightened ages, are made with equal blindness to the future; and nations stumble upon establishments, which are indeed the result of human action, but not the execution of any human design.[29]

[24] *Insts.*, 173. Cf. *Essay*, 55.

[25] *Insts.*, 123.

[26] Ibid., 130.

[27] John Calvin, *Institutes of the Christian Religion*, quoted in *Objections against the Essays on Morality and Natural Religion Examined*, by Hugh Blair et al. (Edinburgh, 1756), 13.

[28] *Analysis*, 27.

[29] *Essay*, 122.

It is not difficult to see why this well-known passage has appealed so strongly to modern social conservatives wishing to minimize the ability of human beings to redesign their institutions by means of rational planning.[30] But to understand Ferguson's meaning fully, it is necessary to read this passage in the context of the Moderates' faith in the existence of an all-powerful, benevolent deity guiding human history according to divine purposes. Thus, the realization that history often proceeds according to no human plan does not lead Ferguson to conclude that history is unplanned or chaotic. It is just that the planning is being done by God rather than by man.

If the organization of the universe is wholly under the direction of God, then it is well for human beings to resign themselves to the divine order of things and strive to be virtuous and happy in their God-given stations:

> *I am in the station which God has assigned me,* says Epictetus. With this reflection, a man may be happy in every station; without it, he cannot be happy in any. Is not the appointment of God sufficient to outweigh every other consideration? This rendered the condition of a slave agreeable to Epictetus, and that of a monarch to Antoninus. This consideration renders any situation agreeable to a rational nature which delights not in particular interests, but in universal good.[31]

The example of the Greek slave Epictetus is somewhat misleading, since Ferguson, Blair, and the other Moderates were opposed to slavery on humanitarian grounds.[32] Yet they were all very much in favor of the hierarchical organization of society,[33] and their Christian-Stoic principles served to bolster their socially conservative views.

The classic Moderate statement on this matter was John Drysdale's sermon "On the Distinction of Ranks," which argued that opposition to the existing, hierarchical structure of society is not only necessarily ineffectual as a means of improving the lot of the lower orders (since virtue and happiness are equally attainable at all social levels) but also blasphemous and anarchical (since it constitutes implicit rebellion against divine government). Although Drysdale died in 1788,

---

[30] See, for example, F. A. Hayek, "The Results of Human Action but not of Human Design," in Hayek, *Studies in Philosophy, Politics and Economics* (Chicago, 1967), 96–105.

[31] *Insts.,* 173–74.

[32] Ibid., 219–20; *Sers.,* 1:144; Stewart, lxxiv.

[33] After conversing with Blair and Robertson on the subject of "subordination and government," Samuel Johnson confided to Boswell: " 'Sir, these two doctors are good men, and wise men' " (*Tour,* 388). On few other matters were Johnson and the Moderates in such close agreement.

"On the Distinction of Ranks" did not appear in print until the beginning of 1793, when a collection of his sermons was published by his son-in-law Andrew Dalzel.[34] The book's chief promoter was William Robertson, who helped to prepare it for the press and sent complimentary copies and glowing accounts to several prelates in the Church of England immediately after publication.[35] Although Robertson was probably motivated in part by his family ties to Drysdale and Dalzel, ideological considerations also played an important role. Thus, in a letter of February 1793 Robertson wrote: "There is one Sermon, *On the Distinction of Ranks*, which seems as [if] it had been written with foresight of some of the wild tenets of the present day, and may be considered as a very usefull antidote against them."[36]

Robertson apparently approved of Drysdale's Christian-Stoic logic as well as his conservative conclusions. According to his eldest son, Robertson was a zealous student and "great admirer" of Stoic philosophy even before he acquired a taste for history.[37] His earliest literary project was a translation of the *Meditations* of Marcus Aurelius, which he gave up following the publication of Francis Hutcheson's translation in 1742.[38] The first Latin discourse that he delivered in his capacity as principal of Edinburgh University is said to have been "a beautiful panegyric on the Stoical Philosophy."[39] Some years later Robertson reaffirmed his Stoic principles in the appendix to his *Historical Disquisition concerning the Knowledge which the Ancients had of India* (1791). In this work, the moral philosophy of the ancient Brahmins turns out to be identical to the "manly active philosophy" formulated much later by Greek and Roman Stoics.[40] It is also almost identical in meaning and tone to the ethical principles laid down in Adam Ferguson's *Institutes of Moral Philosophy*. The critical passage is worthy of quotation:

Man, [the ancient Brahmins] taught, was formed not for speculation or indolence, but for action. He is born, not for himself alone, but for his fellow-men. The happiness of the society of which he is a member, the good of mankind, are his ultimate and highest objects. In choosing what to prefer or to reject, the

[34] John Drysdale, *Sermons*, 2 vols. (Edinburgh, 1793).

[35] Robertson to Dalzel, 28 August 1792, in Andrew Dalzel, *History of the University of Edinburgh*, 2 vols. (Edinburgh, 1862), 1:96.

[36] Robertson to Bishop Douglas, 15 February 1793, BL, Egerton 2182:78–79.

[37] Notes by Lord Robertson, NLS, 3979:22–25.

[38] *The Meditations of M. Aurelius Antoninus*, trans. Francis Hutcheson and James Moor (Glasgow, 1742); Notes by Lord Robertson, NLS, 3979:22–25; chap. 1, n. 28 above.

[39] Stewart, lxxv.

[40] *WWR*, 8:313.

justness and propriety of his own choice are the only considerations to which he should attend. The events which may follow his actions are not in his own power; and whether they may be prosperous or adverse, as long as he is satisfied with the purity of the motives which induced him to act, he can enjoy that approbation of his own mind which constitutes genuine happiness, independent of the power of fortune or the opinions of other men.[41]

Robertson maintains that this ancient Indian philosophy is "the most generous and dignified which unassisted reason is capable of discovering." But he considers it unfortunate that the ancient Brahmins supplemented their Stoic moral principles with false religious beliefs, such as pantheism and reincarnation, which were also held by leading Stoics in ancient Rome.[42] He approves, in other words, of the Brahmins' ethical values but regrets that they were pagan, rather than Christian, Stoics.

The greatest Moderate preacher of Christian Stoicism was Hugh Blair, whose five-volume collection of sermons was among the most popular English-language works of the late eighteenth and early nineteenth centuries. Blair defined Christianity chiefly in terms of virtue or benevolence grounded in faith in Christ. For this reason he considered "a religious and a thoroughly virtuous character" to be identical.[43] Selfless love and "humanity of manners" were in Blair's view what Christ stood for in his own life on earth.[44] These values were responsible for Christianity's historical role as a civilizing force, helping to reduce the severity of warfare, abolish slavery, and increase equality between the sexes.[45] In regard to human conduct, then, the essence of the Christian message was that "humanity is what man, as such, in every station, owes to man."[46]

According to Blair, it is precisely this "sense of humanity"—"the favourite and distinguishing virtue of the age"[47]—that entitles the

---

[41] Ibid., 312.

[42] Ibid., 338. "These doctrines of the Brahmins, concerning the deity . . . coincide perfectly with the tenets of the Stoical school. It is remarkable, that after having observed a near resemblance in the most sublime sentiments of their moral doctrine, we should likewise discover such a similarity in the errors of their theological speculations."

[43] *Sers.*, 3:4–5. Cf. Alexander Carlyle, *The Usefulness and Necessity of a Liberal Education for Clergymen* (Edinburgh, 1793), 30: "To make men pious and virtuous, through the knowledge of the truth as it is in Christ Jesus, is the object of our ministry."

[44] Blair, "On the Moral Character of Christ," *Sers.*, vol. 5, no. 3.

[45] *Sers.*, 1:144. Cf. Blair's s.p.c.k. sermon of 1750, discussed in chap. 2 above.

[46] *Sers.*, 1:145, 2:136.

[47] Ibid., 3:34.

eighteenth century to consider itself an enlightened era. For all this humanity and enlightenment, however, modern man is limited in his knowledge of the world and his ability to control it. His knowledge is limited because his vision is blurred: "For now we see through a glass, darkly."[48] Unforeseen consequences continually upset our plans and calculations, leaving us with a feeling of impotence about our capacity to direct events. As Blair puts it:

> The life of every man is a continued chain of incidents, each link of which hangs upon the former. The transition from cause to effect, from event to event, is often carried on by secret steps, which our foresight cannot divine, and our sagacity is unable to trace. Evil may, at some future period bring forth good; and good may bring forth evil, both equally unexpected.[49]

It would seem that the human plight is rendered hopeless by incorrigible ignorance and almost complete impotence.

Yet this pessimistic view is to Blair entirely unjustified. In the first place, he never tires of pointing out that the events of this world are under the governance of God's wise and just Providence. Normally, God employs "human means" to achieve his ends, but the effect is often the same "as if he were beheld descending from his throne, to punish the sinner with his own hand."[50] As the Bible says in one of Blair's favorite passages, "a man's heart deviseth his way; but the Lord directeth his steps."[51] Even what appears to be human evil—"the wrath of man," in the words of the psalmist—turns out in the last analysis to be part of God's plan and subservient to God's glory.[52] Once we fully understand the extent of the power and goodness of Providence, our sense of despair about our limitations disappears, and we cheerfully "resign ourselves to God."[53] The theme is by this time a familiar one: "Follow wherever his Providence leads; comply with whatever his will requires; and leave all the rest to him."[54] It is up to men and women to act virtuously by loving God and their neighbor;

---

[48] This line from 1 Corinthians 13:12 forms the text for one of Blair's sermons (vol. 1, no. 3) and is frequently quoted in the body of others (e.g. *Sers.*, 2:271, 4:400).

[49] Ibid., 1:196–97; 4:173, 325; 5:383–84.

[50] Ibid., 1:367, 5:386.

[51] This passage from Proverbs 16:9 serves as Blair's text in "On the Government of Human Affairs by Providence" (*Sers.*, vol. 5, no. 18). See also *Sers.*, 4:43.

[52] In addition to his sermon on the '45 discussed in chap. 1 above, Blair used this popular passage from Psalm 76:10 as his text for another sermon (*Sers.*, vol. 2, no. 14) and referred to it in others (e.g. *Sers.*, 4:43).

[53] Ibid., 1:205–206, 3:395.

[54] Ibid., 1:207.

it is up to Providence to govern the universe according to the dictates of divine wisdom and justice.

A second line of reasoning leads Blair to the same conclusion. Let us suppose that there were no correlation between virtue and success in this world. Would it then follow that the wicked are as well off in this world as the virtuous? Blair's answer to this question relies on his Stoic conception of happiness as an internal quality that cannot be affected by "external circumstances."[55] Wealth, physical pleasure, social prestige, and other signs of worldly success do not necessarily bring us true happiness. In fact they are very often the cause of unhappiness by making us slaves to our passions and victims of the unpredictable vicissitudes of fortune, which Blair poetically terms "the perpetual drunkenness of life."[56] The opposite extreme—complete retreat from the world in the manner of Roman Catholic monasticism—is equally pernicious, since human beings are social animals meant for social action.[57] The best course lies in the happy medium between worldliness and withdrawal, which is exactly what "true religion" recommends.[58] It is only by acting a virtuous part in the world, and yet maintaining a proper distance from the world, that true happiness can be attained.

This Stoic position frees Blair from having to explain every instance of unrewarded virtue or unpunished vice. "The distribution of the goods of fortune, indeed, may often be promiscuous; that is, disproportioned to the moral characters of men," he concedes; "but the allotment of real happiness is never so."[59] "Real" happiness comes only from virtue and the sense of inner peace and self-respect that virtue invariably produces:

> It is the peculiar effect of virtue, to make a man's chief happiness arise from himself and his own conduct. A bad man is wholly the creature of the world. . . . But to a virtuous man, success in worldly undertakings is but a secondary object. To discharge his part with integrity and honour is his chief aim. If he has done properly what was incumbent on him to do, his mind is at rest; to Providence he leaves the event.[60]

The logic of this argument leads Blair to endorse socially conservative conclusions similar to those found in John Drysdale's "On the Distinction of Ranks." After insisting, for example, that "among the

---

[55] Ibid., 1:183, 2:31–33.
[56] Ibid., 1:218.
[57] Ibid., 1:145, 218; 5:386.
[58] Ibid., 1:157–58. Cf. ibid., 218–19.
[59] Ibid., 170.
[60] Ibid., 411–12.

different conditions and ranks of men, the balance of happiness is preserved in a great measure equal," Blair adds:

In a state, therefore, where there is neither so much to be coveted on the one hand, nor to be dreaded on the other, as at first appears, how submissive ought we to be to the disposal of Providence! How temperate in our desires and pursuits! How much more attentive to preserve our virtue, and to improve our minds, than to gain the doubtful and equivocal advantages of worldly prosperity![61]

In passages like this one, it is sometimes difficult to distinguish between submission to Providence and submission to the existing system of social "ranks" and orders.[62] To men as comfortable in their social milieu as Blair and the other Moderate literati of Edinburgh, the divine and social orders blended easily into a single entity; resignation to one implied resignation to the other.

It was in their attitude toward death that the Moderate literati expressed most vividly their sense of Christian-Stoic resignation. They were deeply concerned about the Stoic ideal of dying well, by which they meant facing death with a sense of fortitude, courage, and inner calm that comes only from the realization that one has lived a life of virtue and that death is a matter beyond one's control and, therefore, unworthy of one's anxiety. "What divine Providence hath made necessary, human prudence ought to comply with cheerfully," Blair stated in the first of his two published sermons bearing the title "On Death."[63] Adam Ferguson went further, remarking in an unpublished essay that in a world governed by a wise and benevolent Providence "it is joyous to live and it is a triumph to die."[64] Ferguson was impressed that his cousin Joseph Black had passed away so peacefully that a glass of milk resting on his lap had remained undisturbed, and he characteristically concluded the epitaph that he penned for the tomb of Alexander Carlyle with the recollection that in old age Carlyle had "calmly prepared to die in peace."[65] Carlyle himself had been touched by the dignity displayed at the end of life

---

[61] Ibid., 174–75. Cf. ibid., 5:149, where Blair states that "there must be inequality of ranks" in a well-ordered society, though happiness does not depend on one's social rank. The broader implications of Blair's sort of thinking are discussed in Jacob Viner, *The Role of Providence in the Social Order* (Princeton, 1976), esp. chap. 4: "The Providential Origin of Social Inequality."

[62] Cf. Adam Ferguson's comments on the beauty of "a distinction of ranks, in which providence has made the order of society to consist." *Princs.*, 2:379.

[63] *Sers.*, 2:206.

[64] Adam Ferguson, "Of Perfection and Happiness," EUL, Dc. 1.42:25.

[65] Adam Ferguson, "Minutes of the Life and Character of Joseph Black, M.D.," *TRSE* 5 (1805), pt. 3:117; *Auto.*, 604.

by William Robertson, whom he described as "calm and collected, and placid, and even gay."[66] This was the Stoic way of death.

As Christians, furthermore, the Moderate literati had another reason for accepting death with dignity: the Christian promise of eternal life. In Blair's first sermon on death, Stoicism provides only a preliminary argument; it is religion that completes the picture by teaching that, for the virtuous at least, death is not an end but a gateway to "life and liberty."[67] The sermon that follows—"On the Happiness of a Future State"—elaborates on this point. In the *Institutes,* similarly, Adam Ferguson employs rational arguments to demonstrate the high probability of the reality of a future state where the righteous and wicked receive their just due.[68] Moderate preachers frequently stressed the danger of people becoming so immersed in the here and now that they forget about the more important world to come.[69] Thus, the Moderates' view of death, like their view of personal ethics, was essentially an amalgamation of Christian and Stoic principles, emphasizing virtue and submission to the will of God as the surest means of attaining happiness in this world and the next.

[66] Carlyle to Sir John Macpherson, 1796, in *Auto.,* 576. Cf. the similar remarks on the "fortitude," "Christian resignation," and "composure" with which Robertson and Blair faced death, in Stewart, xlvii, and John Hill, *An Account of the Life and Writings of Hugh Blair* (Edinburgh, 1807), 224, as well as the revealing anecdote about Robertson's last days in a letter from Sir Walter Scott to Joanne Baillie, 10 January 1813, in John Gibson Lockhart, *Memoirs of the Life of Sir Walter Scott,* 5 vols. (Boston, 1901), 2:310.

[67] *Sers.,* 2:200.

[68] *Insts.,* pt. 3, chap. 3, esp. 133–34. As Ferguson neared death his belief in an afterlife appears to have grown stronger, and his dying words are said to have been: "There *is* another world!" (quoted in Fagg, 327). Cf. Ferguson's remarks in Brougham, 320.

[69] For example, Alexander Carlyle, *A Sermon on the Death of Sir David Dalrymple, Bar^t Lord Hailes* (Edinburgh, 1792), 5.

WHIG-PRESBYTERIAN CONSERVATISM,
OR "PUBLIC VIRTUE"

He declared from his pulpit, that no man could be a good Christian that was a bad subject.

John Hill, *Hugh Blair*, 1807

He was a constitutional whig, equally removed from republican licentiousness and tory bigotry.

[Robert Bisset], "Dr. Adam Fergusson," 1799

As the Moderate literati of Edinburgh were spreading their Christian-Stoic ethical theory during the third quarter of the eighteenth century, Scotland was undergoing a period of modest but steady agricultural and commercial prosperity that broke the nation's long-standing pattern of poverty and prepared the way for the more dramatic "take-off" of the Scottish economy in the half-century following the end of the American War of Independence.[70] The literati of the Scottish Enlightenment reacted to the phenomenon of economic growth in three basic ways. One was actively and self-consciously to endorse it, encourage it, and spread it—the so-called ideology of improvement that inspired clubs like the Edinburgh Society for Encouraging Arts, Sciences, Manufactures, and Agriculture (1755–1765), breakthroughs in bleaching and other fields of applied science, and efforts by improving lairds to increase food production by means of more efficient farming techniques. A second way, practiced by David Hume and Adam Smith, among others, was to describe it, analyze it, and explain it—the celebrated Scottish science of political economy. Here approval of economic progress continued to be expressed, but the approach was more rational, critical, and detached. The third alternative, which was the one most characteristic of the attitude of the Moderate literati of Edinburgh, was to focus on identifying and mitigating the potentially harmful effects of economic development on morality, religion, and society as a whole.

In practice, all these responses to economic growth can be found to some degree in almost every Scottish man of letters who concerned himself with such matters. Yet it is precisely the question of

[70] T. C. Smout, "Where Had the Scottish Economy Got to by the Third Quarter of the Eighteenth Century?" in *WV*, 45–72.

degree that is of most interest. Adam Smith commented on the paradoxical nature of economic progress, but his doubts and fears were expressed within the context of enthusiastic support for the principle of modernization. For their part, the Moderate literati of Edinburgh were not entirely unresponsive to the new science of political economy, and they sometimes spoke the activist language of the economic improvers, particularly in regard to agriculture and other traditional forms of economic life.[71] Their primary concern, however, lay with the moral and social ramifications of economic development. They were troubled by the tension they perceived between the selfish, materialistic, "corrupt" values associated with economic growth and the Christian-Stoic principles of their own ethical program. In their view, the teachings of the political economists and ideologists of improvement were wont to concede too much to self-interest and modernization and to provide too weak a foundation for moral and social consensus. Although they recognized that competition, division of labor, and other characteristics of modern economic life could be effective means of achieving economic progress, just as competition in the political realm could serve the cause of political liberty, they feared that these features of a modern, pluralistic, commercial society would "break the bands of society" (as Ferguson put it) by fostering factionalism, excessive luxury, and other manifestations of moral "corruption" as well as social evils such as alienation.[72] They yearned for a moral society in which all individuals not only would live up to their ideals of "private" virtue by practicing benevolence in their personal relations with others but also would extend that principle into the social and political world by practicing "public" virtue—in the civic humanist sense of selfless patriotism and identification of the private and civic personality.[73] Their priorities are revealed in the concluding lines of John Home's poem of 1753 on the occasion of laying the foundation stone of the new Edinburgh exchange—an obvious symbol of the town's nascent commercial identity:

> BRITONS, this Day is laid a PRIMAL STONE;
> Firm may it be! But trust not that alone!

---

[71] See, for example, Alexander Carlyle, *Journal of a Tour to the North of Scotland*, ed. Richard B. Sher (Aberdeen, 1981).

[72] *Essay*, 218; Duncan Forbes, "Adam Ferguson and the Idea of Community," in *Edinburgh in the Age of Reason*, by Douglas Young et al. (Edinburgh, 1967), 40–47.

[73] There are stimulating discussions of the concept of public or civic virtue in the context of the virtue-commerce debate of the eighteenth century in J. G. A. Pocock, *The Machiavellian Moment: Florentine Political Thought and the Atlantic Republican Tradition* (Princeton, 1975), chap. 14, and various articles by the same author.

On Public Virtue sound, His Favour gain,
Without whose Aid *the Builders build in vain.*[74]

The Moderate literati never doubted that a social edifice resting on a purely material foundation was bound to fall and that, along with religion, "Public Virtue sound" would be necessary to ensure the success and endurance of a modern, commercial society.

Besides its role as an antidote to the special social and moral ills generated, or at least exacerbated, by economic modernization, the concept of "public" virtue was vital to the Moderate literati of Edinburgh for another reason. As upholders of the ideology that I have termed "Whig-Presbyterian conservatism," the Moderate literati were committed to defending the Hanoverian establishment in Britain against challenges from the Jacobite "right" as well as from the radical Whig "left." Activism on behalf of the political and ecclesiastical status quo was at once the hallmark of their political thought and practice and a critical component in their interpretation of public virtue. Their calls for public virtue were always loudest when the existing institutional order appeared to be in danger, and their sole proposal for a major institutional innovation—the militia scheme—was motivated less by a desire for reform as such than by a belief that a militia was necessary to prevent moral corruption and ensure the stability of established institutions. Although they condemned slavery, campaigned aggressively for religious tolerance, freedom of expression, and other enlightened principles, and sometimes spoke the language of classical republicanism, they rejected virtually every politically progressive proposal and movement of their day, including most varieties of parliamentary, burgh, and ecclesiastical reform, colonial independence, and repeal of the test act.[75]

From the standpoint of the ideology of Whig-Presbyterian conservatism, the most important task of political theory was to justify

---

[74] John Home, *Verses on laying the Foundation of the Exchange of Edinburgh* ([Edinburgh], 1753).

[75] On the last of these issues see G. M. Ditchfield, "The Scottish Campaign against the Test Act, 1790–1791," *Historical Journal* 23 (1980): 37–61. On issues such as slavery, a distinction should be made between the Moderate literati's sincere but essentially theoretical opposition to slavery on humanitarian grounds and the zealous antislavery propaganda of other Scottish ministers and moralists, such as Thomas Somerville and James Beattie. It is true that on rare occasions the Moderate literati gave support to political reforms, but on closer inspection their position usually turns out to be conservative (see, for example, Alexander Carlyle's discussion of burgh reform in his account of Inveresk in the *Statistical Account of Scotland*, ed. Sir John Sinclair, 21 vols. [Edinburgh, 1795], 16:48–49). It is therefore misleading to dub the Moderates "enlightened radicals," as Anand Chitnis has done in *The Scottish Enlightenment: A Social History* (London, 1976), 241.

support for the existing institutional order and to equate such support with the practice of public virtue. This task entailed, among other things, propagating a spirit of civic virtue for conservative purposes while preventing that spirit from operating in the service of reform, revolution, or reaction. After the demise of Jacobitism as an insurrectionary, rather than merely sentimental, ideology in 1746, establishment or conservative Whigs had little to fear from reactionaries. But they were soon faced with two other ideological challenges that were all the more serious because they emanated from within the broad boundaries of Whiggism itself. The first of these challenges was Humean "skeptical" or "scientific" Whiggism, which has been so splendidly scrutinized by Duncan Forbes.[76] As Forbes has persuasively argued, among the most important features of Hume's political writings were their air of moderation and "clinical" or "scientific detachment" and their devastating critiques of "vulgar" Whig "fictions" such as the social contract, ancient constitution, and exaggerated distinction between continental despotism and British liberty. Although Hume was careful to express approval of the "Glorious" Revolution and Hanoverian establishment—which is why it makes sense to call him a Whig—his approval was based chiefly on the principles of expediency and support for establishments as such. Forbes has shown that such principles could not justify the Revolution at the time it occurred. More seriously, they could not justify the present political order at all except on grounds of "time and custom," and they could not stir up very much patriotic fervor for a political order resting on so feeble a foundation—or at least they could not do so when delivered in Hume's self-consciously impartial, "philosophical" manner. In short, both as a political theorist and as an ideological propagandist, Hume was the sort of friend that conservative Whigs would have been glad to be without.

Moreover, although it had once been possible for the Whig-Presbyterian establishment in Scotland to refute Hume simply by ignoring and excluding him, by the mid-1750s Hume was far too popular, and far too bold in his skeptical thinking about both politics and religion, for this tactic to succeed. It was then that some of the most uncompromising Presbyterians in the Scottish kirk went to the opposite extreme by instituting their infidelity campaign against Hume

---

[76] Duncan Forbes, *Hume's Philosophical Politics* (Cambridge, 1975), esp. chaps. 3 and 5, and "Sceptical Whiggism, Commerce, and Liberty," in *Essays on Adam Smith*, ed. Andrew S. Skinner and Thomas Wilson (Oxford, 1975), esp. 182. My debt to these works will be obvious to anyone familiar with them. Cf., however, the stimulating "civic" interpretation of Hume's political theory by John Robertson in "The Scottish Enlightenment at the Limits of the Civic Tradition," in *WV*, 137–78.

in the church courts. Between these two extremes lay the approach of the Moderate literati of Edinburgh, who were prepared to befriend Hume when other clergymen shunned him, defend him when other clergymen attempted to persecute him, and take seriously his scientific pretensions and his powerful attacks on the traditional props of Whig ideology when other clergymen were appalled by them—all the while rejecting or radically modifying the unorthodox and, from their point of view, unsatisfactory arguments that Hume put forward as a substitute for those he had demolished.

The second challenge to establishment Whig ideology came from the new species of radical Whiggism that arose in Britain and America during the 1760s and 1770s.[77] The new Whiggism was more political, more radical, more "focused," more boisterous, and in its Scottish incarnation more closely tied to radical Presbyterianism than were either the "country" ideology of the English gentry or the versions of civic ideology taught by Francis Hutcheson and other Whig-Presbyterian moralists in Scottish universities during the first half of the eighteenth century.[78] Whereas Hutchesonian civic moralism had used classical republican or commonwealthman rhetoric chiefly in an effort to strengthen the moral fiber, civic consciousness, and "gentlemanly republican culture" of the landed classes, the new Whiggism appropriated that rhetoric for more radical causes, such as burgh and parliamentary reform and American independence.[79] In Scotland it first manifested itself in the context of a vociferous ecclesiastical and municipal reform movement that I have described elsewhere.[80] Later it resurfaced in other guises, including support for the American and French Revolutions. The significant point here is that the rhetorical artillery of the commonwealthman tradition was being turned on the Whig-Presbyterian establishment in the name of "real" Whiggism and "true" Presbyterianism.[81] The dilemma confronting the Moderate

[77] See John Brewer, *Party Ideology and Popular Politics at the Accession of George III* (Cambridge, 1976), pt. 4, and H. T. Dickinson, *Liberty and Property: Political Ideology in Eighteenth-Century Britain* (London, 1977), chap. 6.

[78] Brewer, *Party Ideology*, 180, 253–57; Peter Jones, "The Scottish Professoriate and the Polite Academy, 1720–46," in *WV*, 89–118, which contains the phrase quoted in the next sentence (90).

[79] See, for example, Iain Hampsher-Monk, "Civic Humanism and Parliamentary Reform: The Case of the Society of the Friends of the People," and Carla H. Hay, "The Making of a Radical: James Burgh," both in *Journal of British Studies* 18 (1979): 71–89, 90–117.

[80] Richard B. Sher, "Moderates, Managers and Popular Politics in Mid-Eighteenth-Century Edinburgh: The Drysdale 'Bustle' of the 1760s," in *NP*, 179–209.

[81] See *Henry the Corby's Nest: or, The Cry of Liberty, Civil and Sacred* [Edinburgh, 1763] and *The Citizen* (Edinburgh, 1764). The title of the latter pamphlet is significant, for in the common parlance of eighteenth-century Scottish burghs like Edinburgh and

literati, then, was how to provide a justification for prevailing authority that could incorporate the scientific respectability of Humean "skeptical" Whiggism and the rhetorical and moral power of "real" Whiggism while avoiding the cool detachment of the one and the potential radicalism of the other.

In the remainder of this chapter and in portions of the next I shall investigate attempts by the Moderate literati of Edinburgh to resolve the two closely related moral and political problems that I have attempted to clarify in this brief introduction: the problem of the place of patriotism and public virtue in a modern, commercial society and the problem of the defense of the prevailing institutional order in the context of a changing and challenging ideological climate. In this chapter the focus will be on the political teaching of Adam Ferguson and the political preaching of Moderate ministers such as Alexander Carlyle. As in the case of Christian Stoicism, we shall once again see close parallels in the use of classroom and pulpit oratory to spread the ideological tenets of Moderatism.

Our inquiry begins with the important, though generally neglected, discussion of political constitutions in the concluding part of Adam Ferguson's popular textbook, *Institutes of Moral Philosophy*.[82] Ferguson's starting point is Montesquieu's typology of "simple" constitutions, comprising republic (democracy and aristocracy), monarchy, and despotism.[83] Each has its appropriate principle of behavior necessary for proper functioning: public (or political) virtue in democracy, moderation in aristocracy, honor in monarchy, and fear in despotism. In addition to these four "simple" forms of government, Ferguson seeks to refine Montesquieu's typology by adding two "mixed" forms. "In mixed republics," first of all, "the supreme power has been shared betwixt the collective body, and a senate or conven-

---

Glasgow the term "citizen" not only included, but was actually restricted to, producers (i.e. merchants and tradesmen) who would have been excluded from that designation by Fletcher of Saltoun and other older civic thinkers employing an aristocratic-agrarian model of politics and society. This point helps to explain both the looseness with which mid-eighteenth-century Scottish thinkers used terms like "citizen" and the ease with which civic terminology could be appropriated by burgh reformers.

[82] Although the first edition of the *Institutes* (1769) bore the subtitle *For the Use of Students in the College of Edinburgh*, the book soon gained international popularity. A second, revised edition appeared in 1773 and began to attract interest in London, as its author informed the publisher, William Creech, in a letter of 1 April 1774 (SRO, Dalguise Muniments), and an expanded third edition (the one used here) was published in 1785. There were translations into German (Leipzig, 1772), French (Geneva, 1775), and Russian (Moscow, 1804), as well as English editions published at Basel (1800) and Madras (1828).

[83] *Insts.*, 42–44, and *Essay*, 64–71.

tion of nobles," whereas "in mixed monarchies the supreme authority has been shared betwixt a king and nobles or betwixt king, nobles, and people."[84]

Which of these constitutions is best? Following Montesquieu, Ferguson refuses to give a definitive answer to this question. The only universal criteria for judging governments are the "self-evident" principles of public "safety" (synonymous with "security of rights" and "civil and political liberty") and public "happiness."[85] Otherwise there are for Ferguson no absolutes in politics. The formulation of universal models of government "equally adapted to all mankind" is thought to be an exercise in vanity and futility because "every political question must have reference to some particular case and must be determined according to the circumstances of that case."[86] For Ferguson, as for Montesquieu, the excellence of political laws and institutions depends on the degree of their conformity to the special "character" and "condition" of each nation. By "character" Ferguson means a people's degree of virtue or other guiding principle; by "condition" he means a nation's size and social structure, which is closely bound up with its economic system. Once these moral, geographical, social, and economic variables are known, it becomes possible by means of "hypothetical" reasoning to determine the best constitution for a given society.

Ferguson proceeds to construct a series of "suppositions" about the characters and conditions of various imaginary peoples. He first imagines "a people perfectly virtuous, distinguished from one another only by their original [i.e. natural] differences, and forming states of small extent."[87] Such a people would be well suited for pure democracy, just as "a people perfectly vicious, without sense of honour, or hereditary distinctions" would be ideally suited for despotism.[88] These two instances form the hypothetical extremes of human character. Like Montesquieu's Troglodytes, who run the full gamut from absolute vice to absolute virtue, they illustrate the bounds within which real nations exist, without ever having existed themselves.[89] The characters of *real* peoples are always mixtures of virtue and vice, Ferguson remarks, and their conditions nearly always admit of complex social gradations.[90]

---

[84] *Insts.*, 44.

[85] Ibid., 280–87.

[86] Ibid., 288.

[87] Ibid., 289–90.

[88] Ibid., 290, 296.

[89] Ibid., 291, 297; Montesquieu, *The Persian Letters*, trans. George R. Healy (Indianapolis, 1964), 22–30.

[90] *Insts.*, 291.

Suppose, then, a people among whom vice, in the form of vanity, prevails over virtue, and whose system of social subordination is pronounced and varied. Here pure monarchy is the best constitution, and the principle of "honour" is the cement that holds together the political system. In such a society, the monarch alone attends to "public safety and public order"; yet to the extent that his power is limited by the herditary dignities of the nobility and the persistence of tradition, he is actually obliged to govern according to "fixed and determinate laws."

The last hypothetical supposition in Ferguson's analysis concerns peoples among whom virtue greatly prevails over vice. Such peoples are too virtuous to be subjected to despotism or pure monarchy, but they are not virtuous enough to govern themselves unless their country is very small and their social system not highly differentiated. If their country is small and their inhabitants divided into different ranks on the basis of economic distinctions only, they are suited for either "mixed republic" or aristocracy. If their system of social subordination is marked by a single great division between the elite and the common people, then aristocracy is best. Finally, if their country is large and their inhabitants divided into a variety of ranks, they are best suited for "mixed monarchy."[91]

By means of this sociological approach to politics derived chiefly from Montesquieu, his avowed mentor in political theory,[92] Ferguson plainly intended to demonstrate the superiority of the British constitution for the British people, given their particular "character" and "condition." To accomplish this objective he had no need of "vulgar" Whig concepts such as the "social compact"—which he dismissed in the Humean manner as "a mere fiction in theory"[93]—or the Whig myth of the "Glorious" Revolution as a restoration of the "ancient constitution." Rather, his justification lay in the propriety of the fit between a particular constitution and a particular set of circumstances. "Mixed monarchy" was best for Great Britain because the character of the British people was predominantly though not completely virtuous, the size of the country considerable, and the system of ranks well developed. The same logic also provided an implicit justification for the Revolution, which could now be interpreted as a successful constitutional adjustment necessitated by the failure of a particular monarch (or succession of monarchs) to rule in accordance with the character and condition of his (or their) subjects.

[91] Ibid., 291–94.
[92] See Ferguson's famous tribute to "this profound politician and amiable moralist" in *Essay*, 65.
[93] *Insts.*, 217–18.

But the ideological import of Ferguson's theory of politics was not limited to justifying the British constitution. In fact, Ferguson did not dwell on the British situation in the *Institutes*, even though his political theory was obviously intended in part as an explanation and apology for it. What Ferguson had in mind was a good deal grander: a *universal* theory of political conservatism that would provide a sociological justification for supporting virtually every existing government. Thus, in the conclusion to his chapter on politics he argues that "men generally accommodate their establishments to their circumstances," leaving "little room for improvement."[94] This tendency of societies to adapt their political institutions to their particular character and condition is dubbed "the law of political expedience." The conservative implications of this law are clearly drawn:

> Where we cannot materially change the character and circumstances of the people, it would be folly to attempt any radical change in the form of government.
>
> In speculation we form general views and look into distant consequences; but the first maxim of sound speculation is, where matters go tolerably well, to beware of change.[95]

Of course, Ferguson does not categorically deny the possibility of political change, but he believes that such change should, and normally does, occur gradually, through "small alterations" over long periods of time, and he insists that it can never go further than the character and condition of a people will allow.[96] "The Greatest injury that wicked men can commit," reads the final sentence of the *Institutes*, "is the overthrow or corruption of [just] institutions."[97]

At first glance Ferguson's "law of political expedience" looks very Humean in its emphasis on the merits of establishments as such and its lack of concern with justifying the "Glorious" Revolution. On closer inspection, however, important differences come into focus. Hume's case was built chiefly on the principles of "time and custom," which "give authority to all forms of government": Hanoverian rule and existing constitutional arrangements were to be accepted primarily because they had been instituted so long ago that it was no longer worth arguing about them.[98] They existed and they worked; that was enough. This exceedingly pragmatic species of conservatism was the

---

[94] Ibid., 312.

[95] Ibid., 313.

[96] Ibid., 314–15.

[97] Ibid., 317.

[98] David Hume, *A Treatise of Human Nature*, 2d ed., ed. L. A. Selby-Bigge and P. H. Nidditch (Oxford, 1978), 566, and "Of the Protestant Succession," in *Philosophical Works*, ed. T. H. Green and T. H. Grose, 4 vols. (1882; reprint, Darmstadt, 1964), 3:470–79.

product of Hume's overriding desire to discredit all arguments for or against the status quo based on old-fashioned and philosophically indefensible principles, whether "vulgar" Whig or "vulgar" Tory. Hume's message was to stop fighting the ideological wars of the seventeenth century and to concentrate instead on making the best of eighteenth-century political reality. It was a message that may justly be termed moderate and perhaps even enlightened but can hardly be considered powerful or compelling, especially from an ideological point of view. By contrast, Ferguson sought to ground his case for political establishments on a systematic, sociological theory of politics. His "law of political expedience" functioned both as a description of how politics actually works and as a prescription for the future—a reminder that the ultimate check to constitutional change is the "condition" and "character" of a nation. Whereas Hume's political conservatism was based on expediency of a common-sensical, leave-well-enough-alone variety, Ferguson's appealed to expediency as a scientific principle or "law" of politics. In this sense Ferguson bound together his science of society and his ideology more tightly than did Hume—so tightly, in fact, that they frequently appear indistinguishable.

Besides attempting to provide establishment Whig ideology with a sounder sociological foundation, Ferguson was far more concerned than Hume with the twofold task of identifying that ideology with virtue and spreading it throughout the land. This didactic objective permeates Ferguson's two celebrated works of "conjectural" and narrative/philosophical history, respectively: the *Essay on the History of Civil Society* (1767) and the *History of the Progress and Termination of the Roman Republic* (1783). In those works Ferguson worked out some of the implications of his belief that a constitution tends to reflect a nation's "character" (a moral category) and "condition" (a geographical and above all socioeconomic category). Though most historians of social science have stressed the latter factor, by emphasizing Ferguson's typically Scottish discussions in the *Essay* of the connections between particular socioeconomic conditions and the corresponding forms of political organization and cultural life, anyone who reads the *Essay* in the context of Ferguson's ideological concerns and thought as a whole is likely to discover that the social scientist was usually subordinate to the moralist.[99] Viewed in this way, the *Essay* can be regarded as an attempt to prevent a deterioration of the British

---

[99] *Essay*, introduction by Duncan Forbes, xxv. See David Kettler's subtle examinations of this tension in Ferguson's thought between the moralist and social scientist—actor and spectator—in "History and Theory in Ferguson's *Essay on the History of Civil Society*: A Reconsideration," *Political Theory* 5 (1977): 437–60, and "Ferguson's *Princi-*

"character" that would in turn bring about the deterioration of British "mixed monarchy." This interpretation takes us back to the basic difference between Hume's and Ferguson's conceptions of the discipline of moral philosophy as discussed in the preceding chapter—the difference between a detached, impartial, and analytical conception and a didactic, normative, moralistic one. It seems probable that Hume's well-known disapproval of the manuscript of Ferguson's *Essay*, which he tried to keep from being published on account of its alleged deficiencies of "Style" and "Reasoning," "Form" and "Matter," was rooted in his aversion to the *Essay*'s heavily moralistic rhetoric and content.[100] And it is significant that Hugh Blair, speaking on behalf of William Robertson as well as himself, cited "the Rousing and animating Spirit" that "runs thro'" the *Essay* as a principal reason for rejecting Hume's harsh assessment of that work.[101]

The moral and ideological dimension of Ferguson's political thought is nowhere more apparent than in the *Essay*'s treatment of the liberty-slavery antithesis. Since Ferguson followed the jurisprudential tradition in defining liberty as security before the law,[102] he had no trouble admitting, along with a "skeptical" Whig like Hume, that almost any form of government can be free so long as it guarantees such security or "safety." The exception is despotism, which is based on the principle of "fear" and is by definition synonymous with political slavery. Since constitutions tend to conform to national characters, however, despotism is really nothing more than a symptom of a much greater evil: moral corruption, particularly in the form of selfishness, materialism, factionalism, and loss of concern for the public welfare. In Ferguson's view, the great irony of social life is that moral corruption and the despotic form of government that almost always accompanies it are more likely to arise in free and prosperous societies. In such societies the acquisition of money becomes the highest

---

ples: Constitution in Permanence," *EC* 19 (1978): 208–22, both of which make use of Ferguson's unpublished lecture notes in the Edinburgh University Library.

[100] Hume to Blair, 11 February 1766, *HL*, 2:12. Hume's aversion to the moralistic component in Ferguson's *Essay* may also have derived from his belief in what Duncan Forbes calls "the primacy of political institutions": the belief that manners and morals are shaped by institutions rather than the other way around (*Hume's Philosophical Politics*, chap. 7). Cf. Quentin Skinner, *The Foundations of Modern Political Thought*, 2 vols. (Cambridge, 1978), 1:44–45.

[101] Blair to Hume, 24 February 1766, RSE, 3/56.

[102] The jurisprudential definition of liberty as "safety" or security of rights under law—freedom *from* rather than freedom *to*—was present in all of Ferguson's writings on moral philosophy (e.g. *Essay*, 156; *Insts.*, 285; *Princs.*, 2:461) and was also the basis for Ferguson's refutation of Richard Price during the American crisis. See Fagg, 145–47, and Kettler, *Adam Ferguson*, 244.

standard of value, and attainment of "luxury" becomes the principal object of life.[103] The division of labor produces a sense of frustration among the lower orders and leads to a harmful separation of the civil and military spheres.[104] Peace and security themselves cause citizens to become lazy and indifferent about political affairs.[105] Individuals left to pursue "private advantage" become "effeminate, mercenary, and sensual."[106] In short, "society is made to consist of parts, of which none is animated with the spirit of society itself."[107] At such times, Ferguson is saying, socioeconomic "conditions" threaten to corrupt the national "character" and pave the way for despotism. But the process of corruption is not irreversible. Indeed, the purpose of the *Essay* was not only to alert the public to the immediate danger but to inspire them to avert it by counteracting the harmful byproducts of civilization and prosperity with a self-conscious renewal of virtue.

Thus, the *Essay*'s ideological message was not fundamentally different from that found in Ferguson's sermon on the '45 and numerous other Moderate jeremiads: national degeneration brings national calamities that can be avoided or overcome only by moral revitalization on a grand scale. The difference between the two modes was largely a matter of rhetoric—the difference between Christian terminology (sin, God, Providence, regeneration) and the secular language of eighteenth-century civic humanism and moral philosophy (commerce, luxury, corruption, despotism, public virtue). In using the civic or civic humanist paradigm, however, Ferguson was selective. He avoided any concepts that could have radical implications, such as the definition of liberty as the duty of each citizen to participate in political affairs, and he restricted the paradigm's application to preservation of an already virtuous national character and an already free constitution. Public virtue was equated with an intense yet rather vague sense of patriotism and civic responsibility in support of the prevailing institutional order.

The ideological component in the *Essay* becomes clearer when one considers the question of human control over the political environment. As a conservative "social scientist," Ferguson was partial to explanations of political affairs that emphasized socioeconomic and even biological considerations rather than rational planning and meaningful action. The "law of political expedience" and the famous passages in the *Essay* on unintended consequences, the mythic status of

[103]*Essay*, 237–39, 247–48.
[104]Ibid., 150, 218–19, 230.
[105]Ibid., 213–14.
[106]Ibid., 250.
[107]Ibid., 218.

ancient lawgivers like Lycurgus, and the primacy of "instincts" and "circumstances" over "speculations" all reflect this conviction that political organization is not a matter of deliberation. "No constitution is formed by concert, no government is copied from a plan," Ferguson states.[108] As a conservative *moralist*, however, Ferguson could not allow this line of reasoning to preclude the possibility of the effective exercise of civic or public virtue for conservative purposes. He therefore qualified his remarks on the limitations of constructive political action by arguing that "although free constitutions of government seldom or never *take their rise* from the scheme of any single projector, yet are they often *preserved* by the vigilance, activity, and zeal of single men."[109] As political innovators men appear to be helpless against the forces of instinct and circumstance, but as preservers of established political orders they are endowed with the capacity for acting rationally and effectively in the realm of politics. By means of this rather dubious distinction between originating and maintaining political institutions, Ferguson attempts to show both the folly of radical constitutional alterations and the efficacy of public virtue in defense of the status quo.

Like the *Essay on the History of Civil Society*, the *History of the Progress and Termination of the Roman Republic* used the dynamic, moralistic rhetoric of the civic humanist tradition in the service of conservative Whig ideology. Once again Ferguson's inspiration was Montesquieu, whose *Considerations on the Causes of the Greatness of the Romans and Their Decline* had introduced the "Roman question" to the political and social theory of the Enlightenment half a century earlier. The aim of Ferguson's book on Rome was to explain "the great revolution by which the republican form of government was exchanged for despotism."[110] Specifically, Ferguson was fascinated by the pattern of liberty and prosperity / corruption / political despotism that the Roman model seemed to exemplify. From the outset he made it clear that he viewed his subject as a moral lesson for affluent societies everywhere: "To know [Rome] well, is to know mankind," for Rome is "a signal example of the vicissitudes to which prosperous nations are exposed."[111]

Elaborating on an idea suggested by Montesquieu,[112] Ferguson ar-

---

[108] Ibid., 223.

[109] Ibid., 134. Emphasis added.

[110] Adam Ferguson, *The History of the Progress and Termination of the Roman Republic* (Philadelphia, 1845), 10.

[111] Ibid.

[112] Montesquieu, *Considerations on the Causes of the Greatness of the Romans and their Decline* (1734), trans. David Lowenthal (Ithaca, N.Y., 1968), On the similarities be-

gued that the decline of the Roman republic could be traced to moral corruption in the form of Epicureanism. According to this argument, Epicureanism in the late republic represented maximization of personal pleasure, the denial of Providence, the reduction of all ethical issues to pleasure and pain, and the insistence that all goodness is restricted to private affairs.[113] Ferguson was aware that this account of Epicurean values was rather simplistic, and he admitted that when pressed by their opponents the Epicureans had made certain concessions to "religion and morality." He refused to admit, however, that these concessions blunted the practical effect of Epicurean philosophy as he had described it. In spite of the Epicureans' formal contention that true pleasure consists in virtue alone, Ferguson argued,

> the ordinary language of this sect, representing virtue as a mere prudent choice among the pleasures to which men are variously addicted, served to suppress the specific sentiments of conscience and elevation of mind, and to change the reproaches of criminality, profligacy, or vileness, by which even bad men are restrained from iniquity, into mere imputations of mistake, or variations of taste.[114]

The danger of Epicureanism, in other words, stemmed from its indirect tendency to encourage selfishness by viewing morality as private, subjective, and therefore relative.

As Ferguson saw the matter, the conflict between Stoicism and Epicureanism in the late Roman republic was essentially a struggle between self-interest and public virtue, carried on with all the intensity of a religious crusade.[115] The Stoics scorned the love of pleasure and proclaimed the proper choice of right over wrong, good over evil, to

---

tween Ferguson's *Roman Republic* and Montesquieu's *Considerations*, see F. T. H. Fletcher, *Montesquieu and English Politics (1750–1800)* (London, 1939), 38–43, and Alan Baum, *Montesquieu and Social Theory* (Oxford, 1979), 80–82, 115.

[113] Ferguson, *Roman Republic*, 179.

[114] Ibid. Cf. the similar remarks spoken by William Cleghorn in Ferguson's unpublished "Dialogue on a Highland Jaunt" (EUL, Dc. 1.42:16–17): "The Epicurean says Pleasure is the chief good & leaves his Pupils to chuse their pleasure; many of them, I'm afraid, will take the first that Comes; altho he owns that Virtue is the highest, yet many who set out in the pursuit of Pleasure may never Arrive at Virtue." By failing to mention the entire speech in which these important remarks appear, Ernest Mossner misses Cleghorn's (and Ferguson's) point in "Adam Ferguson's 'Dialogue on a Highland Jaunt' with Robert Adam, William Cleghorn, David Hume, and William Wilkie," in *Restoration and Eighteenth-Century Literature*, ed. Carroll Camden (Chicago, 1963), 297–308, esp. 303.

[115] *Roman Republic*, 179–80.

be the sole means of attaining true happiness. They renounced purely selfish interests and steadfastly claimed that a man's "affections, and the maxims of his station, as a creature of God, as a member of society, lead him to act for the good of mankind."[116] Above all, they insisted that there could be "no private good separate from the public good" and that "the same qualities of the understanding and the heart, wisdom, benevolence, and courage, which are good for the individual, are so likewise for the public."[117] In terms of political personalities, Epicureanism was associated with Julius Caesar, Stoicism with Ferguson's beloved Cato. Ferguson implied that Caesar's will to political power was directly linked to his Epicurean will to personal pleasure.[118] The eventual predominance of Epicureanism over Stoicism was for Ferguson a clear indication that the moral character of the Roman people had been corrupted, thereby paving the way for the abolition of Cato's republic of virtue and the establishment of Caesar's despotic empire.

Owing, perhaps, to the appearance of the brilliant first volume of Edward Gibbon's monumental study of the Roman Empire just seven years earlier, Ferguson's Roman history was not very well received by the British press and reading public at the time of its publication.[119] Yet a small group of the author's Moderate friends in Scotland "could not refrain from saying," as Alexander Carlyle put it, "that Ferguson's was the best history of Rome."[120] While helping Ferguson's manuscript through the press Hugh Blair assured the publisher that "it is out of all sight the best Roman History that we have. In my opinion it will extinguish any other."[121] Blair added that he considered Ferguson's study "political and profound," by which

---

[116] Ibid.

[117] Ibid., 179.

[118] Ibid., 181: "When [Caesar] emerged from the avocations of pleasure, from the sloth which accompanies the languor of dissipation, his ambition or desire to counteract the established government of his country, and to make himself master of the commonwealth became extreme." Cf. John Home, "The Fate of Caesar," in *A Collection of Original Poems by Scotch Gentlemen*, ed. Thomas Blacklock, 2 vols. (Edinburgh, 1760–1762), 2:141–43.

[119] *Auto.*, 298. On 2 November 1783 Bishop Douglas wrote to Carlyle: "I always dreaded the want of a rapid sale for Dr Ferguson's History owing to the subject being destitute of novelty: and to his not having followed Mr Gibbon's plan of making the Narrative only a vehicle for attacking the Religion of his Country" (NLS, 3464:37). Ferguson's history did not come into vogue in Britain and America until the early nineteenth century.

[120] *Auto.*, 298. Cf. Carlyle's undated letter to Henry Dundas, ibid., 568. Among Ferguson's most avid supporters was the Moderate minister, poet, and philosopher of history John Logan.

[121] Blair to [William Strahan], 17 December 1781, NLS, 2257:9–10.

he may have meant that he approved of it ideologically. Like the Moderates' Anglican friend John Douglas, Blair was offended by Gibbon's attacks on religion in the *Decline and Fall*,[122] and in the pulpit he adopted the belief of certain unnamed "historians"—undoubtedly Montesquieu and Ferguson—that the growth of Epicureanism had hastened the disintegration of the Roman republic by promoting self-interest and irreligion.[123]

Of course, the fascination of Ferguson and his friends with ancient Rome reflected their concerns about moral and political corruption in their own society.[124] The new Epicureanism—represented by such code words as "factionalism" in politics, "effeminacy" in manners, and "luxury" in economics—seemed to them as dangerous in eighteenth-century Britain as the original sect was thought to have been during the last stages of the Roman republic. If this was how Ferguson intended his Roman history to be read, there is evidence that his message was not misunderstood. For example, in 1783 a London banker wrote to a British colonel: "We are reading Ferguson's new Roman history which shows too clearly what our country is fast coming to. Rome was never more venal than we are already."[125]

Although the example of republican Rome served the Moderate literati as a powerful historical lesson in public virtue, it could not answer the question of just when and how such virtue was applicable in the eighteenth-century British context. A republic, after all, was built on the principle of public virtue and continued to rely on it at every moment of its existence. But the status of public virtue was far more ambiguous in a "mixed monarchy" like Great Britain's. In his most moralistic moments Ferguson simply ignored constitutional distinctions and insisted that "a continual preference of public safety, and public good, to separate interests, or partial considerations," is the duty of "every member of any community."[126] This lofty ideal, however, was not only unrealistic in a commercial society but inappropriate in a "mixed" constitution that was, by Ferguson's own definition, sustained by a balance of powers and interests rather than by a subordination of private interests to public ones. In his earliest

---

[122] "Gibbon has given us an Elegant and masterly Book," Blair wrote to Adam Smith on 3 April 1776. "But what the Deuce had he to do with attacking Religion?" *The Correspondence of Adam Smith*, ed. Ernest Campbell Mossner and Ian Simpson Ross (Oxford, 1977), 189.

[123] *Sers.*, 5:134.

[124] Kettler, *Adam Ferguson*, 201.

[125] Thomas Coutts to Col. J. W. Crawford, 29 June 1783, quoted in Fagg, 239.

[126] *Insts.*, 247.

publication on moral philosophy Ferguson described the British constitution as "a plurality of collateral powers, as *King, Nobles,* and *People,*" in which "men are separated into different orders and classes; and the state is supported by the balance of opposite interests and principles."[127] Even in the moralistic *Essay* we find him arguing that

> the public interest is often secure, not because individuals are disposed to regard it as the end of their conduct, but because each, in his place, is determined to preserve his own. Liberty is maintained by the continued differences and oppositions of numbers, not by their concurring zeal in behalf of equitable government.[128]

But if the liberty and stablility of a commercial, pluralistic "mixed monarchy" derived from a "balance of opposite interests and principles" or the competitive interplay among various individuals, corporations, orders, parties, and institutions, what role remained for public virtue in eighteenth-century Britain? How could a British subject recognize a "Machiavellian moment," and supposing he were able to recognize one, what sort of action could he take in a society with few institutional mechanisms for participatory, civic liberty on behalf of the public welfare? How and when did a self-interested subject become a virtuous citizen?

Insofar as Ferguson ever resolved this dilemma, which he inherited from Montesquieu and the civic tradition itself,[129] his solution involved the institution of a militia and the principle that public virtue becomes imperative in times of public danger. The Moderates' involvement in the militia controversies of their day will be treated more fully in the next chapter; for the moment it is only necessary to point out that Ferguson and the Moderate literati regarded this traditionally republican institution as a critical device for counteracting the harmful effects of commercial civilization and providing a vital institutional outlet for the expression of public virtue in a modern "mixed monarchy." The militia's function as a school for virtue was for Ferguson inseparable from its function as a school for defense of the status quo against threats of internal disorder and external invasion. It is no coincidence that agitation for a Scots militia was most intense during periods of national emergency, such as the Seven Years' War and American Revolution. At such times, Fergu-

---

[127] Ferguson, *Analysis*, 55.

[128] *Essay*, 128.

[129] As J. G. A. Pocock put it, "the problem had always been that of deciding when the particular or private goods should be seen as contributory to the universal or public good, when as competitive with it." *Machiavellian Moment*, 500.

son believed, all subjects must band together to support their government by sacrificing private interest to the public good. It was in this spirit that Ferguson, in the dark days of 1792, drew a distinction between "ordinary times," when an army might safely be restricted to professional soldiers, and "emergency" situations requiring military participation by a larger proportion of the nation in order to ensure the preservation of the established order.[130]

Thus, in Ferguson's view the factionalism and self-interest that are to some degree unavoidable and perhaps even useful in a free, commercial society become intolerable whenever such a society is threatened with disruption from rebellion, riot, or foreign war. "While the Constitution is safe, Ambition and Faction will be Vigorous and Free, and we may owe to them very great and Material Favours," Ferguson explained in an important letter to William Eden during the American War.[131] "But I would not be carried by this Consideration so far as to justify Faction in any Single Instance in which it made a Sacrifice of the Public Safety to Private Ambition or Interest." Whenever we are guilty of "evading and disfiguring the Truth or serving the Enemys of our Country in order to hurt our Rivals in Power," we have crossed the thin line separating factionalism as "a Physical appendage of our Constitution" from factionalism as a sinister force. Ferguson goes on to emphasize the need for a strong militia and to lament the complete separation of "Statesmen" and "Warriors" in eighteenth-century Britain, citing republican Rome as an alternative. He agrees with Eden's call for national unity in the struggle against the American rebels. Moreover, he expresses his sentiments on the American crisis in religious terms that reveal how close he remained to the enduring tradition of the Presbyterian jeremiad:

> I am not fond of National Animositys but I feel and indulge the Indignation of the present Case with much Satisfaction. Every well meaning Clergyman ought to stuff his Sermon with it on the approaching Fast Day. And to tell the Americans in Particular how they were spared by Providence while their wishes were in appearance sincere for the Redress of Grievances, but how they and their mighty Friends have been scourged since they rejected the Redress of Grievances to become Traytors to their King and their Fellow Citizens and the Instruments in the Hands of Inveterate Ennemys for the Destruction of Both.

With this passage we are about to bridge the narrow chasm between Moderate political philosophy and Moderate political preach-

---

[130] *Princs.*, quoted in Kettler, *Adam Ferguson*, 267.
[131] Ferguson to Eden, 2 January 1780, BL, Auckland 34417:3–12.

ing. Before doing so, however, it will be useful by way of summary to consider Ferguson's political theory in the context of the two ideological issues discussed in the introduction to this section. In regard to the virtue-commerce debate, first of all, Ferguson was willing to concede that a certain amount of luxury and economic self- or group interest was unavoidable in a free, commercial society, and that the liberty and prosperity of modern civilization justified that much of a sacrifice. Yet the main thrust of his work was to exalt virtue as the only possible solution to the serious problems posed by modernization. Unless a way were found to limit selfish desires to maximize personal wealth and pleasure at the expense of virtue, the progress of civilization would prove to be an illusion. The *Institutes* made this point with a "hypothetical" typology of societies, showing that virtue is a vital element not only among the people of a republic but also among those residing in an economically advanced, socially stratified society with a "mixed" constitution. The *Roman Republic* made it with a historical case study, showing how a great and prosperous republic was corrupted and then destroyed by selfish, "Epicurean" values. The *Essay* made it with a social evolutionary model, showing that the road from savagery to civil society could all too easily lead to decadence and doom. In each case the point was to demonstrate the close correlations between modernization and moral corruption on the one hand, moral corruption and social and political decline on the other. For Ferguson, political economy was literally a division of *moral* philosophy.

Second, Ferguson's political theory served the cause of conservative or establishment Whig ideology. The public virtue demanded of British citizen-subjects was in practice restricted to the conservative task of constitutional preservation, especially in times of national danger. Only in that limited sense was Ferguson prepared to invoke the language of the civic or civic humanist tradition. By using civic rhetoric in this fashion, he gave warning that the civic tradition and its characteristic institution—the citizens' militia—were not the exclusive domain of nostalgic Tories, utopian dreamers, republicans, radicals, reformers, or members of parliamentary oppositions of one sort or another. Public virtue was rather to be equated with a spirited, patriotic defense of the prevailing order—a defense that could be deployed as effectively against the emerging radical Whig "left" as against the moribund Jacobite "right."

If the civic or civic humanist tradition constituted one ground of support for Ferguson's conservative Whig ideology, the comparative method of political analysis that Ferguson adapted from Montesquieu constituted another. Among other things, the latter provided a theoretical framework for viewing the existing system of British "mixed monarchy" as the form of government best suited to the particular "character" and "condition" of Great Britain and her people. Armed with this theory, Ferguson could safely follow Hume in dispensing with "vulgar" Whig fictions like the social contract and ancient constitution, in adopting a "scientific" approach to political institutions, and in defining political liberty in jurisprudential terms that did not confine it—as some "vulgar" Whigs would have wished—to Britain. Such concessions represented not an abandonment of conservative Whig principles but a realization that such principles could no longer be sustained in the "vulgar," pre-Humean manner. In this way Ferguson joined the scientific ethos of Humean "skeptical" Whiggism with the moralistic rhetoric of "real" or "republican" Whiggism and the conservative ends of "constitutional" or "establishment" Whiggism, forging a lively and resourceful defense of the political status quo.

Just as moral philosophy could be used for spreading conservative Whig principles of patriotism and public virtue from a university lectern, so could the power of the pulpit be put to work for the same end. The Moderate literati's attempts to employ pulpit oratory in this manner, by accounting for national crises like the '45 and American Revolution in terms of a moral and providential logic of history, placed them within a distinctively, though by no means exclusively, Scottish Presbyterian preaching tradition that warrants closer scrutiny. The heart of this tradition was the belief that whole peoples or nations may enter into political and religious convenants with the Lord in conscious imitation of the Old Testament covenent between God and the Jews.[132] Such covenants are of an essentially defensive nature, in that they are designed to preserve the political and religious status quo from the threat of corruption, revolution, or invasion. This point emerges clearly in William Robertson's account of the Reformation origins of the Scottish covenant idea:

> A bond was framed for the maintenance of true religion, as well as the defence of the king's person and government, in opposition to all enemies, foreign and domestic. . . . When roused by an extraordinary event, or alarmed by any public danger, the people of Israel were accustomed to bind themselves, by a solemn covenant, to adhere to that religion which the Almighty had

---

[132] James Walker, *The Theology and Theologians of Scotland* (Edinburgh, 1872), 58–60.

established among them; this the Scots considered as a sacred precedent, which it became them to imitate.[133]

Although critical of the "violent and unconstitutional" uses that were made of the national covenant in the seventeenth century, Robertson was quite sympathetic to the original concept. "At the juncture in which it was first introduced," he stated, "we may pronounce it to have been a prudent and laudable device for the defence of the religion and liberties of the nation."[134]

According to covenant theoreticians, a national covenant not only gives a people special status in the eyes of God but also imposes enormous burdens.[135] A covenanted nation has a greater responsibility than its neighbors to practice virtue and piety, and it therefore deserves to be judged more harshly than other nations if it should fail to do so. Furthermore, it is entitled to interpret historical events in terms of its special relationship with God. As long as the covenant endures, wars, rebellions, epidemics, famines, and similar afflictions are not merely random occurrences but divine reprimands, just as national prosperity and success are signs of divine favor. At such critical junctures the government or the church should set aside designated "fast days" for the purpose of collective penance or thanksgiving. In the latter case all credit goes to God for bestowing peace and happiness on his undeserving people. In the former case the nation must humble itself, acknowledge its sinful ways, pray for forgiveness, and, most important, renew the national covenant by means of a self-conscious commitment to moral and religious reformation.

Although the popular doctrine of the national covenant had lost much of its urgency by the eighteenth century, Presbyterian ministers in Scotland, like many clergymen in America and elsewhere, continued to preach jeremiads that interpreted national events as manifestations of God's pleasure or (more frequently) wrath at the conduct of his people, and governments and churches continued the practice of proclaiming "fast days" at times of national crisis or public thanksgiving. Of course, the precise meaning that a preacher gave to national events on such occasions depended primarily on his prior ideological preferences. John Witherspoon's famous fast-day sermon of May 1776, "The Dominion of Providence over the Passions of Men," used the logic of the jeremiad in support of the American cause,

[133] *History of Scotland*, in *WWR*, 2:155.

[134] Ibid., 156.

[135] The present paragraph is based largely on Perry Miller's brilliant discussion in *The New England Mind: From Colony to Province* (Boston, 1961), 21–24. See also Sacvan Bercovitch, *The American Jeremiad* (Madison, Wisc., 1978), esp. 7–9.

whereas Alexander Carlyle's fast-day sermon of the same year, "The Justice and Necessity of the War with our American Colonies Examined," employed similar logic but reached the opposite conclusion. The success of the Moderates as political preachers lay not in their originality but in their skill at using the thoroughly orthodox preaching tradition of the jeremiad to express their moral and ideological beliefs.

Consider, for example, the following passage from one of Hugh Blair's sermons from the late 1770s:

> When wars and commotions shake the earth, when factions rage, and intestine divisions embroil kingdoms, that before were flourishing, Providence seems, at first view, to have abandoned public affairs to the misrule of human passions. Yet from the midst of this confusion, order is often made to spring; and from these mischiefs lasting advantages to arise. By such convulsions, nations are roused from that dangerous lethargy into which flowing wealth, long peace, and growing effeminacy of manners had sunk them. They are awakened to discern their true interests, and taught to take proper measures for security and defence against all their foes. Inveterate prejudices are corrected; and latent sources of danger are discovered. Public spirit is called forth; and larger views of national happiness are formed.[136]

Here is an eloquent statement of the providential logic of the jeremiad, expressed in a highly generalized form. The ideological significance of the passage lay in its application to the American Revolution, which Blair viewed as the latest providential sign of the need for a revival of British virtue and "public spirit" in order to preserve the nation from moral corruption and eventual ruin. The jeremiads preached against the Americans by Alexander Carlyle, Alexander Gerard, and other Moderates employed the same rhetorical tradition for the same ideological purpose, as I shall show in chapter 7. During the French Revolution Moderate preachers were even more outspoken. Hugh Blair's blatantly chauvinistic fast-day sermon of 18 April 1793, "On the Love of Our Country," recommended piety and public virtue as the only remedies for visionary thinking, Jacobinism, republicanism, atheism, and other dreaded French social diseases.[137] Three yeats later, at the age of seventy-four, Alexander "Jupiter" Carlyle boasted that he could still "preach like a son of thunder . . . against the vile leveling Jacobins, whom I abhor."[138]

[136] *Sers.*, 2:386–87.
[137] Ibid., vol. 5, no. 6.
[138] Carlyle to Sir John Macpherson, 1796, in *Auto.*, 577.

An examination of the fairly typical sermon that Carlyle preached against the French Revolution on a fast day in February 1794 will demonstrate how the Moderate literati expressed their political ideology within the framework of Scottish Presbyterian pulpit oratory. Titled *National Depravity the Cause of National Calamities*, Carlyle's sermon draws its scriptural inspiration from Jermiah 6:8: "Be thou instructed, O Jerusalem, lest my soul depart from thee: lest I make thee desolate, a land not inhabited."[139] Title and text prepare the listener or reader for a traditional Presbyterian jeremiad, in which the nation will be castigated for deviating from its appointed course and warned of the disastrous effects certain to befall it unless a moral and religious reformation is forthcoming. Carlyle proceeds to develop the logic of this argument in four carefully delineated steps. The first is the assertion that "the Almighty governs the world, not merely by general laws, but by constant superintendence and frequent interposition." In making this point, Carlyle emphasizes the pervasive Moderate theme of unintended consequences. Secular leaders may make their plans, but "unexpected events proceed from all their designs." Similarly, "empires and kingdoms rise or fall, yet all depends on the secret designs and operations of Providence." Carlyle's second point is that Providence always gives nations fair warning of imminent danger, providing an opportunity for people to "repent." Third, "sin is the cause of all national evils, and if persisted in by any people, will provoke the Almighty to *cause his soul to depart from them*." Once this occurs the covenant with God has been violated, and the nation is left "at the mercy of human passions uncontrouled." The fourth step in the logical chain is simply the inevitable conclusion that "the certain consequence of this departure [of the soul of God] must be, *that the kingdom shall become desolute, a land not inhabited*."

In the remainder of the sermon, Carlyle attempts to fit the political crisis of the 1790s into this scheme of providential logic. The fundamental question is, why have the prosperity and happiness of Great Britain been destroyed by foreign war and the threat of internal upheaval by a "Determined Band of dark Conspirators"? The answer is unequivocal: it is national depravity that is to blame for the nation's ills. Carlyle enumerates four particular sins that are responsible for Britain's woes. The first is "our ingratitude to God, by whom we have been so highly favoured, and our spirit of murmering and discontent." Although God has blessed the British nation with an ideal political constitution, uniting the best parts of the three simple forms

---

[139] Alexander Carlyle, *National Depravity the Cause of National Calamities* (Edinburgh, 1794).

of government in a perfectly balanced whole, certain deluded elements among the British people have responded not with thanks but with dissent in the name of liberty and social equality. For the sins of the ungrateful few, Carlyle implies, the entire nation has been forced to suffer.

The second sin derives from the "spirit of faction and party," which Carlyle treats in a distinctly Fergusonian manner. He admits that political parties are tolerable, perhaps even useful, in constitutional governments, but he insists that factionalism must not be allowed to exceed certain limits determined ultimately by the criterion of public safety. In this context Carlyle unleashes a furious attack on the Friends of the People and voices approval of the notorious sedition trials, which he views as a necessary response to excessive factionalism. The third sin is "disregard of the public, and the extinction of the love of our country." Here again Carlyle is in fundamental agreement with his friend Adam Ferguson. Like Ferguson, he recognizes the special danger that selfishness poses in a commercial society, in which

> all ranks pursue pleasure, and the gratification of vanity, with impetuous desire; and to fulfill that desire, seek after wealth and riches with a rage that seems to approach to madness. They lose sight of the public in the midst of those interested views.

Finally, Carlyle cites "abuse of our religious privileges" as a fourth sin for which the British people have been forced to pay. Under this head he includes both irrelgion, in the form of "atheism and infidelity," and "the endless fanatical divisions" that have racked the established churches of England and Scotland since the Revolution "introduced true religious liberty."

Taken together, these four sins constitute the "national depravity" that Carlyle considers the root cause of his country's misfortunes. Unless these sins are expiated during the warning period God has provided, "national calamities" of unprecedented magnitude are certain to occur. Fortunately, the situation can be remedied: it is only necessary to atone for the nation's collective guilt by enthusiastically supporting the war with France, the British constitution, "true religion," and the public interest in general. In this way democracy, atheism, factionalism, and self-interest will be restrained, and Great Britain will be restored by Providence to its former position of greatness.

Thus, Carlyle reaches the same moralistic and conservative conclusion by means of Presbyterian logic that Adam Ferguson had reached by means of moral philosophy. The histories of ancient Israel and classical Rome tell the same story. It is the story of great and prosperous nations destroyed from within as a result of excessive selfishness and factionalism, luxury and "effeminacy," passiveness and indifference, pride and conceit, and similar manifestations of moral corruption. Yet the process of decline is neither inevitable nor irreversible. Indeed, for the Moderate literati ancient Israel and classical Rome were deemed useful as sacred and profane historical models precisely because they seemed to demonstrate that moral corruption could be averted through the practice of public virtue, in the sense of zeal for the political and religious status quo. National crises like the '45 and the American and French Revolutions were perceived as tests of the level of public virtue in Great Britain. If the level were too low, the constitution and the established churches would be toppled, and despotism would eventually triumph. If, on the other hand, the level of public virtue could be kept high—as high, that is, as might be reasonably hoped for in a large, commercial, "mixed monarchy"—then the constitution and established churches would be safe, and the Whig-Presbyterian establishment in Scotland would endure.

From the standpoint of ideology and rhetoric, the primary goal of Moderate moral teaching and preaching was to make men virtuous and happy, which is to say, benevolent in thought and deed and appreciative—to the point of personal sacrifice and civic commitment—of the established social, political, and religious order. In order to achieve this goal, elements of Stoicism, orthodox Presbyterianism, civic humanism, and conservative Whiggism were skillfully, if sometimes superficially, combined, and the resulting ideological "system" was preached politely but enthusiastically from the church pulpits and university lecterns that the Moderates controlled.

In its emphasis on spreading morality and happiness, Moderatism was typical of the Enlightenment everywhere. Yet it was also a distinctively Scottish, or in some respects British, phenomenon. It was the ideology of a group of self-satisfied Scottish Presbyterian ministers seeking to promulgate humane, enlightened principles without altering in any significant way the existing structure of religious, social, and political institutions. This helps to explain why Moderate moral teaching and preaching took on a decidedly conservative cast, stressing the limits of rational control over the universe, the prevalence of unintended consequences, the wisdom and power of God and Providence, the Stoic definition of happiness as a virtuous state of mind, the importance of social order and subordination, the danger of moral and political corruption, and the need for patriotism and public spirit in order to guarantee the preservation of free, established institutions. Such principles and the particular modes by which they were communicated were central to the spirit and style of the Scottish Enlightenment. There was no need to astound the world in the manner of a Rousseau or d'Holbach. Nor was it necessary to conceal one's true meaning in the manner of a Voltaire or Diderot. Rather, the dominant tone in Scotland was one of straightforward didacticism—a tone better suited to pulpit and classroom oratory than to subtle exotic tales, witty social satires, or irreverent attacks on accepted values and established institutions.

"Ferguson was in politics what Blair was in theology," wrote Leslie Stephen in 1876, "—a facile and dexterous declaimer, whose rhetoric glides over the surface of things without biting into their substance."[140] No doubt Stephen overstated his case, but from an ideological point of view he was at least partially correct. Ferguson was in politics, or rather in moral philosophy, what Blair and other Moderate ministers were in theology. They were evangelists of Moderatism, teachers and preachers of the principles of Moderate morality and ideology. Each was to some degree what Victor Cousin called Ferguson: "un publiciste vertueux."[141] Seen in this light, the Moderates' struggle to obtain prestigious churches, ecclesiastical offices, and university positions takes on a new meaning. It was not simply a matter of advancing their careers or enhancing the general stature of the Moderate party. It was also a matter of securing the most important academic and ecclesiastical platforms for the transmission of moral and political values. Insofar as this was true, it was a matter of building an institutional base from which to direct Scotland's cultural development and spread the principles of Moderatism and the Scottish Enlightenment throughout Scotland, Britain, and the Western world.

[140] Sir Leslie Stephen, *History of English Thought in the Eighteenth Century*, 2 vols. (New York, 1962), 2:182.
[141] Victor Cousin, *Philosophie écossaise*, 4th ed. (Paris, 1864), 521.

CHAPTER SIX

For the Glory of Scotland

--- ❋ ---

THE CALL TO ARMS

Each chief his seven-fold shield display'd,
And half unsheath'd the shining blade,
And rocks and seas, and skies resound,
To arms, to arms, to arms!

John Home, *Agis*, 1758

They have drawn a line of separation between us and them: they
have broken the sacred bond which tied us together. They have
refused us the badge of distinction between freeman and slaves.

Alexander Carlyle, *Letter to the Duke of Buccleugh on National
Defence*, 1778

We have been considering the moral teaching and preaching of the
Moderate literati of Edinburgh as parts of a relatively coherent "system" of Moderate ideas and values—a system that was the established philosophy and religion of Scotland during the age of the
Scottish Enlightenment. In order to understand Moderatism in its
entirety, however, it is necessary to look beneath the formal lectures,
sermons, and treatises that constitute the proper subject matter of
"high" intellectual history. In this chapter and the one that follows I
therefore examine four contemporary disputes in which the Moderate literati of Edinburgh applied their ideological principles to
contemporary affairs. Chapter 6 shows how controversies over the
Scots militia and the poems of Ossian brought the Moderate literati
into contention with "John Bull." Chapter 7 focuses on differences
with their brethren in the kirk over the American Revolution and
Roman Catholic relief. By studying these disputes in some detail, we
shall see that Moderatism was not simply an intellectual movement
or "mood" in the established church and universities of Scotland but
also a practical and generally consistent ideological program for advancing such causes as religious tolerance, political conservatism, civic
virtue, and Scottish nationalism.

. . .

Along with most other Scottish literary men of their generation, the Moderate literati of Edinburgh suffered from what David Daiches has called "cultural schizophrenia."[1] They enthusiastically endorsed the ideal of union with England and easily assimilated a variety of English manners and customs in order to translate that ideal into cultural reality. Yet they were also proud Scotsmen who were in some ways unwilling or unable to renounce their native culture. The result of this paradox has been described as "national pride in the native heritage accompanied by a nervous desire to do the genteel thing"— which was often the English thing.[2] One thinks in this regard of David Hume boasting of Scotland's literary superiority to England while endeavoring to purge unsightly "Scotticisms" from his written prose; of Lord Kames joking in broad Scots when at home but speaking an affected form of English from the bench; of the Edinburgh literati patronizing the career of the young Robert Burns while discouraging his robust, impolite use of Scots language. At once cosmopolitan and provincial, the literati of the Scottish Enlightenment struggled to integrate Scottish and English culture without losing their own identities in the process.[3]

The Moderate literati's ambivalent attitude toward England is most evident from their feelings about London, which they viewed with a mixture of resentment and respect. It was because of their concern about winning the admiration of London that the Moderates were so deeply hurt whenever Londoners like Samuel Johnson slighted Scottish culture for seemingly chauvinistic reasons. London could be cruel to Scotsmen, as young Boswell learned when the cry of "No Scots! No Scots! Out with them!" rang out at Covent Garden theater in December 1762,[4] but it was nevertheless the place where opinion most mattered and important things were most likely to happen. For this reason it normally inspired feelings of provincial deference among the Scottish literati. "You know how much we Provincials love to hear from the capital," William Robertson once wrote to David Hume in London.[5] As self-conscious provincials, Robertson and his friends were sometimes overwhelmed and perhaps a little frightened by London, which always retained a foreign aura in their eyes. Visits there were

---

[1] David Daiches, *The Paradox of Scottish Culture: The Eighteenth-Century Experience* (London, 1964), 66.

[2] Ibid., 34.

[3] On the self-conscious provincialism of the Scottish literati, see the paragraph in the bibliographical essay citing studies of Scottish national identity.

[4] James Boswell, *Boswell's London Journal, 1762–1763*, ed. Frederick A. Pottle (New York, n.d.), 71.

[5] Robertson to Hume, 27 March 1767, in R. B. Sher and M. A. Stewart, "William Robertson and David Hume: Three Letters," *Hume Studies* (1985).

sometimes essential, but permanent residence was not deemed desirable. Agreeing with Robertson's refusal to reside in London while writing his proposed history of England, Lord Cathcart remarked that "it is a Study of it's self to learn to be in a Strange Country and amongst strangers (for so I must reckon England to you)."[6] Hugh Blair was filled with apprehension as he prepared to visit London at the age of forty-five.[7] When Adam Ferguson was stuck in London for a period of months as a result of government business, he grew restless and homesick and commented to Carlyle: "I pant after Scotland as the Hart Panteth after the Water Brooks."[8] Even John Home, who for several years lived mostly in London as Bute's secretary, and whose fame and fortune rested on the London stage, greatly preferred his native Scotland to England. "If it was not for my attachment to Lord Bute," he once stated, "I would never cross the Tweed."[9] Yet cross the Tweed he often did, not only to be with his patron but also to compete for the applause of the very London audiences for which he sometimes professed disdain.

Only on certain special occasions did all traces of ambivalence vanish and the Moderate literati become staunch Scottish nationalists. These were the times when the English appeared to them reluctant to grant the Scots their due in cultural and political affairs. The two most important examples concern the Scots militia question and the Ossian affair. In both these controversies the sides eventually divided along national lines, and in both cases it was the Moderate literati who took the lead in pleading the cause of Scotland.

Agitation for a Scots militia was one of the liveliest themes of Scottish history during the second half of the eighteenth century, particularly during the latter part of the Seven Years' War and again during the War of American Independence. In order to place the issue in historical perspective, it will be helpful to note the existence of three earlier manifestations of militia spirit in Scotland and Britain generally. One was the indigenous medieval and early modern Scottish martial heritage that generated, in the absence of strong counter-

[6] Lord Cathcart to Robertson, 7 August 1761, NLS, 3942:46–47. Cf. Robertson's discussion of his reasons for preferring Edinburgh to London in his letter to William Mure of 25 November 1761, Bute, uncatalogued (partially published from a rough draft in Stewart, xx).

[7] Blair to Boswell, 19 February 1763, YUL, C156.

[8] Ferguson to Carlyle, 9 February 1779, EUL, Dc. 4.41:47. Cf. David Kettler's perceptive reading of a letter that Ferguson sent to his brother or friend "Jack" (possibly John Home) on the occasion of his first visit to London in 1745, in "History and Theory in Ferguson's *Essay on the History of Civil Society*," EC 5 (1977): 440.

[9] Home to [Col. James Edmonstone], [1761], NLS, 1005:3–4.

vailing political institutions, a highly militaristic conception of Scottish national identity.[10] Another was the antiarmy ideology associated with James Harrington and other English commonwealthmen of the seventeenth century.[11] This ideology was linked to the indigenous Scottish martial heritage, as well as to the literati of the Scottish Enlightenment, through the brilliant Scottish classical republican Andrew Fletcher of Saltoun, whose works were known to the Moderate literati of Edinburgh and whose nephew, Lord Milton, was their friend and patron. In a famous pamphlet of 1697–1698 that was still being reprinted in the 1740s and 1750s, Fletcher had presented a civic humanist argument against standing armies on constitutional grounds: such armies were tools of despots and subversive of political liberty. A militia, by contrast, was not only a method of national defense compatible with liberty but "a school of virtue," by which Fletcher meant an institution for training citizens to be strong, brave, and independent in a Spartan sense.[12]

The third and most recent manifestation of militia spirit was the one associated with the Pittite militia campaign of the mid-1750s, which set off a debate that culminated in the enactment of militia legislation in the spring of 1757.[13] By this time the issue was no longer essentially militia *versus* standing army, as it had been in the seventeenth century; the militia was now regarded by most of its champions as a supplement to a standing army—a domestic force that would free the army and navy to fight the French on the European continent and throughout the colonial world without either compromising Britain's defenses or necessitating the importation of foreign mercenaries. In this way the militia campaigners of the 1750s sought to transform the militia from a regressive military liability into a military asset that would appear all the more progressive and useful as it became clear that the current conflict with France was a war of a new type, fought on many fronts far from home. These military ar-

[10] John Robertson, *The Scottish Enlightenment and the Militia Issue* (Edinburgh, 1985), chap. 1.

[11] Lois G. Schwoerer, *"No Standing Armies": The Antiarmy Ideology in Seventeenth-Century England* (Baltimore, 1974); J. G. A. Pocock, *The Machiavellian Moment: Florentine Political Thought and the Atlantic Republican Tradition* (Princeton, 1975), chaps. 11 and 12.

[12] Andrew Fletcher of Saltoun, *A Discourse of Government with Relation to Militias* (Edinburgh, 1698), in Fletcher, *Selected Political Writings and Speeches*, ed. David Daiches (Edinburgh, 1979), 2–26, esp. 24. This pamphlet first appeared in London in 1697 in slightly different form. There is a contextual discussion in Schwoerer, *"No Standing Armies,"* chap. 8, and perceptive analyses in Pocock, *Machiavellian Moment*, 428–32, and Robertson, *Militia Issue*, chap. 2.

[13] J. R. Western, *The English Militia in the Eighteenth Century: The Story of a Political Issue, 1660–1802* (London, 1965), chap. 6; *Parl. Hist.*, 15:704–70, 782.

guments in favor of militias were supplemented with the constitutional and moral rhetoric of the antiarmy, classical republican tradition. Thus, whereas opponents of Pitt's militia bills generally stressed economic and social factors such as depopulation and expense, supporters tended to emphasize military readiness and national security on the one hand, the preservation of liberty and prevention of moral decay on the other.

The Moderate literati of Edinburgh drew inspiration from all three of these earlier varieties of militia spirit. They made admiring references to the heritage of Scottish, and especially Lowland, militarism; employed the rhetoric of the antiarmy, classical republican tradition when it suited their purpose; and participated directly in the militia campaign of 1756–1757. The last two points are particularly important, for they demonstrate that the Moderate literati's interest in the militia question was rooted in a broadly British context. Only when Scotland was excluded from the provisions of the militia act of 1757—a concession that Pitt and his friends were obliged to make to the two leading opponents of the militia idea, the duke of Newcastle and the earl of Hardwicke—did the militia issue become a Scottish national cause. With the possible exception of Hugh Blair, all the Moderate literati were militia men before they were *Scots* militia men. Scottish national pride would eventually become a vital component in their militia consciousness, but it was not their original motivation. That motivation came, it would seem, from several other factors, such as their conservative zeal for preserving the Whig-Presbyterian—and more broadly, Hanoverian—status quo, their strong sense of civic virtue, and their sensitivity to the military vulnerability of Britain generally and the Scottish Lowlands in particular, as demonstrated by the humiliating ease with which the Lowlands had succumbed to the Jacobite army during the '45.

The earliest evidence of the Moderate literati's involvement with the militia question before it became a predominantly Scottish issue comes from the minutes of the Select Society and is infuriatingly scanty. It is known that the subject of a militia was frequently debated in one form or another in the two years preceding the passage of Pitt's militia bill, as it would be again in 1759–1760, and it has been plausibly suggested that a handwritten militia pamphlet circulated in 1756 by Robert Wallace grew out of these Select Society debates.[14] For the rest, one can only assume that the Moderate literati

[14] Robert Wallace, "Scheme for a Militia in Brittain," EUL, La. 2/620[6]. On militia debates in the Select Society and their possible connection with Wallace's pamphlet, see Robertson, *Militia Issue*, chap. 3. Wallace's surprising lack of involvement in subsequent agitations for a Scots militia may have had something to do with his growing

and their friends in the Select Society who would later distinguish themselves as leading advocates of a militia, such as Lord Elibank and Gilbert Elliot (if he happened to be in Edinburgh), played a major role in these debates on the side of the militia and martial spirit.

There are other indications of the Moderate literati's participation in the British militia campaign of 1756–1757 besides the Select Society debates. "I am sorry to say, that in Scotland the Clergy are the only body, who re-echo the sound of English liberty," John Home wrote to Gilbert Elliot (then a young Pittite M.P. in London) in a pro-Pitt, promilitia letter of November 1756.[15] The kind of liberty Home had in mind is best defined by Lord Randolph's remark in *Douglas*: "Free is his heart who for his country fights."[16] That play about patriotic resistance to a foreign invasion of medieval Scotland opened in Edinburgh on the very day (14 December 1756) that Pitt's militia bill was reintroduced in the House of Commons by George Townshend. Patriot ideology and militia propaganda help to explain Pitt's role in personally arranging the London production of *Douglas* three months later.[17] Furthermore, in November 1756 Home, Carlyle, and Robertson managed to put criticisms of the Newcastle government's military policy into an address to the king from the general assembly's commission—an unprecedented step that even Pitt's new ministry apparently considered too imprudent to be included in the official version of the commission's address that appeared in the *London Gazette*.[18]

The Moderate literati's biggest contribution to the British militia debate of 1756–1757 came from Adam Ferguson. Fresh from a decade spent as a "warlike chaplain" in a Highland regiment, Ferguson published at London in December 1756 what Alexander Carlyle would later call a "very superior militia pamphlet" that contained "all the genuine principles of that kind of national defence."[19] *Reflections Previous to the Establishment of a Militia* began with the problem of military vulnerability, as it lamented Britain's "bare and defenceless" state in the present war with France.[20] But improved national defense was only part, and the less important part, of Ferguson's argument for a

political and ecclesiastical estrangement from the Moderate leaders of the Scots militia movement during the late 1750s and early 1760s.

[15] Home to Elliot, 5 November 1756, NLS, 11008:17–18.

[16] Home, *Douglas*, act 2, line 30. Cf. the discussion of *Agis* in chap. 2 above.

[17] Home to Milton, February 1757, NLS, 16700:190.

[18] *Annals*, 2:99–101.

[19] *Auto.*, 420.

[20] Adam Ferguson, *Reflections Previous to the Establishment of a Militia* (London, 1756), 2–3.

militia. The main point of the pamphlet was to show the importance of a militia in helping the inhabitants of Great Britain "to mix the military Spirit with our civil and commercial Policy."[21] According to Ferguson, the general progress of society, and the progress of commerce in particular, had raised wealth above the ancient virtues of valor and courage as the measure of social honor and distinction.[22] For this reason the nation was in danger of becoming "a Company of Manufacturers, where each is confined to a particular Branch, and sunk into the Habits and Peculiarities of his Trade."[23] Even the gentry and nobility had sacrificed their traditional martial spirit and standards of honor on the altar of "Profit and Interest."[24] Ferguson intimated that by inculcating the love of arms, along with such praiseworthy qualities as courage, discipline, and honor, a militia would help to offset the selfish, materialistic values nurtured by modern, commercial society. In his view the militia was first and foremost a school for virtue.

Ferguson's moralistic vision of the militia obviously owed much to the civic humanist perspective of Andrew Fletcher and the antiarmy ideology of the seventeenth century. Yet the differences between Ferguson and Fletcher are equally significant, especially since they serve to illuminate fundamental changes in the nature of the militia question in Scotland between the 1690s and the 1750s. Fletcher's emphasis was constitutional or political rather than moral. His primary concern was preventing the crown from upsetting the proper historical and constitutional balance, and for this reason his ideology was at least as much antiarmy as promilitia. Since Fletcher's notions of liberty, virtue, and economic prosperity all centered on the idea of independence for the gentry, he had no trouble seeing a citizens' (i.e. gentlemen's) militia and economic development as compatible and even complementary components of a unified civic conception of society.[25] By Ferguson's time, however, the terms of the debate had been radically altered. On the one hand, the existence of a standing army was no longer being vigorously challenged on constitutional grounds; antiarmy ideology as such was dead except for rhetorical purposes. On the other hand, Fletcher's assumption that a citizens' militia and economic prosperity were two sides of the same civic humanist coin was becoming increasingly untenable. For Ferguson, who wrote in

[21] Ibid., 3.
[22] Ibid., 8–9.
[23] Ibid., 12–13.
[24] Ibid., 13.
[25] For an excellent discussion of this point, see John Robertson, "The Scottish Enlightenment at the Limits of the Civic Tradition," in *WV*, 137–78.

the prosperous 1750s rather than in the dismal 1690s and conceived of economic development chiefly in commercial rather than traditional agrarian terms, the militia had a greater role to play as a moral counterweight to the harmful consequences of prosperity. Corruption was no longer essentially dependence but rather selfishness. The militia was a "school of virtue" less because it forged independent citizen-warriors capable of withstanding monarchical incursions than because it countered the new commercial standards of "Profit and Interest" with those of public virtue and patriotism. This variation on a civic humanist theme would continue to occupy a central place in the Moderates' militia program for the next quarter of a century.

Aside from its concern with the militia's moral and military functions, the *Reflections* is noteworthy in three respects. In the first place, Ferguson followed Harrington and Fletcher, among others, in viewing the militia as a socially conservative institution. "We are very happy in the Degrees of Subordination already established in Britain," he stated,[26] and his discussion of the structure of his proposed militia clearly reflected this sense of social complacency. Not only would cottagers, laborers, servants, and former convicts be barred from militia service, but the ranking of officers "should follow, as nearly as possible, the Subordination in point of Dignity and Wealth already subsisting in this Nation."[27] In this way Ferguson hoped both "to exclude the Rabble," as he privately put it some years later, and to reinforce the existing system of social ranks by ensuring the establishment of "the proper Degree of Authority and Subordination" in the militia.[28]

Second, if Ferguson's conception of a militia was socially conservative, it was also remarkably humane. In Ferguson's militia, imprisonment, corporal punishment, fines and all varieties of "compulsion" would be unknown.[29] Rather, men would be motivated to perform their duty by positive and negative sanctions based on the respective principles of honor and disgrace. Among the common people, for example, dutiful service in the militia might entitle a man to a place of honor at elections, in church, and in juries, whereas negligence or insubordination would incur an appropriate form of public disgrace.[30] Refusal to join the militia or to present a suitable

---

[26] Ferguson, *Reflections*, 37.

[27] Ibid., 31, 34–35, 50–51.

[28] Ibid., 20; Ferguson to William Eden, 2 January 1780, BL, Auckland 34417:3–12. See also David Kettler, *The Social and Political Thought of Adam Ferguson* (Columbus, Ohio, 1965), 88–89.

[29] *Reflections*, 33, 43, 47.

[30] Ibid., 40–47.

substitute when called would be punished by the revocation for life of one's right to serve in the militia.[31] This enlightened, if unrealistic, scheme for maintaining military discipline forms a vivid contrast to Fletcher's rigorously Spartan ideal of compulsory service, harsh discipline, and brutal punishments—including the death penalty for sexual offenses.[32]

Finally, the *Reflections* is notable for its delicate handling of the Scottish question. Without ever mentioning Scotland by name, Ferguson contended that denying the militia to one allegedly factious part of Great Britain would have the effect of increasing disaffection and hostility in that area.[33] Moreover, the absence of a militia in the disaffected region would place the entire nation at the mercy of a truly factious minority residing there. Alluding obviously to the '45, Ferguson remarked that "a few Banditti from the Mountains, trained by their Situation to a warlike Disposition, might over-run the Country, and, in a Critical Time, give Law to this Nation."[34] When, however, "the Lovers of Freedom and their Country have an equal Use of Arms, the Cause of a Pretender to the Dominion and Property of this Island, is from that Moment desperate."[35]

It is difficult to say why Ferguson and other militia proponents treated the Scottish question so gingerly in 1756, or why the Scots in general reacted so passively to their exclusion from the provisions of the militia act in the following year. Although this "line of separation between us and them," as Alexander Carlyle later called it, was a violation of the spirit of the Treaty of Union and an insult to loyal Hanoverian Scots, scarcely anyone in Scotland seemed to mind. The press was relatively quiet, and the Select Society, concerned as ever with propriety and politeness, stopped debating the militia question. Years later Alexander Carlyle ingeniously suggested that this passive response on the part of Scotsmen was the cause of subsequent English animosity toward them, since "nothing provokes repeated acts of insolence so much as servility of spirit."[36] Did this remark imply feelings of remorse for the inaction of his own circle of militia supporters in the two years following passage of the English militia act, or was it simply meant to suggest feelings of frustration at their in-

[31] Ibid., 51–52.
[32] Fletcher, *Discourse*, 21–22.
[33] *Reflections*, 22–23.
[34] Ibid., 24–25.
[35] Ibid., 25.
[36] Carlyle, Letters on the Militia (copies), no. 6, NLS, 3464:63–67. John Robertson has informed me that part of this letter was published in the *Caledonian Mercury*, 3 November 1779.

ability to arouse their countrymen in the face of national disgrace?

What finally revived the militia issue were rumors of a French invasion of Scotland in the summer and autumn of 1759. Late in August John Home expressed his views about Scotland's vulnerability in the event of such an invasion in a characteristically vehement letter to Lord Bute:

> I am sorry to say My Lord that this country is in the most wretched situation that ever any country was in which the people were allowed to talk of Liberty. The ignorance of the English and I dont [know] what name to give to the conduct of the Scotch has reduced us in the midst of alarms, to a state totally defenceless. No Poet that ever foamed with inspiration can express the grief and indignation of those Scots that still love there country, to find themselves disarmed. Two hundred men might sack and burn any city in Scotland, except Edinburgh, in the neighbourhood of which there be three paltry regiments of recruits, which the militia of any one county in six weeks would be able to drive to the Devil.

Important people in Scotland were beginning to speak of the need for a militia, Home continued,

> but no man will begin to take the proper steps. I will venture to say that the greatest benefacter that ever Britain saw, will be the man who sires and regulates a Militia in Scotland. It would make the island invincible. I should make an apology for this declamation, but it is the subject nearest to my heart.[37]

It is significant that this impassioned plea for a Scots militia was preceded by a discussion of Home's progress on his latest tragedy, *The Siege of Aquileia*, which David Garrick would stage at Drury Lane Theatre in late February 1760. The play concerns a trying dilemma faced by the commander of the military forces of Aquileia: whether to save the lives of his two captured sons by surrendering to the enemy or to condemn his sons to the gallows by continuing the battle. In the end paternal affection gives way to public virtue, and the commander's sons are sacrificed for the sake of the nation. Home's chief point, of course, was to dramatize the need for public virtue and a martial spirit in the service of national defense. Lest anyone fail to grasp the playwright's narrower meaning, the tragedy was originally set on the Scottish coast and titled "The Siege of Berwick," though it was ultimately deemed wiser to employ a more distant and

---

[37] Home to Bute, [26] August 1759, Bute, box 2 (1759), no. 147.

exotic setting.[38] Not surprisingly, *The Siege of Aquileia* found its most enthusiastic supporters among the playwright's intimate friends who shared his views about the need for public spirit in general and a Scots militia in particular. Blair and Robertson declared the work ready for stage and press despite the objections of David Hume, and Ferguson commented to Gilbert Elliot after reading the fifth act in manuscript that Home's abilities as a dramatist were possibly "too great" to be appreciated in his own time.[39]

Ferguson had the Scots militia cause on his mind when he praised *The Siege of Aquileia* to Elliot, for in the same letter he playfully remarked that he and Home had both been wishing for a French invasion, "he to exhibit his Military Genius & I to practice my Philosophy, which you may remember is the best calculated for invasions of any Philosophy now extant." His efforts to use invasion rumors in order "to horrify people who think we can be secure without a universal Militia" had been "to no purpose," Ferguson conceded, adding significantly that "some of the Methods which are taken to defend us tend to make us not worth defending." As if in answer to Home and Ferguson's prayers, the ominous presence in northern waters of François Thurot's French squadron during the autumn and winter of 1759–1760 had the effect of provoking the Scots militia agitation as never before.[40] The time seemed right for decisive legislative action.

In order to enact militia legislation for Scotland, however, high-level political support in London was necessary. Besides Gilbert Elliot, the two politicians to whom the Scots militia agitators most often looked for guidance at this time were the earl of Bute and Charles Townshend. The latter visited Scotland in the summer of 1759 and aroused militia hopes with a dazzling promilitia speech in Edinburgh.[41] When the French invasion scare became an issue, Scots militia supporters naturally turned to Townshend for help. "Come and compleat the union, and teach us to talk and act like Freemen and Britons," implored Alexander Carlyle.[42] Lord Elibank made an even stronger appeal to Townshend's vanity when he asserted that the person responsible for extending the militia to Scotland would be re-

---

[38] Alice Edna Gipson, *John Home: A Study of His Life and Works* (Caldwell, Idaho, [1917]), 137–42.

[39] Hume to Blair, 11 February 1766, *HL*, 2:12; Ferguson to Elliot, 14 September 1759, NLS, 11015:9–10.

[40] Western, *English Militia*, 162–63.

[41] Alexander Murdoch, *"The People Above": Politics and Administration in Mid-Eighteenth-Century Scotland* (Edinburgh, 1980), 88.

[42] Carlyle to Townshend, 1 November 1759, WLCL, Townshend Papers.

garded as "the real founder of its Liberty."[43] Equally dramatic appeals were made to the earl of Bute, as when John Home remarked that Scotland looked to the earl for deliverance from "the greatest disgrace and calamity that can befall a nation, *sine armis et sine virtute*."[44] Bute and Townshend were both highly susceptible to flattery and more than willing to play the role of Scotland's savior, but neither man possessed political skill, influence, or reliability to match his vanity. The involvement of these "great men" in the Scots militia campaign of 1759–1760 served only to give militia agitators a false sense of confidence about the political strength of their cause.

Buoyed by the verbal support of Bute, Townshend, and most of the Scottish members of Parliament, the Moderate literati proceeded to secure militia resolutions from the Presbytery of Edinburgh and Synod of Lothian and Tweeddale in October and November 1759, respectively.[45] "The Clergy are acting w^t spirit and Dignity," Carlyle commented to Townshend in reference to these resolutions.[46] It was indeed extraordinary for ecclesiastical judicatories in the Church of Scotland to participate in purely political matters of this sort, and the apparent ease with which the militia resolution was enacted in the synod is another indication of the Moderates' skill at ecclesiastical management.[47] The opinion of the church, however, was chiefly symbolic. Far more important from the standpoint of effective political action was a gathering of Scottish gentlemen at Edinburgh on 30 November 1759.[48] The meeting was attended by most of the notables from the Edinburgh vicinity and was chaired by Lord Milton, who evoked memories of his famous uncle Andrew Fletcher.[49] Of the seventy persons in attendance, only one man—representing Lord Advocate Robert Dundas—voiced opposition to a Scots militia.[50] A committee of sixteen was chosen to draft a proposal to serve as the basis for parliamentary legislation. This committee was dominated by men closely linked to the Moderate literati through ecclesiastical, social, or intellectual ties, such as George Drummond, Lord Milton, Lord Elibank, Sir David Dalrymple, Lord Alemoor, Sir Adam Fergusson, and George Dempster.[51] Most of these names will reappear in this

---

[43] "Whatever else others may assert," Elibank added, "you know, that Scotland has never hither to enjoyed real Liberty." Elibank to Townshend, 21 December 1759, ibid.

[44] Home to Bute, 8 November 1759, Bute, box 2 (1759), no. 184.

[45] Robertson to Townshend, 25 October 1759, and Carlyle to Townshend, 15 November 1759, WLCL, Townshend Papers.

[46] Carlyle to Townshend, [early November 1759], ibid.

[47] Carlyle to Townshend, 15 November 1759, ibid.

[48] *SM* 21 (November 1759): 603.

[49] Elibank to Townshend, 21 December 1759, WLCL, Townshend Papers.

[50] Ibid.

[51] *SM* 21 (December 1759): 659.

chapter in connection with the Poker Club and the Ossian controversy.

The plan devised by the Edinburgh militia committee set down strict property qualifications for the various ranks of officers so as not to leave any doubt of the conservative nature of the proposed enterprise.[52] It called for a modest Scottish force of six thousand men, one-fifth the number constituting the English militia. All that remained was the formidable task of convincing uncertain or hostile elements in Scotland and England of the need to enact a Scots militia bill at the earliest possible time. To this end numerous polemical articles and pamphlets were published late in 1759 and early in 1760, including Alexander Carlyle's *The Question Relating to a Scots Militia Considered*. Written at the request of William Johnstone Pulteney and Adam Ferguson and edited by William Robertson,[53] Carlyle's work was the most popular and important pamphlet produced on behalf of the Scots militia cause. "Great and unexpected success it certainly had," Carlyle later recollected; "for it hit the tone of the country at that time, which being irritated at the line that was drawn between Scotland and England with respect to militia, was very desirous to have application made for it in the approaching session of Parliament."[54]

The Question Relating to a Scots Militia began with the event that had so deeply affected Carlyle and his friends fifteen years earlier—the '45. "The alarm of that fatal year . . . will stain our annals for ages to come," Carlyle stated.[55] Had the Scottish Lowlands been armed, "this pitiful insurrection" would never have occurred; instead, loyal Scots were left "without the means and without the capacity of self-defence" and "12,000 of the most despicable foreign mercenaries" were imported to defend the nation.[56] The '45 "had opened the eyes of every thinking man, and shown him our bosom bare and defenceless."[57] Yet the government had failed to realize that the real tragedy of the '45 was not so much that a disaffected minority in the Highlands had rebelled but that the loyal majority in the Lowlands had been unable to do anything about it because they lacked the arms and spirit of a warlike people. Rather than rectify the situation by

---

[52] *SM* 22 (April 1760): 707–708.

[53] *Auto.*, 418–19. Carlyle says that Robertson added one paragraph to this pamphlet and later joked of being responsible for its great success.

[54] Ibid., 419. *The Question Relating to a Scots Militia* passed through four editions in two years. Though the identity of the author was kept secret, it was generally known that he was among three or four members of Carlyle's circle. *Auto.*, 420.

[55] Carlyle, *Scots Militia Question*, 12, 44. All references are to the first London edition unless otherwise noted.

[56] Ibid., 12.

[57] Ibid., 13.

arming the people of Scotland generally and utilizing the martial spirit of the Highlands in foreign warfare, the government had concentrated on disarming and enfeebling the Highlands so that "a warlike spirit might remain in no corner of the island."[58] Even after heaven had provided Britain with a leader capable of rousing her from "the lap of luxury" by instituting a national militia, Carlyle added with obvious reference to Pitt, Scotland had been arbitrarily excluded from participation in this beneficial new policy.[59]

According to Carlyle, the principal issue in the Scots militia controversy was the freedom and dignity of Scotland. The heart of the problem was not England's attitude toward the Scots but the Scots' view of themselves; for freedom was defined in Stoic terms, as a proud and independent spirit that could not be affected by external conditions.[60] The critical question that Carlyle dared to pose was whether the reluctance of Scottish members of Parliament to introduce a Scots militia bill and the indifference of many of their countrymen about the militia cause did not signal the death of Scotland's spirit of liberty and vitality. His answer to this question was ambiguous. On the one hand, he boasted that "the genius of the Scotch never shone with greater lustre than now: In war and in letters we have acquired our share of glory."[61] On the other hand, Carlyle was convinced that the militia issue demonstrated the degree to which many of his countrymen had become excessively slavish and deferential toward the English. "Are we then a province and a conquered Kingdom? . . . What avails it that we are free and independent, while we create ourselves racks and bowstrings in the fear of offending, and wear chains and fetters in servility of mind?"[62] To Carlyle, the apathy and slavishness of Scotland seemed to be making a mockery of the Union, which was supposed to be an equal partnership rather than a provincial conquest. The militia was the issue on which a stand had to be made for the sake of Scottish liberty and integrity. As Carlyle boldly summed up the matter: "With the most hearty approbation of the union, and its salutary effects, I do maintain, that if the militia-bill, now brought into parliament, does not pass, *it had been good for Scotland that there had been no union.*"[63]

[58] Ibid.

[59] Ibid., 15. Cf. Carlyle's laudatory remarks on Pitt's use of formerly rebellious Highland clans in the Seven Years' War in *Plain Reasons for Removing a Certain Great Man from His M———y's Presence and Councils for ever* (London, 1759).

[60] *Scots Militia Question,* 18.

[61] Ibid., 30.

[62] Ibid., 31.

[63] Ibid., 36. Emphasis added.

When Carlyle's militia pamphlet appeared in January 1760, Thurot's ships were merely threatening the Scottish coast. In February reports that Thurot actually had landed on the Hebridean island of Islay threw much of Scotland into a panic.[64] Two months earlier Lord Elibank had called the Scots militia question "the most important event of my Time." Now even William Robertson, who usually remained cool and aloof in the face of political controversy, was moved to declare to Charles Townshend that the militia transaction was "certainly of more importance to Scotland than any that has happened since the Union."[65] Like Elibank and Carlyle, Robertson believed that the militia issue was a critical test of the liberty of Scotland and the viability of the Union. Yet his resentment toward England was tempered by his great respect for its institutions, and he therefore concluded his discussion of the militia issue by remarking: "I will not say that you are better men, but sure I am you are better citizens on your side of the Tweed."[66] The prevailing spirit of the day is indicated by the fact that the Select Society decided at a meeting chaired by Robertson on 5 February to offer a gold medal for the best essay on "means of promoting and supporting Publick Spirit."[67]

The Scots militia agitation of 1759–1760 reached its climax in the late winter and early spring of 1760. On 4 March Gilbert Elliot raised the matter in the House of Commons with a brilliant speech that was well supported by James Oswald of Dunnikier, Sir Harry Erskine, and the Townshend brothers, Charles and George. Their well-organized campaign succeeded in bringing the matter before a parliamentary committee chaired by Oswald (12 March), who skillfully maneuvered a motion for presentation of a Scots militia bill before the full house toward the end of the month (24 March).[68] Meanwhile, the heritors of the shire of Edinburgh met twice in mid-March to petition the government for a militia, and George Townshend wrote a spirited new preface for a London edition of Carlyle's pamphlet.[69] Townshend praised an unnamed parliamentary orator (Gilbert Elliot) for leading the militia fight, scorned the lord advocate for opposing it, and lamented the vulnerability of Scotland in the event of

---

[64] *SM* 22 (February 1760): 99–104.

[65] Elibank to Townshend, 21 December 1759, and Robertson to Townshend, 23 February 1760, WLCL, Townshend Papers.

[66] Ibid. Cf. Carlyle, *Scots Militia Question*, 31.

[67] Select Society Minutes, 5 February 1760, NLS, Adv. 23.1.1.

[68] Western, *English Militia*, 165; Gilbert Elliot to Sir Gilbert Elliot, Lord Minto, 4 March 1760, quoted in George F. S. Elliot, *The Border Elliots and the Family of Minto* (Edinburgh, 1897), 359–60.

[69] Letter Books of Robert Dundas, vol. 6, Appendix on Militia, SRO, RH 4/15/5; *Auto.*, 419.

an invasion such as Thurot had threatened.[70] Other pamphlets and articles helped to nurture an optimistic attitude among advocates of a Scots militia. By the end of March John Home could report from London that the Scots militia bill was likely to be enacted in Parliament, "tho John Bull boggles a little at the Highlanders" and would probably insist on certain additional restrictions and regulations.[71]

Home and his friends were deceived. While supporters were noisily campaigning for passage of the Scots militia bill the duke of Newcastle and earl of Hardwicke were quietly conducting a meticulous canvass of parliamentary votes in hopes of defeating the bill on its second reading in the House of Commons.[72] Their campaign centered on the argument that the economic burden for a Scots militia would fall chiefly on the English, but they were not above adding appeals to base fears about the danger of arming a nation of potential Jacobites.[73] As a cheaper and safer alternative to a Scots militia they endorsed the duke of Argyll's proposal for authorizing private regiments of "fencibles" (so named because their sole concern would be national defense) under the command of trustworthy Scottish peers.[74] Their scheme benefited from Pitt's indecisiveness and from the steady support they received from Lord Advocate Robert Dundas, who openly allied himself with antimilitia forces despite charges of treason leveled against him by disgruntled Scots. When the bill received its second reading in the Commons on 15 April 1760, Pitt spoke ineffectively in favor, Dundas effectively against. Sir Harry Erskine and James Oswald proved to be no match for Charles Yorke and other speakers who participated in Newcastle and Hardwicke's well-orchestrated program, and at the end of the day the bill was thrown out by an overwhelming majority, 194 to 84.[75]

In Moderate circles reaction to news of the militia bill's defeat was shock and resentment. Writing to Gilbert Elliot at the end of April, William Robertson expressed the prevalent view:

---

[70] Townshend's preface, dated 2 March and signed "An Independent Briton," was reprinted in *SM* 22 (March 1760): 167–68.

[71] Home to Milton, 29 March 1760, NSL, 16715:207. In his *Scots Militia Question*, 38, Carlyle asserted that the Scots militia bill "cannot possibly fail of success."

[72] Western, *English Militia*, 167.

[73] Ibid., 164.

[74] Ibid.; Murdoch, *"People Above,"* 88–89. In 1759 Home considered the scheme to raise fencibles an antimilitia ploy (Home to Bute, 8 November 1759, Bute, box 2 [1759], no. 184). In the 1770s, however, he and his friends apparently accepted this alternative as better than nothing. Home himself became a lieutenant in Buccleuch's South Fencibles, which Carlyle praised in the postscript to the Edinburgh edition of his militia pamphlet of 1778.

[75] Western, *English Militia*, 167.

You will easily conceive the astonishment & concern of your friends in this country upon the miscarriage of the Militia Bill. Besides all the other advantages of the measure, I am fully convinced that it would have proved the most effectual security of the present government in this part of the kingdom, & it vexes me to see more done in one day to sower & alienate the minds of the people, than the attention of many years will be able to counterballance.

"I am hopeful," Robertson continued, ". . . that by perseverance we may gain our point in the same manner as the English have done." To this end he proposed a scheme for securing a "vigorous" promilitia resolution at the approaching general assembly. "I am persuaded it may be procured," Robertson wrote, but "the thing shall not be attempted if we are not sure of carrying it." Elliot could help by persuading a particular ruling elder to return to Scotland in time for the opening of the assembly on 15 May; as for the rest, "Home will need only a hint to hunt after any other Elders that may be loitering in London."[76]

Robertson's scheme was only partially successful. On 21 May 1760 the general assembly sent the king an address on the war containing the following sentence: "The inhabitants of this part of the island were unable to exert themselves, in repelling the king's enemies, with such vigour as their principles of religion and loyalty would naturally have inspired." This was thought sufficiently disrespectful by the government to merit expurgation from the published version of the assembly's address in the *London Gazette*,[77] but it was not the "vigorous" militia statement that Robertson had desired. At the close of the general assembly Robert Dundas boasted to Hardwicke that plans for a more forceful promilitia resolution had been dropped, despite "a good deal of private Cabal and faction concerning it," because its proponents came to see that such a measure would certainly have met defeat. In the same letter Dundas noted the personal abuse to which he was continually being subjected in Scotland as a result of his part in the militia affair, adding that he hoped "to obtain an approbation of my Conduct from your Lordship and others."[78] Hardwicke and Newcastle seem to have taken the hint, for two weeks later Dundas was appointed lord president of the Court of Session despite the angry cries

---

[76] Robertson to Elliot, 30 April 1760, NLS, 11009:70–71.

[77] *Annals*, 2:vii, 189–90.

[78] Dundas to Hardwicke, 31 May 1760, BL, Add. 35449:234–35 (courtesy of Alexander Murdoch).

of Scots militia agitators that he had "sold his country for a place."[79]

As far as the Moderate literati of Edinburgh were concerned, the Scots militia controversy of 1760 was merely the latest example of Robert Dundas's steadfast opposition to their policies and programs.[80] It is unlikely that Dundas's antipathy to the Scots militia bill was motivated solely by place-hunting. Equally important was the fact that Dundas viewed the Scots militia agitation as the work of his personal, political, and ideological enemies: Milton, Elliot, Alemoor, Jacobite sympathizers like Elibank, and the Moderate circle of Edinburgh literati.[81] In the late summer or early autumn of 1760 the Moderates and their friends decided to strike a blow at Dundas and his London bosses with a work of satire. The likely choice for such an undertaking was Alexander Carlyle, who had already employed his "ironical style" successfully on two previous occasions. Since Carlyle was then preoccupied with preparations for his wedding, however, the enterprise was secretly entrusted to Adam Ferguson.[82]

The result of Ferguson's labors was a long pamphlet published anonymously in London in December 1760 as *The History of the Proceedings in the Case of Margaret, Commonly called Peg, only lawful Sister to John Bull, Esq.*[83] Inspired by John Arbuthnot's popular pamphlet of 1712,[84] *Sister Peg* describes the adventures of John Bull (England) and his little sister Margaret or Peg (Scotland), whom John leaves unarmed and defenseless in the face of armed incursions by Mac-Lurchar (the Highlanders), Squire Geoffrey (the Jacobite pretenders to the throne), and Lewis Baboon (France). The chief villains are Hubble-bubble (Newcastle), Bumbo (Robert Dundas), and Nurse (Hardwicke), who are held responsible for foiling poor Peg's attempts to arm herself. William Pitt, now openly at odds with Lord Bute and apparently much resented for his sorry performance during the Scots militia debates, is also ridiculed. *Sister Peg*'s controver-

[79] *The Principal Heads of a Speech in P———t concerning the Scots Militia, By a Right Honourable M———R from a certain county in N———H B———N* (1760); *Auto.*, 419–20.

[80] *Auto.*, 248, 333–35.

[81] Ibid., 335, 420; John Ramsay, *Scotland and Scotsmen in the Eighteenth Century*, ed. Alexander Allardyce, 2 vols. (Edinburgh, 1888), 1:327–42; *Principal Heads of a Speech*, where Dundas's arguments against the militia bill are discussed.

[82] *Auto.*, 426–27.

[83] Though the title page reads 1761, the actual time of publication has been pushed back to December 1760 by David Raynor in his recent edition of this pamphlet, *Sister Peg: A pamphlet hitherto unknown by David Hume* (Cambridge, 1982). Reasons for rejecting Raynor's ascription of *Sister Peg* to Hume rather than to Ferguson appear in my review in *Philosophical Books* 24 (1983): 85–91.

[84] John Arbuthnot, *The History of John Bull*, ed. A. W. Bower and R. A. Erickson (Oxford, 1976).

sial nature and biting wit aroused considerable interest that soon called forth a second London edition. Although the author's identity remained a secret, Carlyle says it was commonly supposed that the pamphlet was the work of someone from the Moderates' inner circle, "if not the joint work of us all."[85]

About a year after the appearance of *Sister Peg,* the Moderate literati found themselves at the forefront of another campaign for a Scots militia bill. Their optimism on this occasion was based chiefly on the emergence of what seemed to them a more favorable political climate in London. Not only was Robert Dundas no longer lord advocate, but the earl of Bute, Gilbert Elliot, and Charles Townshend had acquired positions of influence, and promilitia forces in Parliament had been joined by the enthusiastic George Dempster, who dramatically vowed to Alexander Carlyle to resubmit a Scots militia bill every year until one passed.[86] Furthermore, the friends of the Scots militia idea were now more aware of the need for effective organization on the local level. It was apparently for this reason that several of them banded together early in 1762 to establish the Poker or Militia Club, which met once each week for dinner, claret, and "public purpose."[87]

Like the Select Society, to which approximately forty percent of its members belonged, the Poker Club was notable for bringing together many of the leading literary and professional men in the Edinburgh vicinity with elements of the Scottish gentry and nobility.[88] Perhaps because it arose at about the same time that the Select Society was beginning to falter, the Poker has sometimes been viewed as a mere offshoot or extension of the Select. Yet the differences between these two celebrated Edinburgh clubs are more revealing than their similarities. The Select Society was a polite debating club marked by formality and restraint. Participants were required to follow strict rules of conduct, and debate was not permitted on the most controversial topics of the day.[89] By contrast, the Poker Club was firmly

---

[85] *Auto.,* 427.

[86] Dempster to Carlyle, 30 January 1762, EUL, Dc. 4.41:91. Carlyle was told to send this letter back to Dempster as a reminder if the latter should fail to keep his promise.

[87] *Auto.,* 439–40.

[88] Roger L. Emerson, "The Social Composition of Enlightened Scotland: The Select Society of Edinburgh, 1754–1764," *SVEC* 114 (1973); 291–329; Alexander Carlyle, "A Comparison of Two Eminent Characters Attempted after the Manner of Plutarch," in *AC,* 282.

[89] Besides prohibiting debate on revealed religion and Jacobitism, the Rules and Orders of the Select Society stipulated that each member could speak only three times in the course of a debate and that "no person shall be interrupted in his argument, nor shall any person be named in Debate." NLS, Adv. 23.1.1.

committed to a single controversial principle, namely, "zeal for the Militia, and a conviction that there could be no lasting security for the freedom and independence of these islands, but in the valour and patriotism of an armed people,"[90] and its tone was informal, convivial, and at times even rowdy. Writing to Adam Ferguson from luxurious Fontainebleu in 1763, David Hume yearned for "the plain roughness of the *Poker* . . . to correct and qualify so much lusciousness."[91] The same characteristic that so appealed to Hume was scorned by James Boswell, who complained that the members of the Poker were "literary barbarians" out to "destroy politeness."[92] Although Boswell exaggerated, all surviving accounts suggest that the Poker was an exceptionally friendly and lively club that deliberately rid itself of the stiff formality and affected air of "English" gentility associated with the Select Society. The Poker was a place where Scottish gentlemen and literati could relax among themselves without fear of giving offense. In this sense, it is perhaps indicative of an increase in national self-confidence and self-assertiveness on the part of those Scots who most resented the injustice done to their country in regard to the militia issue.

From the outset the Moderate literati were among the prime movers of the Poker. It was Adam Ferguson who gave the club its intentionally cryptic name—which is either an allusion to its intended role as an instrument for stirring up national pride and concern about the Scots militia question or, as David Raynor has plausibly suggested, a reference to a line in *Sister Peg* where Margaret "throws her poker" (militia) at the rebellious Highlanders during the '45.[93] Besides Blair, Carlyle, Ferguson, Home, and Robertson, early members included Lord Elibank, John Jardine, David Hume, William Johnstone Pulteney, George Dempster, John Adam, Sir Adam Fergusson, John Drysdale, George Wishart, John Gregory, Baron Mure, Joseph Black, Adam Smith, John Dalrymple, Andrew Stuart, and James

---

[90] Adam Ferguson, "Minutes of the Life and Character of Joseph Black, M.D.," *TRSE* 5 (1805), pt. 3:113n.; Minutes of the Poker Club, 1774–1784, EUL, Dc. 5.126; *Auto.*, 439. It is unfortunately not known just what the Poker did to advance the Scots militia cause, for the club's minute book is sketchy and chronologically incomplete. Yet Alexander Carlyle has left no doubt that the Poker's "Great Object . . . of which they never lost sight" amidst all their conviviality was the "National" cause of agitation for a Scots militia ("Comparison of Two Eminent Characters," in *AC*, 282). I take this to mean that the members engaged in frequent discussions about the militia issue as well as, perhaps, mild forms of clandestine propaganda, such as pamphlets and letters to the press.

[91] Hume to Ferguson, 9 November 1763, *HL*, 1:410–11.

[92] Boswell, *London Journal*, 300. Cf. *Auto.*, 442–43.

[93] *Auto.*, 439; Ferguson, *Sister Peg*, 57, 110.

Russel, who were soon joined by peers such as the earls of Glasgow, Glencairn, and Haddington and the duke of Buccleuch.[94] After six or seven years the Moderate literati began to feel that increased expenses, an inferior meeting place, and several unfortunate membership admissions were leading the Poker to ruin, so they secretly reorganized the nucleus of their circle into a new club, the Tuesday, which met weekly until the Poker Club itself fell back into their hands around 1771.[95] Surviving club minutes show that the Moderate literati continued to be among the most active members of the Poker Club until its demise in 1784.[96]

In spite of the Poker Club, it soon became clear that economic factors were jeopardizing the chances for passage of a Scots militia bill in 1762. The chief problem was a severe manpower shortage caused by the prolongation of the Seven Years' War. This situation turned many Scottish manufacturers and farmers against the militia and shattered the illusion that all of Scotland was united behind the militia movement.[97] It also provoked the emergence of widespread opposition to the militia among manufacturers and farmers in England. In 1760 Carlyle and other Scots militia proponents had hailed the English militia as "unquestionable proof" that a militia was compatible with modern commerce;[98] now their opponents were using the example of the English militia to support the opposite position.

Early in 1762 an attempt was made to regain momentum for the Scots militia cause by publishing a fourth edition of Alexander Carlyle's *Question Relating to a Scots Militia,* with a new preface designed to refute the latest antimilitia arguments.[99] Denying that the English had tired of their militia and that the militia was to blame for the current manpower shortage, the new preface maintained that the real causes of the British labor shortage were three other factors: the vast size of the army and navy, the growth of trade, and a series of plentiful and productive years that had raised the value of labor. By decreasing the need for demoralizing levies by the regular army and navy, the argument ran, a Scots militia could actually serve to increase rather than diminish the population in general and the labor

---

[94] *AC*, 215.

[95] *Auto.*, 441–42.

[96] Poker Club Attendance Analysis (compiled by Jeremy Cater), EUL, Dc. 5.126*. During the decade covered by existing minutes, the total number of meetings attended by the Moderate literati of Edinburgh was as follows: Ferguson, 33; Robertson, 32; Blair and Carlyle, 28; Home, 22. The most active member, Robert Chalmers, attended forty meetings during this period.

[97] *SM* 24 (January–March 1762): 8–16, 74–76, 161–63.

[98] Carlyle, *Scots Militia Question*, 16, 27–28.

[99] Ibid., 4th ed. (Edinburgh, 1762), 3.

force in particular. A militia would further aid the growth of population in Scotland by strengthening the social and moral fiber of society. Feelings of "tenderness," "esteem," and "mutual confidence" among officers and their men would improve relations between "the high and low" and produce "a regular subordination defined by law, which is the cement of Society."[100]

Such logic proved powerless against prevailing economic and political forces. While Elliot, Oswald, and Dempster continued to press for a Scots militia bill the earl of Bute and some other Scottish politicians were having serious doubts. Bute was in no position to antagonize his many English critics by supporting a partisan Scottish bill with little chance of success in Parliament. In any case he remained unconvinced that the militia was popular with a majority of Scots.[101] Though he asserted that if his friends should insist on pursuing their plan he would "Share their disgrace," Bute made no secret of his preference for restraint.[102] Following his lead, Scottish members of Parliament held a meeting on 22 March 1762 and voted unanimously not to introduce a Scots militia bill. As one of the participants explained it, this decision was prompted both by the manpower shortage in Scotland and by the realization that "we have no chance of getting it, and by moving for it would only put ourselves in the way of being abused and Afronted."[103]

With the coming of peace and the earl of Bute's retirement from government in 1763, the Scots militia cause sank into oblivion for more than a decade. Although the Moderate literati and their friends continued to meet regularly at the Poker and Tuesday clubs, their militia propaganda fell on deaf ears. Yet militia sentiment and feelings of animosity toward John Bull found other forms of expression during this period. As we shall see, the battleground in the war for Scottish national dignity and public virtue sometimes shifted from the militia question to the Ossian controversy, as if poetic genius could somehow compensate for political and military impotence. Adam Ferguson's *Essay on the History of Civil Society* may also be read as an exercise in sublimated Scots militia propaganda; for although the term "militia" is scarcely mentioned in the text, the *Essay*'s emphasis on the need for public virtue and martial spirit and the dangers of the di-

---

[100] Carlyle, *Scots Militia Question*, 4th ed., 11.

[101] Bute to Elliot, 2 March and 14 March 1762, NLS, 11016:24–25, 30–31.

[102] Bute to Elliot, 16 March 1762, Bute, Cdf. 6/142/1–2 (this reference and the next courtesy of Alexander Murdoch).

[103] John Murray of Strowan to John Mackenzie of Delvine, 23 March 1762, NLS, 1404:166–67.

vision of labor and excessive luxury can be fully understood only in the context of the militia question.[104]

The Scots militia issue was revived in the mid-1770s, when discontent and eventual rebellion in America reawakened feelings of national pride and military vulnerability in Scotland. Writing to Alexander Carlyle from London around 1775, George Dempster urged the Poker Club to "take up the Pen" in order to make the country understand the need for a militia.[105] Carlyle had recently embarrassed Dempster by returning the latter's letter of 30 January 1762 pledging unrelenting support for a Scots militia bill.[106] After thirteen years of waiting, he was beginning to feel that the time had come to hold Dempster to his word and mount a new militia campaign.

The man who translated the revitalized militia spirit of the mid-1770s into an actual bid for Scots militia legislation was not George Dempster but the earl of Bute's eldest son, John, Viscount Mountstuart. This was the same young man whom Adam Ferguson had tutored at Harrow in the late 1750s, and it is quite possible that he acquired his zeal for militia from his old tutor.[107] The day before introducing his Scots militia bill in the House of Commons, Mountstuart wrote of his fears and aspirations to Baron Mure, adding that he hoped to hear the Poker Club was thriving.[108] It was not long before Mountstuart himself was paid the honor of being selected for membership in the Poker along with another of Ferguson's former-students, Henry Dundas. On the day following Dundas's election to the Poker in late January 1776, Ferguson reported happily to John Home in London that "the sense of this Country where it has been taken is every where favourable to the Militia."[109]

Matters came to a head in Parliament in March 1776. At the bill's second reading on the fifth of the month, Dempster, Gilbert Elliot, Sir Adam Fergusson, and their friends met stiff opposition,[110] and nine days later they narrowly defeated Grenville's motion for addi-

---

[104] See *Essay*, 191, 218, 230–32, 250, and Duncan Forbes's perceptive comments in the introduction, esp. xxxvi. Cf. Robertson, *Militia Issue*, chap. 7.

[105] Dempster to Carlyle, [1775], EUL, Dc. 4.41:90.

[106] See n. 86 above.

[107] Mountstuart's devotion to Ferguson is evident from his letter to Mure of 23 July 1772, in *Selections from the Family Papers Preserved at Caldwell*, 3 vols. (Paisley, 1883–1885), 2, pt. 2:201.

[108] Mountstuart to Mure, 1 November 1775, ibid., 264–265.

[109] Ferguson to Home, 27 January 1776, NLS, 124:76–77. Cf. James Boswell, *Boswell: The Ominous Years, 1774–1776*, ed. Charles Ryskamp (New York, 1963), 186–87, 214.

[110] *SM* 38 (April 1776): 681–89.

tional taxation at the county level. Supporters of the motion employed economic arguments similar to those used by Samuel Johnson, who told Boswell that "your scheme is to retain a part of your little land-tax, by making us pay and clothe your militia."[111] Offended by his friend's attitude, Boswell retorted: "You should not talk of *we* and *you*, Sir: there is now an *Union.*"[112] Union or no, on 20 March opponents of the Scots militia managed to push through a delaying motion that effectively suppressed the bill.[113] In reporting this development the *Scots Magazine* abandoned its usual sedate tone and harangued against the English for failing to see that "the peace and security of Scotland are the surest basis and best guardians of the wealth and liberties of England."[114]

For the Moderate literati and their friends in the Poker Club, the defeat of the militia bill of 1775–1776 could hardly have occurred at a worse time. Baron Mure had just died, and their beloved David Hume was fading fast. It was in a spirit of dejection caused by "the Loss of one Friend & the Danger of another" that Adam Ferguson drafted a letter to John Home in London telling of Scotland's passive response to the latest militia setback: "I am sorry to tell you that we receive the repulse of the Militia Bill with great Tranquillity. . . . I hope that we may be able to return to the Charge but I confess that I do not foresee a more favourable opportunity."[115]

Upon receiving Ferguson's letter, Home hastened to accompany the ailing Hume on prescribed journeys to London and Bath. To pass the time on their journey, Hume playfully imagined himself the prince of a kingdom bordering states governed by Home and Ferguson. Knowing full well their high regard for "military virtues as essential to every state," Hume joked about the danger that his friends' warlike ways would interrupt his own projects for "cultivating, improving, and civilizing mankind by the arts of peace." He took comfort, however, in the reflection that his neighbors would so neglect their finances and so mismanage their affairs that he would set one upon the other and probably end up "master of all the three king-

---

[111] James Boswell, *The Life of Samuel Johnson*, ed. George Birkbeck Hill and L. F. Powell, 6 vols. (Oxford, 1934–1940), 2:431, and *Ominous Years*, 267–68. Cf. the speeches of Grenville and Thomas Townshend in *Parl. Hist.*, 18:1232–34.

[112] Boswell, *Life of Johnson*, 2:431.

[113] *SM* 38 (April 1776): 681–89, and 40 (May 1778): 236–37.

[114] *SM* 38 (April 1776): 689.

[115] Ferguson to Home, 10 April 1776 (draft), NLS, 1809:1–2. This passage does not appear in the published version of this letter, dated 11 April 1776, in Mackenzie, 167–68.

doms."[116] Although Home's account of this episode concludes with the two travelers doubled up in fits of laughter, the story illustrates a serious point. David Hume, like Adam Smith, had a mentality that was essentially pacific, commercial, and modernizing, whereas Home, Ferguson, and the other Moderate literati of Edinburgh tended to place public virtue and a martial spirit above economic and social progress. Of course, the two sides were frequently ambivalent: Hume and Smith sometimes recommended civic virtue and martial spirit, just as the Moderate literati sometimes demonstrated an interest in economic improvement. Yet their priorities were different, and the anecdote about Hume's imaginary kingdoms demonstrates just how aware of that fact they were.

Differences that were treated lightly in private could give rise to serious confrontations when important public issues were thought to be at stake. Consider the Moderates' reaction to Adam Smith's discussion of national defense in the *Wealth of Nations*, which first appeared while Mountstuart's militia bill was under consideration by Parliament in March 1776. Smith argued that "the history of all ages . . . bears testimony to the irresistible superiority which a well-regulated standing army has over a militia."[117] He supported his position both with historical examples of militias being defeated by standing armies and with logical arguments based on the principle of the division of labor. According to the latter, a standing army is particularly necessary in modern, commercial societies because the majority of citizens are "unwarlike" and because the complexity of modern warfare requires a specialized body of professional soldiers.[118] Smith later modified his position somewhat by arguing that a well-developed "martial spirit" could help to reduce the size of the standing army and prevent the growth of "mental mutilation, deformity and wretchedness" among the people.[119] But he never seemed to realize that those remarks, containing no mention of the word "militia," did little to counteract the effect of his onslaught against militias in the chapter on national defense.[120]

[116] Mackenzie, 181–82. Reprinted in John Home, *A Sketch of the Character of Mr. Hume and Diary of a Journey from Morpeth to Bath*, ed. David Fate Norton (Edinburgh, 1976), 13–25.

[117] Adam Smith, *An Inquiry into the Nature and Causes of the Wealth of Nations*, ed. R. H. Campbell and A. S. Skinner, 2 vols. (Oxford, 1976), 2:701.

[118] Ibid., 694–96.

[119] Ibid., 787.

[120] Smith's ambivalence on the militia issue is stressed in Donald Winch, *Adam Smith's Politics: A Study in Historiographic Revision* (Cambridge, 1978), chap. 5, esp. 112. But see Robertson, *Militia Issue*, chap. 7, for a different view.

At least two of the Moderate literati were deeply troubled by Smith's ill-timed attack on militias. In a letter to Smith devoted chiefly to praising the *Wealth of Nations*, Adam Ferguson stated: "You have provoked, it is true, the church, the universities, and the merchants, against all of whom I am willing to take your part; but you have likewise provoked the militia, and there I must be against you."[121] A letter that Alexander Carlyle prepared for the press around this time seems to be addressed specifically to Smith, for it warns of the dangers of large standing armies of the Prussian variety, which aid the growth of despotism and reduce professional soldiers to mere automatons, worse off than any factory worker. "A man in some Manufacturies converts to become a part of a Machine for a few hours in a day, for his own substanance and that of his family," Carlyle concedes; "but [in a standing army] he is fixed to the Machine for life."[122] Another of Carlyle's essays from this period reiterates the ideas of his friend Adam Ferguson about the special need for militias in commercial societies in order to preserve "the manhood of the people."[123]

The strongest attack on Smith is to be found in an anonymous pamphlet usually attributed to Carlyle, titled *A Letter to His Grace the Duke of Buccleugh, on National Defence: With Some Remarks on Dr Smith's Chapter on that Subject, in his Book entitled . . . the Wealth of Nations*.[124] Here Smith is castigated for treating the militia and standing army as mutually exclusive rather than complementary institutions, for distorting history by calling troops a standing army when they are successful and a militia when they are not, and for creating the impression that the "husbandman" and "manufacturer" in modern, commercial societies are necessarily averse to, or incapable of, bearing arms. The example of Switzerland, which Carlyle probably learned about in detail from Ferguson, is cited as evidence that a militia need not be harmful to agriculture and industry.[125] And even if a martial spirit could be shown to be slightly damaging to commerce, Carlyle adds, "it is surely better to be a little less rich and commerical than

---

[121] Ferguson to Smith, 18 April 1776, in *The Correspondence of Adam Smith*, ed. Ernest Campbell Mossner and Ian Simpson Ross (Oxford, 1977), 193–94.

[122] Carlyle, Letters on the Militia (copies), no. 1, NLS, 3464:51–53.

[123] Ibid., no. 2, 3464:55.

[124] This was the title of the original, London edition of January 1778. Six months later a new edition appeared in Edinburgh without Smith's name in the subtitle. All references are to the Edinburgh edition.

[125] Carlyle, *Letter on National Defence*, 46. Cf. Ferguson's account of his emotional encounter with the Swiss militia in his letter to Carlyle of 29 April 1775, in John Small, "Biographical Sketch of Adam Ferguson," *TRSE* 23 (1864): 620. Cf. also Fletcher, *Discourse*, 18.

by ceasing to be men, to endanger our existence as a nation."[126] Although Smith claimed privately that these charges misrepresented his true position, which was not at all unfavorable to militias,[127] it would be more accurate to say that they reveal a fundamental tension in priorities among the apostles of "wealth" and "virtue" in the Scottish Enlightenment. Smith, like Hume, could sympathize with the Scots militia cause, approve of a martial spirit, and enjoy the company of the Poker Club, but the logic of his position left little room for a militia in modern, commercial societies.[128] For Carlyle, Ferguson, and their Moderate friends, however, the militia was not a secondary consideration but a vital antidote to the poisonous side effects of commerce, modernity, and civilization itself.

For the remainder of the American War, the Moderate literati continued to express themselves from time to time on the need for a Scots militia, especially after John Paul Jones led the motley American navy on successful forays against his defenseless native land.[129] A newspaper notice of February 1780 named Ferguson, Carlyle, and Home among the members of an Antigallican Society pledged to a program for encouraging patriotism and national defense.[130] An anonymous letter published the following month in the same newspaper may also have been the work of one or more of the Moderate literati; it praised the Antigallican Society and asserted that "the national character [of Scotland] has always hinged, and always must, upon *arms* and *letters*" rather than upon agriculture and industry.[131] In May 1782 Carlyle joined a large number of Scottish peers and gentlemen who gathered at a London tavern in an attempt to draft yet another Scots militia bill.[132] Later that year Carlyle, Ferguson, and other members of the Poker Club stirred up still more militia activity, but once again to no avail.[133] Ironically, when Scotland finally got

---

[126] Carlyle, *Letter on National Defence*, 47.

[127] Adam Smith to [Andreas Holt], [26 October 1780], in Campbell and Ross, *Smith Correspondence*, 251 (Smith believed that someone called Douglas was the author of this pamphlet); Smith, *Wealth of Nations*, 2:700 n. 31.

[128] Hiroshi Mizuta, "Two Adams in the Scottish Enlightenment: Adam Smith and Adam Ferguson on Progress," *SVEC* 191 (1981): 812–19.

[129] Ferguson to John Macpherson, 27 July 1779, 25 October 1779, 10 December 1779, EUL, Dc. 1.77, nos. 14–16; Ferguson to Eden, 2 January 1780, BL, Auckland 34415:3–12; Carlyle, Letters on the Militia (copies), nos. 2–7, NLS, 3464:53–71.

[130] *Edinburgh Evening Courant*, 12 February 1780, cited in Davis D. McElroy, "A Century of Scottish Clubs, 1700–1800" (typescript, NLS, 1969), 304–305. McElroy speculates that the Poker Club was behind the Antigallican Society.

[131] Ibid., 306.

[132] *Reformation Interest* (Edinburgh, 1782).

[133] *SM* 44 (August and December 1782): 444–45, 666–68. On the Scots militia agitation of 1782–1783, see Robertson, *Militia Issue*, chap. 5.

a militia during the French wars of the late 1790s, the Moderate literati of Edinburgh played no known role in procuring it and seem actually to have disapproved of it on account of its severity. Their dream of a national militia that would both reflect and maintain the public virtue of Scotland's citizen-subjects had given way to the reality of what Ferguson and Carlyle considered "a sort of press act."[134]

We are now in a position to observe that the spirited participation of the Moderate literati of Edinburgh in the militia agitations of the Seven Years' and American Wars was the result of four interrelated motives. First, the traumatic experience of the '45 had filled them with dread about the vulnerability of the Scottish Lowlands in case of foreign invasion or domestic upheaval. For decades after the event they continued to refer to the '45 as proof of Scotland's defenseless condition, and they were determined to make certain that their country would never again be humiliated in that manner.[135] A second factor is the Moderate literati's "civic humanist" conviction that a militia would be likely to strengthen public virtue, guard liberty, and prevent the growth of "effeminacy," selfishness, excessive luxury, and similar vices likely to afflict a modern, commercial society. In this sense, the militia played a positive role in Moderate ideology as an institutional stimulus for morality and social well-being in a society inclined toward corruption and alienation. Third, both the militia's "military" function as a direct deterrent to catastrophes like the '45 and "moral" function as a stimulus to public virtue cannot be understood apart from the Moderate literati's conservatism. It was their lifelong commitment to the prevailing social, political, and ecclesiastical order that made them so zealous in its defense during times of national danger, so insistent on limiting their definition of public virtue to support for the status quo, and so determined to forge a militia that would reflect and reinforce the traditional social values of landed society. Finally, the militia issue was important to the Moderate literati of Edinburgh because it evoked strong feelings of Scottish nationalism. Whereas the first three factors mentioned above laid the ideological foundation for their militia spirit, it was wounded na-

[134] Ferguson to Carlyle, 2 October 1797, EUL, Dc. 4.41:57. The harsh stipulations of the Scottish militia act of 1797 touched off serious riots that are described and analyzed in Kenneth J. Logue, *Popular Disturbances in Scotland, 1780–1815* (Edinburgh, 1979), chap. 3. Cf. Ferguson's three letters to Henry Dundas of 1802 on his preference for a volunteer militia over a compulsory one, WLCL, Melville Papers.

[135] See, for example, the first paragraph of the short history of the Poker Club that Carlyle prefixed to the club minutes (EUL, Dc. 5.126); Carlyle, *Letter on National Defence*, 27–28; Ferguson, *Sister Peg*, chap. 2.

tional pride that introduced into their militia program a note of urgency, bitterness, and animosity toward England. Was Scotland a free and equal partner with England or merely a conquered province? To Scots staunchly committed to the principle of a "united kingdom," the refusal of a predominantly English Parliament to extend the provisions of the English militia to Scotland and the willingness of many Scots to accept this rebuff without protest seemed to undermine the Union and deprive the Scottish people of their liberty and dignity.

Some of the same principles that motivated the Moderate literati to participate so zealously in the militia campaigns of the 1750s, 1760s, 1770s, and early 1780s also inspired their involvement in another controversial cause of this period. This time the issue was not arms but poems—poems attributed to the legendary third-century Highland bard known as Ossian, son of Fingal.

❧

THE CALL OF THE HIGHLAND BARD

Methinks I hear the Grecian Bards exclaiming,
(The Grecian Bards, no longer worth the naming),
In song the Northern tribes so far surpass us,
One of the Highland-Hills they'll call Parnassus:
And from the sacred Mount *decrees* shall follow,
That Ossian was *himself* the True Apollo.

Prologue to *The Muse of Ossian,* 1763

No reader can rise from him, without being warmed with the
sentiments of humanity, virtue, and honour.

Hugh Blair, *Critical Dissertation on the Poems of Ossian,* 1763

Although a great deal has been written about Ossian and the Ossian
controversy, most of it has been concerned either with the question
of authenticity or with the question of influence. The former category encompasses numerous studies of Ossian's "translator" James
Macpherson and the Gaelic sources that he may or may not have examined. The latter category includes the vast body of scholarship
dealing with Ossian's impact on the primitivist and romantic move-
ments in literature and the arts, particularly in England, France, and
Germany. Since authenticity and influence have virtually monopolized Ossianic scholarship for more than two centuries, other potentially fruitful fields of study have not been thoroughly investigated.
Foremost among them for our purposes is the question of Ossian's
connection with, and attraction to, the Scottish literati who did so much
to advance the Ossianic cause. In addressing ourselves to this question, we shall be searching not for the "real" Ossian of the Highlands
or the romantic Ossian of nineteenth-century France and Germany,
but for the Ossian of the Scottish Lowlands and the Scottish Enlightenment.[136]

When approached in this way, the story of Ossian is not, as is commonly believed, the simple tale of a lone confidence man who per-
petrates a literary hoax. Rather, it is the story of a strange partnership between a brash young poet from Inverness-shire and a group

---

[136] For a different version of the discussion that follows, see Richard B. Sher, " 'Those
Scotch Imposters and Their Cabal': Ossian and the Scottish Enlightenment," in *Man
and Nature: Proceedings of the Canadian Society for Eighteenth-Century Studies,* vol. 1, ed.
Roger Emerson et al. (London, Ont., 1982), 55–63.

of Edinburgh literati—or to put it more dramatically, between the Highlands and the Lowlands. Not surprisingly, it was Adam Ferguson, the person who bridged the gap between the Highland and Lowland worlds more successfully than any other eighteenth-century man of letters, who did the most to bring the two sides together. On the Lowland side, Ferguson was responsible for stimulating John Home's interest in ancient Highland poetry. Although he understood "not one word" of Gaelic, Home was so intrigued by Ferguson's account of a lingering oral tradition of Gaelic balladry among the common people of his native Perthshire that he expressed a strong desire to learn more about the subject.[137] On the Highland side, Ferguson is reputed to have entertained Macpherson at his late father's manse in Perthshire early in 1759. At that meeting he is said to have encouraged Macpherson's professed interest in old Gaelic poetry and provided the aspiring young poet with a letter of introduction to his now famous friend John Home.[138] Thus, the scene was set for Home and Macpherson's historic encounter, which marked the real "beginning of the Ossianic industry."[139]

The meeting took place in September 1759 at Moffat, a popular Scottish spa. Home was there to treat an undisclosed chronic ailment; Macpherson was there in the somewhat demeaning capacity of tutor to the son of a Perthshire laird. Besides quite similar romantic sensibilities, the two poets shared a passion for heroic virtue and patriotism—the dominant values not only in Home's early plays but also in Macpherson's neglected poem, *The Highlander* (1758). Like *Douglas*, *The Highlander* tells of a courageous young Scot (Alpin) who rallies his countrymen against an army of Scandinavian invaders.[140] Even the character of the virtuous and patriotic Alpin seems to have been modeled on that of Home's Douglas.[141] Such resemblances sug-

---

[137] Ferguson to Henry Mackenzie, 26 March 1798 (hereafter cited as "Ferguson's Testimony"), and "Note from John Home" (hereafter cited as "Home's Testimony"), in *Report of the Committee of the Highland Society of Scotland, Appointed to Inquire into the Nature and Authenticity of the Poems of Ossian*, ed. Henry Mackenzie (Edinburgh, 1805), app. 4: 63, 68; Mackenzie, 127.

[138] I have been unable to trace the story of Macpherson's meeting with Ferguson any further back than an article by Allan Sinclair in the *Celtic Magazine* 5 (1880): 311–17. But the credibility of this story is increased by evidence of Ferguson's early involvement in the Ossian affair in Macpherson's letters to the Moderate minister George Lawrie (or Laurie) of Loudon (who was present at the Moffat meeting discussed below), 24 March and 11 April 1760, YUL, C1870 and C1872.

[139] Derick S. Thomson, "'Ossian' Macpherson and the Gaelic World of the Eighteenth Century," *Aberdeen University Review* 40 (1963): 8.

[140] *The Works of Ossian, containing the Poetical Works of James Macpherson*, ed. Malcolm Laing, 2 vols. (Edinburgh, 1805), 2:527–83.

[141] See Malcolm Laing's remarks, ibid., 1:209.

gest that the partnership between Macpherson and Home that gave rise to Ossian grew out of a fundamental similarity of outlook that preceded their meeting at Moffat in 1759. Heroic, patriotic virtue was the fertile common ground in which the seeds of the Ossianic enterprise took root and flowered.

Whatever else may have been said by Home and Macpherson at Moffat, the principal subject of their conversation was ancient Gaelic balladry. Upon learning that Macpherson had several old Gaelic poems in his possession, Home managed "with some difficulty" to coax him into producing an English translation of one of them.[142] The poem in question, "The Death of Oscur," was scarcely seven hundred words long, yet it contained most of the stylistic and thematic traits of Macpherson's later Ossianic poetry, including metaphorical descriptions of wild nature scenes, heroic individual combat, glorification of honor and virtue, and a pervasive concern with romantic themes such as passionate but unfulfilled love, melancholia, and death.[143] In the days that followed Macpherson brought forth several more specimens of this sort for the perusal of Home, who was "highly delighted" with them.[144] On 2 October Alexander Carlyle visited Home at Moffat and learned that his friend "had at last found what he had been long wishing for, a person who could make him acquainted with ancient Highland poetry, of which he had heard so much." Carlyle was introduced to Macpherson and shown several of his supposed translations, which "astonished" him with their "poetical genius."[145]

At this point Carlyle and Home determined that they had made "a precious discovery" that should be "published to the world" as soon as possible.[146] Home accordingly carried Macpherson's translations to a few of his closest literary friends in Edinburgh—Hugh Blair, William Robertson, Adam Ferguson, and Lord Elibank—as well as to several unnamed acquaintances in London, one of whom was almost certainly the earl of Bute.[147] All these critics were impressed by Home's find, but Blair, who was then preparing a course of public lectures on rhetoric and belles lettres, took a special interest. He immediately sent for Macpherson and promised to arrange publication of his collection of ancient Gaelic fragments if enough translations to fill a small

---

[142] "Home's Testimony," 69.

[143] James Macpherson, *Fragments of Ancient Poetry, Collected in the Highlands of Scotland and Translated from the Galic or Erse Language*, 2d ed. (Edinburgh, 1760), no. 7.

[144] "Home's Testimony," 69; Carlyle to William McDonald, 9 January 1802, in Mackenzie, *Highland Society Report*, app. 4 (hereafter cited as "Carlyle's Testimony"): 66.

[145] "Carlyle's Testimony," 66.

[146] Ibid.

[147] Ibid.

book could be produced. As Blair later recollected the incident, Macpherson was "extremely reluctant and averse" and acceded to his request only after "much and repeated importunity."[148] Even then, he continued to have serious doubts about the project:

> Tho' I made a sort of promise to Doctor Blair of sending more of our Highland Rhapsodies, I would rather chuse he would dispense with it upon several accounts. But I am a man of my word, and accordingly have made preparations for satisfying his curiosity, if he does not easily pass from it. . . . I shall transmit a dozen in a few weeks to the Doctor, and let him and the rest of the genii do what seems fit. I am sure they will not readily expose [i.e. publish] me, if they are not realy worth the attention of the Publick, as *it was with reluctance, and out of no desire of applause, I begun to translate them at all.*[149]

Despite his misgivings, Macpherson honored his pledge to Blair, and on 14 June 1760 his poems were published in Edinburgh as *Fragments of Ancient Poetry, collected in the Highlands of Scotland*, with an anonymous preface by Blair himself.

The first edition of the *Fragments* consisted of fifteen brief poems of the sort that Macpherson had shown to Home at Moffat. In the preface Blair stated that these poems could not be dated with certainty but seemed, on the basis of their "spirit and strain," to belong to "the most early state of society."[150] He proceeded to discuss the manner in which the poems had been preserved by Highland bards, "some in manuscript, but more by oral tradition." The translation he described as "extremely literal." Finally, Blair noted that these fragments were thought to be only a small portion of a vast amount of unrecovered Ossianic poetry, including a "heroic poem" or epic about the exploits of an ancient Scottish king called Fingal.[151]

Publication of the *Fragments* produced a minor literary sensation. The *Scots Magazine* printed excerpts, and a second edition appeared "almost immediately" after the first.[152] An advertisement appended to the second edition announced that "measures are now taken for making a more full collection of the remaining works of the ancient Scottish Bards; in particular for recovering and translating the he-

---

[148] Blair to Henry Mackenzie, 20 December 1797, in Mackenzie, *Highland Society Report*, app. 4 (hereafter cited as "Blair's Testimony"), 57.

[149] Macpherson to George Lawrie, 18 March 1760, YUL, C1870. Emphasis added.

[150] Hugh Blair, preface to Macpherson's *Fragments*, iii.

[151] Ibid., vi, viii.

[152] *SM* 22 (July 1760); Bailey Saunders, *The Life and Letters of James Macpherson* (1894; reprint, New York, 1969), 82.

roic poem mentioned in the preface." The "measures" referred to were the various attempts by Blair and his friends to persuade Macpherson to undertake a search for the mysterious Ossianic epic he had earlier described to them. Once again Macpherson showed "extreme unwillingness" to pursue the matter, but the Edinburgh literati won him over at a dinner party organized by Blair.[153]

Since Macpherson had informed Blair two days after publication of the *Fragments* that his present circumstances prohibited a proper excursion to the Highlands, Blair organized a collection to defray expenses.[154] An Edinburgh merchant called Robert Chalmers served as treasurer, and eminent individuals from various walks of life were recruited to supervise the fund raising in their respective circles.[155] A total of £100 was raised in approximately two months from a long list of contributors that included Hume, Boswell, Sir David Dalrymple, John Dalrymple, Sir Adam Fergusson, Dempster, Kames, and Baron Orde.[156] This amount was sufficient to allow Macpherson to terminate his "disagreeable" employment as a tutor, and by the end of August 1760 he was on his way to the Highlands in search of Fingal.[157]

Macpherson's first Highland mission lasted four months and carried him to parts of Perthshire, Argyllshire, and Inverness-shire, to the Hebridean islands of Skye, North and South Uist, and Benbecula, and finally, after a visit to his home village of Ruthven in October, to the Argyllshire coast and the island of Mull.[158] Blair and his friends had provided letters of introduction to clergymen and clan chiefs from whom Macpherson supposedly gathered Gaelic manuscripts and recorded oral recitations.[159] During this period Macpher-

---

[153] "Blair's Testimony," 58. Robertson, Home, Elibank, and Sir Adam Fergusson are known to have attended this dinner.

[154] Macpherson to Blair, 16 June 1760, in Robert Henry Carnie, "Macpherson's *Fragments of Ancient Poetry* and Lord Hailes," *English Studies* 41 (1960): 23; "Blair's Testimony," 58.

[155] "Blair's Testimony," 58; Blair to Sir David Dalrymple, 23 June 1760, in Carnie, "Macpherson's *Fragments*," 22. In this letter Blair mentions William Robertson, John Dalrymple, and Andrew Stuart, along with Sir David Dalrymple himself, as men who might be willing to "lay themselves out among the Circle of their Several Acquaintances for promoting this design." Lord Kames, Baron Orde, and John Balfour the publisher are also mentioned among those willing to help.

[156] Carnie, "Macpherson's *Fragments*"; Elizabeth Montagu to Lord Lyttelton, 31 October 1760, in *The Letters of Mrs. Elizabeth Montagu*, 4 vols. (London, 1809–1813), 4:320. All the Moderate literati of Edinburgh seem to have participated in the subscription drive except Adam Ferguson, who later stated that he was not in Edinburgh at this time. Ferguson to Henry Mackenzie, 3 June 1812, in Mackenzie, 128.

[157] J. S. Smart, *James Macpherson: An Episode in Literature* (London, 1905), 98.

[158] Thomson, " 'Ossian' Macpherson," 8–9.

[159] Saunders, *James Macpherson*, 45.

son wrote often to Blair and his circle about the progress of his expedition. By the middle of January 1761 he was back in Edinburgh,
where he took up lodgings directly beneath those of Blair in Blackfriars Wynd and began translating the epic that he claimed to have
discovered. He continued to report on his progress to Blair, who "saw
him very frequently" at this time, and on at least one occasion he
showed some of his Gaelic manuscripts to Adam Ferguson, who considered them authentic-looking on the basis of his imperfect knowledge of written Gaelic.[160]

Shortly after beginning the "translation" of his "epic," Macpherson set out for London with Robert Chalmers to secure a publisher.[161] Although little is known about the details of his activities on
this London jaunt, it may be assumed that he was frequently in the
company of John Home, who probably introduced him to the earl
of Bute. Home had been so impressed by the ninth poem in Macpherson's *Fragments* that he had begun to prepare a stage adaptation
named for its leading female character, Rivine.[162] Bute soon became
the patron of both Home's play and Macpherson's epic, and it is likely
that he was at least partially responsible for funding the joint expedition to the Highlands made by his two protégés in the late spring
and summer of 1761.[163] On 12 June Home informed Bute that he
would be setting off the following day "with the highland bard to
visit those regions that nursed the genius of Ossian: and to gather if
I can some of natures gems to adorn Rivine the daughter of Kew."[164]
At the end of July the two poets returned to Edinburgh proclaiming
the complete success of their mission. To Bute Home disclosed the
manner in which his Highland jaunt would be likely to enhance his
abilities as a playwright:

[160] "Blair's Testimony" and "Ferguson's Testimony," 59, 63. Blair was under the
impression that Ferguson had actually verified the authenticity of several of Macpherson's translations, when in fact Ferguson had only perused Macpherson's materials.

[161] Saunders, *James Macpherson*, 158; Hume to William Strahan, 9 February 1761,
HL, 1:342–43.

[162] James S. Malek, "The Ossianic Source of John Home's *The Fatal Discovery*," *English Language Notes* 9 (1971): 39–42, and "Eighteenth-Century British Dramatic Adaptations of Macpherson's 'Ossian,'" *Restoration and Eighteenth-Century Theatre Research*
14 (1975): 38.

[163] In a letter to Bute of 26 November 1761, Macpherson referred to "the generous
encouragement" that the earl had provided during the months when *Fingal* was being
prepared for the press. The following summer he wrote to thank Bute for a £100
pension in addition to "that generosity to which I was so much obliged before" (Bute,
box 4 [1761], no. 656, and [1762], no. 228). Bute was undoubtedly the "noble person"
thanked in the advertisement to the first edition of *Fingal*.

[164] Hume to Bute, 12 June 1761, in R. George Thomas, "Lord Bute, John Home
and Ossian: Two Letters," *Modern Language Review* 51 (1956): 73–75.

My expedition to the North fully answered my expectation in all respects. It has enlarged & improved my ideas of natural objects & characters—& I hope will enable me to describe them in another manner than is done by those authors, who bred amongst hedges & ditches, & human beings framed like them, copy from the writings of other men faint pictures of what they never saw nor felt.[165]

As for Macpherson, Carlyle happily reported that he now had accumulated more lines of Ossianic poetry "than all Homer, Virgil, Milton, Tasso and Ariosto put together."[166]

Macpherson's first Ossianic epic, *Fingal, an Ancient Epic Poem,* was published at the end of 1761 (though the title page reads 1762) in a volume that also contained numerous shorter poems attributed to Ossian. It was then that the controversy began in earnest, as critics vied to outdo each other in praising or damning the work.[167] Since few of the participants in the controversy understood Gaelic, and since Macpherson himself was less than cooperative about his sources, no definitive conclusion about the status of the poems was ever reached during his lifetime. Even at a distance of more than two hundred years, all that Gaelic scholars who have studied the "authenticity question" can agree on is, on the one hand, that Macpherson utilized certain authentic names, legends, and stylistic traits drawn from at least fourteen or fifteen old Gaelic ballads and, on the other hand, that he freely manipulated these authentic features (by combining legitimate but traditionally distinct stories, for example) and further altered them by adding romantic touches and other embellishments foreign to genuine Gaelic balladry.[168] Perhaps it is true to say that

---

[165] Home to Bute, 3 August 1761, ibid. Home's "Rivine" eventually opened at Drury Lane (February 1769) with the anglicized title *The Fatal Discovery.* According to Carlyle, it enjoyed a successful run until Home's public declaration of authorship provoked "the jealousy and dislike which prevailed at that time against Lord Bute and the Scotch." *Auto.,* 534–35.

[166] Carlyle to Elliot, 29 July 1761, NLS, 11015:106.

[167] Smart, *James Macpherson,* chap. 6; Larry Le Roy Stewart, "Ossian in the Polished Age: The Critical Reception of James Macpherson's Ossian" (Ph.D. diss., Case Western Reserve University, 1971), chaps. 2 and 3. Stewart shows, however, that the initial controversy over *Fingal* had less to do with charges of forgery or outright fraud than with questions concerning its stature as an epic and its true age and national origins. Only after Macpherson strained credulity by publishing a second epic, *Temora,* in 1763 did the "imposture" issue become prominent, and only after he published his *Iliad* and *History of Great Britain* and acquired a reputation as an arrogant rogue and political hack during the 1770s did the attacks become personal and virulent.

[168] Derick S. Thomson, *The Gaelic Sources of Macpherson's Ossian* (Edinburgh, 1951); Robert P. Fitzgerald, "The Style of Ossian," *Studies in Romanticism* 6 (1966): 22–23.

"Macpherson was not a mere forger," as some of his worst enemies have claimed, and that he successfully "imitated the genuine [Gaelic] ballad style, conventions, and atmosphere."[169] But it is equally true that no epic poem like *Fingal* or its still less authentic sequel of 1763, *Temora,* has ever been known to exist in the Scottish Highlands.

The controversy over Macpherson's *Fingal* rapidly became a national struggle. Soon after it was published some Irish men of letters protested that Macpherson had stolen Ireland's national heroes.[170] Then more abusive references to Ossian began to appear in the English press in the context of radical Whig attacks on Lord Bute. John Wilkes's *North Britain* of 27 November 1762, for example, lampooned Macpherson, Home, and their Scottish "clan" as lackeys of the hated Scots prime minister:

> Macpherson leads the flaming Van,
> Laird of the *new* Fingalian Clan;
> While Jacky Home brings up the rear,
> With new-got pension, neat and clear,
> Three hundred *English* pounds a year.[171]

Charles Churchill struck a similar note in his biting satirical poem, *The Prophecy of Famine: A Scots Pastoral:*

> And if plain nature pours a simple strain,
> Which Bute may praise, and Ossian not disdain,
> Ossian, *sublimist, simplist* Bard of all,
> Whom *English Infidels* Macpherson *call,*
> Then round my head shall honour's ensigns wave,
> And pensions mark me for a willing slave.[172]

Faced with scurrilous criticism of this sort, Ossian's Scottish sympathizers retaliated with extravagant boasts like the one from David Erskine-Baker's stage play *The Muse of Ossian* that is reproduced at the beginning of this section. Such boasting in turn provoked more derisive attacks from English skeptics and bigots.[173] In an effort to gain

---

[169] These quotes are from Thomson, *Gaelic Sources,* 85, and Fitzgerald, "Style of Ossian," 31, respectively.

[170] *Fingal Reclaimed* (London, 1762); Smart, *James Macpherson,* 132; Stewart, "Ossian in the Polished Age," chap. 3.

[171] John Wilkes, "The Poetry Professors," quoted in Ernest Mossner, *The Forgotten Hume: Le Bon David* (New York, 1943), 87. Since English critics frequently attacked Bute for giving preference to Scots, the government pensions bestowed on Macpherson and Home during the Bute years aroused much animosity.

[172] *The Poetical Works of Charles Churchill,* ed. Douglas Grant (Oxford, 1956), 202.

[173] Robert Heron, *Observations Made in a Journey Through the Western Counties of Scotland in the Autumn of 1792,* 2 vols. (Perth, 1793), 1:352. On Scottish boasting as a re-

credibility, Macpherson supposedly deposited some Gaelic manuscripts at the shop of his publisher to be placed on public display. But these papers were ignored by his critics and cannot now be identified with certainty.[174]

Despite some suspicions about the authenticity of *Fingal,* and later *Temora,* as fully formed epics,[175] the Moderate literati of Edinburgh continued to function as the chief supporters of Ossianic poetry. Hugh Blair in particular fancied himself Ossian's champion. Several months after the publication of *Fingal,* Blair delivered a laudatory lecture on Ossian before a distinguished audience at the University of Edinburgh.[176] Soon he was talking of expanding the lecture into a larger work intended for publication in London.[177] The book was completed as planned and sold for fifty guineas to *Fingal's* publisher, Becket and de Hondt.[178] In January 1763 it appeared as *A Critical Dissertation on the Poems of Ossian, the Son of Fingal.* With the publication of this influential work and the withdrawal of Macpherson himself from the controversy, Ossian had become, in David Hume's words, Blair's "child . . . by adoption."[179]

The *Dissertation* begins with one of the century's strongest statements of literary primitivism.[180] According to Blair, every ancient or primitive poet is a kind of child because he lives in a childlike society that places more emphasis on imagination and passion than on reason and understanding. His language will necessarily be metaphorical and figurative, and his poetry will be characterized by those traits "which are the soul of poetry": "enthusiasm," "vehemence," and "fire." The progress of civilization brings forth more regular and polished manners and greater facility of understanding, but these advances

---

sponse to English criticism, and vice versa, see Janet Adam Smith, "Some Eighteenth-Century Ideas of Scotland," in *SAI,* 110.

[174] Saunders, *James Macpherson,* 197, 249; Smart, *James Macpherson,* 140–41.

[175] Blair, Carlyle, and Ferguson all admitted in their Highland Society testimonies that Macpherson had probably pieced together scattered and broken fragments in order to construct his Ossianic epics. Ferguson and Carlyle justified this procedure by arguing that the *Iliad* and *Odyssey* had probably been produced in the same manner.

[176] Blair to [William Strahan], 21 May 1762, in Robert Morrell Schmitz, *Hugh Blair* (New York, 1948), 50.

[177] Blair to Elliot, 17 May 1762, NLS, 11009:140; Blair to ———, [1762], NLS, 3219:1.

[178] Schmitz, *Hugh Blair,* 50. When Thomas Becket disagreed about how much money the *Dissertation* was worth, Blair backed off by saying that his motive for publishing the book was not money but "a Zeal to make Ossian's works be more thoroughly understood & Relished." Blair to Beckett, 19 August 1762, in R. W. Chapman, "Blair on Ossian," *Review of English Studies* 7 (1931): 81.

[179] Hume to Blair, 19 September 1763, *HL,* 1:400.

[180] René Wellek, *The Rise of English Literary History* (Chapel Hill, N.C., 1941), 63.

are achieved at considerable cost. As society develops, language loses its metaphorical quality, and people "subdue or disguise their passions." Poetry closely reflects these social changes by becoming more rational and refined but less vibrant and imaginative. Poetry becomes dry and artificial because it loses touch with its creative essence or "soul."[181]

Great poetry, then, is likely to be ancient or primitive or "oriental" poetry. Homer is the classic example of this poetic type, but Ossian fits the model equally well.[182] Blair paints an idyllic picture of life in the age of Ossian, which he locates somewhere between what Adam Ferguson would call the savage (hunting and fishing) and barbarian (pastoral) stages of society.[183] It was, says Blair, a pure and uncorrupted era, free from vices like "covetousness and effeminacy" that emerged only in a more refined period. Manners were crude and abstract ideas entirely absent, but sentiments were remarkably noble, as befits a heroic age.[184]

In Blair's view, "the two great characteristics of Ossian's poetry are tenderness and sublimity."[185] By the latter term Blair means that Ossian is at all times solemn, grandiose, and forceful in his depictions of natural scenery and events.[186] By "tenderness" Blair means that Ossianic poetry is virtuous and sentimental in its portrayal of human relations. Ossian may be inferior to Homer on several counts, Blair admits, but the Scottish bard far outshines his Greek rival "in point of humanity, magnanimity, virtuous feelings of every kind."[187] Thus Blair esteems Ossian as a poet who unites the raw power and majesty of Homer with the moral and aesthetic sensibilities of the neoclassical age. On the one hand, he is simple, imaginative, noble, and sublime; on the other, he is genteel, humane, sentimental, and prudish. Macpherson himself expressed a similar opinion when he pronounced the ancient Caledonian character that Ossian represented

---

[181] Hugh Blair, *A Critical Dissertation on the Poems of Ossian, the Son of Fingal*, 2d ed. (London, 1765), 1–5. Cf. *Essay*, 173, and Robertson, *History of Charles V*, in *WWR*, 3:66, for similar expressions of literary primitivism. For Ferguson, see also Lois Whitney, *Primitivism and the Idea of Progress in English Popular Literature of the Eighteenth Century* (Baltimore, 1934), 145–54.

[182] Blair, *Dissertation*, 5–6.

[183] Ibid., 30. Blair's *Dissertation* is discussed in the context of the "four stages theory" of social development in Ronald L. Meek, *Social Science and the Ignoble Savage* (Cambridge, 1976), 179–81.

[184] Blair, *Dissertation*, 32–36.

[185] Ibid., 36.

[186] Ibid., 37; *Lects.*, 1:65; Samuel H. Monk, *The Sublime in Eighteenth-Century England* (New York, 1935), 120–29; Stewart, "Ossian in the Polished Age," chap. 5.

[187] Blair, *Dissertation*, 41, 129–30.

to be "happily compounded of what is noble in barbarity, and virtuous and generous in a polished people."[188]

Although Blair was initially pleased with the public response to his *Dissertation,* upon going to London in April 1763 he was dismayed to discover that most men of letters in the capital were inclined to regard Ossian as a worthless imposture.[189] Dr. Johnson insulted him by asserting in his presence that the poems of Ossian could have been written by any man, woman, or child in the eighteenth century, and under Johnson's influence Thomas Percy privately called the whole episode a "cheat" that "could never have succeeded if almost all the Scots had not been simple enough to make it a national affair, and to join in imposing on themselves and others."[190] According to Boswell, Johnson believed that the poems of Ossian would have constituted "a curiosity of the first rate" if authentic, but that as modern productions they were of no literary value whatsoever.[191] By contrast, the most radical Ossianic enthusiasts treasured the poems for their intrinsic beauty as well as their supposed antiquity. One of Ossian's earliest supporters commented that the outcome of the authenticity controversy could in no way affect the excellence of the Ossianic poems: at worst the public had simply been "cheated into pleasure."[192] Adam Ferguson was not far from this view when he remarked that "the Specimens I have seen apart from the curiosity of them are very Interesting as Efforts of the Imagination and the Heart, equal to any poetry I know, and whether genuine or spurious I shall never be ashamed of having mistaken them for Originals."[193] David Hume was more skeptical. In a letter to Blair from London Hume insisted that it was necessary to obtain proof of Ossian's authenticity for inclusion in the planned second edition of Blair's *Dissertation.* "It is in vain to say, that their beauty will support them, independent of their authenticity," Hume warned; only "positive testimony" by respectable Highlanders would be able to save Ossian from falling into oblivion within a few years.[194]

[188] James Macpherson, "A Dissertation concerning the Era of Ossian," quoted (but incorrectly attributed to Hugh Blair) in Daiches, *Paradox of Scottish Culture,* 79–80.

[189] Blair to Boswell, 19 February 1763, YUL, C156; Blair to Hume, 29 September 1763, in John Hill Burton, *Life and Correspondence of David Hume,* 2 vols. (1846; reprint, New York, 1967), 1:468.

[190] Boswell, *Life of Johnson,* 1:396; Percy to Evan Evans, 23 July 1764, in *The Percy Letters: The Correspondence of Thomas Percy and Evan Evans,* ed. Aneirin Lewis (Baton Rouge, 1957), 96–98.

[191] *Tour,* 204.

[192] John Gordon, *Occasional Thoughts on the Study and Character of Classical Athens . . . With some Incidental Comparisons between Homer and Ossian* (London, 1762), 111n.

[193] Ferguson to Bishop Douglas, 21 July 1781, BL, Egerton 2182:47–49.

[194] Hume to Blair, 19 September 1763, *HL,* 1:398–401; *Auto.,* 290.

Blair was hurt and disconcerted by the failure of the English literary world to accept the poems of Ossian as genuine ancient Gaelic masterpieces. "Who but John Bull could entertain the belief of an imposture so incredible as this?" he angrily asked Hume. Annoyed as he was about having to satisfy "such incredulous people," Blair nevertheless agreed to carry out Hume's plan for gathering testimonies of authenticity from the Highlands.[195] With the publication of these testimonies as an appendix to the second edition of the *Dissertation* (June 1765), he felt sure he had refuted all of Ossian's critics, including even "that Barbarian Samuel Johnson."[196] In fact, although the second edition of the *Dissertation* does appear to have silenced the skeptics temporarily, by 1775 both Hume and Johnson were expressing their incredulity in no uncertain terms. Hume wrote, but did not publish, a critical essay on the inconclusiveness of the testimonies Blair had gathered.[197] Dr. Johnson was less discreet: in his *Journey to the Western Islands of Scotland* he openly branded Ossian a fraud and blamed Scottish national prejudice for the success of the hoax.[198] In private he was still more offensive, referring to the Ossian affair as a case of "Scotch conspiracy in national falsehood."[199] Similarly, Horace Walpole lashed out against "those Scotch imposters and their cabal" during a later episode in the Ossian story.[200]

Although they were crude exaggerations, Johnson and Walpole's charges of Scottish conspiracy and cabal were not wholly without foundation. One point of special significance concerns the relatively passive role played by Macpherson himself, particularly in the early days of the Ossian affair. As has been shown, Macpherson was "extremely reluctant" at every stage in the publication process—first to

---

[195] Blair to Hume, 29 September 1763, in Burton, *Life of Hume*, 1:469.

[196] Blair to Hume, 1 July 1765, RSE, 3/53. Blair went to his grave believing that the testimonies assembled in the appendix to the second edition of his *Dissertation* constituted "strong and irrefragable evidence in favour of the authenticity of the Ossianic Poems" ("Blair's Testimony," 60). Cf. Smart, *James Macpherson*, 114.

[197] David Hume, "Of the Authenticity of Ossian's Poems," in *Philosophical Works*, ed. T. H. Green and T. H. Grose, 4 vols. (1882; reprint, Darmstadt, 1964), 4:415–24; Mossner, *Forgotten Hume*, 97.

[198] Samuel Johnson, *Journey to the Western Islands of Scotland*, ed. Mary Lascelles (New Haven, 1971), 118. Johnson's charges prompted Blair to write to Macpherson about the need for "proper measures" to refute Johnson's "frivolous objections" (Blair to Elizabeth Montagu, 1 April 1775, Huntington Library, MO 488). For the sequel, see Robert F. Metzdorf, "M'Nicol, Macpherson, and Johnson," in *Eighteenth-Century Studies in Honour of Donald F. Hyde*, ed. W. H. Bond (New York, 1970), 45–61.

[199] Boswell, *Life of Johnson*, 2:297.

[200] Walpole to William Mason, 22 April 1782, in *Yale Edition of Horace Walpole's Correspondence*, ed. W. S. Lewis (New Haven, 1955), 29:239–40. Walpole's charges concerned a dispute between Adam Ferguson and Thomas Percy that provoked a nasty pamphlet war. See Heinz Maxwell, "Percy und die Ossian-Kontroverse," *Anglia* 58 (1934): 392–401.

provide John Home with translations of Gaelic fragments at Moffat, then to publish those fragments under the patronage of Hugh Blair, and finally to recover and publish an ancient Gaelic epic. "The whole publication, you know, was in its first rise accidental," Blair once re-minded David Hume. *"Macpherson was entreated and dragged into it."*[201] Macpherson's detractors have naturally tried to explain his passive-ness and reluctance in terms of his fears about being exposed as a fraud, whereas his supporters have regarded Macpherson's behavior as proof of his credibility—for what trickster would have to be ca-joled into playing his trick? Yet this aspect of the Ossian story is sig-nificant for another reason: it clearly shows that Ossian was the product of a group effort on the part of Macpherson and a "cabal" of Edinburgh literary men. Macpherson, it is true, produced the Os-sianic "translations" themselves, but the Edinburgh "cabal" provided the inspiration, incentive, financial support, letters of introduction, editorial assistance, publishing connections, and emotional encour-agement that brought Ossian into print. They made it known what they were after and how important it was to them to get it; Mac-pherson gave them what they wanted. For once that proud Highlan-der did not exaggerate when he stated, in a dissertation prefixed to *Fingal,* that the world owed the Ossianic poems in their present form to the "uncommon zeal" of John Home and other "gentlemen" who had first suggested a prose translation rather than verse and had been "earnest in exhorting him to bring more [Gaelic poetry] to the light."[202]

On the basis of testimony submitted to the Highland Society at the turn of the nineteenth century, it is possible to identify only eight members of the inner circle of "gentlemen" who "entreated and dragged" Macpherson into the Ossian affair: Hugh Blair, Alexander Carlyle, Adam Ferguson, John Home, William Robertson, Lord Eli-bank, Sir Adam Fergusson, and Robert Chalmers. To these may be added a few others who aided the cause in one way or another, such as Sir David Dalrymple, John Dalrymple, Andrew Stuart, Lord Kames, and even David Hume before his removal to London, but none of these men can be considered leaders of the campaign on the basis of

---

[201] Blair to Hume, 29 September 1763, in Burton, *Life of Hume,* 1:468. Emphasis added.

[202] *Fingal* (London, 1762), xiv, and preface. Cf. *Works of Ossian,* 1:lxvii. Blair and Ferguson thought so highly of Ossian's "measured prose" that they later persuaded Macpherson to translate the *Iliad* in the same style—a foolhardy venture that was clearly intended as a challenge to English preeminence in the classics and that pleased only his staunchest Scottish admirers, such as William Robertson. See Blair and Robert-son's letters to Macpherson from the early 1770s in Saunders, *James Macpherson,* 220–21, and the account of the whole affair in Wilson M. Hudson, "The Homer of the North Translates Homer," *Library Chronicle of the University of Texas* 4 (1950): 25–43.

currently available evidence.[203] In any case it is fair to say that the Moderate literati and a small number of their friends constituted the nucleus of the Ossianic "cabal." To understand why this was so, we should consider the origins of the Ossianic enterprise in the context of two causes to which the Moderate literati were deeply committed during the 1750s: the struggles for Scottish literary respectability and a Scots militia.

Both these issues exposed the Moderate literati to the deep currents of anti-Scottish feeling that underlay the polite veneer of mid-eighteenth-century England. Their disillusionment with England seems to have begun when David Garrick rejected John Home's first two tragedies as unfit for the London stage. To a transplanted Scotsman like Tobias Smollett, it was plain that the cause of Home's difficulties was the narrowness and ignorance of the English.[204] As the decade wore on the Moderate literati gradually came to share Smollett's stereotypical conception of John Bull as cold, decadent, boorish, and stupid. Shortly before the first London production of *Douglas*, for example, John Home remarked that fashionable Londoners "live so ridiculous a life, that they are scarcely rational creatures, & never think one moment so that they have no sort of taste, but like sheep follow any Leader who has the vogue."[205] The exclusion of Scotland from the militia act of 1757 and the abuse that Home's *Douglas* received from some and Wilkie's *Epigoniad* from nearly all English critics in the same year seemed to demonstrate that Scottish aspirations for political and literary parity were to be treated by the English with indifference or contempt. It is significant, perhaps, that the first of the many known sarcastic references to "John Bull" in the correspondence of the Moderate literati appears in a letter of November 1757.[206]

Despite English literary prejudice, by the late 1750s Hume, Robertson, Smith, and other Scottish authors born after the Union were rapidly shattering the myth that Scotsmen could not write fine English prose. Poetry, however, was a quite different matter. Though Home's *Douglas* had with difficulty earned a place on the London stage, Scots could boast of no nondramatic poetic triumphs in the

---

[203] On the contributions of some of these individuals, see Carnie, "Macpherson's *Fragments*"; Arthur E. McGuinness, "Lord Kames on the Ossian Poems: Anthropology and Criticism," *Texas Studies in Literature and Language* 10 (1968): 67–75; Mossner, *Forgotten Hume*, 82–104.

[204] Smollett to Carlyle, 1 March 1754, in *The Letters of Tobias Smollett*, ed. Lewis M. Knapp (Oxford, 1970), 33.

[205] Home to Milton, 1 February 1757, NLS, 16700:190. Cf. Home to Carlyle, n.d., in Mackenzie, 138.

[206] Carlyle to Elliot, 19 November 1757, NLS, 11014:100–101.

English tongue since James Thomson's "The Seasons" (1726–1730) and Robert Blair's "The Grave" (1743). The poetry of genteel mid-century Scottish versifiers like Thomas Blacklock has been fairly described as little more than "a pale, pale copy of English Augustan verse," and what little native Scots poetry existed in the days before Robert Fergusson and Robert Burns was generally dismissed as a provincial and perhaps vulgar form of amusement.[207] It was a continual source of embarrassment to Scottish men of letters that their country appeared in the eyes of the world to be an unpoetic nation, incapable of producing a Homer, Virgil, or Milton.[208]

These feelings of poetic inferiority help to account for the wild adulation with which the Scottish literati greeted Wilkie's *Epigoniad* (1757), a ponderous, self-consciously Homeric epic in nine books of rhymed couplets. "The whole turn of this new poem would almost lead us to imagine that the Scottish bard had found the manuscript of that father of poetry [Homer], and had made a faithful translation of it into English," David Hume declared in a magazine notice written to promote the second edition of the *Epigoniad* to skeptical English critics and readers.[209] Hume was particularly proud that "the second Epic Poem in our Language" had been written by a Scotsman, and the poet's reputation as a genuine "Rustic" appeared to add an appropriate touch of primitive authenticity to his Homeric image.[210] Yet efforts by Hume and others to sell Wilkie as the "Scottish Homer" came to naught when the second edition of the *Epigoniad* fared almost as poorly in England as did the first. If there were to be found a Scottish poet who could bear comparison with Homer and bear witness to the poetic genius of the Scots, he would have to be someone other than William Wilkie.

For Scottish believers, that someone was Macpherson's Ossian. Whereas the initial Ossianic fragments could not match the epic scope and grandeur of the *Epigoniad, Fingal* and *Temora* could offer those features and more. Ossian had the distinct advantage of appearing to be an authentic, creative epic poet rather than merely an imitator of Homer in the manner of Wilkie. He was not only a rustic but a rustic from a primitive society situated in the distant past. This ele-

---

[207] Daiches, *Paradox of Scottish Culture*, 85 and passim.

[208] Thomas Gray actually cited the poetic incapability of modern Scotsmen as an argument in favor of Ossian's authenticity! Stewart, "Ossian in the Polished Age," 19, 26.

[209] David Hume, "Letter to the Author of the Critical Review" (April 1759), in *Philosophical Works*, 4:425–37. Hume helped to arrange publication of the second edition of the *Epigoniad*, which contained several alterations designed to win over English readers. See Mossner, *Forgotten Hume*, 68–82.

[210] Hume to Elliot, 2 July 1757, *HL*, 1:253–55.

ment of social and temporal authenticity entitled Ossian to direct comparison with Homer as an "original genius"[211] whose epic power transcended, and yet somehow conformed to, the formal rules of poetic composition developed in a later, more rational age.[212] As an authentic ancient Highland epic bard who united the power and passion of the primitive imagination with the humanity and poetic discipline of more polished societies, Ossian alone was worthy of the epithet the "Scottish Homer" and capable of elevating Scotland to a new place in the national history of poetry. Perhaps this is why Hugh Blair was in the habit of referring to *Fingal* as "our Epic" before Macpherson had even set out to recover it, and why he later suggested to Mrs. Montagu that Macpherson should give priority to defending Ossian rather than writing history because "his chance for immortality" depended on his being what the French translator of Ossian had termed *"The Restorer of the British Homer."*[213]

Literary nationalism, then, was one major reason for the strong and passionate attraction to Ossian among the literati of the Scottish Enlightenment. But literary nationalism alone cannot fully explain the nature and timing of that attraction. Why was the Edinburgh "cabal" that sponsored and defended Macpherson led by the Moderate literati of Edinburgh, Lord Elibank, and a few others? Why was David Hume—a leading spokesman for Scottish literary nationalism—not more conspicuous in his support for Ossian? And why did the Ossian affair occur at the particular time that it did?

Questions like these can be answered satisfactorily only by considering the early history of the Ossian affair in the broader context of the Scots militia controversy of the late 1750s and early 1760s. It is

[211] The concept of "original" genius was developed by another Scottish Presbyterian minister, William Duff, in *An Essay on Original Genius* (London, 1767) and its sequel, *Critical Observations on the Writings of the Most Celebrated Original Geniuses in Poetry* (1770; reprint, Delmar, N.Y., 1973), where Ossianic poetry and Blair's account of it are accorded high praise. See also Donald M. Foerster's discussion of Blair, Duff, and other Scottish "heralds of original genius" in "Scottish Primitivism and the Historical Approach," *Philological Quarterly* 29 (1950): 307–23, esp. 312.

[212] H. T. Swedenberg, Jr., *The Theory of the Epic in England, 1650–1800* (1944; reprint, New York, 1972), 115–18. For the contemporary debate on *Fingal* as epic, see Stewart, "Ossian in the Polished Age," chap. 2.

[213] Blair to Sir David Dalrymple, 23 June 1760, in Carnie, "Macpherson's *Fragments*," 22, and 9 May [1760], NLS, Acc. 7228/15:96 (both of which use the phrase "our Epic"); Blair to Elizabeth Montagu, 1 April 1775, Huntington Library, MO 488. The term "British Homer" carried even more of a punch than "Scottish Homer" or the still narrower epithet "Homer of the ancient Highlanders" that was used in Rev. John Macpherson's book of 1768 on the ancient Caledonians (quoted by Donald Foerster in *Studies in Philology* 40 [1943]: 438) because it implied that the English had no poet to rival Ossian.

significant that the foremost Scottish opponent of the Scots militia cause, Lord Advocate Robert Dundas, was a confirmed enemy of Ossian, whereas almost all of Ossian's early promoters were friends of the Scots militia scheme who gravitated to the Poker Club after its establishment in 1762.[214] Moreover, there is evidence that many of them were preoccupied with the Scots militia issue during the critical months when Macpherson's Ossian was being coaxed into existence. The last known letter by John Home before his historic meeting with Macpherson at Moffat in September 1759 identifies the Scots militia as "the subject nearest to my heart," and his first known letter after that meeting refers to the militia as "my chief desire."[215] While the manuscripts of Macpherson's Ossianic fragments were circulating among the Edinburgh literati in late 1759 and early 1760, Lord Elibank and William Robertson both pronounced the Scots militia the most important issue in modern Scottish history,[216] and Alexander Carlyle composed (with the encouragement of Ferguson and the assistance of Robertson) his popular militia pamphlet *Question Relating to a Scots Militia*. Carlyle and Ferguson's extant correspondence from this period reveals a veritable obsession with the Scots militia question. It is surely not fortuitous that the "Scottish Homer" was discovered and readied for the press at the same time that so many of his patrons were strenuously engaged in the first campaign for a Scots militia bill. Nor is it mere coincidence that these same Ossianic patrons came together, shortly after the parliamentary defeat of the Scots militia bill in April 1760, to arrange and finance Macpherson's first expedition to the Highlands in search of *Fingal*. The pattern suggests that many of Ossian's earliest and most dedicated supporters were motivated largely by feelings of resentment and despair about the continued failure of the Scots militia agitation. For them Ossian was, at least in part, a poetical response to a political crisis. By contrast, Scottish literary men who were not so passionately involved with the Scots militia cause at this time, such as Robert Wallace and David Hume, found it easier to entertain doubts about Ossian.[217]

---

[214] *Auto.*, 290. These included all eight of the men named in the Highland Society report of 1805, plus John Dalrymple, George Dempster, and Andrew Stuart among secondary figures. Another early promoter of Ossian, Sir David Dalrymple, was not a member of the Poker Club but did serve on the committee of gentlemen that drafted a proposal for a Scots militia bill late in 1759.

[215] Home to Bute, [26] August and 8 November 1759, Bute, box 2 (1759), nos. 147 and 184.

[216] See n. 65 above.

[217] On Robert Wallace's emphatic opposition to Ossian, see Norah Smith, "The Literary Career and Achievement of Robert Wallace" (Ph.D. diss., Edinburgh University, 1973), 487–90.

Wounded national pride was not the only link between the Scots militia and Ossian. The values that predominate in *Fingal* and most Ossianic poetry—honor, military valor, heroism, and public virtue—were precisely those values considered most conducive to the cultivation of a martial spirit. The "general moral" that Blair found in *Fingal* was that "Wisdom and Bravery always triumph over brutal force."[218] Like Macpherson's *The Highlander* and Home's *Douglas*, *Fingal*, "The Battle of Lora," "Carric-Thura," and other Ossianic poems deal with the theme of proud and warlike Scots successfully defending the British Isles against invading armies of fearsome Scandinavians. Although Ossianic battle scenes are not so violent or inhumane as those in Homer,[219] this concession to neoclassical taste does nothing to weaken the poems' message about the nobility of just and heroic warfare, especially when directed against a foreign invader. Fingal is the archetypal Stoic hero, bravely performing his duty as king and warrior in a world of almost continuous adversity. His prowess in battle is surpassed only by his courage. "Fingal never flies," he announces in the epic that bears his name. "Where danger threatens, I rejoice in the storm of spears."[220] Yet Fingal and his "noble race" fight only for just and good causes; virtue is Fingal's avowed "aim" and chief consolation as a warrior.[221] This unwavering devotion to the principle of heroic virtue appealed to the Moderate literati as a means of arousing patriotism and martial valor among their countrymen. As one member of the Poker Club put it in a vigorous tribute to Ossian: "There we see displayed the highest martial spirit, exerted only in the defence of their friends and their country."[222]

To the Moderate literati of Edinburgh and their kind, Ossian demonstrated the poetic genius of Scotland while projecting a particularly praiseworthy national image. It is an image in which the

---

[218] Blair, *Dissertation*, 43.

[219] Ibid., 47–48. Ossianic heroes frequently bind and later release their worst enemies after defeating them in personal combat. In "The Battle of Lora" Fingal allows "the feeble foe" to withdraw after their leader has been slain (*Works of Ossian*, 1:288). Nearly all Scottish critics praised this characteristic.

[220] *Works of Ossian*, 1:111. "We find humanity blended with courage in all their actions," wrote Lord Kames of the Ossianic heroes in *Sketches of the History of Man*, 2d ed., 4 vols. (1778; reprint, Hildesheim, 1968), 1:421–98, esp. 439. Kames was neither a supporter of the Scots militia campaign nor a member of the Poker Club, but his views on national defense and the need "to unite the spirit of industry with that of war; and to form the same man to be an industrious labourer, and a good soldier" (ibid., 3:40) were quite similar to those of the Moderate literati and most of their friends. Cf. David Lieberman's discussion in *WV*, 203–34, esp. 222.

[221] Macpherson, *Works of Ossian*, 1:109, 279.

[222] John Gregory, *A Comparative View of the State and Faculties of Man with Those of the Animal World*, new ed. (London, 1798), preface, vii.

militarism and heroic virtue of a rude society coexist with the refinement and gentility of a more civilized era. It is a true golden age, not because it is free from warfare, but because it is peopled by a race of heroes who raise warfare to the highest level of virtue and nobility. "Effeminacy," luxury, and other dangerous manifestations of modern, commercial societies are completely unknown. Ossianic heroes reveal no traces of the personal flaws that mark the heroes in Homer's epics, and moral ambivalence is never apparent.[223] Although Ossian's infatuation with heroic perfection is apt to strike modern readers as superficial, it was evidently quite appealing to contemporary readers seeking moral myths and lessons rather than complex character development and dramatic tension. And it was particularly attractive to a group of Scottish literati who believed that their country was in need of a healthy dose of primitive vitality and public virtue as a remedy for the ills of modernity.

Like the militia agitation, the Ossian controversy cannot be reduced entirely to an expression of Scottish national pride on the part of the Moderate literati and their "cabal." Both the militia and Ossian causes drew their interest and support at least partially because they were associated with the broader moral and ideological ideals for which they stood—particularly the ideal of a nation-in-arms fighting for the sake of virtue and the established order. But if national pride was not the only issue in the Scots militia and Ossian controversies, it soon became the most important one. Indeed, it was not long before both affairs had degenerated into loud national squabbles between blind English prejudice and blind Scottish faith, with an occasional voice of moderation like that of David Hume barely audible over the din.

It was not by chance that the Moderate literati of Edinburgh were among the leaders of the Scottish side in these matters. Like the anonymous author of the newspaper letter approving of their Antigallican Society, the Moderate literati were convinced that "the national character [of Scotland] has always hinged, and always must, upon *arms* and *letters*."[224] They were angry and resentful that "John Bull" seemed intent on depriving Scotland of both these attributes by rejecting its bid for a militia and belittling its greatest bard. They were upset by the intensity and scurrility of anti-Scottish feeling in

---

[223] See Malcolm Laing's critical remarks on Ossianic heroes in *Works of Ossian*, 1:208–209, and John L. Greenway, "The Gateway to Innocence: Ossian and the Nordic Bard as Myth," in *Studies in Eighteenth-Century Culture*, vol. 4, ed. Harold E. Pagliaro (Madison, Wisc., 1975), 161–70.

[224] McElroy, "Century of Scottish Clubs," 306.

England. And they were more than a little hurt by the condescension and prejudice that they regularly encountered in their personal relations with eminent English literary men like Samuel Johnson and Horace Walpole.

By means of their zealous involvement on behalf of the militia and Ossian, the Moderate literati fought back against the prejudice of the English as best they could. At times they too were guilty of narrow provincialism and national prejudice, as was perhaps inevitable in the charged atmosphere of their day. For the most part, however, they wished only to see their country strong and proud as an equal partner in a truly united and enlightened kingdom. Their behavior may have been schizophrenic in regard to numerous issues, but concerning the Scots militia and poems of Ossian they were firm and unyielding in their Scottishness. On these matters there could be for them no compromise because the stakes were nothing less than the honor, virtue, and glory of Scotland.

The Tolerant Conservatives

---   ❀   ---

"DANGEROUS AND UNNATURAL REBELLION"

I love my country, I revere her constitution. No form of government ever diffused such equal happiness over the human race. And shall I see that sacred temple of liberty reduced to ruins, on the uncertain project of rearing an Utopia in a distant land?

Alexander Carlyle,
The Justice and Necessity of the War with our American Colonies, 1777

The names, which I thought the true names of things, seem changed, and the love of rebellion is called the love of liberty.

John Home, Letter to Col.———,
ca. 1780

If the controversies over the Scots militia and Ossian demonstrate the Moderate literati's feelings of Scottish national pride, the two issues to be discussed in this chapter reveal different, and seemingly paradoxical, aspects of Moderate ideology. The paradox involves the tension between the Moderates' exceptionally liberal views on such matters as intellectual freedom, religious tolerance, and the need for politeness, learning, and enlightenment, and their staunchly conservative stance on most questions of social, political, and ecclesiastical law and order. The Moderate party was founded in the early 1750s out of a commitment to order and elitism on the one hand, enlightenment and politeness on the other, and this dualism remained a fundamental feature of Moderatism throughout the eighteenth century. It is clearly evident in the Moderate literati's attitudes and actions during the American and Roman Catholic crises of the late 1770s. The Moderate literati of Edinburgh had no sympathy for American "rebels" but approved of Roman Catholic relief, whereas many of their ecclesiastical opponents in the Popular party were sympathetic to the Americans' struggle for political rights but

262

could not accept the idea of Roman Catholics worshiping freely in Presbyterian Scotland. One side stood for political liberalism and religious intolerance, the other for enlightened elitism and tolerant conservatism.

At the onset of hostilities between Great Britain and its American colonies, William Robertson was especially interested in the American situation because he was then at work on a comprehensive history of American colonization. Robertson had been optimistic about American affairs in 1766, when he told his publisher that "a very little skill and attention in the art of governing may preserve the supremacy of Britain as long as it ought to be preserved."[1] Within a decade, however, he was forced to concede that the government had mismanaged American affairs by failing to take tough preventive measures against the colonies' securing arms and consolidating themselves into "a regular systematical confederacy." "As a lover of mankind," Robertson was deeply troubled that the Americans' aspirations for economic independence demanded a firm response that would probably jeopardize their prosperity; "but as a subject of Great Britain," he had no doubt that such a response was necessary and proper.[2] From this point on there could be no middle ground, he told another correspondent in 1776: the American colonies would either gain their independence or else, as Robertson hoped, "be reduced to a more perfect dependence than formerly."[3]

Robertson's views on the need for forceful measures against the rebellious American colonies were shared to some degree by all the Moderate literati of Edinburgh. John Home expressed this position strongly in an anonymous pamphlet published first in London in January 1776 and later that year in Edinburgh as *A Letter from an Officer Retired, to His Son in Parliament*. Tracing the origins of the American rebellion to Rockingham's "feeble ministry," which had encouraged resistance by repealing the stamp act instead of enforc-

[1] Robertson to William Strahan, [1766], in Stewart, xxxi.

[2] Robertson to Strahan, 6 October 1775, ibid., xxx–xxxi. "If our leaders do not at once exert the power of the British Empire in its full force," Robertson warned, "the struggle will be long, dubious and disgraceful. We are past the hour of lenitives and half exertions."

[3] Robertson to [the earl of Hardwicke?], 26 August 1776, BL, Add. 35350:60–61. Henry Brougham's claim that Robertson was "the warm friend" of American independence (Brougham, 315) was the wishful thinking of a nineteenth-century Whig relation and the opposite of the truth, even if Robertson did tell an American visitor in 1772 that America would one day be the seat of a "mighty Empire." Quoted in Andrew D. Hook, *Scotland and America: A Study of Cultural Relations, 1750–1835* (Glasgow, 1975), 68.

ing law and order, Home called for a vigorous war against the Americans as the only honorable policy for Britain to pursue. To strive for a peaceful settlement would be sheer folly, he argued, because

> it is vain to think of peace till you have proved your superiority in war. We must fight and conquer, before we can treat with the rebellious, and hitherto triumphant, Americans. . . . I trust we shall regain our honour, and compel the insolent Americans to own the superiority of English valour. Till then we cannot, we ought not to make peace.[4]

After receiving a copy of Home's *Letter from an Officer,* David Hume addressed a playful reply to Tyrtæus—the poet of Spartan militarism—in which he chided the author for sounding "the trumpet for war against the Americans" without proposing a plan "for governing them, after they are subdued."[5] Adam Ferguson was more sympathetic. Despite some reservations about the wisest course of action under such difficult circumstances, Ferguson observed that he "never had any doubt of the rights [of Great Britain] Established in this Pamphlet."[6]

It was not long before Ferguson joined his friend as a pamphleteer for the government's cause against the Americans. The occasion was the publication in February 1776 of Richard Price's *Observations on the Nature of Civil Liberty, the Principles of Government, and the War with America*—the boldest and most provocative pamphlet on behalf of the Americans yet to be published in Great Britain.[7] As the *Observations* passed through five editions within one month of publication, worried ministers of state turned to their best hacks for retaliation. Adam Ferguson was recruited, explained Sir Grey Cooper of the Treasury, because the government wished to print at least one moderate and well-reasoned reply to Price by a "good and able writer."[8] By 23 March the manuscript of Ferguson's *Remarks on a Pamphlet Lately Published by Dr. Price* was in Cooper's hands, awaiting publication in London at government expense.

Unlike most of Price's respondents, Ferguson was willing to admit

[4] John Home, *A Letter from an Officer Retired, to His Son in Parliament* (Edinburgh, 1776), 19–21, 24.

[5] Hume to Home, 8 February 1776, *HL,* 2:307–308.

[6] Ferguson to Home, 27 January 1776, NLS, 124:76–77.

[7] Price's *Observations* has been reprinted, along with his other pamphlets on America and an introduction that attempts to explain them in terms of Price's moral and epistemological principles, in *Richard Price and the Ethical Foundations of the American Revolution,* ed. Bernard Peach (Durham, N.C., 1979).

[8] Sir Grey Cooper to Ferguson, 23 March 1776, in John Small, "Biographical Sketch of Adam Ferguson," *TRSE* 23 (1864): 625–26.

that the British government had made serious blunders in its handling of American affairs and that changed circumstances might well require a new and somewhat more lenient American policy. He was adamant, however, in his opposition to the radical implications of Price's position. Ferguson believed that Price's entire argument rested on his erroneous definition of political liberty as the right of autonomy.[9] He countered with the view that political liberty consists not in freedom from restraint but in "the security of our rights."[10] Citing Montesquieu on the need for carefully distinguishing between "the Power of the People" and true liberty, he proceeded to argue that although it may be reasonable to extend participation in government as far as the "circumstances and character" of a people will allow, it is "extremely dangerous to confound this advantage with Civil and Political Liberty; for it may often happen, that to extend the participation of power, is to destroy Liberty."[11] Thus, the citizens of ancient Rome had lost their liberty as power shifted from the senate to the popular assemblies.[12]

The idea that "the liberty of every class and order is not proportioned to the power they enjoy but to the security they have for the preservation of their rights" had already been expressed in Ferguson's earlier books on moral philosophy.[13] The American crisis, and above all Price's radical response to it, presented an opportunity for removing this idea from the realm of pure theory and classroom pedagogy and applying it directly to contemporary affairs. Against Price's insinuation that the people of Great Britain were not free because they were inadequately represented, Ferguson could claim that since the British constitution provided "more security than ever was enjoyed by any people," British subjects possessed "higher degrees of Liberty than any other people are known to enjoy."[14] In this way the principle of virtual representation could be defended by appealing not to the special rights and privileges of men of property but to the common rights and privileges, the constitutional safeguards, enjoyed by every British citizen. Ferguson then applies this logic to the American crisis. As long as British citizens in America or any other colony have received "all the benefits of subjects," they may be said to possess liberty regardless of whether or not they have an actual

---

[9] Adam Ferguson, *Remarks on a Pamphlet Lately Published by Dr. Price, Intitled, Observations on the Nature of Civil Liberty* (London, 1776), 2. A brief excerpt is reprinted in Peach, *Richard Price*, 253–60.

[10] Ferguson, *Remarks*, 7.

[11] Ibid., 14.

[12] Ibid., 14, 52.

[13] Ibid., 11.

[14] Ibid., 13.

voice in political affairs.[15] Their liberty consists in the security of their rights rather than in their autonomy. The latter is Price's true aim, Ferguson suggests, and Price's definition of liberty as self-government is really a ploy for justifying "the desire of national independence, under the name of Civil Liberty."[16]

Besides the question of liberty, Ferguson differs with Price about the extent to which Britain's American policy ought to be based on past precedent and experience as opposed to abstract principles of reason and justice or equally abstract appeals to the essence or spirit of the constitution. The right of colonial legislation, including reasonable tax laws, has always been and therefore should remain a parliamentary prerogative, Ferguson contends.[17] It will not do to build a case for the Americans on grounds of "reason, of equity, and humanity" in place of "precedents, statutes, and charters," for to do so "is to set human affairs afloat upon the sea of opinion and private interest, or to deprive men of those charts, landmarks, and rules of sailing, by which they were in use to be guided."[18] Nor is it permissible to invoke the "spirit" or "design" of the British constitution in support of American self-government, since the British constitution is in fact nothing but the existing balance between king and Parliament as it has evolved, slowly and without conscious design, from the feudal order.[19] Appeals to the "ancient establishment" or "primæval state" of the nation are unacceptable because almost nothing is known with certainty about that era and because what little is known cannot take priority over "subsequent establishments and compacts."[20] Price's neglect of "the experience of Europe, Asia, and Africa," of ancient Rome, of Cromwellian England, and of all the other dismal lessons of real history "shows the danger of going so fast in search of ideal perfection, which is apt to make us despise what is attainable and obtained, for the sake of something impracticable, and sometimes ab-

---

[15] Ibid., 17–18. Cf. the similar defense of virtual representation in a fast-day sermon preached against the Americans by another Moderate admirer of Montesquieu, Alexander Gerard, in *Liberty the Cloke of Maliciousness, Both in the American Rebellion and in the Manners of the Time* (Aberdeen, 1778), 9. That Gerard's sermon was part of a concerted Moderate attack on the American Revolution is suggested by the author's request that his Edinburgh distributor send complimentary copies to three party leaders: Blair, Robertson, and John Drysdale. Gerard to William Creech, 8 April 1778, SRO, Dalguise Muniments.

[16] Ferguson, *Remarks*, 25–27.

[17] Ibid., 24.

[18] Ibid., 27.

[19] Ibid., 13, 39–40.

[20] Ibid., 24–25, 39.

surd."[21] "We may wish for improvements in the laws of the state," Ferguson remarks, "but till these are made we must abide by the law as it stands."[22]

Thus, the *Remarks* restated several of the politically conservative ideas and sentiments expressed more generally in Ferguson's moral philosophy lectures and writings, such as the jurisprudential definition of liberty as security of rights rather than as autonomy or freedom to participate in government, belief in the unplanned origin and development of political constitutions, respect for established laws and institutions, and deep commitment to the Hanoverian establishment—especially when threatened by rebellion or foreign war. Ferguson's opposition to the American Revolution was consistent with these principles. He was favorably disposed toward the idea of granting modest concessions that might lead to a negotiated peace and was hopeful that a proposed commission (soon to be constituted under the brothers Howe) would be able to achieve that result. Should compromise fail, however, he was convinced that "the sword must strike" in the name of justice and the sovereignty of Great Britain.[23]

On the basis of contemporary newspapers, magazines, and other printed sources, it appears that Scottish public opinion was much closer to Ferguson's conservative *Remarks* than to Price's radical *Observations*.[24] Yet a minority of Scots openly sided with the opposition on the American question. A noticeably high proportion of these political dissidents were clergymen affiliated with the Popular party in the established church.[25] During the American crisis the loyal Scottish press continually attacked the "wild party" in the church for siding with the "Wilkites" at home and abroad, and government officials kept a close watch on zealous Scottish Presbyterians for fear that their propensity toward "republicanism" in ecclesiastical affairs would put them in league with rebels and democrats.[26] Ties between Popular party ministers and America grew stronger when John Witherspoon left Scotland in 1768 to become president of the College of New Jersey (Princeton) and subsequently used his influence to support the cause of American independence. It is worth noting in this regard

[21] Ibid., 14.

[22] Ibid., 40.

[23] Ibid., 33, 46.

[24] D. B. Swinfen, "The American Revolution in the Scottish Press," in *Scotland, Europe and the American Revolution*, ed. Owen Dudley Edwards and George Shepperson (New York, 1976), 66–74.

[25] Dalphy I. Fagerstrom, "Scottish Opinion and the American Revolution," *William and Mary Quarterly*, 3d ser., 11 (1954): 265.

[26] Ibid., 266, 268 n. 47.

that Witherspoon's foremost Scottish disciple, Rev. Charles Nisbet of Montrose, was pro-American to the point of scandal during the Revolution and emigrated to Pennsylvania soon afterward.[27] Even if Witherspoon had decided—as he very nearly did—not to go to Princeton, many clergymen in the Popular party probably would have felt a strong affinity for the plight of the Americans because of the powerful bond connecting them with leading American Presbyterians, particularly of the New Light or evangelical variety.[28]

Nowhere is this bond more evident than in the career of John Erskine of Edinburgh. As noted earlier, one of Erskine's first publications had portrayed the religious revivals in western Scotland and New England around 1740 as related aspects of a single glorious phenomenon. Later Erskine kept up a regular correspondence with men like Jonathan Edwards, Thomas Prince, and William Cooper (some of whose religious writings he edited for British publication), took a special interest in the missionary activities of the Scottish s.p.c.k. among American Indians, and showed great concern about the possibility of Roman Catholicism spreading south from French Canada.[29] Erskine also sympathized with the political outlook of his friends in America.[30] His first pamphlet on the subject, *Shall I Go to War with My American Brethren?*, appeared anonymously in London as early as 1769. This modest work raised doubts about the efficacy and wisdom of a possible American war and sounded a warning about the alleged growth of Roman Catholicism in England, the Scottish Highlands, and America. It castigated the government for pursuing a policy of "gentleness, not to say encouragement to Jesuits, and harshness to colonies, steadily attached to Protestant principles, and to the succession in the illustrious house of Hanover."[31] Subsequent events, such as the Boston Tea Party and the Quebec act (which granted religious freedom to Catholics in Canada), served to reinforce Erskine's ar-

[27] Samuel Miller, *Memoir of the Rev. Charles Nisbet* (New York, 1840), 74–78; *Auto.*, 73–74n.; Robert Kerr, *Memoirs of the Life, Writings, and Correspondence of William Smellie*, 2 vols. (Edinburgh, 1811), 1:495–96.

[28] See especially L. H. Butterfield, *John Witherspoon Comes to America* (Princeton, 1953), where there is much correspondence showing the close ties between the Popular party in Scotland and the New Lights in America. In a letter of 6 February 1767, for example, one of Witherspoon's Edinburgh friends refers to some of the New Lights' opponents as "the Robertsons and Carlisles of that side of the water" (28).

[29] See Sir Henry Moncreiff Wellwood, *Account of the Life and Writings of John Erskine* (Edinburgh, 1818), 159–64, 196–226, 283–84, 484–85, and Hook, *Scotland and America*, 26–34.

[30] Moncreiff Wellwood, *Life of Erskine*, 265–82.

[31] John Erskine, *Shall I Go to War with My American Brethren?* (London, 1769), 23, 34–40.

guments, and in the spring of 1776 he boldly republished his pamphlet in Edinburgh under his own name, with a new preface drawing attention to his foresight. Later that year he published two other pamphlets that called for moderation and compromise in British relations with the American colonies and warned again of Roman Catholic encroachments there.[32] In these works he attacked the government's handling of the Boston tea crisis, cited the authority of the Bible on the need for moderation between nations, protested Anglican discrimination against American Presbyterians, justified the colonies' resentment against taxation as an unfair innovation, criticized the rigidity of conservative pamphleteers such as Samuel Johnson, John Wesley, and Sir John Dalrymple, and declared a return to the pre-1764 state of affairs to be "the only safe line of peace." Though he stopped short of independence for America, Erskine was quite radical by the standards of his time and country, and he later confided to Edmund Burke that he had suffered "much reproach" for his "feeble efforts" on behalf of the Americans.[33]

Erskine's principles helped to raise expectations that the general assembly of 1776 would feature a major confrontation between the Moderate and Popular parties on the American question. It was known that the government and the Moderates wanted to secure a loyal address from the Church of Scotland, and it was rumored that a large faction in the Popular party was planning to address the king on the need for an immediate withdrawal of troops and an end to the war with America.[34] But the anticipated debate between these two ideological camps never materialized. Instead, James Boswell and other curious spectators who jammed the galleries of the assembly on 27 May watched with surprise as an address espousing the cause of law and order against "the present dangerous and unnatural rebellion" was enacted without a word of dissent.[35] Hugh Blair was pleased to relate this happy news to David Hume in London:

> Tell John Home we have so moderate an Assembly that it was a
> pity there was not more business before them. All that they had

[32] John Erskine, *The Equity and Wisdom of Administration, in measures that have unhappily occasioned the American Revolt, tried by the Sacred Oracles* (Edinburgh, 1776) and *Reflections on the Rise, Progress, and Probable Consequences of the Present Contentions with the Colonies* (Edinburgh, 1776).

[33] Erskine to Burke, 24 January 1779, in *The Correspondence of Edmund Burke*, ed. John A. Woods, 10 vols. (Chicago, 1963), 4:63. See the critical comments on Erskine's Edinburgh edition of *Shall I Go to War* in SM 38 (May 1776): 265. Cf. Moncreiff Wellwood, *Life of Erskine*, 272.

[34] Fagerstrom, "Scottish Opinion," 267.

[35] Ibid.; James Boswell, *The Private Papers of James Boswell from Malahide Castle*, ed. Geoffrey Scott and F. A. Pottle, 18 vols. (New York, 1928–1934), 12:4.

to do they have done well. We have sent up a dutiful and Loyal Address. A violent debate was expected before it. However it did not follow; the Factions were afraid to show themselves; though the words *Unnatural and dangerous Rebellion* went very ill down with them.[36]

Though the vote for the loyal address was unanimous, the matter was somewhat more complicated than one might infer from Blair's account. Correspondence between the government's commissioner, Lord Cathcart, and the secretary of state shows that unanimous passage of the address was the result of careful management that left Charles Nisbet and other Popular party ministers in attendance with no hope of success.[37] The following year William Robertson correctly surmised that opposition to the American War had declined among his fellow clergymen, making it considerably easier to secure a loyal address in the general assembly. "Tho it required some little management to procure one that was decent for last year," he told the new commissioner shortly before the assembly of 1777 was to meet, "I think zeal for America begins to cool among the few partizans of the malecontents whom we have here."[38]

While Robertson and his friends were keeping pro-American sentiments under control in the church courts Moderate ministers were opposing the American cause in sermons preached on specially designated fast days. On the first such fast day appointed by the king (12 December 1776), Hugh Blair and Alexander Carlyle were among those known to have delivered powerful attacks on the Americans from their pulpits. Blair's sermon on that occasion has unfortunately been lost, but his justification for delivering it appears in a letter to James Boswell of February 1777. Offended that one nation would "pray to GOD, for success in destroying another nation," Boswell had reacted so strongly to Blair's fast-day sermon that for a short time he gave up his regular Sunday worship at St. Giles Church.[39] Early in 1777 he told Blair of his feelings and asked that on future fast days

[36] Blair to Hume, [early June 1776], RSE, 3/63. Blair inadvertently reversed the terms in the phrase he emphasized.

[37] Fagerstrom, "Scottish Opinion," 267. The plan apparently called for Lord Cathcart to arouse the members of the assembly with a strong speech against the Americans, after which William Robertson moved that a committee be established to draft a loyal address. The next day this committee, which was dominated by Robertson and his friends, introduced the patriotic address that was unanimously passed by the assembly and later printed in the *London Gazette* as a sign of support for the government's American policy. *SM* 38 (May 1776): 271–73.

[38] Robertson to the earl of Dalhousie, 17 April 1777, SRO, Dalhousie Muniments, GD 45/13/355.

[39] Boswell, *Malahide Papers*, 12:98–99.

he preach in a less offensive manner, adding that in the case of the Americans "Resistance is not Rebellion."[40] Blair's reply begins by noting that the appointment of a fast day left him with little choice: if he remained silent on America or expressed himself in the "very general terms" recommended by Boswell, his actions would be construed as a sign of opposition to the government's American policy, which would be "contrary to my principles." The Americans are held to be wrong because "the war upon their side is a war grounded on speculation, not on the grievances of actual oppression." It was not an actual attack on their "religion, property, or liberty" or constitutional rights, but the "apprehension" of such an attack, that had driven them to arms. Under these circumstances, Blair concludes, "their resistance is in my view rebellion in its most criminal extent."[41] Though Boswell was not persuaded by his pastor's "very pretty Answer" to his protest, he was "flattered" by its eloquence and impressed by its politeness and sincerity.[42]

The sermon delivered by Alexander Carlyle on the fast day on 12 December 1776 was published early in 1777 as *The Justice and Necessity of the War with our American Colonies Examined*. The scriptural text was the same passage that John Erskine had employed in his published sermon on the American crisis: "Shall I yet again go out to battle against the children of Benjamin my brother, or shall I cease?" (Judges 20:28); but whereas Erskine had interpreted this passage as a mandate for moderation and restraint in American affairs, Carlyle viewed it as justification for a vigorous American war.[43] After refuting defenses of the American position on the basis of "ancient right" and "recent provocation," he ended the first part of the sermon with a paternalistic appeal for strict disciplinary action against Britain's wayward "child."[44]

The second part of Carlyle's sermon examined the various sins that may have caused God to punish Great Britain with a colonial rebellion. In addition to general sins of the age, such as immorality, corruption of the common people, and "everlasting gaming and voluptuousness" among the upper classes, Carlyle enumerated three particular sins committed by Great Britain and her colonies since the

[40] Boswell to Blair, 24 February 1777, YUL, L59.

[41] Blair to Boswell, 26 February [1777], in *Boswell in Extremes, 1776–1778*, ed. Frederick A. Pottle (New York, 1970), 359–60.

[42] Boswell, *Malahide Papers*, 12:136.

[43] Alexander Carlyle, *The Justice and Necessity of the War with our American Colonies Examined* (Edinburgh, 1777), 2. It is likely that this biblical passage was meant as a pun on Benjamin Franklin, who was well known in Scotland.

[44] Ibid., 29.

end of the Seven Years' War: "unbounded ambition, and national pride," "unbounded licentiousness," and "the murders, and rapines, and enormities that have been committed in various places of the British empire." His chief example of unbounded pride and ambition was the greedy desire for excessive territorial acquisition that had flourished at the end of the Seven Years' War—an apparent reference to the critics of Bute's modest peace plan. In regard to the second of the nation's sins, Carlyle referred specifically to Richard Price among those radical Englishmen whose writings had prepared the way for "a revolution of government" by carrying the principle of liberty too far in the direction of licentiousness. "With what other view, than to a revolution, have those elaborate treatises been composed?" he demanded.[45] To refute the "utopian" and democratic vision of radicals like Price, Carlyle closely paraphrased a passage from Adam Ferguson's *Remarks* about a republic the size of America being an untried experiment that had failed on a much smaller scale in seventeenth-century England.[46] Finally, Carlyle's reference to the sin of murder and rapine was a device for reproving the inhuman treatment of Indians and African slaves by the same American colonies that freely invoked the principle of liberty in their struggle with Britain.[47]

Carlyle's fast-day sermon on America was another demonstration of the Moderates' skill at using the traditional format of Presbyterian political preaching, the jeremiad, as a platform for the expression of conservative ideology. If sin were the root cause of the American problem, then the solution to that problem would be to give thanks to God for one's undeserved blessings, to reform one's private life, and to rally behind the government's righteous policy against "those degenerate and rebellious colonists" in America.[48] Only by vigorously pursuing the American War, Carlyle concluded, would it be possible to preserve "a government, the most favourable to human nature that ever existed, and to prolong the period of light, and liberty, and happiness among mankind."[49]

Early in 1778 Carlyle reiterated his conservative position on the American crisis in his *Letter on National Defence.* In that work he pronounced the American rebellion more dangerous than even the

---

[45] Ibid., 35, 39–40. Cf. the similar views in George Campbell's fast-day sermon, *The Nature, Extent, and Importance of the Duty of Allegiance,* 2d ed. (Aberdeen, 1778), esp. 7, 43, 70.

[46] Carlyle, *War with our American Colonies,* 40. Cf. Ferguson, *Remarks,* 23.

[47] Carlyle, *War with our American Colonies,* 41–42.

[48] Ibid., 33, 43–45, 47–48.

[49] Ibid., 50.

dreaded Jacobite rebellions of the first half of the eighteenth century. For whereas the latter "aimed only at altering the succession of the crown from one family to another," this one threatened "the throne itself," the "supremacy of parliament," and the very "sovereignty of the state of Britain."[50] Since the American rebellion was inspired by "republican principles of the most levelling kind," an American victory would be likely to trigger a democratic revolution in the British Isles. Too much was at stake, and too much had occurred, to hope for compromise; the war would have to be won on the battlefield.[51]

Adam Ferguson remained more flexible than Carlyle in his approach to American affairs. Although he too believed that the Americans deserved "a sound drubbing,"[52] Ferguson realized that military subjugation would be less likely to reestablish a mutually satisfactory colonial relationship than would peaceful reconciliation. He therefore did not hesitate to accompany his friend George Johnstone, William Eden, and the earl of Carlisle on their conciliatory peace mission to America in the spring of 1778—a mission that Carlyle believed had "Degraded the Nation beyond all example, in sueing for Peace to America."[53] At the outset Ferguson seems to have had no official postion on the peace commission, which was authorized by Parliament to grant extensive concessions drawn up by Alexander Wedderburn,[54] but upon reaching Philadelphia in June the commissioners appointed him their secretary. Three days later they entrusted him with the task of representing them before George Washington and Congress. The latter, however, had no intention of negotiating with a British commission that refused to recognize American sovereignty, and Ferguson's hopes of participating in a historic settlement were ingloriously dashed when the Americans denied him a passport. Throughout the summer of 1778, first at Philadelphia and later at New York, the peace commissioners and their secretary continued to experience humiliation and frustration as their

[50] Alexander Carlyle, *A Letter to His Grace the Duke of Buccleugh, on National Defence* (Edinburgh, 1778), 53.

[51] Ibid., 66.

[52] Ferguson to John Macpherson, 27 October 1777, EUL, Dc. 1.77, no. 7.

[53] Carlyle to William Johnstone (later Pulteney), 12 March 1778, Huntington Library, PU 88. On the peace mission and Ferguson's role in it, respectively, see Charles R. Ritcheson, *British Politics and the American Revolution* (Norman, Okla., 1957), 258–86, and Fagg, 157–201.

[54] For example, full amnesty for all, suspension of all American legislation since 1763, possible American representation in Parliament, increased American autonomy, and even acceptance of Congress (with restricted powers). See Ritcheson, *British Politics,* 268–71.

efforts to negotiate were rejected and then ignored by Congress. The painful fact was that the generous peace overtures that Carlyle found so disgracefully conciliatory were no longer enough to satisfy colonial leaders who had recently tasted victory at Saratoga, weathered the hard winter of 1777–1778, and secured French intervention. The time for compromise had passed.

Under the circumstances, the peace commissioners grew desperate and sometimes rash. Late in the summer the commision was embarrassed by a scandal over Johnstone's attempts to bribe two members of Congress with hints of personal preferment in exchange for their cooperation. The discredited Johnstone returned to England in September, and the remaining commissioners prepared to follow suit. Before doing so, however, they published a "Manifesto and Proclamation" that appears to have been largely, if not wholly, the work of their secretary. It was a tactless, foolhardy appeal to the individual colonies and private citizens of America to meet with the commissioners and arrange a reasonable compromise before it was too late. By blaming the war on Congress, insulting France, and above all threatening a full-scale assault in the event of continued colonial intransigence, the "Manifesto and Proclamation" provoked the indignation of Paine and Lafayette in America and of the parliamentary opposition in Britain. Moreover, some of that indignation was aimed directly at Adam Ferguson, who was cited in Paine's *Crisis* no. 6 and named by the Marquis of Rockingham in the House of Lords as the alleged author of this "ingenious literary production."[55]

After his return to London in December 1778, Ferguson went on functioning as secretary of the ill-fated peace commission until its formal demise in late May 1779. During this period he seems to have given up any lingering hopes of a negotiated settlement with America and to have moved closer to the position of uncompromising conservatives like Carlyle, to whom he wrote that "proper measures" (of a military nature) could probably reduce the influence of the "Johnny Witherspoons" in America to "the small Support of Franklin Adams & two or three more of the most Abandoned Villains in the World."[56] This was the language of conservative ideology intensified by personal resentment and disillusionment. As late as January 1780 Ferguson was still advocating a vigorous military policy as the only hope for Great Britain—not only in colonial affairs but also in

---

[55] *Parl. Hist.*, 20:3; Fagg, 185–90. The "Manifesto and Proclamation" was dated 3 October 1778 and published in numerous newspapers and magazines on both sides of the Atlantic.

[56] Ferguson to Carlyle, 9 February 1779, EUL, Dc. 4.41:47.

the struggle against the Yorkshire Association movement at home.[57] His views were shared by Hugh Blair, who praised James Macpherson's harsh attack on the parliamentary opposition for its "spirit of exertion and unanimity" against the Americans.[58]

Eventually, of course, it was necessary to admit that America could not be regained for the empire by any available means. All the Moderate literati must have been distressed by this realization, but for William Robertson the loss of America was particularly unsettling for personal reasons. Following the outbreak of war with the colonies, Robertson had postponed completion of the portion of his proposed history of America dealing with British colonization, which he apparently considered an inappropriate topic under the circumstances.[59] At that time he had hoped that the defeat of America and the return of normal colonial relations would enable him to complete his work as planned.[60] With the victory of the colonies, however, Robertson decided that "America is now lost to the Empire & to me."[61] His original plan for a comprehensive study of early America had died with the British cause there, a casualty of the "dangerous and unnatural rebellion" that he and his friends had so vigorously opposed.

While the Moderate literati were beset by feelings of bitterness and disappointment during the last years of the American War, their opponents in the Church of Scotland were growing more politically assertive.[62] At the general assembly of 1782, for example, Rev. William Porteous of Glasgow proposed that the assembly's annual address to the king include a note of congratulations on the recent change of ministers, referring to the fall of North and the rise of Rockingham. Though Porteous's proposal was enthusiastically supported by several friends of the Popular party and reform, such as Henry Erskine, the Moderates managed to defeat it after a warm debate.[63] A

---

[57] Ferguson to William Eden, 2 January 1780, BL, Add. 34417:3–12; Ferguson to John Macpherson, 10 January 1780, EUL, Dc. 1.77, no. 18; David Kettler, *The Social and Political Thought of Adam Ferguson* (Columbus, Ohio, 1965), 86–88.

[58] Blair to William Strahan, 3 August 1779 (copy), EUL, Dc. 2.76[10]; James Macpherson, *A Short History of the Opposition during the Last Session of Parliament* (London, 1779).

[59] Preface to the *History of America*, WWR, 6:5. In 1796 two surviving books of Robertson's history of British America were posthumously published by his son.

[60] Robertson to [the earl of Hardwicke?], 8 March 1784, BL, Add. 35350:70–71.

[61] Ibid.

[62] Blair to [William Strahan], 17 December 1781, NLS, 2257: 9–10; Fagerstrom, "Scottish Opinion," 268.

[63] Fagerstrom, "Scottish Opinion," 268; Henry W. Meikle, *Scotland and the French Revolution* (1912; reprint, London, 1969), 2–3. The substance of this debate of 25 May

---

spirited antipatronage campaign waged by the Popular party and Whig reformers in the early 1780s was also defeated by the Moderates.[64] Despite their outcomes, however, these contests are significant because they demonstrate that the Moderates were increasingly being put on the defensive by a loose coalition of Popular party churchmen and radical Whigs whose ideology and rhetoric had been shaped and sharpened by the experience of the American War. The American crisis had forced to the surface the liberal and sometimes radical undercurrents in the ideology of the Popular party as well as the deep-seated political conservatism of the Moderate literati of Edinburgh.

---

was reported in successive issues of the *Caledonian Mercury* from 29 May to 5 June 1782.

[64] Meikle, *Scotland and the French Revolution*, 35–40.

THE CRY OF INTOLERANCE

As certainly as the blasts of the north kill all the genial productions of spring, as certainly does the rage of fanatical zeal banish
arts and sciences, and all the Christian virtues, from a wretched
land.
                                    Alexander Carlyle,
            General Assembly Speech on Catholic Relief, 1779

The evil itself, which is ignorance, points out the cure. Introduce
the light, and the darkness is dispelled.

                                    George Campbell,
                    Address to the People of Scotland, 1779

It would be misleading, however, to leave the impression that the
ideological war between the Popular and Moderate parties reflected
a straightforward contest between liberals or radicals and conservatives. It would be equally misleading to imply that the Moderates were
powerful enough to defeat their opponents in every ecclesiastical
conflict. An examination of the "No Popery" affair of 1778–1779 will
provide a somewhat different perspective on late eighteenth-century
kirk politics. This struggle was not so much between liberal or radical and conservative ideologies as it was between popular prejudice
and enlightened elitism. And, as in practically all such ecclesiastical
confrontations during the era of the Moderate Regime, it soon became a test of the authority of William Robertson and the Moderate
literati in the Church of Scotland. By demonstrating that the combined efforts of government and the Moderates could not force
Catholic relief on a hostile nation, the "No Popery" affair helped to
define the boundaries beyond which the Scottish Enlightenment could
not pass. The retirement of William Robertson from church politics
shortly after the conclusion of this controversy represented, among
other things, a kind of public admission that the Moderate Revolution in the kirk was finally grinding to a halt.

Although anti-Catholic sentiment in Scotland had a long history
dating back to the days of John Knox and the Reformation, the Scottish "No Popery" affair of the late 1770s must be examined in its
contemporary British context. Like Scotland, England had enacted
harsh legislation against Roman Catholics around the turn of the
eighteenth century. Yet a relief bill for English Catholics sailed through

both houses of Parliament with no difficulty in May 1778 and received a relatively muted reception among the English populace; the mere prospect of a similar bill for Scotland, however, set off months of agitation that culminated in violent civil disturbances. It would be quite wrong to attribute these circumstances to a simple contrast between polite English tolerance and stubborn Scottish Presbyterian bigotry. England had her own anti-Catholic riots in 1780, and on an unprecedented scale; conversely, in 1793 a Scottish relief bill much like the one under consideration in 1779 provoked no outcry from the Scottish people. Anti-Catholic feeling may well have been more widespread and intense in Scotland than in England during the second half of the eighteenth century, but this factor alone cannot explain the different ways in which the two nations reacted to Catholic relief proposals during the late 1770s.

With the exception of Edmund Burke and a few other enlightened members of Parliament, there is no reason to believe that the easy passage of the English relief bill of 1778 was prompted chiefly by genuine humanitarian concern for an oppressed minority. In the first place, that bill gave English Catholics little they did not already have in practice. It did, however, repeal the two most repressive and odious restrictions from the reign of William III—the ban on Catholics inheriting or purchasing property and the penalty of "perpetual imprisonment" for any Catholic priest saying Mass or maintaining a school—both of which had long since ceased to be enforced except in extraordinary circumstances. John Dunning even observed in his seconding speech in the Commons that other laws on the books would technically keep a Catholic priest in England liable to a year in prison and a substantial fine![65] In exchange for the little relief they received, professed Catholics would be required to swear an oath of allegiance to King George, repudiate the principles of Jacobitism, renounce the right to break faith with heretics, and disclaim the power of the pope in civil affairs. Relief of this sort was acceptable even to the notoriously anti-Catholic Parliament of Ireland, which narrowly passed a similar relief bill the following summer after a second act of the British Parliament gave it leave to do so.

Yet modest as it was, the English relief bill of 1778 would never have been considered, let alone enacted, if many members of Parliament had not been swayed by various ulterior motives that arose from the problems of administering an extensive and volatile empire during the age of the American Revolution. Catholic relief was deemed desirable by the North government and its supporters as a means of

[65] *Parl. Hist.*, 19:1140.

increasing the number of Catholic recruits in an army about to engage in war on several fronts and, more generally, as a means of
winning or maintaining allegiance in vulnerable, predominantly
Catholic areas such as Ireland and French Canada.[66] The Quebec act
of 1774, which granted relief to Canadian Catholics, had been the
product of the same kind of thinking. In the case of Ireland, economic and demographic factors may also have been at issue, since
members of Parliament who owned Irish estates (such as the bill's
sponsor, Sir George Savile) stood to lose income if enough Irish
Catholic farmhands emigrated to the tolerant New World.[67] Yet it
was clearly inconsistent for Parliament to grant or approve relief for
Irish or Canadian Catholics while denying even the most basic rights
to Catholics at home. The logic of empire—political, military, economic, and demographic—must therefore be considered a major
reason for this remarkable display of parliamentary unanimity on an
issue so traditionally controversial as the status of Roman Catholics
living on British soil.

It is in this context that the exclusion of Scotland from the English
relief bill of May 1778 can be explained. Scotland's youthful lord advocate, Henry Dundas, addressed this point in the House of Commons by noting that the English and Scottish penal acts against Catholics required separate repeal legislation because they predated the
Union.[68] But this was no more than a legal technicality that could
easily have been overcome by introducing either a properly worded
joint bill or a separate Scottish bill to accompany the English one.
Bishop George Hay, the ranking Roman Catholic prelate in Scotland, later expressed the opinion that if something like this had been
done in 1778 "there probably would have been no disturbance."[69]
Scottish and English Catholics had jointly petitioned the king for relief on 2 May 1778. Why, then, was relief granted only to the latter?

The answer lies in the nature and importance (or lack of it) of the
Roman Catholic community in Scotland and the miscalculation of
Henry Dundas and the government. In 1778 the Scottish Catholic
population was still extremely small,[70] for the most part geographi-

---

[66] Christopher Hibbert, *King Mob: The Story of Lord George Gordon and the Riots of 1780*
(London, 1958), 17.

[67] Thomas H. D. Mahoney, *Edmund Burke and Ireland* (Cambridge, Mass., 1960), 70.
Mahoney stresses the behind-the-scenes role of Burke, who later observed that Irish
relief was the ultimate goal of Savile's bill (71, citing an article by A. Paul Levack).

[68] *Parl. Hist.*, 19:1142.

[69] Quoted in Christine Johnson, *Developments in the Roman Catholic Church in Scotland,
1789–1829* (Edinburgh, 1983), 30.

[70] Catholics constituted only about one or two percent of the population of Scotland
in 1779, though their visibility in Lowland towns like Edinburgh may have been in-

cally isolated in northern and western pockets of poverty, and almost completely without power or influence. It therefore lacked both the size and economic importance of the Catholic populations in Ireland or Canada and the high social standing of a significant portion of the Catholic minority in England, who soon regretted their association with their unfortunate Scottish coreligionists and refused to include them in a joint relief bill. The only ulterior motive for Catholic relief that applied in Scotland was the government's wish to attract more soldiers from Catholic clans in the Highlands, but this point was rendered less than urgent by the relatively small number of Highland Catholics and the ease with which many of them got into the army without a formal relief bill, either by swearing the anti-Catholic oath or by being permitted to omit the offending clauses.[71] Moreover, in spite of three decades of loyal military service and assurances of allegiance to the government, Scottish Catholics were still tainted with Jacobitism because of their part in the uprisings of 1715 and 1745, and it was feared that the Church of Scotland—whose general assembly happened to be meeting at Edinburgh just as the English and Irish relief bills were under consideration—might have rocked the boat and started an anti-Catholic tidal wave if a Scottish relief bill had also been proposed at this time. In short, Scottish Catholics were too few, too poor, too unpopular, and too economically, politically, and even militarily insignificant to justify the risk of a relief bill in the spring of 1778. Under these circumstances, Dundas and the government elected to proceed cautiously, apparently believing that postponing a Scottish bill would give Scottish Protestants additional time to accustom themselves to the idea of limited relief for their Catholic countrymen.

With the benefit of hindsight, one can see how flawed such logic was. Two weeks after informing the House of Commons that a Scottish relief bill would probably be proposed sometime in the future (14 May), Dundas was giving the same message to the general assembly of the kirk (27 May).[72] In private he was more specific, pledging on his honor to Bishop Hay that a Scottish relief bill would definitely be introduced during the next session of Parliament.[73] Hay was also told that the chief reason for delaying Scottish relief legislation was

creasing slightly. James Darragh, "The Catholic Population of Scotland since the Year 1680," *Innes Review* 4 (1955): 49–66; Peter F. Anson, *The Catholic Church in Modern Scotland, 1560–1937* (London, 1937), 104.

[71] Johnson, *Roman Catholic Developments*, chap. 2.

[72] *Parl. Hist.*, 19:1142; *SM* 40 (May 1778): 267–71.

[73] Hay to Mr. Grant, 24 July 1778, in *Memoirs of Scottish Catholics during the Seventeenth and Eighteenth Centuries*, ed. William Forbes Leith, 2 vols. (London, 1909), 2:372.

the concern of its supporters about the possibility of an embarrassing display of opposition in the general assembly. That concern proved groundless, however, as an attempt by Rev. John Gillies to establish a standing assembly committee to guard against a Catholic relief bill for Scotland was handily defeated, 118 to 24. The vote followed a heated debate in which William Robertson denied that legislation modeled on the English relief bill would pose a threat to the Protestant interest in Scotland and defended such legislation by drawing attention to the cruelty of existing Scottish laws against Roman Catholics. Robertson was supported by Alexander Gerard, John Home, Joseph McCormick, Allan Maconochie, and other speakers, just as Gillies was backed by several Popular party men, such as Charles Nisbet.[74] After this debate the sides in the Church of Scotland were clearly drawn along party lines, with the Moderates invoking their cherished principle of religious tolerance and their ecclesiastical opponents appealing to traditional Presbyterian fears and prejudices about the dangers of "Popery."[75]

Now Dundas knew, or at least was in a position to know, that the general assembly of 1778 would be overwhelmingly Moderate and therefore ideally suited to voice support for Catholic relief legislation. If that assembly had been given the opportunity to express its approval of an actual parliamentary bill, rather than merely of a proposed and as yet unwritten one, the "No Popery" agitation might have been averted, as Hay later suggested. Instead Dundas in effect opened the door to an opposition movement by consulting public opinion long before the projected bill reached the floor of the Commons. Even so, the most remarkable fact about the Scottish opposition to the proposed Catholic relief bill was how long it took to develop. Despite occasional expressions of disapproval in the press, there were at first few signs of widespread popular feeling against extending Roman Catholic relief legislation to Scotland. As late as September 1778 Scottish Catholics were on the offensive, meeting at Edinburgh to plan their strategy;[76] as late as October of that year the *Scots Magazine* could feature a supportive front-page article. Far from being a spontaneous explosion of deep-seated hatred, the Scottish agitation against Catholic relief had to be nurtured deliberately among a Protestant populace that had little contact with Catholics and no reason to feel threatened by them. Age-old prejudices and passions had

---

[74] *SM* 40 (May 1778): 267–71.

[75] Among the few exceptions to this pattern were Andrew Crosbie and George Hill, who broke with the Popular and Moderate parties, respectively, on this question. On Hill see George Cook, *The Life of the Late George Hill* (Edinburgh, 1820), 298–300.

[76] Johnson, *Roman Catholic Developments*, 17.

to be revived and aroused. Three distinct groups were responsible for cultivating this anti-Catholic spirit, which finally took hold among the people during the autumn and winter of 1778–1779. One was the Popular party in the Church of Scotland, led in this instance by John Erskine. Another was the Edinburgh-based grass-roots organization of tradesmen and merchants who called themselves the Committee for the Protestant Interest. The third, and most unexpected, was the nonjuring Scottish Episcopal Church, or at least its leading spokesman William Abernethy Drummond, later bishop of Brechin. By giving these diverse groups additional time to mobilize their opposition to a Scottish relief bill, Dundas and the government committed a tactical blunder that would soon have severe repercussions.

The first major Scottish pamphlet against Roman Catholic relief was published in September 1778 in the form of a "letter to Mr. G[eorge] H[ay]." It was the work not of a Presbyterian but of the nonjuring Episcopalian William Abernethy Drummond, who argued that the loyalty oaths required of Roman Catholics as a prerequisite for relief would be worthless since their religion condoned "breaking faith with heretics."[77] After Hay denied these charges, Drummond directed a second pamphlet against him at the end of the year, and he may also have been responsible for a harsher anonymous work of 1779.[78] It would seem that a primary objective of these writings against Hay and the Roman Catholics was to gain respectability for Scottish nonjuring Episcopalians, who had long been associated with Jacobitism and Catholicism in the minds of Scottish Presbyterians.[79] The fruits of this policy began to appear in November 1778, when John Erskine and William Robertson each praised Drummond's efforts to

[77] William Abernethy Drummond, *The Lawfulness of Breaking Faith with Heretics proved to be an Established Doctrine of the Church of Rome, in a letter to Mr. G. H.* (Edinburgh, 1778). Drummond and Hay had already engaged in a polemical exchange on points of doctrine in 1776.

[78] George Hay, *An Answer to Mr. W. A. D.'s Letter to G. H.* (Edinburgh, 1778); William Abernethy Drummond, *A Second Letter to Mr. G. H.* (Edinburgh, 1778). The harsher work of 1779 was *A Letter to all Opposers of the Repeal of the Penal laws against Papists in Scotland* (Edinburgh, 1779), which drew the invective of Burke.

[79] On the Episcopalian-Jacobite connection in Scotland, see the relevant studies by D. H. Whiteford and Bruce Lenman cited in the bibliographical essay below. Hay's biographer stated that Drummond was said to have been motivated by anger at the Catholics for having suddenly renounced Jacobitism and "outbid the Non-jurors in the favour and protection of Government" (quoted in Johnson, *Roman Catholic Developments*, 9–10). No doubt Drummond's bitterness was intensified by the fact that the man leading the Scottish Catholics at this time had been born into a nonjuring Episcopalian family and had acquired his taste for Catholicism while serving time in a London prison for complicity in the '45. Perhaps this explains why most of Drummond's anti-Catholic pamphlets took the form of personal attacks on Hay.

differentiate Scottish Episcopalians from Roman Catholics—a point to which Drummond himself proudly alluded in print.[80]

The "No Popery" zeal of John Erskine and his colleagues in the Popular party of the established church had deeper roots than that of Scottish Episcopalians like Drummond. For Erskine, the struggle against Catholic relief began nearly a decade before passage of the English relief bill and was closely bound up with the American crisis. As we have seen, in 1769 Erskine wrote that "Popery" was increasing in England and Scotland because the government foolishly regarded its Protestant colonists in America as a more serious threat to the stability of Great Britain than the Catholics. The Quebec act and the outbreak of war with America seemed to confirm Erskine's suspicions, and his pro-American pamphlets of 1776 reemphasized the evils of "Popery" and the folly of relaxing restrictions against it. In these works Erskine appears to view legal tolerance of Roman Catholicism as tantamount to persecution of Protestants. "The nation seems asleep, insensible of danger, and not like to awake, till guarding against it becomes too late," he warned two years before Catholic relief became a major issue.[81] The fact that such warnings were expressed in the context of support for the American colonies indicates that for Erskine and his party the two issues were inseparable: by alienating British Protestants in America and encouraging French Catholics in Canada, Britain was demonstrating a fatal inability to perceive its true priorities, true friends, and true enemies.

Following the lead of Erskine and other clergymen affiliated with the Popular party, the Synod of Glasgow and Ayr declared itself against Roman Catholic relief in October 1778, thereby touching off a small anti-Catholic riot in Glasgow.[82] As other synods and presbyteries began coming out against Catholic relief, national interest focused on the November meeting of the influential Synod of Lothian and Tweeddale to see whether William Robertson's policy of religious tolerance or John Erskine's policy of continued legal sanctions against Roman Catholics would prevail. The outcome was in the main a victory for Robertson, who saw to it that the synod declared its "firm adherence to the principles of liberty, and the rights of private judgment" as well as its desire that no person "should be deprived of his inheritance, or subjected to civil penalties for conscience sake."[83] But

---

[80] Drummond, *Second Letter to Mr. G. H.*, in *SM* 40 (December 1778): 677.

[81] Erskine, *Equity and Wisdom of Administration*, 15.

[82] Eugene C. Black, *The Association: British Extraparliamentary Political Organization, 1769–1793* (Cambridge, Mass., 1963), 136–37.

[83] "Resolution of the Synod of Lothian and Tweeddale," 11 November 1778, *SM* 40 (October 1778): 566.

representatives of the Popular party did manage to enact a significant qualifying statement warning of the need for "effectual provision" by Parliament "to prevent all the dangers that are apprehended" following repeal of restrictions against Roman Catholics.[84] Was this statement intended as a prophecy or as a threat of Protestant violence in the event that relief legislation was extended to Scotland?

In December 1778 and January 1779 Erskine and his friends produced a number of pamphlets in opposition to Catholic relief, such as William Porteous's *The Doctrine of Toleration, applied to the Present Times,* John MacFarlan's *A Defence of the Clergy of the Church of Scotland who have appeared in Opposition to the Intention of an Unlimited Repeal of the Penal Laws against Roman Catholics,* and Erskine's own *Considerations on the Spirit of Popery.* All three of these pamphlets accepted the principle of religious tolerance in theory but attempted to demonstrate that Roman Catholicism was unworthy of such tolerance because it was itself intolerant. Erskine was willing to grant "that Roman Catholics have naturally as much humanity, and honour, and conscience as other men," but he insisted that these qualities were nullified—particularly in the case of "such poor illiterate Papists as the greater part of those in Scotland"—by the fact that all Roman Catholics "must believe what the church believes" and are little more than willing slaves of the dreaded Jesuits.[85] He proceeded to enumerate the usual examples of alleged Catholic treachery and persecution of Protestants in British and European history, including rumors of Scottish Catholics breaking into homes to disturb the deathbeds of Protestants.[86]

Were the pamphlets of Erskine, Porteous, MacFarlan, and other Popular party ministers partially responsible for provoking the serious "No Popery" riots that occurred in Edinburgh and Glasgow in February 1779? Erskine steadfastly maintained that he and his friends had been appalled by the riots and had done what they could to stop them. According to one account, Erskine personally helped to calm and disperse the mob that tried to burn down Principal Robertson's house on the second day of rioting in Edinburgh.[87] In April Erskine

---

[84] Ibid. An account of the debate that preceded the adoption of this resolution was printed in the *Caledonian Mercury,* 23 November–23 December 1778.

[85] John Erskine, *Considerations on the Spirit of Popery* (Edinburgh, 1778), 1–4, 36. Erskine apparently believed that the Jesuits were still operating in Scotland even though the pope had dissolved their order in 1773.

[86] Ibid., 7.

[87] "Account of the Public Life and Character of the Late Dr Erskine, of Edinburgh," *SM* 65 (February 1803): 81.

sent copies of the anti-Catholic pamphlets by Porteous, MacFarlan, and himself to Edmund Burke, the leading parliamentary spokesman for Roman Catholic rights, in an effort to demonstrate that "no set of men felt or expressed a deeper sorrow, and a warmer indignation at these unchristian and disorderly proceedings" than the local clergy.[88] "The ministers of Edinburgh who disapproved the Popish bill, equally disapproved the February riots, and took the earliest opportunity of reproving them from the pulpit," Erskine informed Burke in another letter. Indeed, he himself had preached warmly against the riots while they were in progress.[89] The pamphlets that he sent to Burke are relatively moderate in tone, and all of them contain explicit admonitions against attacks on Roman Catholics or their property.[90] "It is not the *men* of this religion whom we detest," William Porteous reminded his audience in the course of a warning against "a mobbish and seditious behavior"; "it is the *religion* of these deluded men."[91]

Though Erskine and his associates in the Popular party were certainly the least fanatical of the main forces constituting the "No Popery" movement, they were not quite so moderate as Erskine claimed. Despite their relatively mild tone and their occasional warnings against violence, the pamphlets that this group produced repeated most of the standard slanders of the day against Roman Catholicism and encouraged resistance toward even the smallest amount of Catholic relief. Moreover, they contained several loose remarks that easily could have been read as justifications for violent actions against Catholics. Erskine, for example, stated that "the revolution-settlement has much to fear from indifference about Popery; but can never be endangered by honest endeavours to kindle zeal against it."[92] MacFarlan was more direct when he noted that "if by the indiscreet zeal of the Papists, popular tumults are raised against them, they only can be *accountable* for consequences."[93] Remarks like these lend credence to the view that Popular party pamphleteers were most responsible for the anti-Catholic hysteria of 1779.[94] Edmund Burke

[88] Erskine to Burke, 24 April 1779, *Burke Correspondence*, 4:63.

[89] Erskine to Burke, 16 July 1779, ibid., 104.

[90] Erskine, *Considerations on Popery*, 41; John MacFarlan, *A Defence of the Clergy of the Church of Scotland who have appeared in Opposition to the Intention of an Unlimited Repeal of the Penal Laws against Roman Catholics* (Edinburgh, 1779), 31; William Porteous, *The Doctrine of Toleration, applied to the Present Times* (Edinburgh, 1778), 38.

[91] Porteous, *Doctrine of Toleration*, 38.

[92] Erskine, *Considerations on Popery*, 33.

[93] MacFarlan, *Defence of the Clergy*, 30.

[94] Robert Kent Donovan, "Voices of Distrust: The Expression of Anti-Catholic Feeling in Scotland, 1778–1781," *Innes Review* 30 (1979): 62–76.

suggested as much in a caustic letter to Erskine in which he also pointed out the latter's inconsistency in opposing the religious liberty of Roman Catholics while nobly championing the cause of political liberty in America.[95]

The bulk of Burke's invective, however, was directed not against Erskine's circle of Popular party clergymen but against the Committee for the Protestant Interest, which the *Annual Register* later ridiculed in an unmistakably Burkean manner as a "self-created body" of "a few obscure zealots in Edinburgh" who assumed a "specious and pompous title" in an effort to conceal their humble occupations and insignificant numbers.[96] Six weeks after the Scottish "No Popery" riots, Burke castigated that organization for publishing and distributing inflammatory pamphlets such as *A Short View of the Statutes at Present in Force in Scotland against Popery*.[97] The riots, he charged, were "little more than a practical inference from the principles there laid down."[98] Like John Erskine, the Committee for the Protestant Interest emphatically denied that it had in any way encouraged or condoned the "No Popery" riots.[99] Yet Burke's accusations are not easily refuted. Even if the members of the Committee for the Protestant Interest sincerely disapproved of violence against Roman Catholics—and there is reason to suspect their sincerity on this point—their words and deeds, together with those of Erskine, Drummond, and other zealous and influential opponents of Catholic relief, created an atmosphere of such intense hatred and hostility that anti-Catholic violence was almost inevitable. Indeed, one could argue that such violence was necessary in order for the campaign against Catholic relief to be taken seriously and finally triumph.

The violence began in Edinburgh toward the end of January 1779 with a week of general rowdiness following reports that the Scottish relief bill was already framed and ready for parliamentary consid-

---

[95] Burke to Erskine, 12 June 1779, *Burke Correspondence*, 4:83–88.

[96] *Annual Register* 23 (1780): 27.

[97] This pamphlet by one John Dickson was widely distributed by the Committee for the Protestant Interest in December 1778 and January 1779 and was reprinted in its massive collection of antirelief documents, *Scotland's Opposition to the Popish Bill* (Edinburgh, 1780). In a speech of 18 March 1779 Burke had blamed this organization for publishing another pamphlet, *A Letter to all Opposers of the Repeal of the Penal Laws against Papists in Scotland*, which is thought to have been the work of William Abernethy Drummond. *Caledonian Mercury*, 24 March 1779, and Burke to Patrick Bowie, [31] March 1779, *Burke Correspondence*, 4:53–57.

[98] Burke to Patrick Bowie, [31] March 1779, *Burke Correspondence*, 4:55.

[99] *Scotland's Opposition to the Popish Bill*, x; Bowie to Burke, 25 March 1779, in *SM* 41 (March 1779): 135–40; Thomas Blacklock, *Protestant Interest Vindicated. In a Series of Letters to Edmund Burke, Esq. and Other Eminent Persons* (Edinburgh, 1779).

eration.[100] Although these disturbances were serious enough for the lord justice clerk to warn his superiors in London about the danger of anti-Catholic mobs becoming vehicles for the expression of political radicalism regarding America and other issues,[101] local authorities did virtually nothing to check the escalation of hostilities. Sympathy for the mobs' objectives was probably one reason for the town council's inaction. But principle may have mattered less than politics in this case, since Sir Laurence Dundas, the real power behind the town council, was not one to pass up a chance to embarrass the rival political interest led by the duke of Buccleuch and the relief bill's chief sponsor, Henry Dundas. During the worst days of rioting the town council did little to restore order and actually prevented Buccleuch from doing so with his regiment of fencibles; only when it was clear that the riots had achieved their goal did the council issue a tough proclamation that infuriated Burke by implying that all previous rioting was excusable and by presuming to speak for Parliament concerning future legislation. There was considerable justice, as well as irony, in John Wilkes's later calling Henry Dundas to account in the House of Commons and charging him with capitulation to the mob on the Catholic relief question.[102]

Encouraged by the town council's apathy, crowds gathered on 30 January to break windows at the home of Bishop Hay. Serious rioting began three days later, when large numbers of people responded to anonymous handbills exhorting them to assemble at Leith Wynd for the purpose of demolishing Hay's new house and chapel. In two days of furious rioting, that building and several others—including Hay's old chapel and personal library in Blackfriars Wynd—were burned down or pillaged, despite the efforts of James Boswell to pacify the enraged mob.[103] On the second day of the riots (3 February) the mob even tried to attack the homes of two Presbyterian friends of Catholic relief, William Robertson and Andrew Crosbie (who had drafted the bill), but the presence of dragoons foiled this attempt. Sporadic violence continued in Edinburgh until 6 February, when the town council issued its proclamation announcing that plans for a Scottish relief bill had been set aside and promising that those

---

[100] Unless otherwise noted, the following account of the "No Popery" riots is drawn from these sources: *SM* 41 (February 1779): 106–10; George Hay, *A Memorial to the Public, in Behalf of the Roman Catholics of Edinburgh and Glasgow* (London, 1779); Hay's "Pastoral Letter" of 8 February 1779 in Leith, *Scottish Catholics*, 2:381–83; *Annual Register* 23 (1780): 25–33; *Association*, esp. 142–44.

[101] Fagerstrom, "Scottish Opinion," 268 n. 47.

[102] *Parl. Hist.*, 20:280–82. This confrontation occurred on 18 March 1779.

[103] James Boswell, *Laird of Auchinleck, 1778–1782*, ed. Joseph W. Reed and Frederick A. Pottle (New York, 1979), 47–48.

responsible for further disorders would be severely punished. But no sooner had anti-Catholic rioting subsided in Edinburgh than it flared up in Glasgow, where its leaders were described by a prominent Popular party minister as ignorant of "whether there are seven or two sacraments" and so "blasphemous and impious" in their language that even heathens might be disgraced by it.[104] Finally, the "No Popery" disturbances were brought to an end by the publication on 12 February of a letter from the acting secretary of state for the North, Lord Weymouth, to the lord justice clerk stating that the government had no intention of introducing or approving a Catholic relief bill for Scotland.

Reactions to the Scottish "No Popery" riots were predictably varied. James Boswell was convinced that the riots were forebodings of the bloody rebellion that would surely erupt if Catholic relief were extended to Scotland.[105] Edmund Burke was horrified that extraparliamentary forces of intolerance had won a complete victory.[106] Along with other opposition Whigs he used the affair to embarrass the North government, but it was necessary to renounce any further plans for relief legislation in order to concentrate on the more pressing problem of securing just compensation for victims of the riots.[107] The most zealous Scottish opponents of Catholic relief were defensive about the riots and resented Burke's criticisms of their behavior. "It may be doubted if ever rioters had greater cause to be angry," wrote one anonymous pamphleteer who placed all blame for the "No Popery" disturbances on the Scottish Catholics themselves.[108] More moderate opponents of relief followed the example of John Erskine by denouncing the riots while continuing to support the cause that had inspired them.

With the single exception of George Campbell's *Address to the People of Scotland*, which advocated Catholic relief legislation as late as April 1779,[109] the Moderate party remained conspicuously silent in

---

[104] John Gillies to Sir David Dalrymple, Lord Hailes, 23 February 1779, University of Virginia, Newhailes Papers (microfilm copies), reel 1.

[105] Boswell to Burke, 22 February 1779, *Burke Correspondence*, 4:44.

[106] Burke to Boswell, 1 March 1779, ibid., 45.

[107] *Parl. Hist.*, 20:322–27.

[108] *An Answer to Mr. Burke's Speech in Parliament in Favour of the Scots Roman-Catholics residing in Edinburgh and Glasgow on the 18th of March 1779* (Edinburgh, 1779), iv–v, 14–15.

[109] Though he published his pamphlet in the safety of tolerant Aberdeen, Campbell saw to it that one hundred fifty copies were placed on sale in Edinburgh in time for the meeting of the general assembly, with a promise of more to come. He took no money for his efforts but expressed great concern about sales due to the importance of the topic. Campbell to William Creech, 15 May 1779, SRO, Dalguise Muniments.

the weeks and months following the "No Popery" riots. The silence of William Robertson is particularly noteworthy since Robertson's liberal views on the Catholic relief question had made him the target of much personal abuse. One scurrilous broadside used the "Popery" issue as a springboard for a vicious attack on Robertson's alleged immorality, impiety, political inconstancy, and vanity.[110] Another of Robertson's enemies, Gilbert Stuart, took this opportunity to cast aspersions on Robertson's competence as a historian and integrity as a man in a scholarly work published in January 1779.[111] That Stuart's attacks caused Robertson much pain is clear from the latter's remark to Thomas Somerville in 1792: "At a time when I was fighting for a cause so sacred as religious liberty, [Stuart] concluded his History of the Reformation with reflections evidently intended to expose me to popular odium and personal danger."[112]

In using the phrase "personal danger," Robertson was alluding to the anonymous death threats that he had begun receiving in the winter of 1778–1779. Three of these death threats that have been preserved among Robertson's papers provide insight into the mentality of the fanatical fringe in the "No Popery" affair.[113] The first one, from "A Lover of Truth," is almost unintelligible, but the gist of it seems to be that Robertson must either publicly renounce the idea of Catholic relief or else "take your chance for you may depend if otherwise you shall not be the Bulwark nor Pope's agent longer, your out and in coming shall be watched etc etc." The second death threat is the most explicit about the means by which the principal's life is to be taken: "I have now a pair of pocket pistols, well loaded, which I purpose to give you the contents of one of them." The third threat is the most ominous of all because it hints at a well-organized popular conspiracy similar to the one that brought "Black Jock" Porteous to justice in a famous incident of 1736:

> If you consult your own safety and y^t of your family take refuge
> in Ed^r castle along with Dr. Hay alias his Grace the Archbishop
> of St. Andrews & remember y^t ye death of Sharp ye apostate is still

---

[110] *Character of a Certain Popular Historian, now Ministerial Agent, for reconciling our complasant clergy to the Church of Rome* (1779).

[111] Gilbert Stuart, *Observations Concerning the Public Law and Constitutional History of Scotland* (Edinburgh, 1779).

[112] Somerville, 275–76. Cf. William Adam, *Sequel to the Gift of a Grandfather* (1839), 54, where it is said that Robertson spoke warmly of taking Stuart to court. In a characteristically haughty letter to his anxious publisher, William Creech, Stuart vehemently denied that the forthcoming *Observations* was primarily an attack on Robertson. 17 November 1778, SRO, Dalguise Muniments.

[113] NLS, 3943:85–89.

no murder in the opinion of 20000 people inhabitants of this city of Ed^r who are soon to be reinforced by ye inhabitants of Glasgow—take this warning from one who once esteemed you much; and therefore wishes to save your life—we are resolute and determined—our plan is laid—our officers are chosen of which no. I am one—we are furnished w^t every necessary viz. arms, ammunition, etc., etc.,—we are therefore to resist unto blood and our plan is laid all over Scotland—therefore save yourself and thank me when you have burnt this, *Vivere vel Morire.*

Since this letter is dated "Wednesday evening," it is likely that Robertson received it on Wednesday 3 February, when the mob did in fact attempt to burn down his house while Robertson and his family took refuge in Edinburgh Castle,[114] just as the anonymous letter writer had recommended.

As the opening of the general assembly of 1779 drew near, attention was focused on the question of how William Robertson and the Moderate party would conduct themselves regarding the issue of Catholic relief. Would the Moderates be able to secure a majority in the assembly? Would Robertson remain silent or humbly admit defeat by supporting an anticipated overture calling for a standing committee to lobby against Catholic relief legislation? Or would the Moderates continue their struggle for Catholic relief despite the severity of popular demonstrations against it and the desertion of the government? One anonymous pamphlet called *Scots Anticipation* attracted considerable interest by imagining the substance and outcome of the anticipated "Popery" debate between members of the Moderate and Popular parties in the assembly. According to this pamphlet, the Moderates would command the same overwhelming majority that they had enjoyed the previous year, and the assembly would unanimously approve resolutions by William Robertson condemning the violent actions of the Edinburgh and Glasgow mobs and calling on ministers to exhort the people to behave moderately and peaceably at all times.[115]

When the Moderate candidate for moderator soundly defeated the "No Popery" candidate on the opening day of the general assembly,

[114] Alexander Kincaid, *The History of Edinburgh* (Edinburgh, 1787), 95.

[115] *Scots Anticipation; or, A Summary of a Debate; containing the Substance of some of the Principal Speeches that are to be delivered in the G———l A———y of the C———h of S———d, upon an Overture . . . Relating to Popery* (Edinburgh, 1779). The April issue of *Scots Magazine* commented on this pamphlet (which is sometimes ascribed to John Witherspoon), and on 24 May the *Caledonian Mercury* reprinted the imaginary speech by William Robertson.

it was evident that the author of *Scots Anticipation* had accurately predicted the Moderates' numerical superiority. Opponents of Catholic relief had reason to rejoice, however, when the lord high commissioner reassured the assembly that the government definitely would not introduce a Scottish relief bill.[116] These developments set the tone for the "Popery" debate that took place five days later. On the one hand, it was clear that the Moderates would be forced to give up any lingering hopes for securing a resolution in favor of Catholic relief legislation for Scotland. On the other hand, it was equally clear that the extremist element in the assembly would lack the votes needed to enact an overture calling for establishment of an independent standing committee to guard against a Catholic relief bill. This radical overture was therefore replaced early in the debate by John MacFarlan's milder declaration and resolution, which placed the responsibilities for vigilance in the general assembly's commission rather than in a standing committee of doubtful constitutionality, denounced the "No Popery" riots, and supported the government's decision to refrain from introducing relief legislation for Scottish Catholics. The Moderates eventually accepted MacFarlan's compromise measure in slightly amended form, but before doing so they were determined to have their say in ecclesiastical court. It fell to Alexander Carlyle and William Robertson to explain the principles of the Moderate party in this important affair.[117]

Carlyle's speech began with an affirmation of the speaker's identity as a "Revolution Whig," ever respectful of the opinions of "the people." On the basis of this principle Carlyle admitted that it appeared "highly inexpedient" to press for Catholic relief legislation "now that the commons of Scotland have shewn such a warm aversion against it." Yet the fact that the will of the people must be heeded does not mean that the will of the people is necessarily correct; for though the people "cannot be corrupted or overawed, yet alas! Sir, they can be sadly misled." Understanding no "rules of proportion, the multitude are to be excused," Carlyle insisted. The deliberate implication of these characteristically paternalistic remarks was that responsiblity for the "No Popery" riots lay with antirelief leaders, particularly in the Popular party. The remainder of Carlyle's speech was

---

[116] *SM* 41 (May 1779): 277.

[117] The following account of the speeches of Carlyle and Robertson is based on the versions published in *A Narrative of the Debate in the General Assembly of the Church of Scotland, May 25, 1779, Occasioned by the Apprehensions of an intended repeal of the Penal Statutes against Papists*, ed. John Erskine (Edinburgh, 1780), 32–36, 49–61. Most of the speeches in this debate were originally reported in successive issues of the *Caledonian Mercury* (31 May to 10 July 1779) and *SM* (May to September 1779).

chiefly a plea to "endeavour to make our people worthy, in some future period, of having these sanguinary penal statutes [against Roman Catholics] repealed . . . by propagating among them the mild, generous, and Christian principles of toleration." In conclusion, Carlyle reminded the assembly that religious fanaticism is incompatible with enlightened principles and urged them to oppose Roman Catholicism with reason and humanity instead of persecution.

Shortly after Carlyle had completed his eloquent oration against intolerance, William Robertson rose to deliver what would prove to be his last and perhaps greatest speech in the general assembly. For the first and only time in his distinguished career Robertson elected to preface his general remarks with personal ones, explaining that "when one's character has been unjustly traduced, one owes it to himself, and to his station in life, to vindicate it." He proceeded to trace the history of his involvement with the Catholic relief question during the previous year. Despite "the rapid progress of liberal sentiments in this enlightened age," he had originally doubted that Parliament would actually enact any relief legislation because of "the deep-rooted aversion of Britons to the doctrines and spirit of Popery." After both houses of Parliament had passed the English relief bill, however—with government and opposition, the "Old Whigs" and the bench of bishops, all joining to support it—he had decided to take a closer look at its specific provisions. Upon doing so, "all my apprehensions vanished," for it appeared that the relief given to Roman Catholics was "neither too great nor too little." English Catholics who agreed to swear an appropriate oath were granted basic legal and religious liberties but were denied all political rights. In short, "an English Papist has not acquired the privileges of a citizen; he is restored only to the rights of a man."

Having come to appreciate the "temperate wisdom of legislature" in this matter, Robertson had begun to work for extension of the English relief act to Scotland. He had played an important part in the proceedings of the general assembly and November meeting of the Synod of Lothian and Tweeddale in 1778 and had taken great pride in the moderate resolution passed unanimously by the latter judicatory. To his great dismay, however, his actions had set off a "general alarm" as "the dread of some dark machination to introduce Popery spread through synods, presbyteries, corporations, parishes, and descended at last to bodies without a name, and to men whose station in life little intitled them to deliberate or decide on public measures." As soon as he had perceived the extent of the animosity aroused by the prospect of extending a limited amount of Catholic relief to Scotland, Robertson had begun to have second thoughts about the advisability of proceeding with the proposed Scottish relief bill. Like Carlyle, he was convinced that "the prejudices of the people" must be respected, "however ill-founded their apprehensions might be." For this reason he had applied to the lord advocate and solicitor general for a less liberal relief bill that would prevent Catholic priests from founding religious schools in Scotland. Finally, when it had become clear to him that matters had gone too far for the people of Scotland to accept Catholic relief in any form, Robertson had informed the lord advocate of this fact, adding that the situation was similar to the one that had induced the government to retract the Jewish relief bill of 1753 due to widespread but "ill-grounded" public opposition in England.[118] Robertson implied that he had been personally responsible for persuading the government to abandon its plan for a Scottish relief bill. He had done so reluctantly, not because he disapproved of such a bill but because "I preferred the public good to my own private sentiments."

What recompense had Robertson received for his conscientious conduct in this affair?

> My character as a man, as a citizen, and a minister of the gospel, has been delineated in the most odious colours: I have been represented as a pensioner of the Pope, as an agent for Rome, as a seducer of my brethren to Popery, as the tool of a king and ministry bent on overturning the Protestant religion: In pamphlets, in news-papers, and hand-bills, I have been held out to an enraged mob, as the victim who deserved to be next sacrificed, after they had satiated their vengeance on a Popish bishop [George Hay]. My family has been disquieted: my house has been attacked; I have been threatened with pistols and daggers; I have been warned, that I was watched in my going out and coming home; the time has been set beyond which I was not to live; and, for several weeks, hardly a day passed on which I did not receive incendiary letters.

Like a true Stoic, he had gone about his business as usual, not even mentioning the death threats to his family until the danger had passed. What had irked him most of all, he stated, was the fact that "it was in the name of *Jesus* I was warned that my death was resolved, and the instruments for cutting short my days prepared."

At this point Robertson concluded his dramatic personal narrative and turned his attention to the particular question under considera-

---

[118] Cf. George Campbell, *An Address to the People of Scotland, upon the Alarms that Have been Raised in Regard to Popery* (Aberdeen, 1779), 53.

tion, namely, what action the Church of Scotland should take in regard to the controversy over Catholic relief. His chief point was that the assurances of government that a Catholic relief bill for Scotland would not be submitted to Parliament, coupled with the paucity and poverty of Scottish Catholics, made it unnecessary for the church to adopt an extreme measure that would "foment in the nation the dread of extraordinary danger, which she certainly knows to have no longer any existence." He therefore praised John MacFarlan for giving up the "unconstitutional" plan to establish an independent standing committee to guard against Catholic relief and proposed a somewhat milder version of MacFarlan's resolution for the consideration of the assembly. When the "Popery" debate came to an end later that day, the general assembly unanimously adopted a compromise version of MacFarlan's and Robertson's resolutions.[119] This action both preserved the unity of the kirk and effectively terminated the "No Popery" crisis. Like the Scots militia that the Moderate literati so fervently desired, relief for Scottish Catholics would not become reality until the 1790s, when radically different economic and political circumstances would accomplish what the rational and humanitarian arguments of William Robertson and his Moderate friends could not.[120]

The Scottish "No Popery" affair of 1778–1779 had important consequences for the personal career of William Robertson, the status of the Moderate party in the Church of Scotland, and the Catholic relief question in England. Concerning the last of these points, there is little doubt that the Scottish "No Popery" disturbances were the model for the Gordon Riots that ravaged London in June 1780.[121] This is true not only because the Gordon Riots were motivated initially by anti-Catholic sentiment and inspired by an eccentric Scot (Lord George Gordon) affiliated with the Committee for the Protestant Interest and its sister organization in London, the Protestant Associa-

---

[119] Erskine, *Narrative of the Debate*, 78–79.

[120] The Scottish relief bill of 1793 gave Catholics freedom of worship and basic property rights. At the time George Campbell marveled that "a motion which raised a flame throughout the whole island no longer back than fourteen years, is now allowed to pass as it were unanimously, not a single person daring to utter a syllable against it" (Campbell to William Creech, 14 September 1793, SRO, Dalguise Muniments). The reasons for this dramatic reversal on the Catholic question included growing reliance on cheap Catholic labor in the developing Glasgow cotton industry; fear of Jacobinism and atheism, sympathy for French Catholics, and need for an expanded military force due to the French Revolutionary crisis; and the fact that the bill was enacted quietly and quickly, with almost no public debate, under the leadership of a more experienced and more powerful Henry Dundas. See Johnson, *Roman Catholic Developments*, chap. 4 (esp. Bishop Geddes's comments quoted on 31) and 87.

[121] Black, *Association*, 147–73.

tion, but also because the Scottish "No Popery" riots had demonstrated just how effective persistent popular agitation could be as a means of affecting the decisions of policy makers. In Scotland peaceful protests, pamphlets, and petitions had not changed government policy—it was urban violence that had forced government to honor, however reluctantly, the prejudices of the people against an unpopular minority. Would it not be possible to employ the same tactics successfully in England? To Alexander Carlyle, along with most modern historians, it seemed undeniable that the "mighty Blaze which had very nearly consum'd the Capital, and overturn'd the Government in June 1780" had been kindled by the "Small Spark" of anti-Catholic protest ignited in Scotland in the autumn of 1778.[122]

Within the Church of Scotland the effects were more enduring, if less dramatic. The "No Popery" affair exposed the vulnerability of William Robertson and the Moderate party and marked the beginning of the end of "Dr. Robertson's Administration" in the kirk. In a letter of November 1779 recommending a Moderate clergyman for an academic chair at St. Andrews, Robertson noted that this appointment was particularly necessary "at a time when a spirit of fanaticism and disorder is spreading among our Order."[123] The Moderate principle of tolerance had been called into question, and Robertson himself had been subjected to an extremely trying personal experience. These factors, along with failing health, remain the most plausible explanations for Robertson's rather sudden retirement from ecclesiastical politics in 1780,[124] leaving the Moderate party in a state of confusion at a critical time. Alexander Carlyle summed up the matter in a letter to a friend in England:

> The Principal . . . has abdicated the Government of the Church which leaves us at a Loss for some time. By means of his Great Abilities for Debate (for no Man ever excelled him in the Inside of a Court) he created himself a new office, for he has not only been the Leader in Ecclesiastical Affairs, but the Assembly Or-

---

[122] Carlyle to Bishop Douglas, 14 March 1781, BL, Egerton 2185:103–104. The same metaphor had been used by Burke in *Annual Register* 12 (1780): 27.

[123] Robertson to Lord ———, 15 November 1779, Public Record Office, SP 54/47:364–65. In addition to the "No Popery" affair, Robertson may have been thinking of the recent victory of Andrew Hunter over the Moderate candidate James Macknight in the contest for the chair of divinity at Edinburgh University.

[124] Cf. Ian D. L. Clark, "From Protest to Reaction: The Moderate Regime in the Church of Scotland, 1752–1805," in *SAI*, 213, and Clark diss., app. C, where it is suggested that the primary reason for Robertson's ecclesiastical retirement was the strained relationship between the principal and the man who had emerged as the dominant force in Scottish political management, Henry Dundas.

ator for 20 Years. We shall now return to our old State, which was to let the Management fall into the Hands of a Few Friends at or near Edin^r, and trust to chance to bring us up annual Debaters.[125]

Although they deeply regretted Robertson's decision to withdraw from participation in church politics, Carlyle and other leading Moderates were not about to surrender their church to the "spirit of fanaticism" that had inspired the "No Popery" disturbances. "For my part," wrote Carlyle, "after what has happen'd, I shall exert any little force I have till Death, in guarding against the Progress of Fanaticism, and in Supporting the Liberal minded Clergy who are still, thank God! the Great Majority among us."[126]

With dedicated men like Carlyle sharing the party leadership, and with their friend Henry Dundas gaining complete control of Scottish ecclesiastical and academic patronage, the Moderates managed to maintain their hold on the administration of Scottish ecclesiastical affairs for some time after Robertson's retirement. Yet their party was changing and their hold was gradually slipping. The outcome of the American War was seen as a clear victory for the Popular party and their allies, and it was only with great difficulty that the Moderates defeated their opponents' aggressive campaign against church patronage in the early 1780s. At the climax of that campaign in August 1784, William Robertson himself made an appearance at the Edinburgh general sessions to speak against an important antipatronage resolution. In the course of his speech Robertson drew a damning analogy between the "No Popery" agitation of 1778–1779—which he called "an eternal and irreparable disgrace to this country"—and the current agitation against church patronage: "Sir, the same causes will ever produce the same effects; and once open the gate of novelty, bold is the man who will pretend to foretell when it will be shut."[127] The "No Popery" affair had opened the "gate of novelty" by encouraging "anarchy" and popular tumult, and Robertson was uncertain if it would ever again be closed.

This appearance by William Robertson in the Edinburgh general sessions was the last he is known to have made in any ecclesiastical court. Some months later a scurrilous pamphleteer seized the opportunity to publicize Robertson's recent political failures:

---

[125] Carlyle to Bishop Douglas, 14 March 1781, BL, Egerton 2185:103–104.
[126] Ibid.
[127] *Caledonian Mercury*, 21 August 1784. The general sessions consisted of all the ministers, elders, and deacons in Edinburgh's nine establishment churches.

Recollect what were your sentiments of the late American War? Did you not approve of it as just, and look upon its success as altogether certain? Were not such also your sentiments of the popish bill? And have you not found yourself miserably disappointed in both? So I trust you will be with respect to the bill anent Patronage.[128]

The anonymous pamphleteer had underestimated the tenacity of the Moderate party, the government, and the landed interest in regard to the matter of church patronage, but he had deftly struck a nerve concerning the American and Catholic relief crises. In the former instance Robertson and his Moderate friends had won over the kirk to their principles of loyalty, order, and patriotism, only to be embarrassed by the eventual triumph of the Americans. In the latter instance they had struggled to establish religious tolerance but were finally forced to accede to the demands of an intolerant and sometimes fanatical populace. Although not decisive in themselves, these developments were cracks in the Moderate wall: they signaled the vulnerability and impending decline of the Moderate literati of Edinburgh and their vision of the Enlightenment during the closing years of the eighteenth century.

[128] *The Evils of Patronage Considered* (Edinburgh, 1785), 30.

The Passing of
the Moderate Enlightenment

---------------- ❁ ----------------

"GHOSTS . . . ON THEIR MIDNIGHT TOMBS"

I am now so prodigiously old, that it becomes time to think of
decamping. I have been preaching within a few years of half a
century. Time runs fast away.

Hugh Blair,
Letter to James Boswell, 1789

There was a general feeling that Home's death [in 1808] closed
an era in the literary history of Scotland, and dissolved a link
which, though worn and frail, seemed to connect the present
generation with that of their fathers.

Sir Walter Scott,
"Life and Works of John Home," 1827

In the years between the "No Popery" affair of 1778–1779 and the
death of William Robertson in 1793, the Moderate literati of Edinburgh gradually ceased to function as a leading force in the cultural
and intellectual life of Scotland. This decline was caused in part by
political and economic events that significantly altered the nature of
Scottish and European society at the end of the eighteenth century.
Personal factors also contributed to this process. As they passed into
their sixties and seventies, the Moderate literati began to reduce their
herculean loads as ecclesiastical politicians, pastors, authors, and
professors. Their withdrawal was hastened by the security of their
financial situations and by the discomfort of various physical ail-
ments from which they suffered during this period. By the 1790s most
of their connections with Scottish institutions had been severed, and
their days of creative intellectual activity were by and large over.

The first of the Moderate literati of Edinburgh to show signs of
physical decline was William Robertson. In a letter of 1784 recount-
ing his recent medical history, Robertson explained that his frenzied
efforts to complete and publish the *History of America* during the 1770s

had brought on an attack of rheumatism "which shattered my constitution so much that it cost me three years attention, & three journeys to Buxton, to re-establish my health."[1] The severity of this illness helps to account for Robertson's retirement from church politics in 1780, after which he was granted a pension of £200 per annum as a demonstration of appreciation for his ecclesiastical, academic, and literary accomplishments. For a decade after publishing the *History of America* Robertson was unable to endure the rigors of historical research and composition,[2] though he seems to have regained some of his old vitality toward the end of his life. In 1788 he preached a vigorous sermon commemorating the Glorious Revolution,[3] and three years later his *Historical Disquisition* on India appeared. The £416 he received for that brief work was barely a tenth of the amount paid to him some years earlier for *Charles V*, but the combined annual income of nearly £700 from his pension and his offices as principal, parish minister, and historiographer royal for Scotland would have made Robertson one of the wealthiest Scottish ministers up to this time even if he had never earned a single pound from his histories.

John Home's medical problems began at about the same time as William Robertson's. Shortly after his career as a playwright came to an inglorious end with the complete failure of his last play, *Alfred* (February 1778), Home suffered a more serious blow. While training with the regiment of fencibles in which he served as lieutenant he was thrown from his horse and knocked unconscious.[4] Most accounts blame this accident for seriously impairing Home's faculties. Whether the accident, senility, or some other disorder was to blame, Home's mental powers seem to have been greatly reduced during the last decades of his life. Fortunately, Home had few financial worries during his final years. He continued to draw his government pension and conservator's stipend, and the death of James Macpherson in 1796 brought him a handsome inheritance of £2000—presumably in thanks for his efforts on behalf of Ossian almost forty years earlier.[5]

The third member of the Moderate literati's circle to endure a serious physical affliction was Adam Ferguson. Toward the end of 1780

[1] Robertson to [the earl of Hardwicke?], 8 March 1784, BL, Add. 35350:70–71.

[2] Ibid.; Stewart, xxxii–xxxiii.

[3] A typescript of Robertson's sermon of 1788, coedited by Doris H. Sher, appears in Richard B. Sher, "Church, University, Enlightenment: The Moderate Literati of Edinburgh, 1720–1793" (Ph.D. diss., University of Chicago, 1979), app. B.

[4] "Biographical Notice of the Late John Home," *New Monthly Magazine* 57 (1839): 475.

[5] Alice Edna Gipson, *John Home: A Study of His Life and Works* (Caldwell, Idaho, [1917]), 26.

Ferguson was stricken with a sudden attack of paralysis that threatened to make him a cripple for life. On the orders of his physician, Joseph Black, he spent several months at Bath, became a vegetarian, gave up alcoholic beverages, and wore heavy clothing in all seasons.[6] This peculiar regimen gave rise to Ferguson's reputation as an eccentric old man who "looked like a philosopher from Lapland" in his fur-lined coat and felt hat and could be found "rioting over a turnip" with his cousin Black.[7] Peculiar or not, the treatment seems to have worked. Ferguson gradually regained the use of his limbs, resumed his academic functions, and outlived almost all his contemporaries. Enthusiastic students once again filled the gallery when the professor returned to his moral philosophy class in the autumn of 1782.[8] With the help of Blair, Carlyle, and other friends Ferguson managed to publish in 1783 the history of the Roman republic that he had finished shortly before his illness,[9] and during the next decade he produced a third edition of his *Institutes* (1785) and the expanded version of his moral philosophy lectures titled *Principles of Moral and Political Science* (1792). He even toured Italy in 1793 to study ancient battlefields for use in a projected second edition of his Roman history. But Ferguson's constitution was never again so strong as it had been before his paralytic attack in 1780, and his intellectual activities after that time were little more than footnotes to his work from the 1760s and 1770s. When he retired from active teaching in 1785, with an academic salary of £113 from a sinecure appointment as professor of mathematics, £300 a year from two pensions, and profits from book sales, he was assured of a comfortable income for the remainder of his life.

Hugh Blair had stopped teaching a year before Ferguson did so. His retirement in the spring of 1784 may have been due to troublesome attacks of gout, or to his age (sixty-six), or perhaps to the fact that he was financially secure without the extra income to be gained from class fees. Like Ferguson, Blair worked out an arrangement that enabled him to receive an academic salary (in this case £70) for life

---

[6] Joseph Black, "The Case of Professor Ferguson," *Medico-Chirurgical Transactions* 7 (1816), cited in Fagg, 219.

[7] Henry Cockburn, *Memorials of His Time* (Edinburgh, 1910), 45.

[8] "Ferguson has the pleasure to find that his former fame is again revived," wrote Andrew Dalzel to Sir Robert Liston on 30 November 1782. "He has got a most crowded class. The students are sitting, some of them, in the gallery, in the manner they did when we attended him in his vigorous days, and, though he is living on vegetables and water, he is lecturing with uncommon spirit." Andrew Dalzel, *History of the University of Edinburgh*, 2 vols. (Edinburgh, 1862), 1:39.

[9] Blair to [William Strahan], 14 December 1781, NLS, 2257:9–10; Carlyle to Bishop Douglas, 14 March 1781, BL, Egerton 2185:103–104.

while a younger assistant (in this case William Greenfield) did the lecturing. He also had his regular church stipend and a £200 government pension that Henry Dundas procured for him in 1780 after the king and queen had heard some of his sermons.[10] His lectures on rhetoric and belles lettres fetched £1500, and the final volumes of his *Sermons*, which absorbed nearly all his literary energy during the last two decades of his life, yielded an additional £1000.[11]

Alexander Carlyle was the only member of his inner circle of friends whose constitution and faculties remained largely unimpaired during the 1780s and 1790s. In December 1779 Carlyle finally received governmental recognition for his services as an ecclesiastical politician and pamphleteer in the form of a deanery worth £200 a year. The successful resolution in 1782 of the window tax issue with which he had long been involved and the rise to political prominence of the Buccleuch-Dundas interest with which he was closely connected raised his standing in the church, and during the 1780s he shared the leadership of the Moderate party with John Drysdale and a handful of younger clergymen. After Drysdale's death in 1788, however, Carlyle was narrowly defeated by Andrew Dalzel in a hotly contested election for Drysdale's prestigious office as principal clerk of the general assembly. The clerkship election of 1789 split the ranks of the Moderate party, made Carlyle resentful of William Robertson for quietly supporting Dalzel, and hastened the transition of party and church leadership to a younger generation of Moderates. Along with Blair, Carlyle continued to be regarded as one of the grand old men in the Moderate party, but his role grew increasingly symbolic as actual party management passed to George Hill of St. Andrews.[12]

The decreasing vitality of the Moderate literati of Edinburgh during the 1780s and 1790s is also apparent from their diminishing role in Edinburgh club life. The Poker Club, which had been so closely identified with the ideology and personalities of the Moderate literati since its inception in 1762, disbanded in 1784 without having achieved its goal of establishing a Scots militia. Some time later Carlyle, Home, Blair, and five other former members tried unsuccessfully to revive the Poker Club in conjunction with a group of sixteen younger men that included William Roberston *secundus*, John Playfair, Henry Mackenzie, and Dugald Stewart. In a lively and somewhat fanciful account of this "Young Poker Club," Sir Walter Scott claimed that it began "long after" the dissolution of the original Poker and met only

---

[10] John Hill, *An Account of the Life and Writings of Hugh Blair* (Edinburgh, 1807), 190.
[11] Robert Morrell Schmitz, *Hugh Blair* (New York, 1948), 84, 118; "Dr. Hugh Blair," *Public Characters of 1800–1801* (Dublin, 1801), 240–45.
[12] Clark diss., 102–104.

once because the older members had grown too ill and inactive to enjoy "the gaity and frolic of a convivial evening."[13] A more credible account of the Young Poker was recorded by Alexander Carlyle, who noted that the club began just two or three years after the demise of the original Poker, met not once but "4 or 5 Times," and disbanded not because the older members were enfeebled but because the *younger* members did not attend regularly![14] Whatever the real reasons for the collapse of the Poker and Young Poker, it appears that by the late 1780s the Moderate literati of Edinburgh were no longer playing a major part in the city's convivial clubs.[15]

That the Moderate literati's role in formal, scholarly clubs and societies also declined during this period is evident from an examination of their involvement with the Royal Society of Edinburgh. The formation of the Royal Society in 1783 owed much to the efforts of William Robertson, who successfully presented the idea at a joint meeting of the senatus academicus of Edinburgh University and the Philosophical Society of Edinburgh late in 1782.[16] It is significant that the plan was modeled not on exclusively scientific, British organizations like the Royal Society of London and Philosophical Society of Edinburgh but rather on "foreign academies" dedicated to the cultivation of all forms of polite learning.[17] The Royal Society of Edinburgh was accordingly made to consist of a "physical class" that continued the scientific activities of the Philosophical Society and a larger "literary class" for the study of history, literature, philosophy, and related subjects.[18] Though the Moderate literati of Edinburgh contributed no original papers to the Royal Society, their early influence was considerable. Ferguson, for example, was chosen to be one of the society's original twelve counselors, and at the first meeting of the literary class in November 1783 Robertson and Blair were elected to serve as two of that body's four presidents.[19] Most of the papers

---

[13] Quoted in Davis D. McElroy, *Scotland's Age of Improvement: A Survey of Eighteenth-Century Literary Clubs and Societies* (Pullman, Wash., 1969), 168.

[14] *AC*, 295.

[15] Blair, Ferguson, and Robertson were members of another late eighteenth-century convivial club, the Oyster, but it seems to have stopped meeting soon after the Young Poker (McElroy, *Scotland's Age of Improvement*, 168–69). In a letter to the duke of Buccleuch of 1 March 1793 (WLCL, Townshend Papers), Carlyle refers to a lively meeting of the Old Hens Club at which all ten of the attending members were more than seventy years old.

[16] Alexander Fraser Tytler, Lord Woodhouselee, "History of the Society," in *TRSE* 1 (1788): 7.

[17] Ibid.

[18] Ibid., 12.

[19] Ibid., 98–100.

published in the society's first volume of *Transactions* (1788) were the work of younger ministers and professors affiliated with the Robertson circle and the Moderate party, such as William Greenfield, John Playfair, and John Walker in the physical class and Andrew Dalzel and John Hill in the literary class. Alexander Carlyle read an unpublished ode by William Collins; an appendix included biographies of two recently deceased Moderate ministers (John Drysdale and William Lothian); James Hutton deferred to William Robertson in regard to a proposed preface to his famous paper on geology; and Robertson himself wrote the dedication to the king.[20]

But if the Royal Society of Edinburgh initially represented another step in the process of institutionalizing the values and intellectual concerns associated with the Enlightenment of the Moderate divines, it soon became something quite different. The key development was the deterioration of the branch of the Royal Society in which the personal influence and intellectual interests of the Moderate literati were strongest—the literary class. In the early 1790s meetings of that body were held less frequently than before, and by the end of the century it had ceased to function at all.[21] Thus, the Royal Society was transformed into a predominantly scientific organization, and groups whose interests were mainly nonscientific, such as the clergy, steadily lost influence.[22] Although the fate of the literary class may be explained in part by the growing preoccupation with science all over Britain and Europe at the end of the eighteenth century,[23] and in part by the fact that the formal, scholarly paper is a more suitable medium for communication of scientific knowledge than for communication of knowledge relating to humanistic disciplines,[24] there is also the possibility that the literary class succumbed because of the failure of its founding fathers either to maintain personal control over Scottish cultural institutions or to transmit their intellectual interests and values to younger disciples as the eighteenth century came to an end.

[20] Dennis R. Dean, "James Hutton on Religion and Theology: the Unpublished Preface to his *Theory of the Earth* (1788)," *Annals of Science* 32 (1975): 187–93; Andrew Dalzel to Sir Robert Liston, 24 December 1787, in Dalzel, *University of Edinburgh*, 1:73.

[21] Steven Shapin, "The Royal Society of Edinburgh: A Study of the Social Context of Hanoverian Science" (Ph.D. diss., University of Pennsylvania, 1971), 228–30.

[22] Shapin has calculated the proportion of ministers in the Royal Society as nineteen percent in 1783 and eleven percent in the 1790s (ibid., 317). With very few exceptions, such as Playfair, Walker, Greenfield, and Matthew Stewart, these clergymen were members of the literary class, and the great majority of them were also friends of the Moderate party.

[23] McElroy, *Scotland's Age of Improvement*, 81.

[24] Shapin, "Royal Society of Edinburgh," 233.

A major cause of that failure was the economic, social, and political upheaval taking place in Scotland and throughout the Western world at this time.[25] One aspect of that upheaval was the rapid expansion of the Scottish economy, particularly after the conclusion of the American War in 1783. Besides many obvious advantages, accelerated economic growth brought higher inflation—which was further exacerbated by the long years of war with Revolutionary and Napoleonic France—as well as abrupt demographic transitions and other characteristics of an industrializing economy that appear incompatible with the stability, complacency, and politeness of Lowland Scotland in the days of the Enlightenment. Even Edinburgh, which was far less radically altered by industrialization and Irish immigration than Glasgow, underwent extraordinary growth and unprecedented social and physical fragmentation along class lines during this period; its fundamental character changed from "aristocratic" to "bourgeois."[26] Economic development also encouraged the heightened concern with science and technology that contributed, as we shall see, to a reorientation of Scottish intellectual life.

Another critical factor was the changing political and ideological climate of the late eighteenth century. The radical Whigs who began to make themselves heard in Scotland during the 1760s and 1770s helped to politicize the Scottish intellectual world and to break down the polite, elitist spirit of the Moderate literati and the Scottish Enlightenment generally. So long as the radicals confined their activities to political issues like the American crisis and burgh reform, and ecclesiastical issues like church patronage, they posed no immediate threat to the literati's control of Scottish cultural life. In the early 1780s, however, the eccentric, radical Whig antiquarian David Stewart Erskine, eleventh earl of Buchan, polarized the Scottish literati by petitioning for a royal charter for his upstart Society of Antiquaries. As Steven Shapin has shown, it was largely in response to this challenge that conservative Whigs and Tories established the Royal Society of Edinburgh.[27] Much of their hostility to Buchan's scheme apparently stemmed from doubts and fears about the scholarly and ideological integrity of an organization that was led by a radical Whig

[25] Anand Chitnis, *The Scottish Enlightenment: A Social History* (London, 1976), 238–40.

[26] N. T. Phillipson, "The Scottish Enlightenment," in *A Companion to Scottish Culture*, ed. David Daiches (London, 1981), 344; Laurence J. Saunders, *Scottish Democracy, 1815–1840: The Social and Intellectual Background* (Edinburgh, 1950), 79–96.

[27] Steven Shapin, "Property, Patronage, and the Politics of Science: The Founding of the Royal Society of Edinburgh," *British Journal for the History of Science* 7 (1974): 1–41.

and Freemason and that contained, in William Robertson's words, "many Members neither Gentlemen nor men of Erudition."[28] In the face of intense opposition from the intellectual establishment, Buchan privately branded Robertson "an obscure priest" and his associates a "Junto of Jacobites and Tories who insult the best men in Scotland, and determine the Existence of Literary Societies, Militias, Armaments, and Constitutional Rights."[29] Some years later he publicly assailed the tyranny of the "despicable club" of reigning literati in a speech honoring one of Robertson's most virulent enemies, Gilbert Stuart.[30] As tempers flared, Henry Mackenzie remarked in 1783 that "the voice of the Muses is at Present Crown'd in the Debates of Politics and the clamour of Party."[31]

The trend toward greater politicization of Scottish intellectual life reached its climax during the era of the French Revolution. At the outset many Scottish literati, including William Robertson and Adam Ferguson, were hopeful that the Revolution would bring about constructive changes of a moderate nature in French government and society.[32] In November 1791, however, Alexander Carlyle reported with some satisfaction that early zeal for the Revolution was beginning to cool in Scotland, and fourteen months later he added that "Disrespect at last is smother'd" due to widespread disapproval of the execution of Louis XVI.[33] As an outspoken enemy of the Revolution, Carlyle must have been pleased to see all his Moderate friends, as well as most of his ecclesiastical opponents in the Popular party, turn against what Adam Ferguson would later call "Antichrist himself in the form of Democracy and Atheism."[34] Egged on by Carlyle, Thomas Somerville, Thomas Hardy, and other Moderates, the Scottish literati became almost unanimous in their antipathy to the Revolution and all the things for which it stood.

Yet the price paid for near unanimity was high. The few Scottish men of letters suspected of republicanism during the 1790s, such as

---

[28] Ibid., 28. Cf. Andrew Dalzel's comments on the large number of "ragamuffins" recruited by Buchan, in Dalzel, *University of Edinburgh*, 1:39.

[29] Quoted in Shapin, "Property, Patronage, Politics of Science," 29.

[30] McElroy, *Scotland's Age of Improvement*, 77.

[31] Henry Mackenzie to [Joseph Carmichael] (copy), [1783], NLS, 646:1–11. The tentative date and identification of the recipient of this letter are taken from C. R. Fay, *Adam Smith and the Scotland of His Day* (Cambridge, 1956), 1.

[32] Henry W. Meikle, *Scotland and the French Revolution* (1912; reprint, London, 1969), 48–49; Ferguson to ———, 19 January 1790, NLS, 1809:3–4.

[33] Carlyle to Bishop Douglas, 14 November 1781, BL, Egerton 2186:57; Carlyle to the duke of Buccleuch, 1 March 1793, WLCL, Townshend Papers; Carlyle to Henry Dundas, 1793 (copy), NLS, 3463:96–98.

[34] Ferguson to Carlyle, 23 November 1796, EUL, Dc. 4.41:56.

John Leslie and the Francis Jeffrey circle of young Whig lawyers, were watched carefully and sometimes subjected to abuse by the literary and professional establishment.[35] After the harsh sedition trials of 1793–1794 Scotland fell prey to a psychological "reign of terror" characterized by subservience to the iron will of Henry Dundas and intellectual stagnation.[36] A dearth of scholarly activity in this period is evident in every field except science, though even scientific matters sometimes acquired an extraordinary degree of political significance.[37] Surviving accounts by contemporaries testify to the disastrous effects of the Revolutionary era on Scottish polite literature. Thomas Somerville attributed the commercial failure of his history of the Glorious Revolution (1792) to the fact that the French Revolution had "diverted public attention from every other subject" and "made the very name of revolution, for the time, odious."[38] Somerville's remarks are indirectly supported by Henry Brougham's anecdote about William Robertson the younger refusing to publish or even show privately the manuscript of his father's sermon of 1788 commemorating the Glorious Revolution for fear that it would be viewed as a Jacobin tract.[39] When Somerville's second history was ready for the press in the mid-1790s, the author was compelled to accept a smaller amount of money from his publishers than had originally been offered because "the alarming state of public affairs had in the meantime depreciated all literary property."[40] Later in the decade Rev. James Macdonald informed a German correspondent that "love of learning or enthusiasm for knowledge, once the characteristic of the Scotch nation, . . . is all gone, and not a shadow of it remains."[41]

In lamenting the decline of Scottish literature, Macdonald was thinking specifically of Robertson, Blair, Ferguson, and other leading literati of their age. His attitude was not unusual: time and again younger men expressed the view that the great day of Scottish letters

---

[35] Meikle, *Scotland and the French Revolution*, 153–57; J. B. Morrell, "Professors Robison and Playfair and the *Theophobia Gallica*," *Notes and Records of the Royal Society of London* 26 (1971): 43–63.

[36] Cockburn, *Memorials*, 76:79; Meikle, *Scotland and the French Revolution*, 153–57 and chap. 6.

[37] See, for example, Arthur Donovan, "Scottish Responses to the New Chemistry of Lavoisier," in *Studies in Eighteenth-Century Culture*, vol. 9, ed. Roseann Runte (Madison, Wisc., 1979), 237–49.

[38] Somerville, 256.

[39] Brougham, 270–71.

[40] Somerville, 293.

[41] James Macdonald to K. A. Böttiger, June 1798, in Alexander Gillies, *A Hebridean in Goethe's Weimar: The Reverend James Macdonald and the Cultural Relations between Scotland and Germany* (New York, 1968), 79.

was passing away as the literary generation of William Robertson died out. In a letter of 1783 Henry Mackenzie contrasted the physical beauty of the New Town of Edinburgh with the beginnings of the decline of "Our Scottish Literature." "The brilliant Era seems rather to be past," he commented, meaning that Hume was dead and Robertson, Ferguson, Blair, and Smith were all past their prime. "After the mention of such great names," Mackenzie added, "it were Presumption to talk of myself."[42] To Scottish men of letters even younger than Mackenzie, the leaders of the Scottish Enlightenment assumed almost mythological stature. Sir Walter Scott described Mackenzie himself as "the last link of the chain which connects the Scottish literature of the present age with the period when there were giants in the land—the days of Robertson, and Hume, and Smith, and Home, and [John] Clerk of Eldin, and [Adam] Fergusson."[43] Elsewhere Scott elaborated on the achievements of these "giants of the North," and in *Guy Mannering* he asserted that this list of eighteenth-century literati, augmented by Kames, Black, and Hutton, "has perhaps at no period been equalled, considering the depth and variety of talent which it embraced and concentrated."[44] William Adam termed this period "the Augustan age of the ancient Metropolis of Scotland"; Cosmo Innes called it the "golden age."[45] The greatest tribute of all came from the pen of Henry Cockburn, who fondly recalled associating with Robertson, Ferguson, Carlyle, and other eminent members of the "retiring generation" of Scottish literati during the 1790s and early nineteenth century:

> We knew enough of them to make us fear that no such other race of men, so tried by time, such friends of each other and of learning, and all of such amiable manners and such spotless characters, could be expected soon to arise, and again ennoble Scotland. Though living in all the succeeding splendors, it has been a constant gratification to me to remember that I saw the last remains of a school so illustrious and so national, and that I was privileged to obtain a glimpse of the "skirts of glory" of the first, or at least of the second, great philosophical age of Scotland.[46]

---

[42] Mackenzie to [Carmichael], (copy), [1783], NLS, 646:1–11.

[43] *The Miscellaneous Prose Works of Sir Walter Scott*, 28 vols. (Edinburgh, 1834–1835), 4:7.

[44] Ibid., 19:284; Sir Walter Scott, *Guy Mannering*, chap. 39. See also Jane Millgate, "Guy Mannering in Edinburgh," *Library* 32 (1977): 238–45.

[45] William Adam, *Sequel to Gift of a Grandfather* (1839), i; Dalzel, *University of Edinburgh*, 1:62.

[46] Cockburn, *Memorials*, 52.

Actually, Scottish intellectual life did not deteriorate quite so completely or dramatically as the testimony of Cockburn and his contemporaries would suggest. Indeed, Henry Brougham, Francis Jeffrey, Sir James Mackintosh, Sir Walter Scott, James Hogg, Thomas Carlyle, John Galt, Thomas Brown, Sir William Hamilton, and other philosophical and literary figures, not to mention many great names in science and medicine, kept the intellectual reputation of Scotland and her capital on a high plane until well into Victorian times. What Cockburn and his contemporaries were in fact describing was not so much the *decline* as the *reorientation* of Scottish intellectual life. The particular values and genres associated with the Scottish Enlightenment were dying out, but new values—such as romanticism, sentimental Jacobitism, evangelicalism, patriotic bibliomania, and nineteenth-century Whig and Tory ideologies—and new genres—such as the historical novel, extended critical essay or review, and specialized scientific journal—were emerging to take their place. As these changes occurred the polite, didactic treatises, histories, lectures, and sermons of the Moderate age lost popularity. It was a sign of the times that Adam Ferguson's hefty *Principles of Moral and Political Science* received a chillier reception in 1792 than had the same author's similar but much less developed *Institutes of Moral Philosophy* in the late 1760s.

It was also a sign of the times that Ferguson had chosen to put the term "science" into the title of his last book, for the growing interest in things scientific and technical was one of the primary characteristics of the new Scottish intellectual outlook. Of course, natural science and medicine had played a vital role during the heyday of the Scottish Enlightenment, when the likes of Joseph Black, William Cullen, and John Gregory had been active among the Edinburgh literati.[47] But in the closing years of the eighteenth century and opening decades of the nineteenth century scientific interest in Scotland, and above all in Edinburgh, became particularly keen. Thomas Jefferson remarked in 1789 that "no place in the World can pretend to a competition with Edinburgh" in matters of science.[48] From Jeffer-

[47] See in particular J. R. R. Christie, "The Origins and Development of the Scottish Scientific Community, 1680–1760," *History of Science* 12 (1974): 122–41, and "The Rise and Fall of Scottish Science," in *The Emergence of Science in Western Europe*, ed. Maurice Crosland (London, 1975), 111–26; A. L. Donovan, *Philosophical Chemistry in the Scottish Enlightenment: The Doctrines and Discoveries of William Cullen and Joseph Black* (Edinburgh, 1975); and Roger L. Emerson's series of articles on the Philosophical Society of Edinburgh in *British Journal for the History of Science*.

[48] Quoted in D. B. Horn, *A Short History of the University of Edinburgh, 1556–1889* (Edinburgh, 1967), 64. The place of science in Edinburgh University during the late eighteenth century is discussed in J. B. Morrell, "The University of Edinburgh in the

son's time until well into the nineteenth century the faculty of the University of Edinburgh could boast of a long line of eminent scientific and medical men, including Andrew Duncan, John Thomson, John Robison, John Playfair, Robert Jameson, Sir John Leslie, James Syme, James Young Simpson, and James Forbes—the teacher of James Clerk Maxwell. The first layman to become principal of the university was the physicist Sir David Brewster, a prominent man of science. One striking indication of the trend is the fact that eleven of thirteen academic chairs founded at Edinburgh between the beginning of Robertson's tenure as principal in November 1762 and the appointment of Brewster in 1859 were scientific or technical in nature.[49] At the University of Glasgow, meanwhile, scientific education gained stature during the tenures of Lord Kelvin's teacher William Meikleham in natural philosophy (1803–1846) and Thomas Thomson in chemistry (1817–1846).[50]

The epidemic of science fever in turn-of-the-century Scotland was not limited to the academic community. Publication of James Hutton's *Theory of the Earth* (1788, 1795) and John Playfair's *Illustrations of the Huttonian Theory* (1802) brought controversy and excitement to the field of geology. Sir James Hall introduced Lavoisier's new chemistry in a paper of 1788,[51] and before being called to Glasgow University Thomas Thomson popularized that subject in private lectures and demonstrations in Edinburgh (1800–1811) and in his best-selling textbook, *A System of Chemistry* (1802). While the physical class of the Royal Society of Edinburgh flourished Henry Brougham's circle of young Edinburgh Whigs established their own little scientific society, the Academy of Physics (1797–1800).[52] Other Edinburgh-based scientific and technical societies from this period include the Chirurgo-Physical Society (1788), Hibernian Medical Society (ca. 1790), James Edward Smith's Natural History Society (1782), and Robert Jameson's Wernerian Natural History Society (1808)—all of which

---

Late Eighteenth Century: Its Scientific Eminence and Academic Structure," *Isis* 62 (1971): 158–71.

[49] The scientific and technical chairs were astronomy (1786), agriculture (1790), and technology (1855) in the arts faculty, conveyancing (1825) in the law faculty, and seven new medical chairs established between 1767 and 1831. The only exceptions to this pattern were music (1839) and biblical criticism (1846).

[50] J. B. Morrell, "Thomas Thomson: Professor of Chemistry and University Reformer," *British Journal for the History of Science* 4 (1969): 245–65.

[51] V. A. Eyles, "The Evolution of a Chemist: Sir James Hall," *Annals of Science* 19 (1963): 153–82.

[52] G. N. Cantor, "The Academy of Physics at Edinburgh, 1797–1800," *Science Studies* 5 (1975): 109–34.

were eventually swallowed up by the Royal Physical Society (royal charter, 1788)[53]—the Highland and Agricultural Society (1784), Caledonian Horticultural Society (1809), the Society of Scottish Arts (1821), the Botanical Society of Edinburgh (1836), the Geological Society of Edinburgh (1834), the Astronomical Institution (1819), and the Phrenological Society (1820), which was the institutional embodiment of a thriving local phrenological movement led by George Combe.[54]

The rush to science is also evident from a look at the Edinburgh periodical and encyclopedic press. The scientifically oriented *Encyclopedia Britannica*, which had begun appearing in 1768, attained widespread popularity at the turn of the century upon publication of the third edition, featuring dozens of new scientific contributions by John Robison and others.[55] The early nineteenth century saw the birth of an astonishing array of encyclopedias and periodicals that devoted much if not all of their space to scientific subjects, such as the *Edinburgh Medical and Surgical Journal* (est. 1805), which later merged with the *Edinburgh Monthly Journal of Medical Science* (est. 1841) to form the *Edinburgh Medical Journal* (est. 1855); the *Edinburgh Monthly Review* (1819–1821); the *Edinburgh Encyclopedia* that David Brewster edited between 1807 and 1829; Brewster's *Edinburgh Philosophical Journal* (est. 1819), which Robert Jameson carried on as the *Edinburgh New Philosophical Journal*; Brewster's *Edinburgh Journal of Science* (est. 1824); the *Edinburgh Journal of Natural and Geographical Science* (1829–1831); the remarkably popular *Chamber's Journal* (est. 1832);

---

[53] McElroy, *Scotland's Age of Improvement*, 136–37; D. E. Allen, "James Edward Smith and the Natural History Society of Edinburgh," *Journal of the Society for the Bibliography of Natural History* 8 (1978): 483–93.

[54] Steven Shapin, "The Audience for Science in Eighteenth-Century Edinburgh," *History of Science* 12 (1974): 111–13. On Edinburgh phrenology see the articles and commentaries by Shapin and G. N. Cantor in *Annals of Science* 32 (1975): 195–256. The argument I am making about the growth of Scottish science is a quantitative rather than qualitative one—a critical distinction for understanding how this explosion of scientific interest could have coexisted with frequent laments about the decline of Scottish science. Steven Shapin provides an explanation for that paradox in "Science," in Daiches, *Companion to Scottish Culture*, 318–22, as well as a fuller account of the popularization process in " 'Nibbling at the Teats of Science,': Edinburgh and the Diffusion of Science in the 1830s," in *Metropolis and Province: Science in British Culture, 1780–1850*, ed. Ian Inkster and Jack Morrell (London, 1983), 151–78. There is also much interesting material on popular science and its ideological implications in J. B. Smith's excellent article, "Manners, Morals and Mentalities: Reflections on the Popular Enlightenment of Early Nineteenth-Century Scotland," in *Scottish Culture and Scottish Education, 1800–1980*, ed. Walter M. Humes and Hamish M. Paterson (Edinburgh, 1983), 25–54.

[55] See the preface to the third edition (Philadelphia, 1798), xiii–xiv, and Herman Kogan, *The Great EB: The Story of the Encyclopedia Britannica* (Chicago, 1958), 23–26.

and the famous *Edinburgh Review* (est. 1802). In articles published in the last-named journal in 1804 and 1810, Francis Jeffrey went so far as to argue that science, through its link with technology and economic progress, could pass the test of utility, whereas the celebrated Scottish metaphysics could not.[56] Jeffrey's attitude reflected, it is true, a long-standing Scottish tradition of respect for practical, improving science,[57] but that tradition was intensified in an era of relatively rapid commercial and industrial growth, English utilitarianism, Whiggish political economy, and inventive Scottish engineers like Watt, Telford, Rennie, and McAdam, who were becoming the new heroes of the incipient industrial age.[58]

Ironically, the growing passion for science at the turn of the nineteenth century extended into the very field that Jeffrey used science to criticize: moral philosophy. The crucial development in this regard was the triumph of the analytical philosophy of common sense. A reader of James McCosh's influential *The Scottish Philosophy* (1875) and similar studies might easily conclude that the common sense "school" dominated Scottish moral philosophy throughout the eighteenth century, and certainly after the publication in 1764 of Thomas Reid's first book, the *Inquiry into the Human Mind*. The real story, however, is not quite so simple. For twenty years after the appearance of Reid's *Inquiry*, the only major attempts to elucidate the principles of common sense philosophy were the crude efforts of James Beattie and James Oswald, who overturned Reid's delicate balance between antiskeptical polemics and the empirical, scientific methodology that Reid had learned from—and then turned against—David Hume.[59] Beattie's book enjoyed great popularity, but it was short-lived and less noticeable among the literati of Edinburgh (despite exceptions like Lord Hailes) than among the social and political elite of London.[60] In 1774 Joseph Priestley published a harsh attack on Reid,

[56] George E. Davie, *The Social Significance of the Scottish Philosophy of Common Sense* (Dow Lecture, Dundee, 1973), 14–16; Chitnis, *Scottish Enlightenment*, 214–17; *Edinburgh Review* 17 (1810): 184–86.

[57] See the sources cited in note 47 above.

[58] The classic Victorian tribute to the achievements of late eighteenth- and early nineteenth-century Scottish engineers is Samuel Smiles, *Lives of the Engineers*, 3 vols. (London, 1861–1862).

[59] On Reid's debt to Hume, see especially his remarks in "An Abstract of the *Inquiry into the Human Mind on the Principles of Common Sense*" [1762], published by David Fate Norton in *Thomas Reid: Critical Interpretations*, ed. Stephen F. Barker and Tom L. Beauchamp (Philadelphia, 1976), 125–32.

[60] Beattie's *Essay on Truth* passed through one edition per year during its first five years in print (1770–1774). A sixth ediction appeared separately and in Beattie's collected *Essays* in 1776 and was reprinted in 1777 and 1778, but that was the last time the book was published in Britain in any form during the eighteenth century. The

Beattie, and Oswald as the proponents of a pernicious new school of Scottish philosophy.[61] While Beattie fumed, and Reid and Kames laughed as the former read passages from Priestley's book aloud,[62] the future of common sense philosophy in Scotland remained very much in doubt. Reid had never been able to command a vast following through his moral philosophy lectures in the manner of a Hutcheson or a Ferguson, and his ties with the Edinburgh intellectual establishment were tenuous except with the aged Lord Kames. There is evidence that at the time of Priestley's attack some Edinburgh men of letters regarded common sense philosophy with suspicion or outright disdain, as a sort of Aberdonian aberration.[63] Ten years later Kames was dead, and Reid was a seventy-four-year-old retired professor who had not published anything substantial on the subject for two decades.

Then came the common sense revolution of 1785. On the one hand, Reid published at Edinburgh, in the space of just three years, two weighty collections of essays that reclaimed common sense philosophy as a scholarly and scientific, rather than merely polemical, mode of inquiry.[64] On the other hand, Dugald Stewart (to whom Reid's first volume of essays was partially dedicated) began popularizing the subject in his moral philosophy lectures at Edinburgh University (1785–1810), which were explicitly designed to highlight, clarify, re-

---

geography of Beattie's appeal is made clear in letters to his publisher William Creech (SRO, Dalguise Muniments) like the one of 27 November 1776, in which Creech is directed to send more than three quarters of the 800 copies of the new quarto edition of Beattie's *Essays* to London for distribution to English subscribers by Beattie's friends, such as Lord Newhaven and Mrs. Montagu. Only fifteen percent of the edition was to be kept by Creech for sale in Edinburgh.

[61] *An Examination of Dr. Reid's "Inquiry . . .," Dr. Beattie's "Essay . . .," and Dr. Oswald's "Appeal . . . ."* (London, 1774); Alan P. F. Sell, "Priestley's Polemic against Reid," *Price-Priestley Newsletter*, no. 3 (1979): 41–52.

[62] Beattie to William Creech, 20 October 1774, and Kames to Creech, 4 October 1774, SRO, Dalguise Muniments.

[63] Almost a year before the appearance of Priestley's *Examination*, John Playfair ridiculed the success of "the great Champion of Common Sense, Beattie" (whose unpopularity among the literati of Edinburgh was no secret) for being "A Satyrist without Wit, & a Philosopher without Science." After the publication of Priestley's book Playfair extended his criticism to include Oswald, and while admitting that "Reid ought to be treated in a different manner, for his book is in many respects the work of a Philosopher," criticized him too for taking "great liberties as to creating new principles in the Mind." Playfair to William Robertson the younger, 3 August 1773 and 6 November 1774, NLS, 3942:136–37, 168–69.

[64] *Essays on the Intellectual Powers of Man* (1785) and *Essays on the Active Powers of Man* (1788). A fourth edition of Reid's *Inquiry* also appeared in 1785—the first new edition since the 1760s.

fine, and systematize—but not vulgarize—Reid's complex metaphysical investigations and to render them applicable to "the practical business of life."[65] As a classroom performer, Stewart could be at least as dynamic and persuasive in the cause of Christian-Stoic virtue and conservative Whig ideology as his predecessor Adam Ferguson.[66] But the focus of his interpretation of moral philosophy turned increasingly toward two technical areas that were associated with Adam Smith and Thomas Reid, respectively, but had been of secondary interest to Ferguson: political economy and the science of mind. The former was deemed important enough to warrant its own course after 1799;[67] the latter formed the basis of Stewart's first and most famous philosophical treatise, *Elements of the Human Mind* (1792). By the time that book appeared, the Edinburgh intellectual establishment had been completely won over to the Reid-Stewart camp—just in time to do battle against the perceived onslaught of French Revolutionary ideas.[68] Despite a streak of apostasy toward Reid on certain issues, Stewart's handpicked successor Thomas Brown—a physician whom his biographer rightly called "in the strictest sense of the word, a man of science"—did even more than Stewart to shift the emphasis of Edinburgh academic moral philosophy toward the analytical study of "mental science,"[69] and this trend would certainly have continued had Stewart's candidate, Sir William Hamilton, been able to win the moral

---

[65] See Nicholas Phillipson, "The Pursuit of Virtue in Scottish University Education: Dugald Stewart and Scottish Moral Philosophy," in *Universities, Society and the Future*, ed. Nicholas Phillipson (Edinburgh, 1983), 82–101, which contains this quote from Stewart on page 94.

[66] Cockburn, *Memorials*, 24. See Stewart's avowedly Fergusonian discussion of Stoicism and lengthy theodicy in *Outlines of Moral Philosophy* (Edinburgh, 1793), 155–226, 263–69, and his laudatory remarks on the "English constitution" in *Lectures on Political Economy* (Edinburgh, 1877).

[67] Stewart's political economy course and its influence are discussed from the point of view of political science in an essay by Donald Winch in Stefan Collini et al., *That Noble Science of Politics: A Study in Nineteenth-Century Intellectual History* (Cambridge, 1983), 25–61.

[68] Thus, Adam Ferguson showed greater respect for Reid and common sense philosophy in his *Principles* than in his earlier works, and in a letter of 1796 Alexander Carlyle remarked that "if Reid is the Aristotle, Ferguson is the Plato of Scotch philosophers," to which he added: "the Faculty of Arts of Edinburgh have adopted my phrase." *Auto.*, 577.

[69] Thomas Brown, *Lectures on the Philosophy of the Human Mind* (Edinburgh, 1840), with an abridged life of Brown by David Welsh, esp. xxv–xxvii; J. Charles Robertson, "A Bacon-Facing Generation: Scottish Philosophy in the Early Nineteenth Century," *Journal of the History of Philosophy* 14 (1976): 37–49; John Gibson Lockhart, *Peter's Letters to His Kinfolk*, 2d ed., 3 vols. (Edinburgh, 1819), 1:175. Like Stewart, Brown intended to offer a separate course on political economy, including politics proper (*Lectures*, 675), but an early death prevented him from doing so.

philosophy chair following Brown's death in 1820.[70] Even so, what came to be called the "Scottish Philosophy" in the nineteenth century was not the broad, humanistic, normative *moral* philosophy of Hutcheson and Ferguson but the highly analytical study of psychology, epistemology, and metaphysics associated chiefly with Reid and Stewart.[71] As Richard Olson and others have demonstrated, with the institutionalization of the common sense school Scottish moral philosophy came to speak a technical language that physical scientists could utilize in formulating their own methodologies.[72]

Perhaps because the triumph of the analytical philosophy of mind threatened to obliterate the traditional pedagogical purpose of Scottish moral philosophy—the training of virtuous Christian gentlemen and good British citizens—the moral philosophy chair at Edinburgh University passed in 1852 to an able but undistinguished member of the resurgent Evangelical party rather than to Hamilton's brilliant metaphysical protégé, James Frederick Ferrier.[73] Yet even the Evangelicals of the Disruption era, as represented by James McCosh, Hugh and James Miller, David Welsh, Sir David Brewster, and Thomas Chalmers, were by no means immune to the nineteenth-century predilection for natural and mental science.[74] Among clergymen associated with the Moderate party a growing interest in science had begun to show itself as early as the 1780s, when younger ministers like William Greenfield, John Playfair, and John Walker had distinguished themselves in the Royal Society of Edinburgh. Table 4, which was utilized for different purposes in the preceding chapter, indicates that the number of scientific works published by a representative group of eighteenth-century Scottish clergymen rose appreciably during the last quarter of the eighteenth century. The late eighteenth century also witnessed several important clerical contri-

---

[70] Hamilton was defeated in 1820 by the Tory littérateur John Wilson in one of the most blatantly political contests in the history of the university.

[71] See James McCosh, *The Scottish Philosophy* (New York, 1875), chap. 1.

[72] Richard Olson, *Scottish Philosophy and British Physics, 1750–1880* (Princeton, 1975); Crosbie Smith, " 'Mechanical Philosophy' and the Emergence of Physics in Britain, 1800–1850," *Annals of Science* 33 (1976): 3–29; G. N. Cantor, "Henry Brougham and the Scottish Methodological Tradition," *Studies in History and Philosophy of Science* 2 (1971): 69–89; L. L. Laudan, "Thomas Reid and the Newtonian Turn of British Methodological Thought," in *The Methodological Heritage of Newton*, ed. Robert E. Butts and John W. David (Toronto, 1970), 103–31.

[73] For a different perspective on this incident and a stimulating general account of moral philosophy instruction in nineteenth-century Edinburgh, see George Davie, *The Democratic Intellect: Scotland and Her Universities in the Nineteenth Century* (Edinburgh, 1961), 286–312.

[74] J. David Hoeveler, Jr., *James McCosh and the Scottish Intellectual Tradition* (Princeton, 1981), 70 and chap. 6.

butions to technology, such as Rev. Alexander Campbell's improved plow of 1794 (itself a refinement of James Small's innovative plow of the 1760s) and the revolutionary invention of the percussion lock by Rev. Alexander Forsyth in 1807.[75]

But if some Scottish ministers were showing signs of becoming more scientifically and technologically proficient in the late eighteenth and early nineteenth centuries, these gains were more than offset by the Presbyterian clergy's staggering losses in the other departments of polite literature and learning. A dramatic shift in the relative importance of clergymen and lawyers in the world of letters is one of the most striking features of Scottish intellectual history of this period. Whereas clergymen had been predominant and lawyers subordinate in intellectual matters during the era of the Scottish Enlightenment, these roles had reversed by the beginning of the nineteenth century.[76] The two prototypes of the new breed of literary lawyers were Henry Mackenzie and John Millar—the former because he exemplified the fruitful association between the legal profession and novels and literary magazines that took hold around the time of *The Man of Feeling* (1771), *Mirror* (1779–1780), and *Lounger* (1785–1787), that reached its apex with Sir Walter Scott's *Waverly* novels, the *Edinburgh Review*, and *Blackwood's Magazine* in the first half of the new century, and that culminated in the late Victorian career of Robert Louis Ste-

---

[75] On Campbell's plow see the advertisement at the end of *SM* for April 1794. Forsyth's invention is described in all the standard histories of firearms and technology.

[76] Important as it was, the role of lawyers in the intellectual life of the mature Scottish Enlightenment has sometimes been exaggerated, particularly by those who would extend the boundaries of the Scottish Enlightenment into the nineteenth century and would confuse the undisputed *social* preeminence of the legal profession—as demonstrated in various works by N. T. Phillipson—with *intellectual* preeminence (e.g. John Clive in *SAI*, 228). In fact, the elite status of eighteenth-century Scottish lawyers and judges may actually have discouraged intellectual activity, first by providing political and administrative opportunities that left many legal men of taste and intelligence— such as Gilbert Elliot, William Mure, Alexander Wedderburn, and perhaps even Henry Dundas—with little time for literary pursuits (though they often kept their hand in by adopting the aristocratic role of literary patron), and second by depriving the legal profession of the financial and social pressures that so frequently stimulated clergymen to better their situations by seeking distinction in the republic of letters. As Principal Leechman commented to Lord Bute when recommending John Millar for the civil law chair at Glasgow University in 1761, "a person who is both proper to fill this office & willing to accept it, is not very easy to be found, so great are the emoluments of a well employed Lawyer, & so small those of a Professor in a College" (Bute, Cdf. 3/167/1–2; courtesy of Alexander Murdoch). Whereas lawyers flocked to quasi-intellectual debating clubs like the Select and Speculative societies, Presbyterian ministers were more plentiful and important in the universities and made a far better showing as authors and scholars in every field of polite literature and learning except fiction, antiquarianism, and law itself.

venson; and the latter because he prepared the way for the close connection between the legal profession and nineteenth-century Whiggism. Not only Scott, Jeffrey, Brougham, and much later Stevenson, but also Francis Horner, Macvey Napier, Sir James Mackintosh, his son-in-law William Erskine the orientalist, Henry Cockburn, Thomas Thomson the antiquarian, Malcolm Laing, Cosmo Innes, his son-in-law John Hill Burton, James Maidment, Alexander Fraser Tytler (Lord Woodhouselee) and his son Patrick, Sir Archibald Alison, John Wilson ("Christopher North" of *Blackwood's*), George Combe, John Gibson Lockhart, Sir William Hamilton, James Frederick Ferrier, John Galt (briefly), eminent jurists such as David Hume and James Reddie, and other intellectual leaders of the nineteenth century came from the ranks of the legal profession. Some, such as the Tytlers, Scott, and the regular contributors to *Blackwood's* (Lockhart, Alison, Wilson, and Burton, for example) were Tories, and many of them were Episcopalians, but more were Presbyterians who subscribed to Whig political principles.[77] These Scottish literary lawyers were as preeminent in Edinburgh literary and philosophical life at the turn of the century and afterward as the generation of Moderate ministers born around 1720 had been several decades earlier. When Scott noted "the predominance of barristers" among the Edinburgh literary class, when Cockburn referred to the law as "the profession the most intimately connected with literature,"[78] they were making observations that probably appeared self-evident in the first half of the nineteenth century but would not have seemed so during the age of the Enlightenment.

A brief consideration of developments in the field of history will be useful for illustrating both the reversal of lawyers and ministers and the rise of new literary attitudes and genres as the Enlightenment came to an end. Scotland's distinction as the historical nation par excellence during the eighteenth century rested chiefly on the Scottish contribution to two overlapping varieties of historical inquiry: "conjectural" history, involving the comparison of different cultures or institutions by means of an evolutionary or developmental model, and narrative/philosophical history, involving accounts of

[77] Robert Mudie, *The Modern Athens: A Dissection and Demonstration of Men and Things in the Scotch Capital* (London, 1825), 241. On the Whiggism of the Jeffrey circle of lawyers responsible for the *Edinburgh Review*, see John Clive, *Scotch Reviewers: the Edinburgh Review, 1802–1815* (London, 1956), esp. chaps. 3 and 4, and Christoph Groffy, *Die Edinburgh Review, 1802–1825* (Heidelberg, 1981), pt. 3.

[78] Sir Walter Scott, "On the Present State of Periodical Criticism" (1812), in Kenneth Curry, *Sir Walter Scott's Edinburgh Annual Register* (Knoxville, Tenn., 1977), 149; Henry Cockburn's journal for 1848, quoted in N. T. Phillipson, "Lawyers, Landowners, and the Civic Leadership of Post-Union Scotland," *Juridical Review* (1976): 98.

particular peoples or places at particular times. If the first of these genres was practiced about equally by clergymen (e.g. Robertson, Ferguson, Blair, and John Logan) and lawyers (e.g. Kames, Millar, Sir John Dalrymple, and Gilbert Stuart), along with a few others such as Adam Smith, the second, which was often more popular in its day, was dominated by Presbyterian ministers (mostly Moderates) and their friend David Hume. The Scottish practitioners of narrative/philosophical history were the most popular and best-paid authors of their time because they produced books that were interesting, well-written, polite, learned, cosmopolitan in outlook and subject matter, morally as well as factually instructive, and reasonably fair or moderate in their handling of controversial issues—in short, "enlightened." These characteristics were to be found in Robert Henry's history of Great Britain (1771–1785), Robert Watson's histories of Philip II (1777) and Philip III (1783), Adam Ferguson's history of the Roman republic (1783), and of course the best-selling histories of Robertson and Hume. Meanwhile, lawyers virtually monopolized two older, and by this time somewhat marginal, historiographical traditions to which they may have been attracted by their fondness for evidence and argument, respectively: that of antiquarian chronicler or annalist (e.g. Sir David and Sir John Dalrymple) and that of contentious Jacobite or Marian controversialist (e.g. William Tytler and Gilbert Stuart).

By the early nineteenth century things had changed. Thanks largely to a new breed of legal men, including Thomas Thomson, Cosmo Innes, James Maidment, William Turnbull, Patrick Tytler (William's grandson), and Sir Walter Scott, the "conjectural" and narrative/philosophical modes of historiography lost ground to the antiquarian and controversial modes, as well as to the quasi-romantic mode found in Scott's historical novels and popular histories. These changes in historical taste had several constructive consequences for the study of history in Scotland, such as an increased concern with rare old documents and texts and the controversies surrounding them, the classification and publication of Scottish records at Register House, the production of valuable books by patriotic publishing clubs like the Bannatyne and Maitland, and the heightened appreciation for the European Middle Ages, and for all periods of Scottish history, fostered by Scott's fiction. They may also have had less admirable consequences, such as an escalation of the old Presbyterian-Episcopalian (or Roman Catholic), Whig-Tory wrangling over the past and, in the case of Scott's historical novels, a tendency to accentuate the most dramatic and quixotic historical events, characters, and situations. Value judgments aside, the point is that the historiographical priorities of the Scottish Enlightenment and the Moderates were displaced by different approaches to the past practiced chiefly by younger lawyers. Even in the field of "orientalism"—a thriving branch of early nineteenth-century Scottish historical research where the role of lawyers was somewhat less conspicuous (despite Mackintosh and Erskine) and the influence of Scottish "conjectural" history somewhat more enduring—one finds that scarcely any clergymen were involved, and that the distinctive historiographical features of the Scottish Enlightenment were for the most part sacrificed either to more technical and specialized investigations into comparative philology or to the more popular but less enlightened exercises in cultural chauvinism promulgated by Anglo-Scots like James Mill and Thomas Macaulay.[79]

The intellectual and social decline of the Scottish Presbyterian clergy was acknowledged by several commentators during the 1790s and early nineteenth century. Henry Mackenzie noted with regret that whereas Blair, Robertson, and other enlightened ministers of their day had appeared regularly "at dinners among literary men, and indeed in all good companies," where they had exerted a powerful effect on "the manners and morals of the company in which they were found," their successors in the clergy generally mingled less with polite society.[80] A German visitor to Scotland omitted the clergy from a list of the social leaders of Edinburgh society in 1795.[81] John Gibson Lockhart attributed the declining influence of the Scottish clergy over "the best educated classes of their countrymen" to "the insignificant part they have of late taken in general literature."[82] Henry Cockburn observed that "the descent of the Scottish clergy throughout the last half of the eighteenth century was steady and marked." The transformation of the Edinburgh clergy provided Cockburn with an appropriate illustration. In 1790 the town still had several eminent ministers from both ecclesiastical parties who were "literary and agreeable gentlemen." By 1820, however, the situation had changed markedly: "I do not recollect a single work of any importance, which any one of our Established clergy contributed during this time to

[79] On particular aspects of early nineteenth-century Scottish historiography discussed in this paragraph, see especially Marinell Ash, *The Strange Death of Scottish History* (Edinburgh, 1980); James Anderson, *Sir Walter Scott and History* (Edinburgh, 1981); Jane Rendall, "Scottish Orientalism: From Robertson to James Mill," *Historical Journal* 25 (1982): 43–69; and J. W. Burrow, *Evolution and Society* (Cambridge, 1966), chap. 2.

[80] *The Anecdotes and Egotisms of Henry Mackenzie, 1745–1831*, ed. Harold William Thompson (London, 1927), 94; Mackenzie, 10.

[81] Shapin, "Property, Patronage, and Politics of Science," 5.

[82] Lockhart, *Peter's Letters*, 1:80.

learning, or to science, or even to theology," he remarked; "and in Edinburgh at least, but I believe everywhere, they had fallen almost entirely out of good lay society."[83]

Cockburn and Alexander Carlyle cited the same two factors to account for the social and intellectual decline of the Scottish Presbyterian clergy at the end of the eighteenth century. First, they maintained that patronage was increasingly abused by irresponsible magistrates and landowners, who frequently used their powers to fill vacant churches and university chairs with lackies and unqualified relations rather than with ministers of intellect and enlightenment.[84] The second factor was that ministers' stipends had not kept pace with inflation.[85] An impoverished clergy was likely to be dedicated and devout, Cockburn pointed out, but it was not likely to be distinguished for its politeness or intellectual accomplishments.[86] Carlyle believed that these circumstances discouraged "superior spirits" from pursuing clerical careers and attracted in their place "young men of low birth and mean education."[87] The Moderate literati hoped that the trends toward abuse of patronage and impoverishment of ministers would both be reversed by their friend Henry Dundas, who dominated Scottish ecclesiastical and academic patronage throughout the 1780s and 1790s. Despite his involvement with the *Mirror* and *Lounger* circle of literary lawyers, however, Dundas dispensed patronage with a view toward political advantage rather than toward encouragement of a polite, well-lettered, Moderate clergy.[88] In regard to ministers' stipends, similarly, the Moderates felt betrayed when the government's stipend augmentation bill of 1793 was quickly withdrawn at the first hint of opposition from the Scottish landowners whom Dundas wished to placate.[89] When significant financial re-

[83] Cockburn, *Memorials*, 225–26; Ian F. Maciver, "Cockburn and the Church," in *Lord Cockburn: A Bicentenary Celebration*, ed. Alan Bell (Edinburgh, 1979), 68–103. The intellectual decline of the Presbyterian ministers of this period may be contrasted with the growing intellectual importance in Scotland of Episcopalian clergymen such as Archibald Alison, Bishop George Gleig, and the Englishman Sydney Smith.

[84] Cockburn, *Memorials*, 226; *Auto.*, 555.

[85] *Auto.*, 554; Cockburn, *Memorials*, 224.

[86] Cockburn, *Memorials*, 224.

[87] Carlyle manuscripts quoted in Henry Grey Graham, *Scottish Men of Letters in the Eighteenth Century* (London, 1908), 99n.

[88] On Dundas see Ian D. L. Clark, "From Protest to Reaction: The Moderate Regime in the Church of Scotland, 1752–1805," in *SAI*, 200–24, and John Dwyer and Alexander Murdoch, "Paradigms and Politics: Manners, Morals and the Rise of Henry Dundas, 1770–1784," in *NP*, 210–48.

[89] The bitter recriminations of Carlyle and Henry Grieve on this occasion inspired John Kay's satirical etching "Faithful Service Rewarded," reproduced on page 320. See *Auto.*, 589.

"Faithful Service Rewarded" by John Kay

lief was finally granted to the clergy, it was both too little and too late to prevent middle class young men with enlightened values and intellectual inclinations from deserting the ministry for more lucrative careers in law, medicine, and the military.[90]

As the clergy in the Church of Scotland lost social and intellectual status, so too did the Moderate party. Once synonymous with polite learning and enlightened principles, the Moderate party gradually relinquished its claims to those traits and became a reactionary force in intellectual as well as political matters.[91] Perhaps it is an exaggeration to say that under the leadership of George Hill of St. Andrews the Moderate party became merely "the Dundas interest at prayer,"[92] but there can be little doubt that the young Scottish divines who called themselves Moderates at the turn of the nineteenth century and afterward were mere shadows of their illustrious predecessors. They were not, as a rule, leading figures in Scottish—let alone British or European—intellectual life; they lacked the integrity and independence of the Robertson Moderates as ecclesiastical politicians; and they did little to promulgate, and sometimes did much to stifle, the enlightened principles to which the Moderate literati of Edinburgh had dedicated their lives. The change in the Moderate party was most evident during the celebrated Leslie case of 1805, when James Finlayson, John Inglis, and other Moderates fabricated a charge of atheism in an unsuccessful attempt to obtain the Edinburgh mathematics chair for a minister of their ecclesiastical party instead of John Leslie, a more qualified but Whiggish lay candidate.[93] It was an intellectually and spiritually bankrupt party of Scottish clergymen that carried the name "Moderate" into the new world of the nineteenth century, where they eventually would find themselves incapable of maintaining the unity of their church in the face of a vigorous challenge by the dynamic and socially responsive Evangelical party of Thomas Chalmers.[94]

The social and intellectual decline of the Scottish Presbyterian clergy generally and the Moderate party in particular; the demise of the Poker and Young Poker Clubs; the collapse of the literary class of the Royal Society of Edinburgh; the emergence of younger genera-

---

[90] Mudie, *Modern Athens*, 260.

[91] Clark, "From Protest to Reaction," 200–24; Andrew J. Campbell, *Two Centuries of the Church of Scotland, 1707–1929* (Paisley, 1930), 163, 168, and chap. 7.

[92] William Ferguson, *Scotland: 1689 to the Present* (Edinburgh, 1968), 227.

[93] See the articles on the Leslie affair cited in the bibliographical essay.

[94] Stewart J. Brown, *Thomas Chalmers and the Godly Commonwealth in Scotland* (Oxford, 1982).

tions of lawyers as the leaders of the Scottish literary world; the relatively rapid economic development of Scotland; the strain of the French Revolution; the politicization and fragmentation of Scottish intellectual life; the shift from the polite, didactic history, philosophy, and literary criticism of the Enlightenment to novels and review essays on the one hand and science, technology, and technical philosophy on the other—a more literary literature and a more scientific science and philosophy—all signaled the end of the Moderate age and the Scottish Enlightenment. Upon the death in June 1793 of William Robertson, the man who most fully represented the Moderate Regime in the church and university, this transformation was given symbolic expression. Expecting Robertson's office as principal of Edinburgh University to be offered to him as a mark of respect, Hugh Blair was deeply hurt when the town council chose instead a much younger minister who lacked impressive literary or academic credentials but possessed powerful political connections.[95] This incident illustrates as well as any other the movement of Blair and his generation of Moderate literati from the center to the periphery of Scottish intellectual and institutional life.[96]

After losing William Robertson and other friends and loved ones, Blair, Ferguson, Carlyle, and Home persevered as best they could in a society and a world that regarded them more and more as relics of a bygone era. They busied themselves with their last literary projects and frequently reminisced together about old times.[97] One such turn-of-the-century gathering of the remnants of the Robertson circle of Moderate literati was later described by Sir Walter Scott in terms that are less than flattering to the so-called "antideluvian" company:

> The subjects of their conversation might be compared to that held by ghosts, who, sitting on their midnight tombs, talk over the deeds they have done and witnessed while in the body. The *forty-five* was a remarkable epoch, and called forth remarks and anecdotes without number.[98]

[95] "The Provost by his influence with the Council conferred the office at once on his son-in-law George Baird, without taking the smallest notice of me. I could not but feel this as an affront." Blair to [Carlyle], 18 March 1795, NLS, 3431:232–33. Cf. Carlyle to Sir John Macpherson, 1796, in *Auto.*, 576, and Hill, *Hugh Blair*, 215–18.

[96] Blair was dealt another personal blow in 1798, when his protégé William Greenfield was charged with an undisclosed immoral act so serious that it cost him his church and his chair and sent him scurrying to England in disgrace.

[97] [Robert Bisset], "Dr. Adam Fergusson," in *Public Characters of 1799–1800* (London, 1799), 455.

[98] Scott, *Prose Works*, 19:321.

The elderly John Home seems to have fitted Scott's description perfectly, for late in life Home lost the ability to deal intelligently with recent events,[99] and his last major literary effort was appropriately a history of the '45. Home's surviving Moderate friends also turned back to the past for literary inspiration after 1793—Blair to revise old sermons that eventually constituted the fifth and final volume of his published collection, Carlyle to compose his memoirs, and Ferguson to revise his history of Rome and to write short biographies of his relations Joseph Black and Col. Patrick Ferguson as well as more than thirty philosophical essays, at least two of which took the form of dialogues featuring David Hume and other friends long since departed.

As the prospect of death grew every day more ominous, the Moderate literati prepared for their fate with Christian-Stoic resignation. "My prime consolation is that I have nothing to do but wait quietly till my time comes," Adam Ferguson commented in 1798.[100] In the previous year Alexander Carlyle had described an amusing dream that reveals the deep sense of camaraderie that continued to prevail among the Moderate literati of Edinburgh in old age. In the dream Carlyle finds himself at the entrance to Elysium, where he sees Robertson, Hume, James Macpherson, and other deceased friends. "There is Carlyle just coming down," exclaims Macpherson, "and John Home and Ferguson cannot be far behind, when I shall have irresistible evidence for the authenticity of Ossian. Blair, I daresay, is likewise on the road."[101] Hugh Blair died three years after this prophecy and was soon followed by Carlyle himself (1805) and John Home (1808). Only Adam Ferguson lived on, "tho' very deaf and almost blind,"[102] until he too passed away at the age of ninety-two (1816). The simple epitaph that Ferguson chose for his tomb in 1798 speaks equally well for the other members of his aging circle of Moderate literati: "I have seen the works of God: it is now your turn: do behold them and rejoice."[103] But Christian Stoicism had no place in a romantic age, and when Ferguson finally died his terse statement was rejected in favor of a long, flattering tribute by his friend and neighbor Sir Walter Scott.[104]

---

[99] Carlyle to Sir John Macpherson, 1797 (copy), NLS, 3464:27–29.
[100] Ferguson to Sir John Macpherson, 3 July 1798, in John Small, "Biographical Sketch of Adam Ferguson," *TRSE* 23 (1864): 660.
[101] Carlyle to Sir John Macpherson, 1797, *Auto.*, 575.
[102] George Dempster to Sir Adam Fergusson, 14 January 1813, quoted in Fagg, 323.
[103] Ferguson to Sir John Macpherson, 3 July 1798, in Small, "Adam Ferguson," 660.
[104] Ibid., 665.

THE MEANING OF MODERATISM

> Moderatism, in the full acceptation of that term, was only another name for the spirit of the age.
>
> William Law Mathieson,
> *The Awakening of Scotland*, 1910

Having traced the careers of Blair, Carlyle, Ferguson, Home, and Robertson to their ends, it may now be useful to summarize briefly the basic tenets of their collective ideology. At the risk of oversimplification, these may be reduced to six overlapping heads: Presbyterianism, Scottish nationalism, Stoicism, civic humanism, conservatism, and enlightenment.

Whatever else they may eventually have become, the Moderate literati of Edinburgh were originally and fundamentally churchmen, and for that reason their values and beliefs cannot be fully understood outside the context of eighteenth-century Scottish Presbyterianism. To be sure, their approach to religion was a far cry from the somber and sometimes rigid Calvinism of their fathers and forefathers, but it was also worlds away from the skeptical, deistic, anticlerical, and occasionally atheistic religious attitudes of so many of their contemporaries. They esteemed a rational, polite form of Presbyterianism that would bridge the gap between John Knox and David Hume, between fanaticism and infidelity, between tradition and modernity. They emphasized the moral lessons of Christianity within a thoroughly Presbyterian framework and remained loyal, active members of their national church despite their other interests and activities.

The Moderate literati's allegiance to the Church of Scotland was partly a function of the strong nationalist component in their ideology. If this aspect of Moderatism has all too often been underestimated or overlooked, it is probably because the Moderate literati were not anxious to glorify the peculiarities of Scottish culture in the manner of later romantic nationalists. Theirs was a cosmopolitan species of nationalism that sought to raise the status of Scotland in the eyes of the world by demonstrating its superiority according to universally accepted standards of taste and conduct. Generally speaking, their national pride was expressed quietly, through gentle boasting about the excellence of Scottish institutions and intellectual accomplishments. Was *Douglas* not a first-rate tragedy, they demanded? Were

the prose works of Scottish men of letters not as polite and profound
as any in England or France? Were the Church of Scotland and University of Edinburgh not deservedly renowned for their urbanity and
learning as well as their rational piety? Only when "John Bull" denied Scotland a fair chance to shine in "arms and letters" did the
Moderate literati exchange this polite style of gentle boasting for a
more overt and belligerent form of Scottish nationalism, as shown by
their nationalist fervor over the Scots militia and Ossian.

In regard to ethics, the dominant philosophical strain in Moderate
preaching, teaching, and scholarly and theatrical writing was Stoicism. The Moderate literati of Edinburgh believed that human beings
attain happiness only by fulfilling ethical obligations to one another
without regard for rewards. They must strive to live the life of virtue—defined chiefly in terms of benevolence, or what Ferguson called
the "love of mankind"—while recognizing that the results of their
virtuous actions are usually beyond their comprehension and always
beyond their control. Instead of employing this Stoic philosophy as
a weapon against Christianity, as Peter Gay's interpretation of the
Enlightenment might lead one to expect, the Moderate literati followed Francis Hutcheson in using it as a foundation for a Christian
Stoic approach to morality. With God instead of impersonal fate as
the ultimate director of events and determiner of outcomes, Stoicism
was stripped of its pessimistic, pagan attributes and reconciled with
the promise—and threat—of the Scottish Presbyterian jeremiad, which
taught that divine Providence rewards or punishes the people of
Scotland or Britain as a whole according to the extent of their faith-
fulness to their ethical and religious "covenant" with the Lord. The
Stoic emphasis on inner purity rather than exterior circumstances and
consequences, on the limitations of human planning and design, and
on the importance of resignation to one's lot in life meshed nicely
with similar beliefs in Presbyterianism as well as with the Moderates'
propensity for social and political conservatism. And other features
of the Stoic outlook, such as natural law (now with divine backing)
and human fellowship, meshed equally well with the Moderates'
commitment to liberal or "enlightened" principles regarding the rule
of law, personal rights, and what Blair called the "sense of humanity."

Particularly when contrasted with Epicureanism, Stoicism was also
in harmony with the Moderate literati's faith in public virtue as the
only effective antidote to the moral and social ills plaguing modern
commercial civilization. Here the languages of Marcus Aurelius and
Cicero on the one hand and the Presbyterian jeremiad on the other
slid easily into the discourse of the civic or civic humanist tradition—

a tradition that appealed to classical ideals of patriotic, martial virtue in the struggle against moral corruption. The Moderate literati of Edinburgh owed too much to prosperous, eighteenth-century commercial society to employ this civic language with all the rigor and severity of the man who had introduced it in Scotland in the 1690s, Andrew Fletcher of Saltoun. They were far more concerned than Fletcher with promoting polite manners, moderate religion, personal or private ethics, and individual rights secured by the rule of law; far more tolerant than he of commercialization, self-interest, and luxury; and far more comfortable than he could possibly have been in a world of convivial clubs, standing armies, national debts, vast networks of political and ecclesiastical patronage, and Scottish union with England.

Recent commentators who have approached the Scottish Enlightenment from this perspective have emphasized the extent to which its leaders transformed Fletcher's political, military, patriotic, "civic" vision into a social, economic, and essentially "civil" language and program of politeness, propriety, and improvement.[105] An interpretation of this sort is valuable for explaining certain features of the Scottish Enlightenment, such as the rage for all kinds of improving schemes and societies and the extraordinary degree to which efforts to effect economic and social improvement were imbued with moral and patriotic significance. Yet it may also exaggerate the social and modernizing component in the ideology of the Scottish Enlightenment at the expense of a component that insisted on the need for patriotic, martial virtue, especially when war, rebellion, or some other national emergency seemed to threaten the established order. The Moderate literati of Edinburgh were the foremost spokesmen for this enduring civic ideal. When William Robertson identified the Scots militia agitation during the Seven Years' War as the single most important issue since the Union; when Alexander Carlyle asserted, in a similar context, that if conflict should arise between virtue and commerce a portion of the latter would have to be sacrificed for the sake of the former; when Hugh Blair idealized the mythical, violent world of the heroic Fingal; when Adam Ferguson and John Home glorified the independent citizen-warrior as the model of uncorrupted virtue, whether he be found in republican Rome or savage America, the Sparta of *Agis* or the Scotland of *Douglas*—they were

---

[105] See the essays by Nicholas Phillipson and J. G. A. Pocock in *WV*, esp. 198–202 and 240–41, as well as other recent studies by these authors cited in the bibliographical essay below and Pocock's more generalized statement of the same thesis in "Virtues, Rights, and Manners: A Model for Historians of Political Thought," *Political Theory* 9 (1981): 353–68.

expressing a point of view that was fundamentally "civic" and militant rather than "civil" and social, and that was as vital a part of the Scottish Enlightenment as the more prophetic, "bourgeois" ideology of commerce and modernization associated with Scottish political economy. And when these same men preached jeremiads against rebels, radicals, and foreign foes; gathered at the Poker Club to agitate for a Scots militia; donated their services to Cope and Cumberland's forces during the '45; or themselves donned the uniforms of an Edinburgh volunteer, an army chaplain, or a fencible officer—they were putting the ideological theory of the Scottish Enlightenment into practice just as much as when they espoused the principles of Addisonian politeness.

Since the rhetoric of civic virtue was rooted in the heritage of classical and Renaissance republicanism, adopted by the parliamentary opposition as part of the country platform, and appropriated by British radicals and American rebels in the 1760s and 1770s, historians have tended to identify this tradition either with the political "left" or with the reactionary "right" of Tories like Bolingbroke. The Moderate literati of Edinburgh, however, belong to the less well-known body of eighteenth-century thinkers who adapted civic rhetoric to serve conservative or establishment ends. They were, of course, Whigs, as were all Scottish Presbyterians of their day, but they were conservative or "constitutional" Whigs who scorned almost every variety of radicalism and reform. Their attempts to inculcate civic or public virtue were not only manifestations of their moralizing mission as Presbyterian divines and university educators but also ideological weapons in their ongoing struggle to defend the existing Whig-Presbyterian order against both the dying Jacobite "right" and the incipient radical Whig (and in Scotland, radical Presbyterian) "left." Similarly, their zealous participation in the Scots militia movement, which cast them in the unlikely role of agitators for institutional reform, was prompted largely, if paradoxically, by a desire to protect the status quo and to reinforce existing morals and mores against the corrupting effects of modernization. It was precisely because they equated public virtue with the patriotic exercise of conservative ideology that the Moderate literati sounded most like commonwealthmen when the prevailing institutional order appeared to be threatened by foreign foes. Moreover, the conservative component in Moderatism was not restricted to or exhausted by the civic humanist paradigm. In their "Reasons of Dissent" of 1752; in their consistently rigorous policy on lay patronage, ecclesiastical discipline, and other issues pertaining to church polity; in their frequent attempts to justify the "distinction of ranks" in society; in their firm opposition to the American and French

Revolutions; in the sociological theory of political constitutions taught by Adam Ferguson; in the fast-day jeremiads preached by Alexander Carlyle and other Moderate ministers at times of political crisis—the Moderate literati of Edinburgh displayed a steadfast commitment to conservative ecclesiastical, social, and political principles that transcended the rhetoric of civic humanism. In short, the Moderate literati were believers in what I have called, for want of a better name, "Whig-Presbyterian conservatism."

Finally, Moderatism was dedicated to propagating many of the leading values of the Enlightenment, especially religious tolerance and freedom of expression, reasonableness and moderation, polite learning and literature, humanitarianism and cosmopolitanism, virtue and happiness. These enlightened values tempered the Moderate literati's religious, ethical, social, and political attitudes, making their Presbyterianism open and polite rather than narrow and intolerant, their nationalism cosmopolitan and restrained rather than parochial and chauvinistic, their Stoicism action-oriented and sensitive rather than escapist and austere, their civic humanism fundamentally moral rather than constitutional and far less severe than that found in Fletcher of Saltoun, their conservatism moderate and humane rather than doctrinaire and reactionary. They also inspired the involvement of the Moderate literati in numerous literary enterprises, in academic affairs, and in important controversies concerning such diverse issues as ecclesiastical censorship, the status of the theater, and the rights of Roman Catholics.

As men of letters, the Moderate literati of Edinburgh were not so radical or innovative as many of their continental counterparts, but in their "moderate" way they were as enlightened and *engagés* as Voltaire and Diderot, and they were considerably more successful than most European *philosophes* at institutionalizing their values during their own lifetimes. Though they may not always rank in the first echelon as philosophers, historians, playwrights, or literary critics, in their day they performed important roles as ecclesiastical politicians, academic administrators, preachers, and teachers. The distinctive attributes of Moderatism were indeed "part-and-parcel of the philosophy of the Scottish Enlightenment."[106] By successfully institutionalizing the principles of Moderatism, the Moderate literati of Edinburgh forged an atmosphere in which the Scottish Enlightenment could thrive and prosper, defined the unique features of the Scottish Enlightenment vis-à-vis the Enlightenment as a whole, and helped to transform their church, their college, their city, and their country into centers of enlightened ideas and values.

[106] Mossner, 284.

BIBLIOGRAPHY

This bibliography consists of three parts: (I) the publications of the Moderate literati of Edinburgh cited in the text and footnotes, listed chronologically by author (using dates of first editions), followed by brief accounts of the secondary literature on their lives and works; (II) an alphabetical list of libraries and other institutions housing relevant manuscript collections; and (III) a select bibliographical essay on eighteenth-century Scotland and the Scottish Enlightenment, with particular attention paid to studies of topics featured in this book.

I. Works by and about the Moderate Literati of Edinburgh

HUGH BLAIR

1739   *De fundamentus & obligatione legis naturæ.* Edinburgh. Blair's M.A. thesis in Edinburgh University Library.

1746   *The Wrath of Man Praising God. A Sermon Preached in the High Church of Edinburgh, May 18, 1746.* Edinburgh.

1750   *The Importance of Religious Knowledge to the Happiness of Mankind.* Edinburgh. Preached before the Scottish s.p.c.k.

1753   ed., *The Works of Shakespear.* 8 vols. Edinburgh.

1755   *Observations upon a Pamphlet Intitled An Analysis of the Moral and Religious Sentiments contained in the Writings of Sopho and David Hume, Esq.* Edinburgh.

1755–   Reviews no. 2 and appendix 1 in the *Edinburgh Review,*
1756   vol. 1, and reviews no. 9 and 12 in the *Edinburgh Review,* vol. 2.

1756   *Objections against the Essays on Morality and Natural Religion Examined.* Edinburgh. With the assistance of Robert Hamilton, Robert Wallace, George Wishart, and presumably Lord Kames (the ostensible author).

1760   Preface to James Macpherson, *Fragments of Ancient Poetry, Collected in the Highlands of Scotland.* Edinburgh. I have used a reprint of the second edition (Edinburgh, 1970).

1763   *A Critical Dissertation on the Poems of Ossian, the Son of Fingal.* London. I have used the second edition of 1765.

1767   *Heads of the Lectures on Rhetoric and Belles Lettres, in the University of Edinburgh.* Edinburgh. I have used the 1771 version of this pamphlet.

1777–   *Sermons*. London. I have used the five-volume, London
1801   edition of 1818.

1783   *Lectures on Rhetoric and Belles Lettres*. 2 vols. London. I have
        used the edition edited by Harold F. Harding (Carbon-
        dale and Edwardsville, Ill., 1965).

1805   Testimony on Ossian in *Report of the Committee of the High-
        land Society of Scotland, Appointed to Inquire into the Nature
        and Authenticity of the Poems of Ossian*. Edited by Henry
        Mackenzie. Edinburgh. Appendix. The same source con-
        tains the testimonies of Carlyle, Ferguson, and Home.

The only modern biography of Blair—Robert Morrell Schmitz, *Hugh Blair* (New York, 1948)—treats its subject chiefly from a literary point of view. More valuable in some respects is John Hill, *An Account of the Life and Writings of Hugh Blair* (Edinburgh, 1807). Blair's ecclesiastical and academic colleague James Finlayson wrote a brief life that is prefixed to several editions of Blair's *Sermons*, but this is less useful than the article on Blair in *Public Characters of 1800–1801* (Dublin, 1801), 233–45, and Carlyle's "Comparison of Two Eminent Characters," in *AC*, 275–82. Thumbnail sketches of Blair and the other Moderate literati can be found in the *Dictionary of National Biography*, Chambers and Thomson's *Biographical Dictionary of Eminent Scotsmen*, Hew Scott's *Fasti*, and Henry Grey Graham's *Scottish Men of Letters in the Eighteenth Century*.

Blair's religious side has never been properly assessed, though it is discussed in several doctoral theses: David Grant, "A Critical Analysis of the Sermons of Hugh Blair" (Stanford University, 1952), which is mainly concerned with rhetoric; William Nelson Hawley, "Hugh Blair: Moderate Preacher" (University of Chicago, 1938); Charles Rogers McCain, "Preaching in Eighteenth-Century Scotland: A Comparative Study of the Extant Sermons of Ralph Erskine, John Erskine, and Hugh Blair" (Edinburgh University, 1949); and, most succinctly and perceptively, Ian D. L. Clark's thesis on Moderatism cited in part III of this essay. Among the many studies of Blair that have appeared in journals of rhetoric are Douglas Ehninger and James Golden, "The Intrinsic Sources of Blair's Popularity," *Southern Speech Journal* 21–22 (1955–1957): 12–30; the latter's "Hugh Blair: Minister of St. Giles," *Quarterly Journal of Speech* 38 (1952): 155–60; Vincent Bevilacqua, "Philosophical Assumptions underlying Hugh Blair's *Lectures on Rhetoric and Belles Lettres*," *Western Speech* 31 (1967): 150–64, which attempts to place Blair within the common sense tradition; and articles by Herman Cohen based on his State University of Iowa Ph.D. dissertation of 1954, "An Analysis of the Rhetoric of Hugh

Blair." There is also much on Blair in the extensive general literatures on Scottish rhetoric and on Ossian and Scottish literary primitivism, and there are good bibliographies in Harding's edition of Blair's *Lectures* and Schmitz's biography.

ALEXANDER CARLYLE

1748   *The Reasons for Applying to the King and Parliament for an Augmentation of Stipend to the Ministers of the Church of Scotland.* Edinburgh. Usually ascribed to Carlyle, though he once remarked that a brief item in the *Scots Magazine* of June 1755 was his first publication (*Auto.*, 322).

1754   Prologue to Charles Hart, *Herminus and Espansia: A Tragedy.* Edinburgh.

1756   *A Full and True History of the Bloody Tragedy of Douglas as it is now to be seen acting at the Theatre in the Canongate.* Edinburgh.

1757   *An Argument to Prove that the Tragedy of Douglas ought to be Publickly Burnt by the Hands of the Hangman.* Edinburgh. Reprinted in Gipson, *John Home*, 189–99.

1758   Review of John Home's *Agis* in the *Critical Review* 5:233–42. This is undoubtedly the review of *Agis* that Carlyle mistakenly remembered publishing in another of Smollett's periodicals, the *British Magazine* (*Auto.*, 375).

1759   *Plain Reasons for Removing a Certain Great Man from His M———y's Presence and Councils for ever.* London.

1760   *The Question Relating to a Scots Militia Considered.* Edinburgh. Republished at London and Edinburgh with a preface attributed to George Townshend (J. Tower, 1760) and again at London in a second edition with a preface by "another hand" (M. Cooper, 1760). In 1762 Hamilton and Balfour, the original publishers, put out a fourth edition featuring an interesting new preface that may well have been by Carlyle himself. I have used the text of the first London edition of 1760.

1763   *Faction Detected.* London.

1767   "Verses on his Grace the Duke of Buccleugh's Birthday, September, 1767." *SM* 29:487.

1767   *The Tendency of the Constitution of the Church of Scotland to form the Temper, Spirit, and Character of Her Ministers.* Edinburgh. Preached before the Synod of Lothian and Tweeddale in May 1767. Reprinted in volume 2 of *The Scotch Preacher* (Edinburgh, 1777).

1769   *Essay upon Taxes, particularly tending to shew That the Ministers of the Church of Scotland cannot in Law, and ought not in Justice and Equity, to be subjected to the Tax upon Houses and Lights.* Edinburgh.

1777   *The Justice and Necessity of the War with our American Colonies Examined.* Edinburgh. A fast-day sermon preached at Inveresk on 12 December 1776.

1778   *A Letter to His Grace the Duke of Buccleugh, on National Defence; With Some Remarks on Dr Smith's Chapter on that Subject, in his Book entitled . . . the Wealth of Nations.* London. I have used the revised edition published at Edinburgh later in 1778 with a different subtitle: *to which is now added, a Postscript, relative to the Regiments of Fencible Men Raising in Scotland.*

1779–
1782   Militia letters in the *Caledonian Mercury,* 3 November 1779, 24 and 31 January 1780, and 14 September 1782. These items represent only a small portion of the militia letters that Carlyle left behind in manuscript. Their partial publication in the *Caledonian Mercury* was pointed out to me by John Robertson.

1788   "An Ode on the Popular Superstitions of the Highlands. Written by the late Mr William Collins." *TRSE* 1:63–75. Read to the literary class of the Royal Society by Carlyle on 19 April 1784.

1792   *A Sermon on the Death of Sir David Dalrymple, Bar^t Lord Hailes . . . With an Address to the Congregation suited to the Circumstances of the Times.* Edinburgh. Preached at Inveresk on 9 December 1792.

1793   *The Usefulness and Necessity of a Liberal Education for Clergymen.* Edinburgh. Preached before the Society for the Benefit of Sons of the Clergy on 28 May 1793.

1794   *National Depravity the Cause of National Calamities.* Edinburgh. Preached at Inveresk on 25 February 1794 and published for the benefit of the parish poor.

1795   Account of the parish of Inveresk in the *Statistical Account of Scotland* 16:1–49. Edited by Sir John Sinclair. 21 vols. Edinburgh.

1860   *The Autobiography of Dr. Alexander Carlyle of Inveresk, 1722–1805.* Edited by John Hill Burton. London and Edinburgh. Includes excerpts from Carlyle's unpublished "Recollections" and a valuable supplementary chapter on his later life. The "new" edition of 1910, which has been used here, adds an index, a note on Carlyle's ancestry, and numerous illustrations.

1973   *Anecdotes and Characters of the Times.* Edited by James Kinsley. London. Another version of the preceding entry, bearing the title that the author intended for it and containing first-rate portraits of Carlyle and his friends and patrons as well as a previously unpublished sketch of Blair and Robertson called "A Comparison of Two Eminent Characters Attempted after the Manner of Plutarch." Discursive footnotes that Burton integrated into the text have been put back where they belong, and some words and sentences that Burton miscopied or eliminated have been corrected and restored. Unfortunately, the text is too slavishly literal a transcription of the original manuscript (which was not meant for publication in that rough form) to make for smooth reading or to displace the revised *Autobiography* of 1910 as the standard edition.

1981   *Journal of a Tour to the North of Scotland.* Edited by Richard B. Sher. Aberdeen. A brief travel journal of 1765 that Carlyle apparently intended for publication at the appropriate place in his autobiography.

As no life of Carlyle has ever been written, biographical information must be carefully culled from his autobiography—which is not always accurate and does not cover the last part of his life—and various unpublished sources. John Hill Burton's supplementary chapter in the *Autobiography* is helpful, but besides this there is little except William Thomas Cairns's appreciative essay, "Jupiter Carlyle and the Scottish Moderates," in his *The Religion of Dr. Johnson and Other Essays* (1946; reprint, Freeport, N.Y. 1969), 81–110; D. L. Carver, "Collins and Alexander Carlyle," *Review of English Studies* 15 (1939): 35–44; and G. M. Ditchfield, "The Scottish Campaign against the Test Act, 1790–91," *Historical Journal* 23 (1980): 37–61, where Carlyle is shown to be among the most avid Scottish opponents of repeal of that restrictive piece of legislation.

ADAM FERGUSON

1746   *A Sermon Preached in the Ersh Language to His Majesty's Highland Regiment of Foot, Commanded by Lord John Murray, at their Cantonment at Camberwell, on the 18th Day of December, 1745.* London. Translated into English by the author and published by Murray's mother, the duchess of Atholl.

1756   *Reflections Previous to the Establishment of a Militia.* London.

1757   *The Morality of Stage Plays Seriously Considered.* Edinburgh.

ca. 1760   *Of Natural Philosophy*. Edinburgh.

1761   *The History of the Proceedings in the Case of Margaret, Com-*
[1760]   *monly called Peg, only lawful Sister of John Bull, Esq.* London.
Recently reprinted by David R. Raynor as *Sister Peg: A pamphlet hitherto unknown by David Hume* (Cambridge, 1982), but the case for Hume's authorship seems highly implausible for reasons discussed in my review in *Philosophical Books* 24 (1983): 85–91.

1766   *Analysis of Pneumatics and Moral Philosophy. For the Use of Students in the College of Edinburgh.* Edinburgh.

1767   *An Essay on the History of Civil Society.* Edited by Duncan Forbes. Edinburgh. 1966. Includes a superb introduction by the editor.

1769   *Institutes of Moral Philosophy. For the Use of Students in the College of Edinburgh.* Edinburgh. I have used the third edition of 1785.

1776   *Remarks on a Pamphlet lately Published by Dr. Price, Intitled, Observations on the Nature of Civil Liberty.* London.

1778   ["Manifesto and Proclamation to the Members of Congress, etc.], 3 October 1778. The swan song of the Carlisle Peace Commission in America, probably wholly or chiefly the work of Ferguson. I have used the text printed in *SM* 40 (November 1778): 603–10.

1783   *The History of the Progress and Termination of the Roman Republic.* 3 vols. London. I have used the one-volume edition published at Philadelphia in 1845.

1792   *Principles of Moral and Political Science; being chiefly a retrospect of lectures delivered in the College of Edinburgh.* 2 vols. London.

1805   "Minutes of the Life and Character of Joseph Black, M.D." *TRSE* 5. Part 3: 101–17.

1817   *Biographical Sketch, or Memoir, of Lieutenant-Colonel Patrick Ferguson.* Edinburgh.

1960   " 'Of the Principles of Moral Estimation: A Discourse between David Hume, Robert Clerk, and Adam Smith': An Unpublished MS by Adam Ferguson." Edited by Ernest Campbell Mossner. *JHI* 21:222–32.

The standard biography is John Small, "Biographical Sketch of Adam Ferguson," *TRSE* 23 (1864): 599–665, which is valuable for its many primary source materials but contains quite a few unsubstantiated or incorrect remarks. A fuller biography is Jane Bush Fagg, "Adam Ferguson: Scottish Cato" (Ph.D. diss., University of North Carolina,

1968). Other useful biographical sources are John Lee, "Adam Ferguson," *EBS*, 4:239–43; an anonymous article in the *Edinburgh Review* 125 (1867): 48–85, which includes unpublished autobiographical excerpts by Ferguson's father; and two interesting sketches believed to be by Burke's biographer Robert Bisset, the son of the elder Ferguson's successor as minister of Logierait and a close family friend: "Dr. Adam Fergusson," in *Public Characters of 1799–1800* (London, 1799), 431–55, and "The Life of Adam Ferguson" (1798), an unsigned fragment in the Edinburgh Room of Edinburgh Public Library. Other sources of this sort will be found in Fagg's bibliography.

David Kettler, *The Social and Political Thought of Adam Ferguson* (Columbus, Ohio, 1965) is a good intellectual biography. Readers of Italian will also be able to consult Pasquale Salvucci, *Adam Ferguson: sociologia e philosophia politica* (Urbino, 1972), reviewed at length by William C. Lehmann in *History and Theory* 13 (1974): 165–81. Lehmann's own *Adam Ferguson and the Beginnings of Modern Sociology* (New York, 1930) and H. H. Jogland, *Ursprünge und Grundlagen de Soziologie bei Adam Ferguson* (Berlin, 1959) emphasize Ferguson's contribution to the development of sociology. Other discussions of Ferguson as sociologist, "conjectural" historian, and moral philosopher can be found in general works on those topics by Gladys Bryson, Alice Wheeler, and others, some of which are cited in part III below. Specialized articles on Ferguson's social thought include Andrew Bernstein, "Adam Ferguson and the Idea of Progress," *EC* 19 (1978): 99–118; Ronald Hamowy, "Adam Smith, Adam Ferguson and the Division of Labour," *Economica* 35 (1968): 249–59; David Kettler, "History and Theory in Ferguson's *Essay on the History of Civil Society*: A Reconsideration," *Political Theory* 5 (1977): 437–60, and "Ferguson's *Principles*: Constitution in Permanence," *EC* 19 (1978): 208–22; and Hiroshi Mizuta, "Two Adams in the Scottish Enlightenment: Adam Smith and Adam Ferguson on Progress," *SVEC* 191 (1981): 812–19. Ferguson and Smith are also compared in chapter 7 of John Robertson's new book on the militia, mentioned below. Among doctoral dissertations of interest are Ronald Hamowy, "The Social and Political Thought of Adam Ferguson" (University of Chicago, 1969); Richard F. Teichgraeber III, "Politics and Morals in the Scottish Enlightenment" (Brandeis University, 1978), chap. 5; and Jean Carolyn Willke, "The Historical Thought of Adam Ferguson" (Catholic University of America, 1962). For the possible impact of Ferguson's Highland background on his thinking, see Duncan Forbes, "Adam Ferguson and the Idea of Community," in Douglas Young et al., *Edinburgh in the Age of Reason* (Edinburgh, 1967), 40–47, and Ernest Campbell Mossner, "Adam

335

Ferguson's 'Dialogue on a Highland Jaunt' with Robert Adam, William Cleghorn, David Hume, and William Wilkie," in *Restoration and Eighteenth-Century Literature*, ed. Carroll Camden (Chicago, 1963), 297–308.

JOHN HOME

1742　　*De republica vel imperio civili.* Edinburgh. Home's M.A. thesis in Edinburgh University Library.

1753　　*Verses on laying the Foundation of the Exchange of Edinburgh.* [Edinburgh]. A printed page found in Edinburgh University Library (La. 3/584.16*) along with a letter from David Herd to Archibald Constable identifying the author and noting that several copies were distributed by George Drummond to gentlemen at the ground-breaking ceremony on 13 September 1753.

1757　　*Douglas.* Edited by Gerald D. Parker. Edinburgh. 1972.

1762　　"Prologue on the Birthday of the Prince of Wales, 1759" and other poems by Home published in volume 2 of *A Collection of Original Poems by Scotch Gentlemen.* Edited by Thomas Blacklock. Edinburgh.

1776　　*A Letter from an Officer Retired, to His Son in Parliament.* London and Edinburgh.

1822　　*The Works of John Home.* Edited by Henry Mackenzie. 3 vols. Edinburgh. This standard edition has been used for references to Mackenzie's biography, Home's history of the '45 (1802), and all of Home's plays except *Douglas,* for which I have used Gerald D. Parker's edition cited above.

1956　　Letters to Lord Bute of 12 June and 3 August 1761, in George R. Thomas, "Lord Bute, John Home and Ossian: Two Letters." *Modern Language Review* 51:73–75.

1976　　*A Sketch of the Character of Mr. Hume and Diary of a Journey from Morpeth to Bath.* Edited by David Fate Norton. Edinburgh. The sketch of David Hume is published for the first time; the travel diary, covering a trip to Bath with the dying Hume, is reprinted from Mackenzie's biography.

Henry Mackenzie, "Account of the Life of Mr. John Home," in the 1822 edition of Home's *Works,* 1:1–184 (also published separately in the same year) is better on the age than on the man. Sir Walter Scott's long review of Mackenzie's biography in *The Miscellaneous Prose Works of Sir Walter Scott,* 28 vols. (Edinburgh, 1834–1835), 19:283–367, is another lively portrait by a younger writer who viewed Home as a symbol of eighteenth-century Scottish literature. Two other useful biographical sketches from the early nineteenth century are John Lee, "John Home," *EBS*, 4:645–49, and "Biographical Notice of the Late John Home," *New Monthly Magazine* 57 (1839): 289–304 and 471–83, and 58 (1840): 164–76, by an anonymous "near relative" who utilized a collection of private papers that seems to have vanished. Since then virtually nothing has been written on Home's life besides the superficial biographical chapter in Alice Edna Gipson, *John Home: A Study of His Life and Works* (Caldwell, Idaho, [1917]).

Nor has there been much scholarship on Home's career as a dramatist. Gipson's book summarizes the plots of his plays and reprints much primary source material on the *Douglas* controversy of 1756–1757 but has little else to offer. The controversy over *Douglas* is also covered in Hugh Compton's doctoral dissertation, cited in part III below. James S. Malek has published several brief studies: "The Ossianic Source of John Home's *The Fatal Discovery*," *English Language Notes* 9 (1971): 39–42; "John Home's *Douglas*: The Role of Providence," *The New Rambler* 15 (1974): 30–35; and "John Home's *The Siege of Aquileia*: A Reevaluation," *Studies in Scottish Literature* 10 (1973): 232–40. Other sources on *Douglas*, many of them dealing with technical aspects of textual accuracy, are noted in the introduction and bibliography of Gerald Parker's excellent edition of that play.

WILLIAM ROBERTSON

1752   "Reasons of Dissent from the Judgment and Resolution of the Commission, March 11, 1752, resolving to inflict no Censure on the Presbytery of Dunfermline for their Disobedience in relation to the Settlement of Inverkeithing." *SM* 14:191–97. Reprinted in *Annals*, 1:231–42, where it was dubbed the Moderate "manifesto" on church polity. It is credited to Robertson, along with a committee that "corrected and enlarged" it, in *Auto.*, 470.

1755   *The Situation of the World at the Time of Christ's Appearance, and Its Connection with the Success of His Religion Considered.* Edinburgh. Preached before the Scottish s.p.c.k.

1755–   Reviews no. 1 and 3, and appendixes 2 and 4 in the *Edin-*
1756   *burgh Review*, vol. 1, and reviews 1, 3, 4, and 11 in the *Edinburgh Review*, vol. 2.

1768   *Memorial Relating to the University of Edinburgh.* Edinburgh. Also published in *SM* and the *Caledonian Mercury*.

1825   *The Works of William Robertson.* 8 vols. Oxford. I have used this edition (to which a few spelling corrections have been added) for all references to Robertson's histories of Scotland (1759), Charles V (1769), America (1777), and India (1791).

1829   *The Works of William Robertson.* 2 vols. Edinburgh. A popular edition that I have used only for Dugald Stewart's biography and Robertson's s.p.c.к. sermon, which are not included in the last entry.

1972   *The Progress of Society in Europe.* Edited by Felix Gilbert. Chicago. The introduction to the *History of Charles V,* slightly abridged.

1985   Letters of 8 March 1762, 27 March 1767, and 31 January 1769, in R. B. Sher and M. A. Stewart, "William Robertson and David Hume: Three Letters," *Hume Studies.*

All the Moderate literati of Edinburgh are in need of good modern biographies, but none more so than William Robertson. Despite the astonishing range of his activities as historian and man of letters, college principal, parish minister, and ecclesiastical leader, the myth persists that Robertson's life was too uneventful to merit much serious attention (see, for example, Felix Gilbert's introduction to his edition of Robertson's *Progress of Society,* xii). The origins of this myth derive in part from a lack of interest in Scottish affairs among commentators on Robertson's histories and in part from the fact that the standard biography by Dugald Stewart (presented to the Royal Society of Edinburgh in 1796, and published in 1801 and subsequently in several editions of Robertson's *Works*) does not bring its subject to life. Robertson's grandnephew Henry, Lord Brougham tried to show a more personal side of his famous relation in his critical review of Stewart's biography in the *Edinburgh Review* 2 (1803): 229–49, in his own attempt at a biography in *Lives of Men of Letters and Science, Who Flourished in the Time of George III,* 2 vols. (London, 1845), 1:256–323, and in his memoirs, *The Life and Times of Henry, Lord Brougham,* 2d ed., 3 vols. (Edinburgh, 1871). But Brougham is not always reliable. Another interesting memoir by a relative is William Adam, *Sequel to the Gift of a Grandfather* (1839). The eulogy preached by Robertson's colleague and ecclesiastical opponent John Erskine, "The Agency of God in Human Greatness," in *Discourses Preached on Several Occasions,* 2d ed., 2 vols. (Edinburgh, 1801–1804), 1:240–77, is very informative and remarkably generous. See also Alexander Carlyle's "Comparison of Two Eminent Characters" in *AC;* George Gleig, *An Account of the Life and Writings of William Robertson* (Edinburgh, 1812); and several brief biographical sketches prefixed to the various editions of Robertson's *Works.*

Robertson liked getting ahead and knew how to do it, and this trait, coupled with his ecclesiastical politics and his moderate stance on Mary Queen of Scots, made him many enemies. A good example is James Boswell's blistering attack on Robertson as too ambitious, too political, and too unsympathetic toward Mary in the unsigned "Skeptical Observations upon a late Character of Dr. Robertson," *London Magazine* 41 (June 1772): 281–83, a response to the glowing sketch of Robertson in the April issue of the same periodical. Two studies of Robertson's rise to power are Jeremy J. Cater, "The Making of Principal Robertson in 1762: Politics and the University of Edinburgh in the Second Half of the Eighteenth Century," *SHR* 49 (1970): 60–84, which is useful despite a tendency to underestimate the influence of the "people above," and James Lee McKelvey, "William Robertson and Lord Bute," *Studies in Scottish Literature* 6 (1969): 238–47.

For Robertson's achievements as a historian, it is unfortunate that the standard account remains a dated chapter in J. B. Black, *The Art of History: A Study of Four Great Historians of the Eighteenth Century* (London, 1926), which can be supplemented with D. B. Horn's little-known article, "Principal William Robertson, DD, Historian," *University of Edinburgh Journal* 18 (1956): 155–68. German scholars have shown interest in Robertson as a diplomatic and cultural historian: see the references to works by Bernhard Pier, Manfred Schlenke, and Friedrich Meinecke in the article just mentioned. Scholarship in English is for the most part highly specialized. R. A. Humphreys's lecture *William Robertson and His History of America* (London, 1954) focuses on Spanish America; Robert Birley, *Sunk Without Trace: Some Forgotten Masterpieces Reconsidered* (New York, 1962), chap. 4, deals only with *Charles V*; E. Adamson Hoebel, "William Robertson: An Eighteenth-Century Anthropologist-Historian," *American Anthropologist* 62 (1960): 648–55, considers Robertson's contribution to anthropology; Jeffrey Smitten, "Robertson's *History of Scotland:* Narrative Structure and the Sense of Reality," *Clio* 11 (1981): 29–47, shows how Robertson's first book achieves narrative coherence by means of patterns of contrast; Thomas R. Brooks, "Transformations of Word and Man: The Prose Style of William Robertson" (Ph.D. diss., University of Indiana, 1967) analyzes Robertson's prose from a linguist's point of view; J. H. S. Burleigh, "The Scottish Reformation as Seen in 1660 and 1760," *RSCHS* 13 (1959): 241–56, examines Robertson's account of the Reformation; Herbert Weisinger, "The Middle Ages and the Late Eighteenth-Century Historians," *Philological Quarterly* 27 (1948): 63–79, treats Robertson's perceptions of medieval culture; and various commentators on Scottish social science and "conjectural" history concentrate on his role as a historical sociologist. Diplomatic historian, ecclesiastical historian, "conjectural" historian, cultural historian, anthropologist, sociologist, and polite stylist—no doubt Robertson was all these things and more, but a fuller appreciation of his work will require a more integrated and comprehensive approach than anyone has yet attempted.

II. Manuscripts

Researching the personal papers of the Moderate literati of Edinburgh entailed a number of special problems. Blair, Ferguson, and Robertson deliberately destroyed most of their private papers late in life (Fagg, 325; John Hill, *An Account of the Life and Writings of Hugh Blair* [Edinburgh, 1807], 5; *WWR,* 8:v); a collection of John Home's papers seems to have disappeared since the mid-nineteenth century; and attempts to gain access to a privately owned collection of Alexander Carlyle's papers proved unsuccessful. Nevertheless, many important manuscript materials remain extant and accessible, mostly in the form of correspondence scattered throughout Great Britain and America. What follows is not a complete list of those materials but a survey of major collections and sources used in the preparation of this book.

British Library. The Egerton Papers, containing letters from Carlyle, Ferguson, and Robertson to their Anglican friend John Douglas, bishop of Carlisle (later Salisbury), are extremely useful. The correspondence of John Home and other Moderates with Charles Jenkinson in the Liverpool Papers is mainly concerned with political affairs. The Auckland Papers feature a long and important letter from Ferguson to William Eden, later Lord Auckland. There are several useful items of correspondence from Blair and Robertson among the Hardwicke Papers.

Edinburgh University Library. The Laing Papers (La.) contain vast amounts of material relevant to this study, including much correspondence, a collection of documents concerning the Carlyle libel case during the *Douglas* controversy of 1757, and the papers of Robert Wallace. Other useful sources include the minutes of the senatus academicus of Edinburgh University, seventy-two letters from Ferguson to Sir John Macpherson, one hundred fifty-six letters to Carlyle from Ferguson and others, minutes of the Poker Club for the years 1774–1784, a collection of Carlyle's poems, Ferguson's unpublished essays and lecture notes, and numerous other sets of lecture notes from the classes of Blair and other Edinburgh professors. A major source for the history of the university is the collection of papers of the late Professor D. B. Horn, which includes transcriptions of town council minutes relating to university affairs from 1718 to 1818.

Glasgow University Library. Besides a small amount of relevant correspondence, this library contains an account book and autobiographical notes by Alexander Caryle that were brought to my attention by David Raynor.

Historical Society of Pennsylvania, Philadelphia. More than a dozen letters from the subjects of this study are housed here, including some interesting ones to the London publishers Strahan and Cadell.

Huntington Library, San Marino, California. The papers of Elizabeth Montagu contain eight letters from Blair and Robertson, and other correspondence from the Moderate literati is scattered through the collection.

Hyde Collection, Somerville, New Jersey. A dozen letters from the Moderate literati of Edinburgh are here, as catalogued in volume 3 of *The R. B. Adam Library Relating to Dr. Samuel Johnson and His Era* (London, 1929).

Mount Stuart, Isle of Bute. The correspondence of the third earl of Bute contains many letters by and about the Moderate literati and their friends, including James MacPherson, and is particularly rich with letters from John Home. Most of this correspondence has been catalogued by the National Register of Archives (Scotland) in survey no. 631, but uncatalogued items were produced for my use by the Bute family archivist, Miss Catherine Armet. Other materials were brought to my attention by Miss Armet or Alexander Murdoch from among the papers of Bute's brother James Stuart Mackenzie and the Bute Papers at Dumfries House. Still another collection of Bute correspondence—identifiable by the prefix "Cdf."—was at Cardiff Public Library in Wales when I examined it in 1974 but has since been transferred to Mount Stuart.

National Library of Scotland. This outstanding library houses by far the best manuscript sources for the study of the Moderate literati and the Scottish Enlightenment. The most important for the writing of this book were the papers of Andrew Fletcher, Lord Milton (Saltoun Papers) and Sir Gilbert Elliot, third baronet of Minto (Minto Papers). Most of the correspondence of another man of affairs connected with the Moderates, William Mure of Caldwell, was published in the nineteenth century, but the originals are worth consulting due to numerous errors and omissions in the printed text. The Robertson-Macdonald Papers contain dozens of letters to William Robertson, along with other personal papers, but this correspondence has apparently been edited for posterity to hide almost all traces of the tough academic administrator and ecclesiastical politician that Robertson could be. The papers of Alexander Caryle's protégé John Lee include copies of Carlyle's religious writings, militia letters for the press, private correspondence, and memoirs. There are several letters from Blair and Robertson to Sir David Dalrymple, Lord Hailes in the Newhailes Papers, most of which are also available on microfilm at the University of Virginia Library. A valuable source for appreciating the active club life in which the Moderate literati participated is the set of Select Society minutes located among the Advocates Manuscripts. Hundreds of other relevant items are scattered throughout this library's fine manuscript collection.

New College Library, Edinburgh. There are a few letters from William Robertson here as well as an assortment of papers of other ministers, such as David Plenderleath, Patrick Cuming, and John Bonar.

Public Record Office. A considerable number of letters and other materials dealing with Scottish ecclesiastical affairs were found among the state and home office papers. Some of these items have been published in the *Calendar of Home Office Papers of the Reign of George III*, vols. 1–4 (1760–1775) (London, 1878).

Royal Society of Edinburgh. The papers of David Hume contain many unpublished letters from the Scottish literati including fourteen from Hugh Blair, and all have been neatly catalogued and summarized in J. Y. T. Greig and Harold Beynon, "Calendar of Hume MSS in the Possession of the Royal Society of Edinburgh," *Proceedings of the Royal Society of Edinburgh* 52 (1931–1932): 3–138.

Scottish Record Office. The papers of the Church of Scotland constitute a valuable resource that has yet to be utilized fully by ecclesiastical and social historians. Correspondence by and about the Moderate literati is in the Clerk of Penicuik Muniments, Dalhousie Muniments, Seafield Muniments, and the letter books of the bookseller/publisher William Creech in the Dalguise Muniments. Volumes 6 and 7 of the letter books of Robert Dundas, Lord Arniston the younger, contain several items of correspondence with William Robertson that were examined on microfilm at West Register House.

William L. Clements Library, University of Michigan. The Townshend Papers (formerly among the Buccleuch Muniments at the Scottish Record Office, where I examined them) include letters from Carlyle, Robertson, and Lord Elibank that proved to be the most important single source for appreciating the intensity of the Scots militia agitation of 1759–1760. Some additional materials relating to the Moderate literati were found among other collections here.

William R. Perkins Library, Duke University. Thirteen letters by William Robertson, mostly to Andrew Strahan concerning publishing matters, are housed in a separate collection.

Yale University Library. The Boswell Papers contain a number of interesting, and as yet unpublished, letters from Blair to Boswell and from James Macpherson to George Lawrie of Loudon.

III. Eighteenth-Century Scotland and the Scottish Enlightenment

The first great age in the historiography of eighteenth-century Scotland was the remarkable decade and a half before World War I, when Henry Grey Graham, William Law Mathieson, Henry W. Meikle, John H. Millar, John Rae, William Robert Scott, and others produced a number of important works that remained unrivaled for decades. Among them were several notable books of a general nature: Graham's *Social Life of Scotland in the Eighteenth Century* (1899; reprint, New York, 1971) and *Scottish Men of Letters in the Eighteenth Century* (London, 1901 and 1908); Millar's *Literary History of Scotland* (London, 1903) and *Scottish Prose of the Seventeenth and Eighteenth Centuries* (Glasgow, 1912); and broadest and most influential of all, Mathieson's *The Awakening of Scotland: A History from 1747 to 1797* (Glasgow, 1910)—the first attempt at a comprehensive presentation of the now hackneyed idea that Scotland underwent an extraordinary period of development in almost every sphere of life after the '45 rebellion. In the second major wave of eighteenth-century historiography during the 1960s, these pioneering books finally began to be replaced by new and better ones. Graham's social history was superseded by T. C. Smout's outstanding *History of the Scottish People, 1560–1830* (London, 1969) while Mathieson gave way to William Ferguson, *Scotland: 1689 to the Present* (Edinburgh, 1968). The economic history of the period was comprehensively treated for the first time, dryly but thoroughly in Henry Hamilton, *An Economic History of Scotland in the Eighteenth Century* (Oxford, 1963), and more readably in part 1 of R. H. Campbell, *Scotland since 1707: The Rise of an Industrial Society* (Oxford, 1965). Complementing these surveys were growing numbers of specialized studies in philosophy, sociology, literature, science, and other disciplines as well as a seminal collection of essays edited by N. T. Phillipson and Rosalind Mitchison, *Scotland in the Age of Improvement* (Edinburgh, 1970).

The works just cited are still among the best general introductions to eighteenth-century Scotland, but they may now be supplemented with more recent ones. Rosalind Mitchison, *Lordship to Patronage: Scotland 1603–1745* (London, 1983) and Bruce Lenman, *Integration,*

Enlightenment, and Industrialization: Scotland 1746–1832 (London, 1981), though not displacing William Ferguson and T. C. Smout's books as the standard surveys of eighteenth-century Scotland, incorporate much recent scholarship and contain useful bibliographical essays that complement those of Ferguson and Smout. None of these surveys, however, is at its best on intellectual and cultural matters. Introductory essays on various aspects of eighteenth-century Scotland may be found in a lovely pictorial book by Harold Orel et al., *The Scottish World: History and Culture of Scotland* (New York, 1981). There are several recent collections of interdisciplinary essays covering this period, including R. H. Campbell and Andrew S. Skinner, eds., *The Origins and Nature of the Scottish Enlightenment* (Edinburgh, 1982); John Dwyer et al., eds., *New Perspectives on the Politics and Culture of Early Modern Scotland* (Edinburgh, 1982); Istvan Hont and Michael Ignatieff, eds., *Wealth and Virtue: The Shaping of Political Economy in the Scottish Enlightenment* (Cambridge, 1983); Michèle S. Plaisant, ed., *Regards sur l'Ecosse au XVIIIe siècle* (Lille, 1977); and T. C. Smout, ed., *Scotland and Europe* (Edinburgh, 1984).

The most up-to-date assessment of the Scottish economy in the age of the Enlightenment is an article by T. C. Smout in *WV*, 45–72. Smout's well-documented conclusion that Scottish economic growth in the third quarter of the eighteenth century was perceptible though decidedly unspectacular is not revolutionary, but it is important for understanding the context of the Scottish Enlightenment. So is R. H. Campbell, "The Enlightenment and the Economy," in *ONSE*, 8–27, which warns against exaggerating the correspondence between the Enlightenment and economic improvement. Thanks to Campbell, Smout, T. M. Devine, and others, the study of eighteenth-century Scottish economic history has experienced its own "take-off" recently. One indication is the appearance of a worthy new journal with good coverage of this period: *Scottish Economic and Social History.* Another is the sudden proliferation of monographs on nearly every kind of industry and institution, including T. M. Devine's examination of the lucrative Glasgow tobacco trade, *The Tobacco Lords* (Edinburgh, 1974); Alastair Durie's *The Scottish Linen Industry in the Eighteenth Century* (Edinburgh, 1979); Enid Gauldie's charming *The Scottish Country Miller, 1700–1900* (Edinburgh, 1981) and its technological companion, J. P. Shaw's *Water Power in Scotland, 1550–1870* (Edinburgh, 1983); and Charles Munn's *The Scottish Provincial Banking Companies, 1747–1864* (Edinburgh, 1981), which takes its place alongside S. G. Checkland's substantial survey, *Scottish Banking: A History, 1695–1973* (Glasgow, 1975). Together with a few older works such as R. H. Campbell's pioneering study of Scotland's first major iron firm, *Car-*

ron Company (Edinburgh, 1961), these specialized monographs are a boon to the discipline and a credit to the dedicated publishing house responsible for most of them, John Donald, Ltd., of Edinburgh.

Still another sign of vitality in this field is the explosion of scholarly essays on a variety of topics, many of which have been conveniently collected in volumes such as L. M. Cullen and T. C. Smout, eds., *Comparative Aspects of Scottish and Irish Economic and Social History, 1600–1900* (Edinburgh, 1977); T. M. Devine and David Dickson, eds., *Ireland and Scotland, 1600–1850* (Edinburgh, 1983); John Butt and J. T. Ward, eds., *Scottish Themes* (Edinburgh, 1976); and T. M. Devine, ed., *Lairds and Improvement in the Scotland of the Enlightenment* (Glasgow, 1978). Though the last of these volumes is disappointing, its subject has been well covered elsewhere: see especially T. C. Smout's article in *Journal of Political Economy* 11 (1964): 218–34; R. H. Campbell's essay in the Cullen and Smout collection cited above, 104–15; Rosalind Mitchison's studies of a prominent improver and editor of the indispensable *Statistical Account of Scotland* in *Agricultural Sir John* (London, 1962), of the communal responsibilities of landowners in *British Journal for Eighteenth-Century Studies* 1 (1974): 41–45, and of the poor law in *Past and Present* 63 (1974): 58–93 (and the exchange on that subject in the next volume of the same journal, 113–21, with R. A. Cage, author of *The Scottish Poor Law, 1745–1845* [Edinburgh, 1981]); Malcolm Gray's classic, though misleadingly titled, essay, "Scottish Emigration: The Social Impact of Agrarian Change in the Rural Lowlands, 1775–1875," *Perspectives in American History* 7 (1973): 95–174, and later variations on that study; E. J. Hobsbawm's "Scottish Reformers of the Eighteenth Century and Capitalist Agriculture," in Hobsbawm et al., *Peasants in History* (Calcutta, 1980), 3–29 (first published in French in *Annales* in 1978), which works better as intellectual history than as social history; and Michael Ignatieff's insightful critique of Hobsbawm in *People's History and Social Theory*, ed. Raphael Samuel (London, 1981), 130–35. The considerable contributions of historical geographers may be found in the concluding chapters of Robert A. Dodgshon, *Land and Society in Early Scotland* (Oxford, 1981); David Turnock, *The Historical Geography of Scotland since 1707* (Cambridge, 1982), chaps. 3–6; an article by Ian D. Whyte in *SHR* 60 (1981): 1–13; and various essays by Dodgshon, Timperley, Whittington, and others in some of the collections cited above and in *The Making of the Scottish Countryside*, ed. M. L. Parry and T. L. Slater (London, 1980) and *An Historical Geography of Scotland*, ed. G. Whittington and I. D. Whyte (London, 1983), which contains good topical bibliographies. An article by H. Jones in the last-named volume surveys demographic developments since 1600, but the fundamental study of eighteenth-century demography is part 4 of *Scottish Population History*, ed. Michael Flinn (Cambridge, 1977).

Whereas economic history and historical geography have been thriving, the same cannot be said of topics in social history that do not fit easily into those disciplines, such as childhood, sexuality, women, and the family. See, however, Craig Beveridge, "Childhood and Society in Eighteenth-Century Scotland," in *NP*, 265–90; Norah Smith, "Sexual Mores and Attitudes in Enlightenment Scotland," in *Sexuality in Eighteenth-Century Britain*, ed. Paul-Gabriel Boucé (Manchester, 1982), 47–73; part 3 of Rosalind K. Marshall, *Virgins and Viragos: A History of Women in Scotland from 1080 to 1980* (London, 1983), which complements the same author's exhibition catalogue *Women in Scotland, 1660–1780* (Edinburgh, 1979); and an interesting essay now being prepared for publication by John Dwyer on perceptions of "youth" in the late eighteenth century. The neglect of family history is particularly unfortunate in light of the special importance of kinship in Scottish history, and particularly conspicious in light of the quantity and quality of recent research in this field by social historians of eighteenth-century America, England, and Europe. At the moment one must still rely on old-fashioned studies of Scottish "domestic life" by Marion Lochhead and Marjorie Plant. Ian Donnachie, "Drink and Society, 1750–1850," *Scottish Labour History Society Journal*, no. 13 (1979): 5–22, provides an interesting but all too brief look at the social side of a topic studied from an economic and technical perspective in works such as Donnachie's *History of the Brewing Industry in Scotland* (Edinburgh, 1979) and Michael S. Moss and John R. Hume, *The Making of Whiskey* (Ashburton, 1981). A very different sort of social question that has received too little scholarly attention is introduced in C. Duncan Rice's articles "Controversies over Slavery in Eighteenth- and Nineteenth-Century Scotland," in *Antislavery Reconsidered: New Perspectives on the Absolutionists*, ed. Lewis Perry and Michael Fellman (Baton Rouge, La., 1979), 24–48, and "Archibald Dalzel, the Scottish Intelligentsia and the Problem of Slavery," *SHR* 62 (1983): 121–36.

Though a comprehensive history of eighteenth-century Scottish politics and administration remains to be written, recent books and doctoral theses have changed the face of this field. Most of these new works focus on "high" politics or management, which invariably raises the complex question of Scotland's relationship with England. The pre-Union status of that relationship is examined from a Scottish point of view in William Ferguson, *Scotland's Relations with England: A Summary to 1707* (Edinburgh, 1977). The period from William to Walpole is dominated by three well-documented monographs by P.W.J.

Riley: *King William and the Scottish Politicians* (Edinburgh, 1979), *The Union of England and Scotland* (Manchester, 1979), and *The English Ministers and Scotland, 1707–1727* (London, 1964). Continuing the story are several doctoral dissertations, including M. S. Bricke, "Management and Administration of Scotland, 1707–1765" (University of Kansas, 1972); Richard Scott, "The Politics and Administration of Scotland, 1725–1748" (Edinburgh University, 1982); and Eric G. Wehrli, Jr., "Scottish Politics in the Age of Walpole" (University of Chicago, 1983), as well as John Simpson's perceptive essay, "Who Steered the Gravy Train, 1707–1766?" in *SAI*, 47–72, and John Stuart Shaw, *The Management of Scottish Society, 1707–1764* (Edinburgh, 1983), which is most useful for the period before the '45. For the 1750s and 1760s, Alexander Murdoch, *"The People Above": Politics and Administration in Mid-Eighteenth-Century Scotland* (Edinburgh, 1980) is unrivaled. Unfortunately, no scholarship of this quality has been published on the latter part of the century. Even the turbulent 1790s have been under-researched, despite Henry W. Meikle's classic *Scotland and the French Revolution* (1912; reprint, London, 1969). But there is now John Brims, "The Scottish Democratic Movement in the Age of the French Revolution" (Ph.D. diss., Edinburgh University, 1983).

Scottish historiography has sometimes been criticized for being overly biographical and political, yet curiously enough there are few decent biographies of eighteenth-century Scottish politicians. Even the dominant political force of the century, Ilay, third duke of Argyll, must be studied piecemeal, using the works just mentioned by Bricke, Murdoch, Riley, Scott, Shaw, and Wehrli for information about different aspects of his career. His elder brother John, second duke of Argyll, is the hero of Patricia Dickson, *Red John of the Battles* (London, 1973), but that study, like its subject, is more military than political and not very illuminating. The life of the duke's influential nephew John Stuart, third earl of Bute must also be pieced together with different sources, such as Murdoch's *"People Above"* for his career as a Scottish manager; James Lee McKelvey, *George III and Lord Bute: The Leicester House Years* (Durham, N.C., 1973) for the background to his role as George's favorite; articles by Karl W. Schweizer in *Albion* 13 (1981): 262–75, and elsewhere for his work as a diplomat; and various studies cited in the bibliographical note to John Brewer's biographical sketch in *The Prime Ministers*, ed. Herbert Van Thal (London, 1974), 105–13 (including of course Brewer's own excellent work) for his rise and fall at Westminster and his personal life. Most of these scholars will be represented in Schweizer's forthcoming collection, *Lord Bute: Essays in Reinterpretation* (Leicester). Bute's brother James Stuart Mackenzie remains a shadowy figure in spite of a valuable chapter on his brief stint as a Scottish manager in Murdoch's *"People Above."* There is an account of Gilbert Elliot, third baronet of Minto, by his Victorian relation George F. S. Elliot in the latter's *The Border Elliots and the Family of Minto* (Edinburgh, 1897), but a full-scale modern biography is called for now that the Minto Papers have become accessible. The same may be said of Andrew Fletcher, Lord Milton, whose importance both as Argyll's subminister and as his own man is demonstrated by John Shaw in his book cited above. On Scotland's leading politician of the late eighteenth century, Henry Dundas, see the standard but by no means fully satisfactory biographies by Holden Furber (Oxford, 1931) and Cyril Matheson (London, 1933) and the fresh interpretation suggested by John Dwyer and Alexander Murdoch in "Paradigms and Politics: Manners, Morals and the Rise of Henry Dundas, 1770–1784," in *NP*, 210–48. Alexander Fergusson, *The Honourable Henry Erskine* (Edinburgh, 1882) is now barely adequate for the life of Dundas's chief Scottish rival, and Christina Bewley, *Muir of Huntershill* (London, 1981) does not do all it might have to show the significance of Scotland's best-known radical of the 1790s and his milieu.

For Scottish members of the House of Commons, there are brief but useful biographical sketches in the two volumes of the *History of Parliament: The House of Commons* covering the years 1715 to 1754, edited by Romney Sedgwick (London 1970) and in the three volumes edited by Sir Lewis Namier and John Brooke on the years 1745 to 1790 (London, 1964). The traditional view of the Scottish representative peers as government lackeys has now been modified somewhat in Michael W. McCahill, "The Scottish Peerage and the House of Lords in the Late Eighteenth Century," *SHR* 51 (1972): 177–96; William C. Lowe, "Bishops and Scottish Representative Peers in the House of Lords, 1760–1775," *Journal of British Studies* 18 (1978): 86–106; and an article by G. M. Ditchfield in *SHR* 60 (1981):14–31. The best, indeed the only, general study of electoral politics is William Ferguson's doctoral thesis, "Electoral Law and Procedure in Eighteenth and Early Nineteenth Century Scotland" (Edinburgh University, 1957). Various studies of electoral politics in particular burghs and shires by W. L. Burn, Sir James Fergusson, William Ferguson, and R. M. Sunter are cited in the thorough bibliography appended to Murdoch's *"People Above."* Frank Brady, *Boswell's Political Career* (New Haven, 1965) is another kind of electoral case study, showing the problems and frustrations of playing at politics at this time. County government and administration have traditionally been ignored except insofar as they could be related to electoral politics, but there is now Ann E. Whetstone, *Scottish County Government in the Eighteenth and*

Nineteenth Centuries (Edinburgh, 1981), which focuses on the functions of sheriffs, justices of the peace, lords lieutenant, and commissioners of supply in maintaining order in the countryside. Although more research is needed on the manner in which eighteenth-century burghs and shires alike fought the most serious threats to such order arising from problems like food shortages, poor sanitation, epidemics, and widespread poverty, a pioneering effort along these lines is Thomas Ferguson, *The Dawn of Scottish Social Welfare* (London, 1948).

On the political situation in Edinburgh during the age of the Enlightenment, see Alexander Murdoch's excellent article, "The Importance of Being Edinburgh: Management and Opposition in Edinburgh Politics, 1746–1784," *SHR* 62 (1983): 1–16, and Richard B. Sher, "Moderates, Managers and Popular Politics in Mid-Eighteenth-Century Edinburgh: The Drysdale 'Bustle' of the 1760s," in *NP*, 179–209. The life of the foremost Edinburgh magistrate of the century is sketched in William Baird, "George Drummond," *Book of the Old Edinburgh Club* 4 (1911): 1–54, and T. C. Smout, *Provost Drummond* (Edinburgh, Town and Gown Lecture, 1978), but a fuller biography of Drummond is needed. The best source for general information about the institutional structure of Edinburgh remains Hugh Arnot, *The History of Edinburgh* (Edinburgh, 1779), which may be supplemented with other works cited in *Edinburgh, 1767–1967: A Select List of Books* (Edinburgh, 1967). Cultural life is surveyed in David Daiches, *Edinburgh* (London, 1978) and Douglas Young, *Edinburgh in the Age of Sir Walter Scott* (Norman, Okla., 1965). An excellent study of the building of the New Town is A. J. Youngson, *The Making of Classical Edinburgh* (Edinburgh, 1966), which may be fruitfully read along with Youngson's "The City of Reason and Nature," in Young et al., *Edinburgh in the Age of Reason*, 15–22; J. Wreford Watson, "Adam Smith, *Wealth of Nations*, and the Edinburgh New Town," in a volume of *Proceedings and Transactions of the Royal Society of Canada* devoted to the Scottish Enlightenment, 4th ser., 14 (1976): 240–54; and Peter Reed, "Form and Context: A Study of Georgian Edinburgh," in *Order in Space and Society: Architectural Form and Its Context in the Scottish Enlightenment*, ed. Thomas A. Markus (Edinburgh, 1982), 115–53, which also contains Markus's fascinating essay, "Buildings for the Sad, the Bad and the Mad in Urban Scotland, 1780–1830," 25–114, and an illuminating piece by Frank Arneil Walker on the making of Glasgow, 155–99. The development of eighteenth-century Scotland's second city is also treated from a cultural point of view in David Daiches, *Glasgow* (London, 1977) and from an economic point of view in Andrew Gibb, *Glasgow: The Making of a City* (London, 1983). I know of nothing comparable for Aberdeen, though some of the same ground is covered in a thin pamphlet called *Polite Society in Aberdeen in the Eighteenth Century* (Aberdeen, 1980); part 4 of Alexander Keith, *A Thousand Years of Aberdeen* (Aberdeen, 1972); and T. Donnelly's article on the Aberdeen Merchant Guild in *Scottish Economic and Social History* 1(1981): 25–41. Other recent studies of urban economic and social life include T. M. Devine's essays on eighteenth-century merchants in *SHR* 58 (1978): 40–67, *ONSE*, 26–41, and Devine and Dickson, *Ireland and Scotland*, 163–76, and A. Dickson and W. Speirs's article on the changing social structure of industrializing Paisley in *SHR* 59 (1980): 54–72. There is more on eighteenth-century Scottish towns in I. H. Adams, *The Making of Urban Scotland* (London, 1978); Colin McWilliam, *Scottish Townscape* (London, 1975); and essays on planned villages by D. G. Lockhart (in Devine and Dickson, *Ireland and Scotland*, 132–45) and T. C. Smout (in *SAI*, 73–106).

Scholarship on Jacobitism has finally begun to transcend its romantic infatuation with Bonnie Prince Charlie: see the concise bibliographical essay by F. J. McLynn in *History Today* 33 (1983): 45–47, for discussion of the most important books and controversies. Bruce Lenman, *The Jacobite Risings in Britain, 1689–1746* (London, 1980) is the best survey. The leading role of nonjuring Episcopalians in Scottish Jacobitism is stressed in D. H. Whiteford, "Reactions to Jacobitism in Scottish Ecclesiastical Thought, 1690–1760" (Ph.D. diss., Edinburgh University, 1965), the same author's articles in *RSCHS* 16 (1967 and 1968): 129–49, 185–201, and Bruce Lenman, "The Scottish Episcopalian Clergy and the Ideology of Jacobitism," in *Ideology and Conspiracy: Aspects of Jacobitism, 1689–1759*, ed. Eveline Cruickshanks (Edinburgh, 1982), 36–48—a volume that also includes a suggestive essay on Jacobite rhetoric by Howard Erskine-Hill. For the '45 specifically, McLynn's bibliography cites valuable books on special subjects by Cruickshanks, W. A. Speck, and McLynn himself, among others; and McLynn's article in *EC* 23 (1982): 97–133, neatly enumerates the major reasons for supporting the Jacobite cause in that rebellion. Annette M. Smith, *Jacobite Estates of the Forty-Five* (Edinburgh, 1982) gives a thorough treatment to one of the thorniest problems generated by the uprising. The general impact of the '45 on the Highlands is addressed in A. J. Youngson, *After the Forty-Five* (Edinburgh, 1973) and Malcolm Gray, *The Highland Economy, 1750–1850* (Edinburgh, 1957). Among more specialized works on the late-eighteenth-century transformation of the Highlands are three recent studies of social and demographic change: J. M. Bumsted, *The People's Clearance: Highland Emigration to British North America, 1770–1815* (Edinburgh, 1982); T. M. Devine, "Highland Migration to Lowland Scotland, 1760–1800," *SHR* 62 (1983): 137–49; and most important Eric Richards, *A History of the Highland Clearances* (London, 1982); two recent studies of linguistic and educational change: Victor Edward Durkacz, *The Decline of the Celtic Languages* (Edinburgh, 1983) and Charles W. J. Withers, *Gaelic in Scotland, 1698–1981* (Edinburgh, 1984); and one classic study of religious change: John MacInnes, *The Evangelical Movement in the Highlands of Scotland, 1688 to 1800* (Aberdeen, 1951). And then there is Hugh Trevor-Roper's stinging exposé of Highland culture as an artificial construct of the eighteenth and early nineteenth centuries, "The Invention of Tradition: The Highland Tradition of Scotland," in *The Invention of Tradition*, ed. Eric Hobsbawm and Terence Ranger (Cambridge, 1983), 15–41.

On the place of the law and legal profession in eighteenth-century culture and society, see the following by N. T. Phillipson: "Lawyers, Landowners, and the Civic Leadership of Post-Union Scotland," in *Juridical Review* (1976): 97–120 (also in *Lawyers in Their Social Setting*, ed. D. N. McCormick [Edinburgh, 1976], 171–94); "The Social Structure of the Faculty of Advocates in Scotland, 1661–1840," in *Law-making and Law-makers in British History*, ed. Alan Harding (Edinburgh, 1980), 146–56; and "The Scottish Whigs and the Reform of the Court of Session, 1785–1830" (Ph.D. diss., Cambridge Univ., 1967). See also Alexander Murdoch, "The Advocates, the Law and the Nation in Early Modern Scotland," in *Lawyers in Early Modern Europe and America*, ed. Wilfrid Prest (London, 1981), 147–63, and chapter 2 of John Shaw's *Management of Scottish Society*.

The large literature on Scottish ecclesiastical history is often parochial, partisan, outdated, or unscholarly—if not all four. Older works are listed in Malcolm B. MacGregor, *The Sources and Literature of Scottish Church History* (Glasgow, 1934). Among the most useful are a number of nineteenth-century studies that must be read with a critical eye: Sir Henry Moncreiff Wellwood, *A Brief Account of the Constitution of the Established Church* (Edinburgh, 1818, as an appendix to his life of John Erskine and 1833 as a separate publication); Nathaniel Morren, ed., *Annals of the General Assembly of the Church of Scotland, 1739–1766*, 2 vols. (Edinburgh, 1838–1840); and John Cunningham, *The Church History of Scotland*, 2 vols. (Edinburgh, 1859). More sympathetic to the Moderates is Andrew J. Campbell, *Two Centuries of the Church of Scotland, 1707–1929* (Paisley, 1930), which is not bad on the eighteenth century though shrill on the nineteenth. There is a brief chapter on the eighteenth-century kirk in J.H.S. Burleigh, *A Church History of Scotland* (London, 1960). Andrew L. Drummond and James Bulloch, *The Scottish Church, 1688–1843: The Age of the Moderates* (Edinburgh, 1973) is poorly researched and frequently unreliable. For theology, nothing has yet replaced James Walker, *Theology and Theologians of Scotland* (Edinburgh, 1872). Indispensable for any research on the Church of Scotland in this period are Hew Scott, *Fasti Ecclesiæ Scoticanæ: The Succession of Ministers in the Church of Scotland*, new ed., 7 vols. (Edinburgh, 1915–1928); the annual reports of general assembly business in the *Scots Magazine*; the unabridged *Principal Acts of the General Assembly*; and various articles in *Records of the Scottish Church History Society*. Little of value has been published on the eighteenth-century seceders since the classic, though often partisan, mid-nineteenth-century studies of MacKelvie, McKerrow, and Struthers (cited in most church history bibliographies) and A. R. Macewen's *The Erskines* (Edinburgh, 1900). The standard histories of the Scottish Episcopal church by G. Grub and F. Goldie, and of the Scottish Roman Catholic church by P. Anson and A. Bellesheim, are inadequate on the Enlightenment era, though the latter subject receives some coverage in a book by Christine Johnson mentioned later in this essay.

On the Church of Scotland in the first half of the eighteenth century, see A. Ian Dunlop, *William Carstares and the Kirk by Law Established* (Edinburgh, 1967); Stewart Mechie, "The Theological Climate in Early Eighteenth-Century Scotland," in *Reformation and Revolution*, ed. Duncan Shaw (Edinburgh, 1967), 258–72; Andrew L. Drummond, *The Kirk and the Continent* (Edinburgh, 1956); Arthur Fawcett, *The Cambuslang Revival: The Scottish Evangelical Revival of the Eighteenth Century* (London, 1971); and Robert Wodrow's *Analecta*, 4 vols. (Edinburgh, 1842–1843). The kirk's liberal element that Wodrow so dreaded is the subject of Henry R. Sefton, "The Early Development of Moderatism in the Church of Scotland" (Ph.D. diss., Glasgow University, 1962) and articles based on that study in *RSCHS* 16 (1969): 1–22, and 19 (1977): 203–16, and in *Church, Politics and Society: Scotland 1408–1929*, ed. Norman Macdougall (Edinburgh, 1983), 186–96. An essay in the last-named volume by Richard Sher and Alexander Murdoch, "Patronage and Party in the Church of Scotland, 1750–1800," 197–220, attempts to reassess the central issue dividing the Moderate and Popular parties in the age of the Enlightenment. Ian D. L. Clark, "From Protest to Reaction: The Moderate Regime in the Church of Scotland, 1752–1805," in *SAI*, 200–24, is a superb condensation of, but no substitute for, his excellent doctoral thesis, "Moderatism and the Moderate Party, 1752–1805" (Cambridge University, 1964). More specialized studies of the Moderates of this period include Sher, "Moderates, Managers and Popular Politics" and John Dwyer, "The Heavenly City of the Eighteenth-Century Moderates," both in *NP*, 179–209, 291–318. Among the few useful biographies of Moderate leaders other than the subjects of this book are George Cook, *The Life of the Late George Hill* (Edinburgh, 1820) and Andrew Dalzel, "Account of the Life of Rev. John Drysdale," in *TRSE* 3 (1794), app. 2: 37–53. Since virtually nothing has been written about the Popular party as such, it is necessary to study it through the generally unsatisfactory surveys of ecclesiastical history cited above or through biographies of some of its leaders, especially Sir Henry Moncreiff Wellwood's essential *Account of the Life and Writings of John Erskine* (Edinburgh, 1818); William Oliver Brackett, "John Witherspoon: His Scottish Ministry" (Ph.D. diss., Edinburgh University, 1935); Varnum Lansing Collins, *President Witherspoon*, 2 vols. (Princeton, 1925); Samuel Miller, *Memoir of the Rev. Charles Nisbet* (New York, 1840), which, like Collins's biography of Witherspoon, is better on its subject's life in America than in Scotland; and Hugh Watt, "Robert Walker of the High Church," *RSCHS* 12 (1958): 82–96.

General studies of Scottish universities in this period include Roger L. Emerson, "Scottish Universities in the Eighteenth Century, 1690–1800," *SVEC* 167 (1977): 453–74; Ronald G. Cant, "The Scottish Universities and Scottish Society in the Eighteenth Century," *SVEC* 58 (1967): 1953–66, and "Origins of the Enlightenment in Scotland: the Universities," in *ONSE*, 42–64; the chapters on the Scottish universities in Anand Chitnis's and Douglas Sloan's books mentioned below; Alexander Morgan, *Scottish University Studies* (London, 1932); and George Elder Davie's pioneering work, *The Democratic Intellect: Scotland and Her Universities in the Nineteenth Century* (Edinburgh, 1961).

On the University of Edinburgh specifically, the standard accounts remain Alexander Bower, *The History of the University of Edinburgh*, 3 vols. (Edinburgh, 1817) and Sir Alexander Grant, *The Story of the University of Edinburgh*, 2 vols. (London, 1844)—both of which must be used with care—and D. B. Horn's more reliable but briefer *Short History of the University of Edinburgh, 1556–1889* (Edinburgh, 1967). Selections from town council minutes relating to the university are printed in Andrew Dalzel, *History of the University of Edinburgh*, 2 vols. (Edinbrugh, 1862) and Alexander Morgan, ed., *Charters, Statutes and Acts of the Town Council and Senatus, 1583–1858* (Edinburgh, 1937), and lists of M.A. degrees and the succession of principles and professors may be found in *A Catalogue of the Graduates . . . of the University of Edinburgh*, ed. David Laing (Edinburgh, 1858). For descriptions of the courses taught by Edinburgh professors, see the "Short Account" by Robert Henderson in *SM* 3 (August 1741): 371–74, and the different editions of Arnot's *History of Edinburgh*.

There is now a sizable literature on particular aspects of Edinburgh University in the eighteenth century. Useful background material may be found in Isabel Kenrick, "The University of Edinburgh, 1660–1715: A Study in the Transformation of Teaching Methods and Curriculum" (Ph.D. diss., Bryn Mawr College, 1956) and Christine M. Shepherd, "Newtonianism in Scottish Universities in the Seventeenth Century," in *ONSE*, 65–85, and "The Inter-relationship between the Library and Teaching in the Seventeenth and Eighteenth Centuries," in *Edinburgh University Library, 1580–1980*, ed. Jean R. Guild and Alexander Law (Edinburgh, 1982), 67–86 (the same volume contains a good historical sketch of the library itself by C. P. Finlayson and S. M. Simpson). On the Edinburgh chair of moral philosophy, see Douglas Nobbs, "The Political Ideas of William Cleghorn, Hume's Academic Rival," *JHI* 26 (1965): 575–86; Nicholas Phillipson, "The Pursuit of Virtue in Scottish University Education: Dugald Stewart and Scottish Moral Philosophy," in *Universities, Society and the Future*, ed. Nicholas Phillipson (Edinburgh, 1983), 82–101; and M. A. Stewart, "Hume, Wishart and the Edinburgh Chair," *Journal of the History of Philosophy*, forthcoming. Other arts and divinity chairs and professors are discussed in Henry W. Meikle, "The Chair of Rhetoric and Belles Lettres in the University of Edinburgh," *University of Edinburgh Journal* 13 (1945): 89–103; D. B. Horn, "The University of Edinburgh and the Teaching of History," ibid., 17 (1954): 161–72; L. W. Sharp, "Charles Mackie, the First Professor of History at Edinburgh University, *SHR* 41 (1962): 23–45; Cosmo Innes's account of the life of Andrew Dalzel prefixed to the latter's *History of the University of Edinburgh*; and Jeremy J. Cater, "James Robertson, 1720–1795: An Anti-Enlightenment Professor in the University of Edinburgh" (Ph.D. diss., New York University, 1976).

Edinburgh scientific and medical education is particularly well documented, though much remains to be done. The origins of the medical school, like so much else at Edinburgh University during this period, must be sought in the Dutch connection discussed by some of the contributors to *The Early Years of the Edinburgh Medical School*, ed. R. G. W. Anderson and A. D. C. Simpson (Edinburgh, 1976). There is an introductory treatment of the rise of the medical school in chapter 4 of David Hamilton, *The Healers: A History of Medicine in Scotland* (Edinburgh, 1981) and a more scholarly account in a recent Edinburgh University doctoral thesis by Rosalie Stott. The contributions of particular professors of medicine are discussed in R. K. French, *Robert Whytt, the Soul, and Medicine* (London, 1969); Roy E. Wright-St. Clair, *Doctors Monro* (London, 1964); and articles in specialist journals like *Medical History*. A. Logan Turner's study of the Royal Infirmary of Edinburgh, *The Story of a Great Hospital* (Edinburgh, 1937) and W. S. Craig's massive *History of the Royal College of*

Physicians of Edinburgh (Oxford, 1976) are part of a large literature on related institutions. There is more on the institutional foundations of science and medicine in Anand Chitnis's *Scottish Enlightenment*; the same author's slight essay, "Provost Drummond and the Origins of Edinburgh Medicine," in *ONSE*, 86–97; and several important articles by J. B. Morrell, including "The Edinburgh Town Council and Its University, 1717–1766," in the Anderson and Simpson volume cited above, 46–65; "The University of Edinburgh in the Late Eighteenth Century: Its Scientific Eminence and Academic Structure," *Isis* 62 (1971): 158–71; and "The Leslie Affair: Careers, Kirk and Politics in Edinburgh in 1805," *SHR* 54 (1975): 63–82, which complements other articles on that incident by Ian D. L. Clark in *RSCHS* 14 (1963): 179–97, and by John G. Burke in *Isis* 61 (1970): 340–54.

One of the critical links between medicine and science in the Scottish universities of the Enlightenment was chemistry, particularly as practiced by the protagonists of A. L. Donovan's *Philosophical Chemistry in the Scottish Enlightenment: The Doctrines and Discoveries of William Cullen and Joseph Black* (Edinburgh, 1975), which has a good bibliography. On the chemistry chair at Glasgow University, and Glasgow science education generally, see Andrew Kent, ed., *An Eighteenth-Century Lectureship in Chemistry* (Glasgow, 1950) and Peter Swinbank, "Experimental Science in the University of Glasgow at the Time of Joseph Black," in *Joseph Black, 1728–1799: A Commemorative Symposium*, ed. A. D. C. Simpson (Edinburgh, 1982), 23–35, which includes other useful essays. In a companion volume R. G. W. Anderson looks at the chemistry chair at Edinburgh: *The Playfair Collection and the Teaching of Chemistry at the University of Edinburgh, 1713–1858* (Edinburgh, 1978).

Outside of scientific education at Glasgow, scholarship on Scotland's four other universities is scarce by comparison with Edinburgh. Glasgow and St. Andrews have been competently handled in general surveys—James Coutts, *A History of the University of Glasgow* (Glasgow, 1909) and J. D. Mackie, *The University of Glasgow, 1451–1951: A Short History* (Glasgow, 1954) for the former, and R. G. Cant, *The University of St. Andrews: A Short History*, 2d ed. (Edinburgh, 1970) for the latter. But none of these works provides really thorough coverage of the eighteenth century, and there is not even a decent introductory survey of this kind on King's and Marischal Colleges at Aberdeen. Though a perusal of back issues of the *Aberdeen University Review* will yield a number of interesting articles, such as E. H. King's on James Beattie as a professor (44 [1971]: 174–85) and Bruce Lenman and J. Kenworthy's on Dr. David Skene (47 [1977]: 32–44), academic life in eighteenth-century Aberdeen remains seriously underresearched in every respect.

More attention has been devoted to the sociology of Scottish education. The backgrounds and careers of Glasgow University graduates are analyzed in W. M. Mathew, "The Origins and Occupations of Glasgow Students, 1740–1839," *Past and Present* 33 (1966): 74–94, and the "geographical provinces" of the Scottish universities are discussed in an essay by Robert Noyes Smart in *The Scottish Tradition*, ed. G. W. S. Barrow (Edinburgh, 1974), 91–106. Vern and Bonnie Bullough have produced several rather simplistic studies on statistical correlations between education and prominence in eighteenth-century Scottish intellectual life, the most accessible being "Intellectual Achievers: A Study of Eighteenth-Century Scotland," *American Journal of Sociology* 76 (1971): 1048–63, and a similar study in *British Journal of Sociology* 24 (1973): 418–30. More work of this kind has been done by the sociologist Charles Camic: "Experience and Ideas: Education for Universalism in Eighteenth-Century Scotland," *Comparative Studies in Society and History* 25 (1983): 50–82, and *Experience and Enlightenment: Socialization for Cultural Change in Eighteenth-Century Scotland* (Chicago, 1983). esp. chaps. 5 and 6. Robert Houston, "The Literacy Myth? Illiteracy in Scotland, 1630–1730," *Past and Present* 96 (1982): 81–102, questions the traditional belief in the existence of widespread literacy in early modern Scotland, but an article by T. C. Smout in the next issue of the same journal, 114–27, effectively qualifies Houston's qualifications by showing that most people at the Cambuslang revival of 1741 could read even if they could not write. On the general subject of Scottish schools and schooling, see Donald Withrington's excellent essay, "Education and Society in the Eighteenth Century," in *SAI*, 169–99; Alexander Law, *Education in Edinburgh in the Eighteenth Century* (Edinburgh, 1965); and James Scotland, *The History of Scottish Education*, 2 vols. (London, 1969), which contains a good bibliography of older studies in the field.

Davis D. McElroy, *Scotland's Age of Improvement: A Survey of Eighteenth-Century Literary Clubs and Societies* (Pullman, Wash., 1969) is the standard published work on its topic, though it is less comprehensive than his Edinburgh University doctoral thesis of 1952, "The Literary Clubs and Societies of Eighteenth-Century Scotland," and in some ways inferior to his "A Century of Scottish Clubs, 1700–1800" (typescript, National Library of Scotland, 1969). Edinburgh club life is placed in a comparative framework in James E. McClellan, *Science Reorganized: Scientific Societies in the Eighteenth Century* (New York, 1985) and Roger L. Emerson, "The Enlightenment and Social Structures," in *City and Society in the Eighteenth Century*, ed. Paul Fritz and David

Williams (Toronto, 1973), 99–124. Emerson has also produced several thorough studies of particular improving societies, such as "The Social Composition of Enlightened Scotland: The Select Society of Edinburgh, 1754–1764," *SVEC* 114 (1973): 291–329; "The Edinburgh Society for the Importation of Foreign Seeds and Plants, 1764–1773," *Eighteenth-Century Life* 7 (1982): 73–95; and a splendid series of three articles on the rise and fall of the Philosophical Society of Edinburgh in *British Journal for the History of Science* 12 (1979): 154–91, 14 (1981): 133–76, and 18 (1985). The last installment in that series dovetails nicely with Steven Shapin's outstanding paper on the establishment of the PSE's successor, "Property, Patronage and the Politics of Science: The Founding of the Royal Society of Edinburgh," ibid., 7 (1974): 1–14. See also Shapin, "The Royal Society of Edinburgh: A Study of the Social Context of Hanoverian Science" (Ph.D. diss., University of Pennsylvania, 1971); Neil Campbell and R. Martin S. Smellie, *The Royal Society of Edinburgh (1783–1983)* (Edinburgh, 1983); and the series of pamphlets and reference works on RSE fellows being published by Edinburgh University's History of Medicine and Science Unit under the general title *Scotland's Cultural Heritage*. Another Edinburgh scientific society of the late eighteenth century is the subject of D. E. Allen, "James Edward Smith and the Natural History Society of Edinburgh," *Journal of the Society for the Bibliography of Natural History* 8 (1978): 483–93. Specialized studies of "provincial" clubs are less plentiful, but see E. H. King's article on the Aberdeen Philosophical Society in *Dalhousie Review* 50 (1970): 201–14, for an introduction to a particularly important one.

Moving from institutions to the lives and achievements of the literati, one may still profit from Henry Grey Graham's marvelous collection of brief, yet lively and deceptively erudite, biographical sketches in *Scottish Men of Letters in the Eighteenth Century*, which has recently been reissued as part of an admirable reprint series by Garland Publishing of New York. The premier full-length biography of a Scottish literatus is Ernest Campbell Mossner, *The Life of David Hume*, 2d ed. (Oxford, 1980), which opened new vistas when first published in 1954 and still is one of the best introductions to the social world of the Scottish Enlightenment. It is unfortunate, however, that the second edition repeats so many of the little errors found in the original version. Mossner's *The Forgotten Hume* (New York, 1943) covers much of the same territory in thematic rather than chronological fashion. Two older biographies by William Robert Scott are still useful: *Francis Hutcheson: His Life, Teaching and Position in the History of Philosophy* (Cambridge, 1900) and *Adam Smith as Student and Professor* (1937; reprint, New York, 1965), which may be read along with Dugald Stewart's biography of Smith (reprinted most recently in the excellent Glasgow Edition of Smith's works); John Rae's *Life of Adam Smith* (London, 1895); C. R. Fay's *Adam Smith and the Scotland of His Day* (Cambridge, 1956); and R. H. Campbell and A. S. Skinner's brief *Adam Smith* (London, 1982). A fuller biography of Smith has been promised by Ian S. Ross, author of *Lord Kames and the Scotland of His Day* (Oxford, 1972). The latter may be supplemented with Alexander Fraser Tytler's biographical memoir of 1807; A. E. McGuinness, *Henry Home, Lord Kames* (New York, 1970); and William C. Lehmann, *Henry Home, Lord Kames, and the Scottish Enlightenment* (The Hague, 1971). An earlier intellectual biography by Lehmann treats the life and thought of *John Millar of Glasgow, 1735–1801* (Cambridge, 1960). Another important thinker from the legal profession is covered in E. L. Cloyd, *James Burnett, Lord Monboddo* (Oxford, 1972); an intellectual biography in Italian by Antonio Verri, *Lord Monboddo* (Ravenna, 1975); and an older work on Monboddo by William Knight (London, 1900). For the life of Dugald Stewart one must still resort to John Veitch's dated memoir in volume 10 of Stewart's *Collected Works* (Edinburgh, 1858). Robert Wallace, an interesting and neglected figure in the Edinburgh Enlightenment, also lacks a good biography, but a step in that direction has been taken by Norah Smith in "The Literary Career and Achievement of Robert Wallace" (Ph.D. diss., Edinburgh University, 1973).

Where the literati of Aberdeen are concerned, biographical neglect is the rule. The older lives of Thomas Reid by Dugald Stewart and A. Campbell Fraser are unsatisfactory, and no biography of Reid has appeared in this century. The story of James Beattie's life has been told in older works by Alexander Bower, Sir William Forbes, and Margaret Forbes, as well as more recently in E. H. King, *James Beattie* (New York, 1977), but there is much more to tell. I know of no adequate biographies of Thomas Blackwell, Alexander Gerard, or George Turnbull, and one must consult a pair of unpublished intellectual biographies for detailed information about two other interesting Aberdonian literati: A. R. McKay, "George Campbell: His Life and Thought" (Ph.D. diss., Edinburgh University, 1951) and Christopher J. Berry, "James Dunbar, 1742–1798" (Ph.D. diss., University of London, 1970). Eighteenth-century Aberdeen's gift to classical scholarship and Jacobite polemics is the subject of Douglas Duncan, *Thomas Ruddiman* (Edinburgh, 1965), which is a good introduction to the surviving Latin humanist culture of this period.

Among the many biographies of prominent eighteenth-century painters, architects, and literary figures, the student of the Scottish Enlightenment may particularly wish to consult John Fleming, *Robert*

Adam and His Circle (Cambridge, Mass., 1962) and Doreen Yarwood, *Robert Adam* (London, 1970); Burns Martin, *Allan Ramsay* (Cambridge, Mass., 1931) and Alastair Smart, *The Life and Art of Allan Ramsay* (London, 1952), on the poet and his son the painter, respectively; Gerard A. Barker, *Henry Mackenzie* (Boston, 1975) and Harold W. Thomson, *A Scottish Man of Feeling* (London, 1931); Frederick A. Pottle, *James Boswell: The Earlier Years, 1740–1769* (New York, 1966); Franklin Bliss Snyder, *The Life of Robert Burns* (New York, 1932), as well as David Daiches's eye-pleasing *Robert Burns and His World* (London, 1971) and the volumes on Boswell and Scott in the same series. Recent studies of Scott have stressed his strong personal and intellectual ties with the literati of the Scottish Enlightenment: see especially Graham McMaster, *Scott and Society* (Cambridge, 1981), chap. 2; Paul Henderson Scott, *Walter Scott and Scotland* (Edinburgh, 1981), chap. 6; Peter D. Garside, "Scott and the 'Philosophical' Historians," *JHI* 36 (1975): 497–512; and books on Scott and history by James Anderson and David S. Brown. The relationships of other transitional figures to the "giants" of the eighteenth century are examined in Donald Winch's essay, cited below, on Dugald Stewart and his pupils and in Esther Lynn Barazzone's intellectual biography of one of those pupils, "The Politic Philosopher: Sir James Mackintosh (1765–1832) and the Scottish Enlightenment" (Ph.D. diss., Columbia University, 1982). More work of this kind is needed, not only on the contemporaries of Scott and Mackintosh but also on Boswell, Burns, Mackenzie, the Ramsays, the Adam brothers, Smollett, and other eighteenth-century men of arts and letters whose relationships to the Scottish Enlightenment have yet to be determined.

When one turns to autobiographies, journals, and the like, nothing can match Alexander Carlyle's autobiographical memoirs for bringing the world of the Scottish Enlightenment to life, but Thomas Somerville, *My Own Life and Times, 1741–1814* (Edinburgh, 1861) is also indispensable. John Ramsay of Ochtertyre, *Scotland and Scotsmen in the Eighteenth Century*, ed. Alexander Allardyce, 2 vols. (Edinburgh, 1888), although very good on certain topics, such as the legal profession, is not the balanced and objective analysis of Scottish intellectual and cultural life that some commentators have taken it to be. Both Somerville's and Ramsay's memoirs are now being reissued, along with dozens of other important titles, in the impressive Scottish Enlightenment reprint project announced by AMS Press of New York. Interesting accounts of Edinburgh are to be found in Edward Topham, *Letters from Edinburgh* (1776; reprint, Edinburgh, 1971) and William Creech, *Edinburgh Fugitive Pieces* (Edinburgh, 1815), containing Creech's *Letters* of 1793 that are part of the AMS reprint series. *The Diary of George Ridpath,* ed. Sir James Balfour Paul (Edinburgh, 1922) provides a glimpse of the life of a relatively obscure but enlightened clergyman-historian. The observations of James Boswell in the many volumes of his journals are always entertaining and often revealing—though perhaps more frequently of Boswell himself than of his subjects. Also useful are *Memorials of the Public Life and Character of the Right Hon. James Oswald of Dunnikier* (Edinburgh, 1825) and *Selections from the Family Papers Preserved at Caldwell,* 3 vols. (Paisley, 1883–1885), which contains the valuable correspondence of Bute's agent William Mure and an illuminating memoir by Elizabeth Mure.

The closing years of the period covered by this study are particularly rich with memoirs and journals that throw light on Scottish thought and culture. These include William Adam, *The Gift of a Grandfather* and its *Sequel* (1836 and 1839); Brougham's *Life and Times;* Henry Cockburn's marvelous *Memorials of His Time* (Edinburgh, 1910); Creech's *Letters* mentioned above; John Gibson Lockhart, *Peter's Letters to His Kinfolk,* 2d ed., 3 vols. (Edinburgh, 1819); *The Anecdotes and Egotisms of Henry Mackenzie, 1745–1831,* ed. Harold William Thomson (London, 1927); and *Memoirs of the Life of the Right Honourable Sir James Mackintosh,* 2d ed., 2 vols. (London, 1836). Scottish travel literature came into its own during the second half of the eighteenth century: besides the famous accounts by Boswell and Johnson, see Robert Heron, *Observations Made in a Journey Through the Western Counties of Scotland,* 2 vols. (Perth, 1793); Thomas Pennant, *A Tour in Scotland, 1769,* 2d ed. (London, 1772), which appears in abridged form along with travel accounts by Burt and Thornton in *Beyond the Highland Line: Three Journals of Travel in Eighteenth-Century Scotland,* ed. A. J. Youngson (London, 1774); and T. C. Smout's discussion in "Tours in the Scottish Highlands from the Eighteenth to the Twentieth Centuries," *Northern Scotland* 5 (1983).

On the Scottish Enlightenment as such there is little to recommend. Anand Chitnis, *The Scottish Enlightenment: A Social History* (London, 1976) is a generally competent if unimaginative and poorly written survey of the institutional context with a scientific-academic slant. The only other booklength treatment of the subject—Charles Camic's *Experience and Enlightenment*—is better at criticizing previous interpretations than at formulating a new one. Nicholas Phillipson has produced several stimulating essays: "The Scottish Enlightenment," in *The Enlightenment in National Context,* ed. Roy Porter and Mikuláš Teich (Cambridge, 1981), 19–40; the briefer entry with the same title in *A Companion to Scottish Culture,* ed. David Daiches (London, 1981), 340–45; "Culture and Society in the Eighteenth-Century

Province: The Case of Edinburgh and the Scottish Enlightenment," in *The University in Society,* ed. Lawrence Stone, 2 vols. (Princeton, 1974), 2:407–48; and "Towards a Definition of the Scottish Enlightenment," in Fritz and Williams, *City and Society,* 125–47—all of which may be read along with the same author's more specialized studies of Hume in *Philosophers of the Enlightenment,* ed. S. C. Brown (Brighton, 1979), 140–61 (which contains other useful studies of Hume and Smith), and of Smith in *WV,* 253–70, to get a sense of the interpretation that may be expected from Phillipson's eagerly awaited book. Enough has been said in the Introduction to indicate my reservations about Hugh Trevor-Roper's two articles titled "The Scottish Enlightenment," *SVEC* 58 (1967): 1635–58, and *Blackwood's Magazine* 322 (1977): 371–88, though credit should go to the first of them for generating interest in the topic. G. E. Davie's slim pamphlet, *The Scottish Enlightenment* (London, 1981), is disappointingly diffuse despite some characteristic flashes of insight. The formative years of the Scottish Enlightenment are emphasized by several of the contributors to *ONSE* and by Jane Rendall in her primary source reader, *The Origins of the Scottish Enlightenment, 1707–1776* (London, 1978).

For Scottish thought and culture generally, Daiches's *Companion to Scottish Culture* is an erratic but often useful reference work. Eighteenth-century music is well covered in Thomas Crawford, *Society and the Lyric: A Study of the Song Culture of Eighteenth-Century Scotland* (Edinburgh, 1979) and David Johnson, *Music and Society in Lowland Scotland in the Eighteenth Century* (London, 1972), as well as a new book by Johnson on fiddling and George S. Emmerson, *A Social History of Scottish Dance* (Montreal, 1972). David and Francina Irwin's *Scottish Painters at Home and Abroad, 1700–1900* (London, 1975) is a fine introduction to that topic. There is still no substitute for John Kay's delightful *Series of Original Portraits and Caricature Etchings,* 2 vols. (Edinburgh, 1837–1842), but Hilary and Mary Evans, *John Kay of Edinburgh* (Aberdeen, 1973) presents a portion of Kay's work. John Dunbar, *The Historic Architecture of Scotland,* 2d ed. (London, 1978) is the standard work on that subject. The student of the Scottish Enlightenment, however, may find more of interest in Ian G. Lindsay and Mary Cosh, *Inverary and the Dukes of Argyll* (Edinburgh, 1973); Geoffrey Beard, *The Work of Robert Adam* (Edinburgh, 1978) and various other studies of the Adam brothers and their style; and the previously cited essays in Markus, *Order in Space and Society.* An important component in the process of ordering physical space was gardening: see the article on it in *Studies in Scottish Antiquity,* ed. David J. Breeze and Nicholas Reynolds (Edinburgh, 1984); A. A. Tait's splendid little book *The Landscape Garden in Scotland, 1735–1835* (Edinburgh, 1980); and Harold Roy Fletcher and William H. Brown, *The Royal Botanic Garden, Edinburgh, 1670–1970* (Edinburgh, 1970).

A booming interest in the history of Scottish science has resulted in a large and rewarding essay literature but curiously few books. Notable among the latter are Arthur Donovan's previously cited study of Cullen and Black; Richard Olson, *Scottish Philosophy and British Physics, 1750–1880* (Princeton, 1975); and A. G. Clement and Robert H. S. Robertson's spotty survey, *Scotland's Scientific Heritage* (Edinburgh, 1961). John D. Comrie, *History of Scottish Medicine*, 2d ed., 2 vols. (London, 1932) is the standard medical reference work, though David Hamilton's previously cited survey *The Healers* makes for easier reading. A comprehensive study of eighteenth-century Scottish technology and its connections with science is badly needed just now; at present one may consult any number of sources on James Watt as well as two outstanding general works: A. E. Musson and Eric Robinson, *Science and Technology in the Industrial Revolution* (Manchester, 1969) and Archibald and Nan Clow, *The Chemical Revolution* (London, 1952). Many of the excellent articles published on Scottish science by Cantor, Christie, Donovan, Emerson, Morrell, Shapin, and others are cited in the footnotes to chapter 8 or elsewhere in this bibliographical essay. See also the annual bibliographies in *Isis* and *Technology and Culture* and the one appended to Christopher Lawrence's suggestive article, "The Nervous System and Society in the Scottish Enlightenment," in *Natural Order: Historical Studies of Scientific Culture,* ed. Barry Barnes and Steven Shapin (Beverly Hills, 1979), 19–40. On natural philosophy see R. L. Emerson's piece in *SVEC* (1985).

Gladys Bryson, *Man and Society: The Scottish Inquiry of the Eighteenth Century* (1945; reprint, New York, 1968) remains the best introduction to Scottish moral philosophy in spite of its limitations. Among older works on that subject cited in Bryson's bibliography, James McCosh, *The Scottish Philosophy* (New York, 1874) is still worth consulting for the odd point of interest, whereas still older accounts by Victor Cousin and H. T. Buckle are now chiefly valuable for the light they throw on nineteenth-century French and English, rather than eighteenth-century Scottish, thought. See especially N. T. Phillipson's insightful critique of Buckle in *History of Education Quarterly* 14 (1974): 407–17. Though the role of Francis Hutcheson as the "father" of Scottish moral philosophy is universally acknowledged, most of the existing literature on Hutcheson focuses rather narrowly on technical philosophical issues connected with the "moral sense" controversy. T. D. Campbell provides a brief outline of Hutcheson's "system" in *ONSE*, 167–85, and promising research by Nicholas

Phillipson, Richard Teichgraeber, and others is now underway; but at present Hutcheson's enormous contributions to the social, political, economic, and educational thought of the Scottish Enlightenment have not been properly analyzed or explained. Other Scottish moral philosophers active during the second quarter of the eighteenth century have attracted even less scholarly interest; see, however, David Fate Norton's discussions of George Turnbull and Lord Kames, as well as Hutcheson, in his book cited below; various articles by G. E. Davie; and three stimulating studies of the moral and philosophical foundations of eighteenth-century education that pay some well-deserved attention to David Fordyce: Peter Jones, "The Polite Academy and the Presbyterians, 1720–1770," in Dwyer et al., *NP*, 156–78, and "The Scottish Professoriate and the Polite Academy, 1720–46," in *WV*, 89–119; and J. C. Stewart-Robertson, "The Well-Principled Savage, or the Child of the Scottish Enlightenment," *JHI* (1981): 503–25.

Research on Thomas Reid's philosophy may begin with Stephen F. Barker and Tom L. Beauchamp, eds., *Thomas Reid: Critical Interpretations* (Philadelphia, 1976), where older studies are cited. Reid's connection with a French precursor is examined in Louise Marcil-Lacoste, *Claude Buffier and Thomas Reid* (Montreal, 1981). The neglected political and mathematical-scientific aspects of Reid's thought are treated, respectively, in J. C. Stewart-Robertson, "*Sancte Socrates:* Scottish Reflections on Obedience and Resistance," in *Man and Nature: Proceedings of the Canadian Society for Eighteenth-Century Studies,* vol. 1, ed. Roger Emerson et al. (London, Ont., 1982), 65–80, and in the important doctoral thesis just completed by Paul Wood at the University of Leeds, "Thomas Reid: Natural Philosopher." On the Scottish "school" of common sense generally, S. A. Grave, *The Scottish Philosophy of Common Sense* (Oxford, 1960) is a technical philosophical work with little sense of history. More interesting to the generalist are G. E. Davie's provocative Dow lecture, *The Social Significance of the Scottish Philosophy of Common Sense* (Dundee, 1973), the same author's article in *McGill Hume Studies*, ed. D. F. Norton et al. (San Diego, 1979), 43–62, and "Hume and the Origins of the Common Sense School," *Revue Internationale de Philosophie* 6 (1952): 213–21, which should be read in conjunction with David Fate Norton, *David Hume: Common-Sense Moralist, Sceptical Metaphysician* (Princeton, 1982) and "Hume and His Scottish Critics," in Norton et al., *McGill Hume Studies*, 309–24, and an article by Louise Marcil-Lacoste in *Dalhousie Review* 60 (1980): 67–86. The moderate varieties of common sense philosophy associated with the likes of Reid, Campbell, and Stewart were compatible with the Moderates' vision of Enlightenment; the strident, vulgar, superficial, or self-righteous varieties were not. On the latter, see N. T. Phillipson, "James Beattie and the Defence of Common Sense," in *Festschrift für Rainer Gruenter,* ed. Bernhard Fabian (Heidelberg, 1978), 145–54; Jeremy J. Cater, "General Oughton *versus* Edinburgh's Enlightenment," in *History and Imagination,* ed. Hugh Lloyd-Jones et al. (London, 1981): 254–71; J. Cooper, "James Oswald and the Application of the Common Sense Philosophy to Religion" (Ph.D. diss., Edinburgh University, 1948); and Gavin Ardley, *The Common Sense Philosophy of James Oswald* (Aberdeen, 1981), which fails to rehabilitate that philosopher.

The civic humanist / classical republican paradigm has emerged as a topic of fruitful research on the Scottish Enlightenment thanks to Caroline Robbins, *The Eighteenth-Century Commonwealthman* (Cambridge, Mass., 1961), chap. 2, and especially J.G.A. Pocock's magnum opus, *The Machiavellian Moment: Florentine Political Thought and the Atlantic Republican Tradition* (Princeton, 1975), chap. 14. Articles in *WV* by Pocock, Peter Jones, Nicholas Phillipson, John Robertson, and others have recently introduced refinements and qualifications designed to demonstrate that the civic or civic humanist tradition endured during the Scottish Enlightenment but in a form very different from that of late seventeenth-century civic purists like Andrew Fletcher of Saltoun. See also the Smithian sequel to Robertson's outstanding article on Hume in *WV,* published in *History of Political Thought* 4 (1983): 451–82. On the other hand, recent scholarship has convinced even Pocock that some aspects of Scottish social thought are better understood in terms of the paradigm of natural jurisprudence than that of civic humanism. See especially James Moore and Michael Silverthorne's article on Gershom Carmichael in *WV,* 73–87 (also published in Emerson et al., *Man and Nature,* 41–54), as well as articles in *WV* on Smith by Donald Winch and—most impressively— by Istvan Hont and Michael Ignatieff; Hans Medick, *Naturzustand und Naturgeschichte der bürgerlichen Gesellschaft* (Göttingen, 1973), esp. chaps. 5 and 6 and app. 1, and David Kettler's review essay of that book in *Journal of Modern History* 48 (1976): 95–100; Peter Stein, "From Pufendorf to Adam Smith: The Natural Law Tradition in Scotland," in *Europäisches Rechtsdenken in Geschichte und Gegenwart,* ed. Norbert Horn (Munich, 1982), 667–79; Knud Haakonssen's and Duncan Forbes's essays in *ONSE,* 186–225; Haakonssen, *The Science of a Legislator: The Natural Jurisprudence of David Hume and Adam Smith* (Cambridge, 1981) and the wider-ranging Edinburgh University doctoral thesis of 1978 on which that book was based; and the opening chapters in Forbes's landmark study *Hume's Philosophical Politics* (Cambridge, 1975), along with Forbes's numerous essays on Hume, Smith, and others.

The secondary literature on the thought of David Hume and Adam Smith is of course immense, and relatively little of it can be mentioned here. Older studies on Hume, among other Scottish philosophers of his age, are listed in T. E. Jessop, *A Bibliography of David Hume and of Scottish Philosophy from Francis Hutcheson to Lord Balfour* (London, 1938). More recent work is cited in Roland Hall, *Fifty Years of Hume Scholarship* (Edinburgh, 1978), which contains a useful subject index, and the specialist journal *Hume Studies*. Smith has been less well served bibliographically, though most of the standard studies, including the essential *Essays on Adam Smith*, ed. Andrew S. Skinner and Thomas Wilson (London, 1975), are cited in the bibliography of Donald Winch's valuable book, *Adam Smith's Politics: A Study in Historiographic Revision* (Cambridge, 1978). But some of the best works on the social and political thought of Smith and Hume have appeared since then, including *WV*; Haakonssen's *Science of a Legislator*; Andrew S. Skinner's collection of essays on Smith, *A System of Social Science* (Oxford, 1979); and David Miller's fine introduction to Hume's social philosophy, *Philosophy and Ideology in Hume's Political Thought* (Oxford, 1981).

Scholarship on Scottish political economy naturally concentrates on Smith, but the subject does not end there. Istvan Hont, "The 'Rich Country-Poor Country' Debate in Scottish Political Economy," *WV*, 271–315, is a splendid exercise in the history of economic words and ideas from Hume to Lauderdale. Andrew Skinner has produced several accounts of the economic thought of Sir James Steuart, the most recent being an article in *Scottish Journal of Political Economy* 28 (1981): 20–42. Other studies by Skinner and Ronald Meek treat Scottish political economy within the framework of "conjectural" history and are cited under the latter topic below. On the development of political economy as an autonomous discipline, see H. F. Thompson, Jr., "The Emergence of Political Economy from the Moral Philosophy Course in the Scottish Universities in the Eighteenth Century" (Ph.D. diss., University of Colorado, 1963) and Donald Winch, "The System of the North: Dugald Stewart and His Pupils," in *That Noble Science of Politics: A Study in Nineteenth-Century Intellectual History* by Stefan Collini et al. (Cambridge, 1983), 25–61.

The Scottish origins of sociology have been much debated since the 1920s and 1930s, when studies by Bryson, Lehmann, Sombart, and others raised the issue in a serious way. In the late 1960s the case for the Scots as sociological pioneers reached its peak in works such as Louis Schneider's introduction to his popular anthology *The Scottish Moralists: On Human Nature and Society* (Chicago, 1967) and Alan W. Swingewood, "Origins Of Sociology: The Case of the Scottish Enlightenment," *British Journal of Sociology* 21 (1970): 164–80, and "The Scottish Enlightenment and the Rise of Sociology" (Ph.D. diss., University of London, 1968), which focuses on Ferguson, Robertson, and Millar. At the same time a reaction was setting in, as David Kettler attacked Schneider's presentism in "The Uses and Abuses of Intellectual History," *EC* 10 (1969): 1267–74, and some sociologists, such as Ronald Fletcher in *The Making of Sociology* (London, 1971), vol. 1, app. 1, minimized the importance of the Scottish Enlightenment for the development of their discipline. Most sociologists who have considered the matter would probably agree with William Lehmann's comment on Louis Schneider's thoughtful paper, "Tension in the Thought of John Millar," *EC* 13 (1971–1972): 2083–2110, that Millar, in company with the other Scottish moral philosophers of his day, was "the pre-sociologist . . . rather than the complete sociologist," but what is the point of such terminology? As Michael Ignatieff has argued in his recent paper on Millar in *WV*, 317–43 (where all the older literature on Millar is cited, including Duncan Forbes's classic essay on "scientific Whiggism" in the *Cambridge Journal* of 1954), all "anticipatory" readings of this type are likely to lead commentators astray in one way or another.

Although a great deal has been written about the Scottish Enlightenment's contributions to what Dugald Stewart dubbed "conjectural" or "theoretical" history, relatively little research has been done on its less glamorous cousins, antiquarian, controversial, and narrative/philosophical history, except perhaps as the last of these was practiced by David Hume and, to a lesser extent, William Robertson. For Hume, see especially chapter 8 of Forbes, *Hume's Philosophical Politics* and Victor G. Wexler, *David Hume and the History of England* (Philadelphia, 1979). Antiquarian historiography is discussed later in this essay. Controversial history may be approached through chapter 8 of David Duncan, *Thomas Ruddiman* and Laurence L. Bongie, "The Eighteenth-Century Marian Controversy and an Unpublished Letter by David Hume," *Studies in Scottish Literature* 1 (1964): 236–52, though these sources merely scratch the surface of an interesting and largely unexplored field. The contributions of several "minor" eighteenth-century Scottish historians, such as James Dunbar, John Logan, Thomas Somerville, and the cantankerous Gilbert Stuart, are noted in D. B. Horn, "Some Scottish Writers of History in the Eighteenth Century," *SHR* 40 (1961): 1–18, and Thomas Preston Peardon, *The Transition in English Historical Writing, 1760–1830* (New York, 1933).

The fullest treatments of Scottish "conjectural" history and the "four-stages" or stadial theory of social development are in Alice Jacoby Wheeler, "Society History in Eighteenth-Century Scotland" (Ph.D.

diss., Emory University, 1966), which is especially good for secondary figures like Dunbar and Logan, and Ronald L. Meek, *Social Science and the Ignoble Savage* (Cambridge, 1979), which supplements essays on this subject in Meek's *Economics and Ideology and Other Essays* (London, 1967), 34–50, and *Smith, Marx, and After* (London, 1977), 18–32. Other notable studies include Searl Spencer Davis, "Scottish Philosophical History: Hume to James Mill" (Ph.D. diss., University of Toronto, 1981); Roger L. Emerson's essay in the CHA's *Historical Papers* (1985), "Conjectural History and the Scottish Philosophers," which demonstrates the importance of the early eighteenth century for the development of this mode of inquiry; chap. 7 of Haakonssen, *Science of a Legislator*; H. M. Höpfl, "From Savage to Scotsman: Conjectural History in the Scottish Enlightenment," *Journal of British Studies* 17 (1978): 19–40; chapter 5 and appendix 2 of Hans Medick, *Naturzustand und Naturgeschichte*; Roy Pascal's seminal paper, "Property and Society: The Scottish Historical School," *Modern Quarterly* 1 (1938): 167–79; Jane Rendall, "Scottish Orientalism: From Robertson to Mill," *Historical Journal* 25 (1982): 43–69; Andrew S. Skinner, "Economics and History: The Scottish Enlightenment," *Scottish Journal of Political Economy* 12 (1965): 1–22, "Natural History in the Age of Adam Smith," *Political Studies* 15 (1967): 32–48, and "A Scottish Contribution to Marxist Sociology?" in *Classical and Marxian Political Economy*, ed. Ian Bradley and Michael Howard (London, 1982), 79–114; and George W. Stocking, Jr., "Scotland as the Model of Mankind: Lord Kames' Philosophical View of Civilization," in *Toward a Science of Man: Essays in the History of Anthropology*, ed. Timothy H. H. Thoresen (The Hague, 1975), 65–89, which cites additional sources in German. The topic is treated in a broadly comparative framework in Robert A. Nisbet, *Social Change and History* (New York, 1969). A more specialized discussion may be found in Peter Stein, *Legal Evolution: The Story of an Idea* (Cambridge, 1980), chap. 2, which complements several excellent articles by the same author on other aspects of eighteenth-century Scottish legal thought (especially his contribution to *SAI*, 148–68); David Leiberman's interesting essay on Kames's approach to that subject in *WV*, 203–34; and Neil MacCormick's "Law and Enlightenment" in *ONSE*, 150–66.

Among other things, "conjectural" history provided a method for dealing with the concept of the primitive, which constituted one of the critical problems of eighteenth-century Scottish thought. The standard general study is still Lois Whitney, *Primitivism and the Idea of Progress in English Popular Literature of the Eighteenth Century* (Baltimore, 1934). The social scientific dimension is emphasized in Meek's *Ignoble Savage*; Roger L. Emerson, "American Indians, Frenchmen, and Scots Philosophers," in *Studies in Eighteenth-Century Culture*, vol. 9, ed. Roseann Runte (Madison, Wisc., 1979), 211–36; and the introduction to J. W. Burrow's important book, *Evolution and Society* (Cambridge, 1966). Aspects of Scottish literary primitivism are discussed in Donald M. Foerster, *Homer in English Criticism: The Historical Approach in the Eighteenth Century* (New Haven, 1947); René Wellek, *The Rise of English Literary History* (Chapel Hill, N.C., 1941), chap. 3; and several articles on the subject—includir.g some that use reactions to Rousseau as a primitivist gauge—published in journals such as *PMLA* and *Philological Quarterly* between 1933 and 1950.

The focal point of interest in literary primitivism during the Scottish Enlightenment was of course Ossian. Most of the voluminous, and often passionately partisan, literature on this topic is listed in George F. Black, *Macpherson's Ossian and the Ossianic Controversy* (New York, 1926) and John J. Dunn, "Macpherson's 'Ossian' and the Ossianic Controversy: A Supplementary Bibliography," *Bulletin of the New York Public Library* 75 (1971): 465–73. Of older studies, the two most important are Bailey Saunders's defense of Macpherson, *The Life and Letters of James Macpherson* (1894; reprint, New York, 1969), which prints some useful materials, and John Semple Smart's critique, *James Macpherson: An Episode in Literature* (London, 1905). Since then it has become commonplace to find Ossian dismissed as nothing more than an elaborate hoax perpetrated by Macpherson, but recent scholarship suggests that this interpretation is too simple. On the one hand, studies such as Derick S. Thomson, *The Gaelic Sources of Macpherson's "Ossian"* (Edinburgh, 1951) and Robert P. Fitzgerald, "The Style of Ossian," *Studies in Romanticism* 6 (1966): 22–23, have shown that there was much that may be considered authentic about Macpherson's Ossianic poetry, and Malcolm Chapman has devoted a chapter to placing Ossian within the Gaelic context in *The Gaelic Vision in Scottish Culture* (London, 1978). On the other hand, Richard B. Sher, " 'Those Scotch Imposters and Their Cabal': Ossian and the Scottish Enlightenment," in Emerson et al., *Man and Nature*, 55–63, presents a slightly different version of the argument made in chapter 6 of this book in order to emphasize that the discovery of Ossian was not the work of Macpherson alone. Several other articles on particular aspects of the Ossian affair are cited in the footnotes to chapter 6 above. Two doctoral theses of interest are J. N. M. Maclean, "The Early Political Careers of James 'Fingal' Macpherson and Sir John Macpherson" (Edinburgh University, 1967) and Larry Le Roy Stewart, "Ossian in the Polished Age: The Critical Reception of James Macpherson's Ossian" (Case Western Reserve University, 1971), which deals with the intensification of the Ossianic controversy in Britain during the 1760s and 1770s. This is not the place to discuss the large literature on the extensive influence of Ossian abroad, but mention may be made of S. N. Cristea, "Ossian v. Homer: An Eighteenth-Century Controversy," *Italian Studies* 24 (1969): 93–111; the catalogue prepared by Hanna Hohl and Hélène Toussaint from the excellent Parisian exhibit of Ossianic art, *Ossian* (Paris, 1974); and the discussion of Ossian's impact on European composers in chapter 2 of Roger Fiske, *Scotland in Music: A European Enthusiasm* (Cambridge, 1983).

The impact of Ossian on the Scottish stage is examined in James S. Malek, "Eighteenth-Century British Dramatic Adaptations of Macpherson's 'Ossian,'" *Restoration and Eighteenth-Century Theatre Research* 14 (1975): 36–41, 52. Terence Tobin, *Plays by Scots, 1660–1800* (Iowa City, 1974) is not very helpful for understanding Scottish theater. Those interested in that poorly researched subject must rely on John Jackson's charming but limited memoir, *The History of the Scottish Stage* (Edinburgh, 1793); James C. Dibden's superficial *Annals of the Edinburgh Stage* (Edinburgh, 1888); and two doctoral theses: Jack McKenzie, "A Study of Eighteenth-Century Drama in Scotland, 1660–1760" (St. Andrews University, 1956) and Hugh Thorne Compton, "Legal, Political, and Religious Controversies over the Stage in Edinburgh in the Eighteenth Century" (University of South Carolina, 1975). See also the substantial literature on David Garrick, the London stage, and eighteenth-century British drama generally.

Wilber Samuel Howell, *Eighteenth-Century British Logic and Rhetoric* (Princeton, 1971) is a superb book that builds much of its case for a revolution in logic and rhetoric around Smith, Blair, Campbell, and other Scotsmen. General works on eighteenth-century literary criticism and aesthetics with good coverage of the Scots are Walter Jackson Bate, *From Classic to Romantic: Premises of Taste in Eighteenth-Century England* (Cambridge, Mass., 1946); James Engell, *The Creative Imagination: Enlightenment to Romanticism* (Cambridge, Mass., 1981); Walter John Hipple, Jr., *The Beautiful, the Sublime, and the Picturesque in Eighteenth-Century Aesthetic Theory* (Carbondale, 1957); Martin Kallich, *The Association of Ideas and Critical Theory in Eighteenth-Century England* (The Hague, 1970), esp. chap. 5; Gordon Mackenzie, *Critical Responsiveness: A Study of the Psychological Current in Later Eighteenth-Century Criticism* (Berkeley, 1949); Samuel Monk, *The Sublime* (New York, 1935); René Wellek, *A History of Modern Criticism, 1750–1950*, 4 vols. (New Haven, 1965), esp. vol. 1, chap. 6; and Scott Elledge's anthology, *Eighteenth-Century Critical Essays*, 2 vols. (Ithaca, N.Y., 1961). Several of these books have good bibliographies or bibliographical notes that cite the large specialist literature in this field, much of which is unfortunately located in doctoral theses and regional speech journals that are not always easily accessible. A recent essay of general interest is Philip Flynn, "Scottish Aesthetics and the Search for a Standard of Taste," *Dalhousie Review* 60 (1980): 5–19.

The standard works on eighteenth-century periodicals and publishing are little more than annotated bibliographies: W. J. Couper, *The Edinburgh Periodical Press*, 2 vols. (Stirling, 1908); Mary E. Craig, *The Scottish Periodical Press, 1750–1789* (Edinburgh, 1931); H. R. Plomer, *Dictionary of Printers and Booksellers . . . 1726–1775* (London, 1932) and supplements to it by R. H. Carnie in *Studies in Bibliography* 12 (1959), 14 (1961), and 15 (1962); and Philip Gaskell, *A Bibliography of the Foulis Press* (London, 1964). But see Warren McDougall, "Gavin Hamilton, John Balfour and Patrick Neill: A Study of Publishing in Edinburgh in the Eighteenth Century" (Ph.D. diss., Edinburgh University, 1974) and "Gavin Hamilton: Bookseller in Edinburgh," *British Journal for Eighteenth-Century Studies* 1 (1978): 1–19. Herman Kogan, *The Great EB: The Story of the Encyclopedia Britannica* (Chicago, 1958) is a popular account of a remarkable enterprise that deserves a more critical study. Also ripe for further research are Henry Mackenzie's two influential literary magazines, the *Mirror* and *Lounger*, which are examined in Robert D. Mayo, *The English Novel in the Magazines, 1740–1815* (London, 1962); Charles A. Knight, "The Created World of the Edinburgh Periodicals," *Scottish Literary Journal* 6 (1979): 20–36; and Dwyer and Murdoch's essay in *NP*, 210–48, as well as in the biographical and critical literature on Mackenzie himself.

Eighteenth-century Scottish literature is surveyed in Maurice Lindsay, *History of Scottish Literature* (London, 1977). Literary giants like Boswell, Burns, Scott, and Smollett have spawned vast numbers of specialized critical studies and their own bibliographies to keep track of them. For the rest, one may keep up by consulting *The Eighteenth Century: A Current Bibliography* and the *Annual Bibliography of Scottish Literature* published by the Scottish library journal *Bibliotheck*. A pioneering attempt to connect Scottish literature and common sense philosophy is M. A. Goldberg, *Smollett and the Scottish School* (Albuquerque, 1959). Two stimulating studies assail the Moderate literati and their kind for sacrificing the native, creative element in eighteenth-century Scottish literature to more English—which is to say more formal and less vibrant—literary modes: David Craig, *Scottish Literature and the Scottish People, 1680–1830* (London, 1961) and David Daiches, *The Paradox of Scottish Culture: The Eighteenth-Century Experience* (London, 1964). An alternative viewpoint, stressing the continuity of different varieties of Scottish poetry with the Enlightenment, is all too briefly sketched in John MacQueen, *The Enlightenment and Scottish Literature: Poetry and Progress* (Edinburgh, 1982).

Other useful studies of eighteenth-century Scottish national identity—literary and otherwise—are John Clive and Bernard Bailyn's important essay, "England's Cultural Provinces: Scotland and America," *William and Mary Quarterly*, 3d ser., 11 (1954): 200–213, the central thesis of which is restated in Clive's piece in *SAI*; Rosalind Mitchison, "Patriotism and National Identity in Eighteenth-Century Scotland," in *Nationalism and the Pursuit of National Independence*, ed. T. W. Moody (Belfast, 1978), 73–95, and the sequel in a collection Mitchison edited under the title *The Roots of Nationalism: Studies in Northern Europe* (Edinburgh, 1980), 131–42; almost everything written by Nicholas Phillipson, but particularly "Nationalism and Ideology," in *Government and Nationalism in Scotland*, ed. J. N. Wolfe (Edinburgh, 1969), 167–88, and "Scottish Public Opinion and the Union in the Age of the Association," in *SAI*, 125–47; Janet Adam Smith, "Eighteenth-Century Ideas of Scotland," in *SAI*, 107–24; G. E. Davie, "Hume, Reid, and the Passion for Ideas," in Young et al., *Edinburgh in the Age of Reason*, 23–39; Ian C. Walker, "Scottish Nationalism in *The Weekly Magazine*," *Studies in Scottish Literature* 16 (1981): 1–13; John S. Gibson, "How Did the Enlightenment Seem to the Edinburgh Enlightened?" (on linguistic assimilation), *British Journal for Eighteenth-Century Studies* 1 (1978): 46–50; most of the contributions to *Eighteenth-Century Life*'s disappointing special issue on Scotland (September 1977); and F. W. Freeman's superb introduction to antiquarian, linguistic nationalism, "The Vernacular Movement," in Daiches, *Companion to Scottish Culture*, 393–96.

For the Scots militia movement, which was, along with Ossian, the most important issue for the expression of Scottish national pride among the literati of the Enlightenment, John Robertson, *The Scottish Enlightenment and the Militia Issue* (Edinburgh, 1985) will be fundamental. J. R. Western, *The English Militia in the Eighteenth Century: The Study of a Political Issue, 1660–1802* (London, 1965) is also important but, true to its title, adopts a narrowly political and primarily English approach to the militia question. Adam Smith's views are discussed in Winch, *Smith's Politics*, chap. 5, and the case for David Hume as a "zealous" militia man is made in the introduction to David R. Raynor's edition of *Sister Peg*. Useful for the broader British context of the Scots militia issue are Lois G. Schwoerer, *"No Standing Armies": The Antiarmy Ideology in Seventeenth-Century England* (Baltimore, 1974); Lawrence Delbert Cress, "Radical Whiggery on the Role of the Military: Ideological Roots of the American Revolutionary Militia," *JHI* 40 (1979): 43–60, and *Citizens in Arms* (Chapel Hill, N.C.,

1982); and the various studies of civic ideology by Phillipson, Pocock, and others. The Scots militia act of 1797 and the reaction it provoked are studied in J. R. Western, "The Formation of the Scottish Militia in 1797," *SHR* 34 (1955): 1–18, and Kenneth J. Logue, *Popular Disturbances in Scotland, 1780–1815* (Edinburgh, 1979), chap. 3.

On the fringes of the Enlightenment lay a different sort of Scottish nationalist spirit, propagated by a peculiar assortment of individuals who shared an antiquarian taste for the past. Here national pride and intellectual inquiry were expressed through nostalgia and the collection, classification, publication, or exhibition of old Scottish things, be they ballads or artifacts, documents or inscriptions. The literature on this long-neglected tradition is suddenly formidable. F. W. Freeman's previously cited article stresses the nationalist aspect. Iain Gordon Brown, *The Hobby-Horsical Antiquary: A Scottish Character, 1690–1830* (Edinburgh, 1980) delightfully delineates the antiquarian "type," of which two case studies from opposite ends of the century are Brown's article on Sir John Clerk of Penicuik in *Antiquity* 51 (1977): 201–10, and Ronald G. Cant's essay on the eccentric founder of the Society of Antiquaries in Scotland, the eleventh earl of Buchan, in *The Scottish Antiquarian Tradition*, ed. A. S. Bell (Edinburgh, 1981), which contains a good bibliography. If Clerk and Buchan's brand of antiquarianism was largely classical, a later strain associated with Sir Walter Scott was largely romantic—a dichotomy skillfully explored in Stuart Piggott, *Ruins in a Landscape* (Edinburgh, 1976), chap. 7. Much work remains to be done on antiquarian historiography, but see T. I. Rae, "The Scottish Antiquarian Tradition" and other essays in *Scots Antiquaries and Historians* (Dundee, 1972); chapter 4 of R. H. Carnie's doctoral thesis on Sir David Dalrymple, Lord Hailes (St. Andrews University, 1954); and Marinell Ash's bright little book, *The Strange Death of Scottish History* (Edinburgh, 1980), which carries the story into the early nineteenth century.

Eugene C. Black, *The Association: British Extraparliamentary Political Organization, 1769–1793* (Cambridge, Mass., 1963), chap. 4 (also published in slightly different form in *Review of Politics* 25 [1963]: 183–211) is a good introduction to the "No Popery" affair of 1778–1779 from the point of view suggested by the subtitle. It may now be supplemented with Robert Kent Donovan, "Voices of Distrust: The Expression of Anti-Catholic Feeling in Scotland, 1778–1781," *Innes Review* 30 (1979): 62–76, and the early chapters in Christine Johnson, *Developments in the Roman Catholic Church in Scotland, 1789–1829* (Edinburgh, 1983). A critical reader will find much useful material on this subject in the life of the indefatigable Bishop George Hay in

Journal and Appendix to Scotichronicon and Monasticon, published as volume 4 of J. F. S. Gordon, *Ecclesiastical Chronicle for Scotland* (Glasgow, 1867), esp. chaps. 9 and 10. Forthcoming articles by Robert Kent Donovan in *Historical Journal* and *Recusant History* trace the origins of Catholic relief schemes of the 1770s to Sir John Dalrymple, a controversial friend of the Moderates whose motives were not entirely altruistic.

Scottish views on the American Revolution are treated in two well-documented studies by Dalphy I. Fagerstrom: "Scottish Opinion and the American Revolution," *William and Mary Quarterly*, 3d ser., 11 (1954): 252–75, and "The American Revolution in Scottish Opinion, 1763–83" (Ph.D. diss., Edinburgh University, 1951). See also Owen Dudley Edwards and George Shepperson, eds., *Scotland, Europe and the American Revolution* (New York, 1976); Shepperson, "The American Revolution in Scotland," *Scotia* 1 (1977): 3–17; and the relevant portions of studies by Andrew Hook and others cited in the next paragraph. Virtually every British pamphlet on America published between 1764 and 1783 is listed in Thomas R. Adams's annotated bibliography, *The American Controversy* (Providence, 1980). Adam Smith's views on America have been particularly well investigated: see William D. Grampp, "Adam Smith and the American Revolutionists," *History of Political Economy* 11 (1979): 179–91; chapter 8 in Andrew Skinner's *System of Social Science*; David Stephens, "Adam Smith and the Colonial Disturbances," in Skinner and Wilson, *Essays on Smith*, 202–17; and Donald Winch, *Classical Political Economy and Colonies* (Cambridge, 1965), pt. 2, and *Adam Smith's Politics*, chap. 7. The ideas and activities of some other Scottish literati are discussed in Caroline Robbins, " 'When It Is That Colonies May Turn Independent': An Analysis of the Environment and Politics of Francis Hutcheson," *William and Mary Quarterly*, 3d ser., 11 (1954): 214–51; J. G. A. Pocock, "Hume and the American Revolution," in Norton et al., *McGill Hume Studies*, 325–44 (though there is less here on this subject than the title would suggest); John M. Werner, "David Hume and America," *JHI* 33 (1972): 439–56; and Christopher J. Berry, "James Dunbar and the American War of Independence," *Aberdeen University Review* 45 (1974): 255–66.

William R. Brock, *Scotus Americanus: A Survey of the Sources for Links between Scotland and America in the Eighteenth Century* (Edinburgh, 1982) and William C. Lehmann, *Scottish and Scotch-Irish Contributions to Early American Life and Culture* (Port Washington, N.Y., 1978) are the most comprehensive introductions to the subject of Scottish-American cultural ties. Andrew D. Hook, *Scotland and America: A Study of Cultural Relations, 1750–1835* (Glasgow, 1975) cleverly explores the paradoxical nature of Scotland's dual image in America as both land of intellect and land of romance. The academic connection is stressed in Douglas Sloan, *The Scottish Enlightenment and the American College Ideal* (New York, 1971); Howard Miller, *The Revolutionary College: American Presbyterian Higher Education, 1707–1837* (New York, 1976); Daniel Howe, *The Unitarian Conscience: Harvard Moral Philosophy, 1805–1861* (Cambridge, Mass., 1970); and D. H. Meyer, *The Instructed Conscience* (Philadelphia, 1972). A pivotal figure in this regard was John Witherspoon of Princeton, whose moral teaching is best approached through Roger Jerome Fechner, "The Moral Philosophy of John Witherspoon and the Scottish-American Enlightenment" (Ph.D. diss., University of Iowa, 1974) and Jack Scott's recent edition of his lectures. The continuity of the Scottish philosophical heritage at Princeton is the subject of James D. Hoeveler, Jr., *James McCosh and the Scottish Intellectual Tradition* (Princeton, 1981). At the heart of that heritage was common sense philosophy, the influence of which is further discussed in Terence Martin, *The Instructed Vision: Scottish Common Sense Philosophy and the Origins of American Fiction* (Bloomington, Ind., 1961); Richard J. Peterson, "Scottish Common Sense in America, 1768–1850" (Ph.D. diss., American University, 1963); and Sydney E. Ahlstrom, "The Scottish Philosophy and American Theology," *Church History* 24 (1955): 257–72. For the Scottish connection with, and influence upon, the American founding fathers, see James Bennett Nolan, *Benjamin Franklin in Scotland and Ireland, 1759–1771* (Philadelphia, 1938); Gilman M. Ostrander, "Jefferson and Scottish Culture," *Historical Reflections* 2 (1975): 233–48; Garry Wills, *Inventing America: Jefferson's Declaration of Independence* (New York, 1978), which is taken to task by Ronald Hamowy in "Jefferson and the Scottish Enlightenment," *William and Mary Quarterly*, 3d ser., 36 (1979): 503–23; Arnaud B. Leavelle, "James Wilson and the Relation of the Scottish Metaphysics to American Political Thought," *Political Science Quarterly* 57 (1942): 394–410; Roy Branson, "James Madison and the Scottish Enlightenment," *JHI* 40 (1979): 235–50; James Conniff, "The Enlightenment and American Political Thought: A Study of the Origins of Madison's *Federalist* Number 10," *Political Theory* 8 (1980): 381–402; a classic paper by Douglas Adair that is reproduced, along with Craig Walton's "Hume and Jefferson on History," in *Hume: A Reevaluation*, ed. Donald W. Livingston and James T. King (New York, 1976); and Garry Wills, *Explaining America: The Federalist* (Garden City, N.Y., 1981).

Surprisingly little comparative research has been done on the Scottish and French Enlightenments. Most of what has been published on this subject deals with the influence or dissemination of

French ideas in Scotland. J. H. Brumfitt, "Scotland and the French Enlightenment," in *The Age of Enlightenment,* ed. W. H. Barber (Edinburgh, 1967), 318–29, sketches French influences through personal contact, the press, and book trade. F. T. H. Fletcher, *Montesquieu and English Politics (1750–1800)* (London, 1939) and John Lough, *"L'Esprit des Lois* in a Scottish University in the Eighteenth Century," *Comparative Literature Studies* 13 (1944): 13–16, are two of the many studies that deal with the influence of Montesquieu. In "The Relations of the Aberdeen Philosophical Society with France," *Aberdeen University Review* 30 (1943): 144–50, Lough discusses the impact of French thought on one "provincial" Scottish club. Michael Ignatieff, "Smith, Rousseau and the Spiral of Needs," in Smout, *Scotland and Europe;* Ronald Grimsley, "Jean-Jacques Rousseau jugé par un pasteur écossais [Blair]," *Revue de littérature comparée* 36 (1962): 558–60; and J. C. Stewart-Robertson, "Reid's Anatomy of Culture: A Scottish Response to the Eloquent Jean-Jacques," *SVEC* 205 (1982):141–64, focus on Scottish reactions to Rousseau. Arthur L. Donovan, "Scottish Responses to the New Chemistry of Lavoisier," *Studies in Eighteenth-Century Culture,* vol. 9, ed. Roseann Runte (Madison, Wisc., 1979), 237–49, treats a critical scientific issue. And Alison K. Howard, "Montesquieu, Voltaire, and Rousseau in Eighteenth-Century Scotland: A Checklist of Editions and Translations of Their Works Published in Scotland before 1801," *Bibliotheck* 2 (1959): 40–63, and Keith Marshall, "France and the Scottish Press, 1700–1800," *Studies in Scottish Literature* 13 (1978): 1–14, document the extent of the Scots' interest in the works of leading French authors. A great deal that cannot be cited here has been written about Adam Smith's relations with Turgot and the physiocrats and David Hume's relations with the French *philosophes.* Aspects of Scotland's image and impact in France are treated in Leonard Adams, "Scotland in the *Encyclopédie,*" *Scottish Tradition* 9/10 (1980): 49–63, and P. P. Dockwrey, "Dugald Stewart and the Early French Eclectics, 1796–1820" (Ph.D. diss., Cambridge University, 1976), but nothing in print reveals who was reading the many Scottish books translated into French in the decades preceding the Revolution—or why.

Comparative studies in English on the Scottish and German Enlightenments are mostly limited to the impact of the Scots philosophers on a few German men of letters, for example, Dushan Bresky, "Schiller's Debt to Montesquieu and Adam Ferguson," *Comparative Literature* 13 (1961): 239–53; Roy Pascal, "Herder and the Scottish Historical School," *Publications of the English Goethe Society* (1938–1939): 23–42; L. R. Shaw, "Henry Home of Kames: Precursor of Herder," *Germanic Review* 35 (1960): 116–27; and Edmund Heier, "William

Robertson and Ludwig Heinrich von Nicolay," *SHR* 41 (1962): 135–40. See also Manfred Kuehn, "Scottish Common Sense in Germany, 1768–1800" (Ph.D. diss., McGill University, 1980) and an article based on that study in *Journal of the History of Philosophy* 21 (1983): 479–96, and Alexander Gillies, *A Hebridean in Goethe's Weimar: The Reverend James Macdonald and the Cultural Relations between Scotland and Germany* (Oxford, 1969), as well as other works on the influence of Ossian. On the Scottish and Italian Enlightenments, there are Basil Skinner, *Scots in Italy in the Eighteenth Century* (Edinburgh, 1966) and Franco Venturi, "Scottish Echoes in Eighteenth-Century Italy," in *WV*, 345–62. It is, however, the influence of the Scottish Enlightenment on Russia and Russians that has received the biggest boost of late: see the papers by Franco Venturi and A. G. Cross in *Great Britain and Russia in the Eighteenth Century*, ed. A. G. Cross (Newtonville, Mass., 1979), 2–47; chapter 5 of Cross, *"By the Banks of the Thames": Russians in Eighteenth-Century Britain* (Newtonville, Mass., 1980); and Paul Dukes, "Some Aberdonian Influences on the Early Russian Enlightenment," *Canadian-American Slavic Studies* 13 (1979):436–51, and other articles cited in the notes to those studies.

INDEX

Library of Congress Cataloging in Publication Data

Sher, Richard B., 1948–
Church and university in the Scottish enlightenment.

Revision of thesis (Ph.D.)
Bibliography: p.
Includes index.
1. Enlightenment.   2. Scotland—Intellectual life.
I. Title.
B1402.E55S54 1985   941.107   84-17911
ISBN 0-691-05445-2 (alk. paper)